Framing the Subjects and Objects of Contemporary EU Law

Framing the Subjects and Objects of Contemporary EU Law

Edited by

Samo Bardutzky

Assistant Professor, Faculty of Law, University of Ljubljana, Slovenia

Elaine Fahey

Reader, City Law School, City, University of London, UK

Edward Elgar
PUBLISHING

Cheltenham, UK • Northampton, MA, USA

Published by
Edward Elgar Publishing Limited
The Lypiatts
15 Lansdown Road
Cheltenham
Glos GL50 2JA
UK

Edward Elgar Publishing, Inc.
William Pratt House
9 Dewey Court
Northampton
Massachusetts 01060
USA

A catalogue record for this book
is available from the British Library

Library of Congress Control Number: 2017931745

This book is available electronically in the **Elgar**online
Law subject collection
DOI 10.4337/9781786435743

MIX
Paper from
responsible sources
FSC® C013056

ISBN 978 1 78643 573 6 (cased)
ISBN 978 1 78643 574 3 (eBook)

Typeset by Columns Design XML Ltd, Reading
Printed and bound in Great Britain by TJ International Ltd, Padstow

Contents

Contributors

Dr Samo Bardutzky, Assistant Professor, University of Ljubljana

Professor Emilios Christodoulidis, University of Glasgow

Dr Joseph Corkin, Senior Lecturer, Middlesex University

Dr Andrés Delgado Casteleiro, Senior Research Fellow, Max Planck Institute Luxembourg for International, European and Regulatory Procedural Law

Professor Sionaidh Douglas-Scott, Anniversary Chair in Law, Co-Director at the Centre for Law and Society in a Global Context, Queen Mary University, London

Professor Michelle Everson, Birkbeck, University of London

Dr Elaine Fahey, Reader, City Law School, City, University of London

Professor Sir Francis Jacobs QC, Professor of Law and Jean Monnet Professor, King's College London

Dr Emilia Korkea-aho, Academy of Finland Research Fellow and Adjunct Professor in EU Law, University of Helsinki

Professor Dora Kostakopoulou, University of Warwick

Dr Damjan Kukovec, Max Weber Fellow, European University Institute; Lecturer, Kent Law School, Brussels; and Visiting Scholar, Harvard University

Professor Sara Poli, Jean Monnet Chair in EU Law, University of Pisa

Professor Siniša Rodin, Judge, Court of Justice of the European Union

Professor Matthias Ruffert, Humboldt University, Berlin

Dr Anastasia Tataryn, Lecturer in Law, University of Liverpool

Dr Alina Tryfonidou, Associate Professor, University of Reading

Dr Josephine van Zeben, Fellow and Tutor, Worcester College, University of Oxford

Dr Samantha Velluti, Reader in Law, Sussex European Institute, University of Sussex

Dr Ilaria Vianello, Senior Research Fellow, Max Planck Foundation for International Peace and the Rule of Law, Heidelberg

Foreword

The title 'subjects and objects of EU law' reminds me of my first steps in international law, when there was much discussion of that topic in international law. The traditional mantra was that 'only states were subjects of international law' – and perhaps later, progressively, international organisations. But international law today takes many different forms. The EU itself has been active as a subject of international law; and individuals can appear before some international courts and tribunals.

(By way of a random example: an introductory textbook: *International Law of Peace* by NA Maryan Green, even in second edition, 1982, about 240 pages in all, seemed to be representative, in having a disproportionate treatment: after two extremely brief chapters, Chapter 3 'Subjects of International Law', over 50 pages, divided into three sections: states, international organisations, and other subjects of international law (the Holy See, etc.). Chapter 4, 30 pages: The position of the individual (including corporations) in international law; Chapter 5, organs of the state. That was most of the book: not much space left (one hundred rather short pages for the rest of international law) ...)

Twenty years earlier, in *Van Gend en Loos* (1963), the Court of Justice proclaimed that the EEC Treaty constituted a new legal order of international law 'for the benefit of which the states have limited their sovereign rights, albeit within limited fields, and the subjects of which comprise not only Member States but also their nationals'.

And direct effect has had a remarkable history in EU law: (1) the Treaty provisions may have direct effect, not only where, as stated in *van Gend*, they are negative and unconditional, but also where they are positive and conditional. (2) Not only the treaties, but regulations may have direct effect: and direct effect is not the same as directly applicable? (3) Not only regulations, but also directives: they are not directly applicable, but may have direct effect. (4) Not only internal EU acts, but treaties concluded by the EU with third states. They may confer rights on third state nationals, which they can claim in EU courts: and they can do so even without reciprocity.

It is interesting to speculate how differently EU law might have been if *van Gend* had been decided differently. This issue is all the more piquant because, although all decisions of the Court of Justice are collective and no separate or dissenting opinions are allowed (except to the Advocate General), and although the deliberations of the Court are secret, and every judge and Advocate General undertakes on appointment to preserve the secrecy of the deliberations, we now know that *van Gend en Loos* very nearly went the other way, and, at a time when the Court had only seven judges, was in the end decided by a 4:3 majority.

This is in fact rather useful as helping to dispel the idea that the Court is a sort of monolith, or even juggernaut, driven onward by a single agenda. In fact there is still, I think, a wide range of views in the Court, which may have implications for considering who or what are the subjects or objects of EU law. For example, those who come from a more traditional international law background may still see the Court as an international court, concerned primarily with disputes between states; they may in consequence be less concerned to protect or develop the right of standing before the court for individuals and undertakings. And there is indeed some basis for the special status of the Member States. Not only are they considered by some as 'masters (or mistresses) of the Treaty', as it is sometimes put. They can of course amend the Treaties, although there is a view that there are limits to that power. And they have, under the Treaties, an unqualified standing before the Court, so that they have the right to appear in any case before the Court, without having to demonstrate any specific interest in the outcome of the case. They are therefore sometimes described as having 'privileged' access before the Court.

Other members of the Court may, however, take a different stance. And they may in any event consider that the views advanced by a Member State carry no special weight in the Court's deliberations.

What is perhaps most remarkable about the EU legal system in this respect is the extent to which, in contrast perhaps to some other international and transnational courts, the Member States have regularly sought to develop and to strengthen the EU's judicial system: by, for example, setting up the General Court to improve the judicial protection of undertakings; by improving the system of judicial remedies generally; by improving the system of judicial appointments and limiting their own prerogatives in that regard; and by introducing the system of sanctions by way of severe financial penalties against the Member States themselves to encourage compliance with judgments of the Court. They have rather often made significant amendments to the Treaties to bring them in line with the case law of the Court. Rarely have their amendments been regressive.

All in all, EU law provides a good example of the rule of law in interstate and intra-European relations.

Professor Sir Francis Jacobs QC
Kings College London

Acknowledgements

We are very grateful to City, University London, City Law School, Institute for the Study of European Laws for the financial support and the hospitality that made it possible for us to meet with the authors and discuss their work in progress on 6 November 2015 and 6 May 2016.

We wish to thank sincerely the Kent Centre for Comparative and European Law at the University of Kent, Kent Law School, for financial support to the project.

We are indebted to the colleagues who have contributed to the exchange of ideas leading to the development of the accounts presented in this edited volume: Cristina Fasone, Marios Costa, Panos Koutrakos, Sir Alan Dashwood, David Seymour, Dan Wilsher and Laurent Pech.

We extend our cordial thanks, also on behalf of the authors of the chapters, to a number of colleagues who accepted our invitation and very generously took the time to review the chapters in the book. Their highly constructive comments and suggestions were greatly appreciated:

Matej Accetto
Tawhida Ahmed
Matej Avbelj
Niels Blokker
Paul James Cardwell
Edoardo Chiti
Richard Collins
Joseph Corkin
Marco Dani
Andrés Delgado Casteleiro
Giacomo Delledonne
Valerie Demedts
Hent Kalmo
Bojan Kovačević
Acar Kutay
Anna Labedzka
Joris Larik
Serena Natile
Amanda Perry-Kessaris
Sara Poli
Michael Schwarz
Nikos Skoutaris
Josephine van Zeben
Martijn van den Brink
Michalis Zivanaris

Our final thanks go to the editors at Edward Elgar Publishing for their support for this project and to the anonymous reviewers of the original publishing proposal for their extremely useful feedback and reflections, which we hope we have done justice to overall.

Samo Bardutzky
Elaine Fahey
London, 8 March 2017

1. The subjects and objects of EU law: exploring a research platform

Samo Bardutzky and Elaine Fahey*

INTRODUCTION

The words 'subject' and 'object' are an important part of the lexicon of Western philosophy, social sciences, humanities, and also law. The dichotomy and the relationship between the subject – the knower, the thinker – and the object – what the knower knows and the thinker thinks about – play a central role in the understanding of knowledge and society. The richness of the term 'subject', whether referring to the politico-legal, philosophical or a human being, illustrates the appeal of this framework to different fields of study. The notions of subject and object belong also to the classical vocabulary of the positivist or doctrinal study of law, especially public international law (PIL). Subjects form an unavoidable part of every contemporary international law treatise. But it is not at the heart of contemporary analysis of European Union (EU) law and policy.

The specific origins of EU law were framed by the Court of Justice (CJEU) by redefining its subjects, in its construction of the EU founding treaties, in a foundational decision in the 1960s, discussed in detail herein. However, for whatever reason, we argue there has yet to be sufficient engagement with these notions in EU law. This book explores whether the logic, the nature and reach of EU law and policy can be persuasively captured by investigating its subjects and objects. Our main claim is that the lexicon of subjects and objects offers a platform to

* The authors wish to thank Faizah Patel and Angelika Braouzi for research assistance, Panos Koutrakos, Marios Costa, Kangle Zhang and David Seymour for comments, and the participants of this research project from 2014 to 2016 for discussions that helped shape this contribution. The authors are grateful for the support of the City Law School and of the Centre for Comparative and European Law of the University of Kent.

capture and analyse three specific issues. These are: the transformations, crises and the external/internal nexus of EU law. This volume is structured so that the contributions and case studies are organised in one normative-theoretical part and three parts that correspond to these three elements, often overlapping or cross-cutting.

The introduction to the volume starts by discussing the subjects of EU law, their original framing by the CJEU in *Van Gend en Loos* and what we might call a 'conventional' meaning of the subject of EU law. It goes on to propose that the subjects of EU law could be captured by a different definition, one that does not rely on the idea of a subject as bearer of rights and duties and a politically and legally active participant in the legal system. By adopting a more critical understanding of the word 'subject', a broader spectrum of the subjects can be captured by scholarly analysis. Capturing a broader spectrum of the legal subjects, however, does not mean that their political capacity cannot be scrutinized. The introductory text continues on to describe the difficulty in defining the objects of EU law and proposes a taxonomy of the different approaches to this issue. It discusses objects of EU law as a question of jurisprudence and procedure and as a construct and considers the constitutional and the administrative approach to the question. The chapter refrains from passing a final judgment on the definition of the object of EU law and accordingly warns against drawing a sharp line between the subjects and the objects of EU law. This text argues that observing EU law from the perspective of its subjects and objects is an alternative to systemic approaches. It also harbours potential to capture and analyse the legitimacy gaps and omissions fostered by contemporary EU law, evident within the three areas of transformations, crises and the internal/external nexus of EU law.

The final section of this chapter aims to establish a connection between the introductory chapter and the contributions collected in this volume. It does so by presenting four sets of questions that were posed to the contributors to facilitate the identification of the three elements considered in the individual case studies (transformations, crises and external/internal nexus).

1. SUBJECTS OF EU LAW

1.1 The Original Framing of Subjects (and Objects) in EU Law

The central claim on which this book is based is that the framing of its subjects and objects is an important element in the development and formulating of EU law. What we could call the 'original' framing of the subjects, the recognition by the Court of Justice of the European Union (CJEU) in its landmark judgment in *Van Gend en Loos* that the subjects of EU law are not only the Member States but also the individuals (nationals of the Member States), carries an importance of what is usually called constitutional character.[1] Miguel Poiares Maduro described this move as a 'subjectivation' of the treaties: EU law has moved from the state-based interpretation of the treaties to the individual-based interpretation.[2] In Daniel Halberstam's account, on the one hand *Van Gend en Loos* contained a 'radical [constitutional] disaggregation of the State', and on the other hand is the beginning of a 'normative [and democratic] recalibration of the Community system', a normative 'turn to the individual'.[3] In absence of an external constitutional author for Europe that is often imagined in constitution-making, the reallocation of roles and redefinition of the Member States and the individuals in *Van Gend en Loos* is considered one of the first elements of 'Europe's piecemeal constitution'.[4]

By and large, the framing of subjects of EU law in *Van Gend en Loos* was a prelude to a drift of EU law from the logic of public international law (PIL). By authoritatively framing the subjects of EU law, the CJEU extracted it from the long-standing debate concerning the dichotomy between subjects (more so than objects) in PIL. There, the perceived

---

[1] 'The Community constitutes a new legal order of international law for the benefit of which the states have limited their sovereign rights, albeit within limited fields, and the subjects of which comprise not only the Member States but also their nationals': *Van Gend en Loos v Nederlandse Administratie der Belastingen* Case 26/62 ECLI:EU:C:1963:1; [1963] ECR 1, 12. De Witte, Bruno, 'The European Union as an International Legal Experiment' in de Búrca, G, and JHH Weiler (eds), *The Worlds of European Constitutionalism* (Cambridge University Press, Cambridge 2012) 19; de Witte, Bruno, 'EU Law: Is it International Law?' in Barnard, C, and S Peers (eds), *European Union Law* (Oxford University Press, Oxford 2014) 174.

[2] Maduro, Miguel Poiares, *We the Court – The European Court of Justice and the European Economic Constitution* (Hart, Oxford 1998), 9.

[3] Halberstam, Daniel, 'Pluralism in Marbury and Van Gend' in Maduro, MP, and L Azoulai (eds), *The Past and the Future of EU Law: Revisiting the Classics on the 50th Anniversary of the Rome Treaty* (Hart, Oxford 2008) 29. See also Halberstam, Daniel, 'The Bride of Messina: Constitutionalism and Democracy in Europe' (2005) 30 ELR 775, 777.

[4] Halberstam, Daniel, 'Internal Legitimacy and Europe's Piecemeal Constitution: Reflections on Van Gend at 50' in Tizzano, A, J Kokott and S Prechal (eds) *50th Anniversary of the Judgment in Van Gend en Loos (1963–2013)* (Office des publications de l'Union européenne, Luxembourg 2013) 116.

redundancy of the subjects' formulation has brought about many alternative theorisations of the 'actors' of PIL. For example, it has caused some to argue for a reformulation from subjects and object to 'participants',[5] so as to escape the so-called 'prison' of the distinction.[6] The entire discourse of PIL has arguably operated as a fight for inclusion as regards subjects and objects.[7]

It is stated that many international lawyers agree what the subjects doctrine is without explaining it.[8] One may note that, in PIL, the subjects doctrine has been argued to act as the 'clearinghouse' between sources and substance.[9] It is a discourse perceived to be perpetuated by subjective or even 'old-fashioned' positivists. It has most famously ignited a debate on the place of non-state actors in PIL. Instead, some call for more elaborate conceptual tools to systematize the lexicon of non-state actors and their role played in contemporary international law. Yet whether the solution lies in 'relativizing the subjects' or 'subjectivising the actors' remains for some time open to doubt.[10]

1.2 The Critiques of the Original Framing of the Subjects of EU Law

What kind of a subject is the subject of EU law as framed in *Van Gend en Loos*? The Court does not offer an extensive reasoning for its redefinition of the circle of subjects and recognition of individuals as subjects of EU law. It relies on the finding that, first, that '[i]ndependently of the legislation of Member States, Community law [...] not only imposes obligations on individuals but is also intended to confer upon them rights which become part of their legal heritage'.[11] Second, behind the Court's framing of the subjects is the fact that the Treaties have

---

5 Eg Higgins, Rosalyn, *Problems and Process: International Law and How We Use It* (Oxford University Press, Oxford 1994), referencing the Yale School.

6 Bianchi, Andrea, *Non-State Actors and International Law* (Ashgate, Aldershot 2009).

7 Bianchi (n.6).

8 See Alvarez, José E, 'Are Corporations "Subjects" of International Law?' (2011) 9 *Santa Clara Journal of International Law* 1; Clapham, Andrew, *Human Rights Obligations of Non-State Actors* (Oxford University Press, Oxford 2006).

9 Klabbers, Jan, '(I Can't Get No) Recognition: Subjects Doctrine and the Emergence of Non-State Actors' in Bianchi (ed.), *Non-State Actors and International Law* (2009) 55.

10 Bianchi, Andrea, 'Relativizing the Subjects or Subjectivizing the Actors: Is That the Question?' in Bianchi (ed.), *Non-State Actors and International Law* (2009) xi ff.

11 *Van Gend en Loos* (n.1).

established institutions 'endowed with sovereign rights, the exercise of which affects Member States and also their citizens'.[12] Lastly, the individual is also a subject as he is accorded political subjectivity in the sense of having a say in the decision-making of the then Community, or in the words of the Court, he is 'called upon to cooperate in the functioning of this Community through the intermediary of the European Parliament and the Economic and Social Committee'.[13]

The quotes reveal the individual as what we refer to as a *liberal subject*. By liberal subject, we refer to the liberal tradition of understanding an individual person and the *self*. Being a subject in the liberal sense equals bearing a number of (legal) rights which enable the subject to participate in society and pursue his project of self-determination.[14]

The subject of EU law as revealed in the quotes from *Van Gend en Loos* is, on the one hand, a bearer of rights and duties, particularly the newly recognized EU law rights. On the other hand, it is the subject of a supranational political order, someone who 'cooperates in the functioning' of the Union. The liberal subject of EU law is 'legally freed from the constitutional confines of her MS and endowed with […] an immediate "jurisgenerative" capacity at the supranational level'.[15]

The individual as legal subject of EU law is exposed to a set of expectations. The individual becomes a 'legal vigilante' (or 'Private Attorney General') of this legal order.[16] By invoking rights and entitlements conferred upon him by EU law, before national courts, he participates in a decentralized system of enforcement of EU law, praised for its efficiency.[17] The vindication of the individual's rights under EU law, which pursues his private interests, is utilized for the public interest of upholding EU law in relation to the Member State.[18] Joseph Weiler's critique of the original framing of subjects and objects of EU law is based primarily on the inadequate democratic legitimacy that would be capable of supporting the transformation of the EU legal order and its relationship with Member State law that ensued from the introduction of

---

12 *Van Gend en Loos* (n.1).

13 *Van Gend en Loos* (n.1).

14 Hughes, Cheryl L, 'Reconstructing the Subject of Human Rights' (1999) *Philosophy & Social Criticism* 49. Hall, Donald E, *Subjectivity (The new critical idiom)* (Routledge, New York and Abingdon 2004) 26–27.

15 Halberstam, Pluralism (n.3) 30.

16 Weiler, Joseph HH, '*Van Gend en Loos*: The Individual as Subject and Object and the Dilemma of European Legitimacy' (2014) I.CON 96.

17 Weiler (n.16).

18 Weiler (n.16).

direct effect and the recognition of the individual as a subject of EU law.[19] For Weiler, this turns an individual citizen into an object rather than a subject of EU law.[20] Yet, while one way to describe the expectations put upon liberal subjects of EU law is as 'instrumentalisation' or 'objectification' of the liberal subject, we explore whether these processes can be captured by a different understanding of what is the subject of EU law.

1.3 Subjects Constituted by EU Law

The proposal made here for such a different understanding is to look beyond the understanding of a legal subject as a bearer of rights and duties and someone who is active in the law-making process. The other dimension to which attention should be paid is that the (legal) subject is defined and recognized by the government and by the law. To apply the term used by Louis Althusser: the subject is constituted when he is 'interpellated'. Althusser's example of interpellation is the following: a person that turns around when called by the policeman on the street.[21] The policeman, by hailing the passer-by, creates out of him a subject answerable to law, to the State or to the legal system.[22] The identity of Althusser's subject had been ascribed to him beforehand. The subject only recognizes himself in the call, by answering accordingly.[23]

The understanding of the subject as an 'interpellated subject' is helpful as it allows for a broad range of entities that can recognize themselves as subjects of EU law due to the fact that EU law constitutes them and ascribes an identity to them. Compared to the idea that EU law has two narrow categories of subjects as proclaimed by the CJEU in *Van Gend en Loos*, based on recognizing the subjects as members of these two categories of politically empowered bearers of rights, this alternative understanding bears the promise of a much wider platform. A wide range of different individuals and entities can find themselves constituted in this way by EU law. The fact that an individual person is not a citizen of an EU Member State does not mean that Union law cannot constitute

---

[19] Weiler (n.16) 99 ff.

[20] Weiler (n.16) 102.

[21] Althusser, Louis, 'Ideology and Ideological State Apparatuses' in Althusser, Louis, *Lenin and Philosophy and other Essays* (Monthly Review Press, London 2001) 118.

[22] Mansfield, Nick, *Subjectivity: Theories of the Self from Freud to Haraway* (NYU Press, New York 2000) 53.

[23] Blunden, Andy, 'Althusser's Subjected Subject', accessed 27 January 2017 at *home.mira.net/~andy/works/althusser.htm*.

him as a subject. Persons who are citizens of countries that are not Member States, or who are stateless persons, can find themselves constituted as asylum seekers, as long-term residents, but also as workers, family members etc.

At the same time, legal persons are a vast and important group of subjects of EU law. Despite the fact that the framing of subjects of EU law was triggered by a corporation, the reasons given by the court to a large extent refer to a *citizen* of a Member State as the 'new' subject of EU law that takes his place next to the Member State. A different understanding of what is a subject can of course lead to a conclusion that corporations are constituted (as subjects) by EU law as natural persons are. Undoubtedly, a vast body of EU law can be seen to regulate, ascribe identity and recognize legal persons. Other entities may be constituted or recognize themselves in this way vis-à-vis EU law – for example, subnational units or organs of the Member States.[24]

Two observations should be made. First, many of the examples given in the preceding paragraphs (workers, citizens etc.) may also be seen as subjects (or enjoying at least traces of subjectivity) in the meaning of the word that was discussed initially: subjects as bearers of (some) rights (or duties), or as entities who enjoy standing in different procedures of EU Law. Second, it is not only EU law and its subject that can be observed by understanding its subjects as constituted or recognized by law. Every legal system could be observed in this way, and this approach allows us to recognize the richness of different legal subjects that it constitutes. It would seem, however, that EU law might offer particularly fertile grounds for the approach where subjects are understood to be constituted by law. Despite limited competences, EU law touches upon a large number of suspects in very different ways, defining countless positions for them. Even if, in a more positivist meaning of the word, a corporation is 'constituted', and thereby furnished with legal personality under the law of a Member State, not under EU law, and even if EU citizens are EU citizens by nature of their citizenship of a Member State, this does not preclude us from observing the many different ways in which an identity is ascribed to these subjects by EU law.[25] A different understanding of the

[24] See Josephine van Zeben in this volume, as well as Fasone, Cristina, 'National Parliaments in the EU. From new subjects to usual objects?' presented at the workshop on Framing the Subjects and Objects of EU Law, City, University of London 6 May 2016 (on file with authors).

[25] Alina Tryfonidou's contribution in this volume offers an insight into the complexity surrounding the fundamental mechanism of recognition of recognizing individuals as citizens of EU law by granting them Member State citizenship.

term 'subject', one that does not rely on being a bearer of rights, is liberating in the sense that we do not need to focus on the rights and entitlements of the subjects in order to observe and describe a wide spectrum of those subjects. It also allows us to use the lexicon of subjects to think of law beyond the rights and entitlements. This gives the exercise of framing the subjects of EU law a strong descriptive dimension. By that we mean that by merely referring to an individual, a corporation, an entity or a State as a subject of EU law, we are putting forward a claim that this subject should enjoy rights, entitlements, standing within EU law, its procedures and decision-making processes.

1.4 Subjects and Law

But if we are to follow the proposal and adopt a wider concept of legal subject (one that looks beyond the meaning of bearer of rights) the question arises: in what sense are thus-constituted and recognized subjects of EU law still 'legal subjects'? We draw on Damjan Kukovec's insight in this volume that '[w]e are all constantly deciding and creating our social and legal life in every social setting'.[26] The power of a legal subject to decide goes beyond what is usually considered to be the power of a legal subject: voting, putting forward initiatives, litigating and so on.[27] A subject acts within the law through a broad array of other actions – for example, purchasing an item from a shop or migrating to another country. These actions that can be performed by a legal subject are foreseen by the law and the law ascribes consequences to them. A subject of EU law, seen in this way, is 'always-already' a subject, practising acts through which he is recognized as a subject.[28]

A dimension of the legal subject that should not be overlooked is the subject's contribution to the understanding of law. The value in studying law using the lexicon of subjects and objects is that we can perceive 'subjects and objects of legal interpretation as equal partners in the constitution of the legal system'.[29] Jack Balkin's account presents a call for a more balanced view of law, one in which it is not only the object (i.e. law, the legal doctrine, the legal system) that is studied, but also the

---

[26] Damjan Kukovec in this volume.

[27] See n.26.

[28] Althusser (n.21) 117.

[29] Balkin, Jack, 'Understanding Legal Understanding: The Legal Subject and the Problem of Legal Coherence' (1993) 103 Yale LJ 134.

legal subject – the interpreter or the 'understander' of law.[30] We find that a balanced role of both subjects and objects of law in observing the law is of particular pertinence in EU law – a legal system that is interpreted by a vast multitude of different entities, natural and legal persons, courts, judges, lawyers, governments etc., belonging to a number of different legal traditions, political and ideological orientations and economic circumstances. In the EU, these traditions, orientations and circumstances vary to a larger extent that in any national legal system. Our interest in the dimension of the subject of EU law as the interpreter of EU law, however, does not mean that we are prepared to overlook the political dimension of the subjects of EU law.

1.5 Political Capacity of the Subjects of EU Law

When observing its political dimension, the subject of EU law again reveals itself as ambiguous and versatile. Two aspects of this issue are discussed here to illustrate the complexity of the political capacity of the subjects of EU law. In this Section, we look at the legal sources. In the following Section, we observe the political capacity of the *citizen* as subject of EU law, recognizing it as a particularly salient case study in the political dimension of the subjects of EU law.

The EU Treaties constituted a variety of political subjects of the European Union. The drafters drew a distinction between representative democracy and participatory democracy, without clarifying the relationship without them, possibly creating tensions between the two approaches to democracy.[31] But representative and participatory democracy are primarily distinguished as there are different circles of subjects drawn by the Treaties. The definition of subjects of representative democracy of the European Union resembles the original framing of subjects of EU law in *Van Gend en Loos*. It is the citizens that are represented in the European Parliament; and it is the Member States that are represented in the European Council and in the Council, and expected to be democratically accountable to *their* citizens (Article 10(2) TEU).[32]

---

30 Balkin (n.29). The work of Siniša Rodin is also an analysis of the subject as understander and interpreter of EU law, focused on the CJEU understanding and interpreting EU law. See Siniša Rodin in this volume.

31 Kutay, Acar, 'Limits of Participatory Democracy in European Governance' (2015) 21 (6) ELJ 803–818.

32 An illustrative example of the perception of the EU citizenship as endowing the subject with political capacity presented by Alina Tryfonidou: Chapter 8 of this volume.

These are the subjects, whose 'involvement [has been] institutionalised through the EU's law-making process'.[33] These circles of subjects also appear in other accounts, for example they are perceived by Jürgen Habermas as the subjects of constitutional change in the European Union.[34]

The subjects of participatory democracy are defined in a number of partly overlapping circles, with only some of the forms reserved for citizens, acknowledging representative associations as well as the civil society, and even reaching the widely defined universe of 'parties concerned' (Article 11 TEU). This, of course, means that the circle of political subjects as constituted by the Treaties transcends the geographical or territorial boundaries of the Union, encompasses foreign or multinational corporations with considerable interest in the end result of the decision-making process of the EU legislature. The lexicon of subjects and objects can serve to identify cases where political capacity as enjoyed by the interested parties from non-EU countries can lead to access deficit between economic and non-economic subjects.[35]

A distinct class of political subjects of the EU, as 'constituted' by Article 12 TEU, are the parliaments of the Member States. Mentioning the national parliaments in the Treaties, a development introduced by the Treaty of Lisbon, is a great illustration of how expectations that EU law has from its subjects, and the identity it assigns to them, go hand in hand with the creation of formal rights and empowerment to participate in the political process.[36]

1.6 Political Capacity of the Subjects and the 'Subjectification' of the European Citizen

We turn for a closer examination to one of the categories of subjects of EU law that were 'originally framed' in *Van Gend en Loos*: the *citizens* of the Member States. The citizen of the EU Member States as subject of EU law is particularly worthy of attention here due to the complexity of this concept. The citizen as a subject is a particularly complex issue because of the political dimension of his subjectivity. The political capacity, as recognized by the Treaties, which was discussed in the

---

[33] See Joseph Corkin, Chapter 5 of this volume.

[34] Habermas, Jürgen, *The Crisis of the European Union: A Response* (Polity, Malden MA 2012) 35.

[35] See further, Emilia Korkea-aho, Chapter 11 of this volume.

[36] Fasone (n.24).

previous section, is only one layer of the political dimension of the subjectivity.

Citizens of the Member States are not only EU citizens and subjects of EU law. In line with the understanding of 'subject' that we have outlined, we argue that they are constituted and defined also by their national legal systems. Competing legal claims of overlapping legal systems can be observed from the perspective of subjects as well.

Furthermore: individuals-citizens of Member States are 'subjectified'. That means that they are exposed to regulatory expectations, strategies and pressures that are exerted by government power. In this understanding of the subject, individuals are made subjects by a form of *power*, and this power 'categorises the individual, marks him by his own individuality, attaches him to his own identity'.[37] The individual faces a 'double bind' as he is not only controlled by the government. The power to which he is exposed also causes his individualization, and he is individualized by the power, in procedures, imposed upon him, through which he understands himself.[38] The understanding that a subject is constituted and shaped by the exercise of governmental power has been used in critiquing EU citizenship law as a progressive narrative.[39] Marco Dani draws our attention to the conflict that can emerge between contradictory supranational and national regulatory strategies, signalling the erosion of a citizen as a constitutional subject.[40]

An additional layer has to be added to the already complex coexistence of the two identities of the subject that is at the same time subject of EU law and citizen of a Member State. EU law has been offered as an answer to the question of external effects of the Member State law on the citizens of other Member States who have no political capacity that they could exercise in relation to the making of this law but are nevertheless affected by it, and, in certain constellations, (part-) constituted by it as its 'quasi-subjects'.[41]

---

37 Foucault, Michel, 'The Subject and Power' (1982) *Critical Inquiry* 781.

38 Foucault (n.37) 785; Hall (n.14) 92.

39 See Dani, Marco, 'The Subjectification of the Citizen in European Public Law' (2015) EUI Working Paper LAW 2015/02, 1–2, accessed 27 January 2017 at *hdl.handle.net/1814/34701*.

40 See n.39.

41 See Joseph Corkin in this volume. See Michelle Everson in this volume for the critique of this perspective.

1.7 Transformations in EU Law

We argue that the transformations that we have witnessed in EU law as the original framing of the subjects and objects to EU law, and ever-increasing growth in the scope, relevance, sphere of application and reach of EU law, can also be depicted as two overlapping layers of the individual citizen's subjectivity beginning in the nineties. Firstly, through the judicial creation of the *Francovich/Brasserie de Pêcheur* doctrine of State Liability for failure to implement EU law;[42] and secondly, through the strengthening of the infringement proceedings with the introduction of financial penalties.[43] The introduction of sanctions for the breach of EU law is a compelling example of how a certain transformation in EU law can be seen in different light depending on whether we observe it, on the one hand from the perspective of EU law as a legal system, and on the other hand from the perspective of the subjects of EU law.

From the former perspective, the introduction of sanctions can be hailed as the 'perfection' of EU law (stemming from *lex perfecta – lex imperfecta* dichotomy).[44] From the perspective of the citizen of a Member State as subject of EU law with a political dimension of his subjectivity, strengthening EU law with sanctions can also translate into more intensive pressure on the subject that is the target of government strategies. If the financial loss as the consequence of a breach of EU law is intended to incentivize the national politics not to breach EU law, then the principal mechanism to achieve this is through electoral accountability of the national government, cascading the pressure to comply with the supranational regulatory strategy down to the individual subject – the taxpayer and voter. At the same time, enforcement of EU law in its current form exemplifies well the schism between the subjects of EU *law* and what is the political dimension of these subjects – their capacity to form political decisions in the Member State. If on the one hand observing financial liability of Member States through the definition of subject as constituted by government regulatory pressures reveals the role of the subject in the functioning of the enforcement system, on the other hand the CJEU and the doctrine perceive the infringement proceedings as

---

[42] See, for example, Schütze, Robert, *European Constitutional Law* (Cambridge University Press, Cambridge 2012) 396.

[43] Art.260 TFEU.

[44] Baquero Cruz, Julio, 'Francovich and Imperfect Law' in Maduro, MP, and Azoulai, L (eds), *The Past and Future of EU Law: The Classics of EU Law Revisited on the 50th Anniversary of the Rome Treaty* (Hart, Oxford 2010).

proceedings of an 'objective character'.[45] The Government of the Member State, standing before the CJEU attempting to defend the Member State from the accusations of infringement, is barred from raising any kind of 'subjective' defence that would link the failure to comply with EU law to the Member State's parliament, courts, or subnational units.[46]

1.8 (In)Coherence of the Subject

In Section 1.4, we posited that the quest for a balanced role of subjects and objects as equal partners of legal interpretation was an important feature of studying law by observing its subjects and objects. Accordingly, we argue that attention ought also be paid to the role of the subject. In Jack Balkin's words: 'instead of seeing legal coherence as a pre-existing feature of an object apprehended by a subject, we should view legal understanding as something that the legal subject brings to the legal object she comprehends.'[47] However, if the contribution of the subject to the law and the subject's legal understanding is not to be overlooked, then we also cannot assume that the subject itself is coherent.[48] In Balkin's account, where the legal subject is an individual person, this is largely because the subject is herself socially constructed. Transplant this idea into the study of EU law, and a broad spectrum of incoherencies of the subject reveal themselves. As an example: the citizenship of one of the Member States or the citizen as subject of EU law (or the person's residence in a certain Member State ...) would seem to be an important determinant of the subject's social construction that influences the subject's understanding of the law. Acknowledging the incoherence of the subject of EU law allows us to factor into our study of EU law, for example, the centre-periphery dynamics at work in EU law, as explored in this volume by Damjan Kukovec.[49]

---

45 See Lenaerts, Koen, *Procedural Law of the EU* (Sweet & Maxwell, London 2006) 146.

46 Take the example of the Data Retention Directive, where Member States were threatened with fines or fined for the non-implementation of a directive that was subsequently found to be in violation of human rights (*Commission v Sweden* (Case C-270/11) ECLI:EU:C:2013:339). The pressure of EU law on the political subject to not only accept but via parliamentary accountability contribute to compliance with EU law is in conflict with the subject's identity as a constitutional subject.

47 Balkin (n.29).

48 Balkin (n.29).

49 See Damjan Kukovec in this volume.

The concept of the subject constituted by interpellation, introduced above in Section 1.3, can be conducive to understanding that the subjects are not all the same and that they are constructed in different ways. Through the lens of Althusser's theory of interpellation of the subject we can also observe how *groups* of subjects are constituted and defined.[50] In EU law, this can help us observe how subjects are interpellated and constituted through different roles: a subject is recognised and constituted as a worker, or as a family member.[51]

1.9 The Subject and the Crises

It is our claim that the platform of subjects and objects of EU law offers a valid starting point for the study of the crises that the European Union has faced in recent years. Indeed, this volume comes at a time when the Union's constitutional settlement and its law is presented with a number of challenges, including the emergence of illiberal regimes in some Member States and the implications thereof for the rule of law as a constitutional value and the arrival of a large number of refugees from Syria in Autumn 2015.[52] The most recent in the series of challenges is the June 2016 decision of the voters in the United Kingdom that their country is to leave the European Union.[53] The financial crisis, however, has so far seen the largest corpus of literature emerge attempting to analyse it within EU law and legal scholarship, mapping the changes in the constitutional landscape of the European Union and its law caused by the crisis and the responses to it.[54] It would seem that the crises have

[50] Zhang, Kangle, 'Border and Authority: Private Credit Rating in Neo-Liberal Society', Paper presented at the Borders, Otherness and Public Law, 2016 Conference of the International Society of Public Law (19 June 2016) (cited with permission of the author).

[51] See also, for example, the interesting discussion on the 'good citizens' and the 'bad citizens' in EU law. Loïc Azoulai, 'The (Mis)Construction of the European Individual: Two Essays on Union Citizenship Law', EUI Department of Law Research Paper No. 2014/14, accessed 28 January 2017 at *ssrn.com/abstract=2515889*, 11.

[52] 'From eurocrisis to asylum and migration crisis: Some legal and institutional considerations about the EU's current struggles, Editorial Comments' (2015) CMLR 1–14.

[53] Craig, Paul P, 'Brexit: A Drama in Six Acts', Oxford Legal Studies Research Paper No. 45/2016, forthcoming in *European Law Review*.

[54] See Menéndez, Agustín J, 'Editorial: A European Union in Constitutional Mutation?' (2014) ELJ 127–141. See also Dawson, Mark, and Floris de Witte, 'From Balance to Conflict: A New Constitution for the EU' (2016) ELJ 386.

touched upon several different categories of subjects. Member States have stepped outside the Treaties on a number of occasions – as was confirmed, this was in compliance with EU law[55] – to develop the responses to the crisis. What at first sight could be interpreted as an empoverment of the sovereign States has led to wide gaps between the creditor nations and the debtor nations. The political capacity of the individual citizen as subject of EU law has taken its toll. National decision-making in Member States where austerity measures have been imposed by the representatives of the lenders is a curious species of democracy without a choice.[56] These diagnoses seem to call for a revisiting of the role of the subject in the crisis situation.

While it may be reliably observed that the pressures exerted on the subject by the government pursuing its regulatory strategies increase as the manoeuvre space of national decision-making narrows, it would seem that these processes have taken on new forms. Is there space for any political capacity of the subject within the broader frame of the subjectification pressures experienced by both categories of subjects with the political dimension, citizens/individuals as well as Member States? The contribution of Emilios Christodoulidis on the substitution of *subjective* choice and decision-making with the *objective* output requirements casts a shadow of doubt on this being possible altogether.[57] Or, from the other perspective, where is the *power* now, in the new *societas economica* analysed by Michelle Everson in her contribution? Rather than the exercise of power from the sporadically conflicting supranational and national government, as we have observed *pre-crisis,* who is the source of the governmental pressures on the subject now, *post-crisis?*[58]

---

[55] *Ledra Advertising ltd and others* (Joined Cases C-8/15 P to C-10/15 P) ECLI:EU:C:2016:701; C-370/12 *Pringle*, EU:C:2012:756.

[56] As phrased by Commission President Jean-Claude Juncker, '*Il ne peut y avoir de choix démocratique contre les traités européens.*' Delaume, Coralie, Du traité constitutionnel à Syriza : l'Europe contre les peuples, *Figaro*, 2 February 2015. Or Germany's finance minister Wolfgang Schäuble: 'Elections change nothing. There are rules.' Hewitt, Gavin, 'Greece: The dangerous game', *BBC News*, accessed 27 January 2017 at *www.bbc.co.uk/news/world-europe-31082656*.

[57] Emilios Christodoulidis in this volume.

[58] Michelle Everson in this volume. Recent ECJ case law confirms the 'informality' of the Eurogroup which indirectly leads to impossibility of judicial review of its decisions (*Konstantinos Mallis and others* (Joined Cases C-105/15 P to C-109/15 P) ECLI:EU:C:2016:702, para.49), echoing the words reported by the former Greek minister of finance Varoufakis: 'Eurogroup does not exist in law'. Lambert, Harry, 'Our battle to save Greece (Interview with Yanis Varoufakis)',

2. THE OBJECTS OF EU LAW

2.1 On Actors and EU Law

The contributions to this volume understand an object of law predominantly in two ways. First, the object is whatever is regulated by law.[59] Second, the object can also mean what the subject thinks, perceives or interprets.[60] They are all nonetheless united in being actor-centric accounts. One practical difficulty in approaching a method to identify the objects of EU law is that there is no agreed definition of an *actor* under EU law.[61] Instead, a sharp distinction is drawn between the masters of the treaties and those amenable to judicial review or those with legal personality – yet it does not inform the framing of EU law's objects. The grant of legal personality under EU law has been accorded on a wholly pragmatic rather than conceptual basis.[62] Many new actors created in recent times are not technically institutional actors: for example, the European External Action Service (EEAS), the European Cybercrime Centre (EC3) or the European Public Prosecutors Office (EPPO). Instead, they are carved up in other ways, for example, in the case of the EC3 as 'desks' of other institutions, e.g. Europol. This does not appear to preclude their autonomous development.[63] Formalist understandings of those who are the objects of EU law are thus unable to capture much about EU law. It lacks realism about autonomy and institutional behaviour.

What might be phrased as increased levels of role circularity is also of relevance to the issue of the objects of EU law not being assisted by its constituent definitions of 'actors'. For example, executive actors of the EU (e.g. the European Council or the Euro group, ECOFIn) increasingly

New Statesman, 13 July 2015, accessed 27 January 2017 at *www.newstatesman.com/world-affairs/2015/07/yanis-varoufakis-full-transcript-our-battle-save-greece*.

[59] This perspective is arguably obscured by a different understanding of how subjects are defined and constituted by power, ideology, law, etc., introduced in Section 1.3 above, which allows us to 'reframe' and have a wide net which catches a wide circle of subjects.

[60] As for example Rodin in this volume, or Balkin (n.29).

[61] See Ruffert, Matthias, 'Personality under EU Law: A Conceptual Answer Towards the Pluralisation of the EU' (2014) ELJ 346.

[62] See n.61.

[63] Gatti, Mauro, 'Diplomats at the Bar: The European External Action Service Before EU Courts' (2014) 39 (5) ELR 664.

impinge upon domestic politics, often significantly so.[64] How do we account for this role circularity when we consider the subjects and objects of EU law? We seek to incorporate a broader perspective on actors in EU law and seek to look at those beyond or outside the analytical capture of EU law.[65] Beyond individual actors per se as entities or objects, the taxonomy or typology of the objects of EU law necessitates further analytical method, to which this account next turns.

2.2 Transformations of the Subject and Object: On Role Circularity

As to the question of how we understand the term 'the objects of EU law' as a term of art, this project adopts the view that a range of analytical approaches warrant exploration. As outlined above, on a purely descriptive (or even 'empirical') analysis, the treaties reference a vast array of terms as to entities other than Member States in the treaties, citizens, third parties, interests, third countries, but do not employ the generic term of objects, or anything specific about 'others'.[66] The limitations of such an empirical approach are thus rather straightforward. The challenge, we argue, lies in that there is an overt circularity at the heart of deciphering subjects and objects. This is principally because in various ways, the 'subject' that we write of includes 'Member States', 'state institutions' and 'individuals'. To an extent, they are all 'subjects', as has been demonstrated above. However, as we have also tried to show, the perception of a subject modelled on the free and autonomous

---

[64] Puetter, Uwe, *The European Council and the Council: New Intergovernmentalism and Institutional Change* (Oxford University Press, Oxford 2014); Curtin, Deirdre, 'Challenging Executive Dominance in European Democracy' (2014) 77 MRL 1; de Waele, Henri, 'Strained Actorness – The "New" European Council in Theory and Practice' in Fahey, E (ed.), *The Actors of Postnational Rule-Making: Contemporary Challenges of EU and Public International Law* (Routledge, Abingdon 2015); Bovens, Mark, and Deirdre Curtin, 'An Unholy Trinity of EU Presidents? The Political Accountability of Post-Crisis EU Executive Power' in Chalmers, D, M Jachtenfuchs and C Joerges (eds), *The End of the Eurocrat's Dream: Adjusting to European Diversity* (Cambridge University Press, Cambridge 2016) 190.

[65] Consider e.g. Jones, E, A Menon and S Weatherill (eds), *The Oxford Handbook of the European Union* (Oxford University Press, Oxford 2012) focusing upon 'personalities' Member State cleavages, Institutions and Member States as the 'typology' of actors in the EU in a multi-disciplinary context.

[66] The Member States of the EU are empirically and explicitly the primary 'subjects' of the EU treaties, receiving more references than any other entity in the treaties: see our calculation as follows using Eur-lex and Curia databases (at the time of writing), with thanks to Faizah Patel also for her assistance.

individual is not likely to cover a broad spectrum of EU law. The subject of EU law is not disenganged from its object cleanly via 'neat lines' in the treaties.[67] Take also, for example, the *treaties* that constitute the EU. They are objects of subjective (i.e. among Member States, the subjects) agreements, but then take on an objective character over those same subjects. There are multiple objects of EU law who are also the subjects of EU law but not involved in its making, for example Norway or Switzerland, hence a construction of participation or active engagement is not necessarily instructive. To sidestep the formalism and positivism that we wish to escape, we may unintentionally fall back into another radical form of separation between 'subjects' and 'objects' and, in so doing, reproduce the legitimacy gap that we want to overcome.

Table 1.1 Empirical count of the subjects and other entities referenced in treaties

Word	TEU	TFEU
'Citizens'	14	5
'Contracting parties'	1	1
'Member States'	99	400
'Subjects of the treaties'	0	0
'Subject of the treaties'	0	0
'Subjects of the agreements'	0	1
'Subject of an agreement'	1	1
'Third Parties'	1	6
'Third Persons'	0	0
'Third countries'	5	45
'Interests'	13	21

2.3 (In)Coherence of the Objects of EU Law: On Taxonomies

As a result, we assert that there is a significance to taxonomizing analytical methods as to the subjects and objects of EU law as part of our framing and reframing exercise. Strictly speaking, the *objects* of EU law remain more troublesome, more opaque and more multifarious than its subjects, even if a perfect or clear separation of them both might be

[67] Taylor, Charles, *Philosophical Arguments* (Harvard University Press, Cambridge MA 1997) Ch 1, 'Overcoming Epistemology'.

unsatisfactory. One method might be to consider approaching the question of the objects of EU law as a descriptive question of *jurisdiction and procedure*, which is of much contemporary significance in case law, heavily centred upon secondary law and specifically environmental and financial and banking regulation in its focus.[68] Such an approach appears to run into difficulties with its singular emphasis upon territoriality in an era of law beyond the nation state, its definition of law and rules, its constructivist tendencies and its limited range of case studies qua fields of law.

A further alternative would be to matter-of-factly consider the objects of EU law as a *construct*, flowing from foundational jurisprudence warranting a broader methodology to engage with its contours. It is one which is commonplace in contemporary environmental law, EU taxation, banking and financial services law, EU refugee and migration law, data protection and EU competition law.[69] Indeed, it is now a regular occurrence of EU law such that it is broadly agreed to have global reach.[70] The claim of global reach is usually substantiated by its authors to the effect that EU policy documents and legislation regularly attempt to link the internal to the external in EU law and policy with much transparency, including more frequently mooting its extraterritoriality. EU politics also emphasizes the global ambitions of EU law as warranting exploitation. Yet this does not necessarily provide us with real analytical clarity as to the category of others, institutions, entities or countries which are the recipients or takers of EU law qua others.

A further method might be a *constitutional analysis* of the boundaries of the internal and external of EU law, reflecting upon the objects of EU law as a tangential issue within an analysis of competence. This is common in mainly external relations scholarship, focusing upon international agreements and secondary legislation and its overlap with the internal market. EU external action may 'lead' or even eclipse internal policy development 'outwards in', which is not necessarily obvious as a

---

68 See Scott, Joanne, 'The New EU Extra-territoriality' (2014) 51 (5) CMLR 1343; Scott, J, 'From Brussels with Love: The Transatlantic Travels of European Law and the Chemistry of Regulatory Attraction' (2009) 57 (4) AJCL 897.

69 See n.68.

70 See Bradford, Anu, 'The Brussels Effect' (2012) Northwestern Univ Law R 1; Fahey, Elaine, *The Global Reach of EU Law* (Routledge, New York and Abingdon 2016); Damro, Chad, 'Market Power Europe' (2012) 19 JEPP 682.

matter of EU law.[71] For example, certain international agreements entered into by the EU have acted as the catalyst for internal EU legislation. The EU-US Passenger Name Records Agreements and EU-US Transatlantic Financial Tracking Programme (TFTP) (Swift) Agreement have triggered the development of comparable internal EU legislative proposals.[72] This analysis is mostly conducted from the perspective of competence and a discussion of the role of the Court of Justice as to its constitutional significance, with a small 'c'.[73] Yet what the precise elements of the objects of EU law are now is not discernible from this. There is also little by way of case law in this area despite the analytical style here which is predominantly 'court-centric'. Contrasting approaches adopted here in this vein but broadly within this genre are adopted by Corkin in this volume (as to transnational constitutional law and the EU as a political community).[74]

A more concrete approach might be to reject the constitutional character of such an analytic method and to focus upon the question of the objects of EU law as one requiring an *administrative approach.* From primary law to secondary law and the plethora of administrative instruments deployed in the treaties, they raise a question as to the evolving nature of their scope beyond the EU and its territories, beyond existing partners and deliberately embed an ambiguity as to the ends of EU law. For example, Art.11(3) Treaty on the European Union (TEU) provides that the Commission is obliged to consult in its administrative rule-making with 'the parties concerned', a phrase that appears to encompass stakeholders irrespective of their country of origin and which is interpreted broadly in EU policy documents. As the accounts of Vianello and Korkea-aho will explore, many EU administrative decisions are addressed to individuals or legal persons in third countries and there are also many obligations under EU law to initiate coordination or to monitor third-country conditions or international progress. The Ombudsman has significantly expanded the remit of her role in internal relations through conducting extensive analysis of the transparency as to third-party

[71] Cremona, Marise, 'EU External Relations: Unity and Conferral of Powers' in Azoulai (ed.), *The Question of Competence in the European Union* (Oxford University Press, Oxford 2014).

[72] See Fahey (n.64), Ch.2.

[73] Cremona (n.71); Eeckhout, Piet, *The European Internal Market and International Trade – A Legal Analysis* (Oxford University Press, Oxford 1994).

[74] See also Fasone (n.24).

interests in EU law.[75] These administrative approaches to the 'others' of EU law appears centrally focused upon EU external relations and environmental law. This is evident in the approaches adopted by Vianello and Korkea-aho in this volume as to EU Administrative and Environmental law.

A further complexity to that approach might suggest that administrative law approaches are themselves limited normatively and their innocuous character creates expectations and consequences which are non-innocuous for third countries and individuals. The question then arises less as to *who* the objects of EU law are but rather *how* they are treated. The Treaty of Lisbon makes clear that the Union, when acting on the international scene, shall not only promote the rule of law but shall also respect it in the development and implementation of its external action.[76] However, as Vianello will argue in this volume, this obligation requires redefining the actorness of the EU in its relations with third countries as well as the actorness of the third countries themselves. Still, the approach of the EU must be gauged by a standard and the most frequent reference point in EU law for conduct is in the form of *equal treatment or non-discrimination and respect for fundamental rights.* We argue that such an approach has a distinguished pedigree at the heart of understanding the evolution of EU law beyond a customs union into a more sophisticated supranational project but yet does not necessarily offer clear answers. For example, in contemporary times, much debate in the context of the TTIP negotiations rests upon the treatment of foreign investors under EU law. Examples of this approach might be evident from the case studies conducted in this volume respectively by Poli (on restrictive measures and the broadening range of objects of EU law, rendering them subjects) and Velluti (on the objects of the EU's conditionality in its trade relations with respect to labour rights).

Yet the lack of a perfect fit in terms of a method (empirical, jurisdictional, constructivist, constitutional, administrative or equal treatment based) need not necessarily cause us concern. Rather, we argue that our project proposes a clearer taxonomy of the *range* of applicable approaches, many of which are evidenced in this book within individual case studies. They remind us of the importance of pushing out the

---

[75] Regulation (EC) No 1049/2001 of the European Parliament and of the Council of 30 May 2001 regarding public access to European Parliament; Transparency of the Transatlantic Trade and Investment Partnership, Decision of 6 January 2015, accessed 27 January 2017 at *www.ombudsman.europa.eu/en/cases/summary.faces/en/58670/html.bookmark*.

[76] See Ilaria Vianello in this volume.

barriers of method that cause us to exclude case studies, lose sight of contemporary significance or overlook the intellectual 'elephant in the room' (by which we could mean the role of the CJEU in EU law).

3. THE SUBJECTS AND OBJECTS AS A METHODOLOGICAL FRAMEWORK FOR EU LAW

3.1 A Narrative for Transformations and Crises

The exercise of framing methodologically and reframing substantively the subjects and objects of EU law is thus motivated by a concern for how to address legitimacy issues of EU law arising from the manifold role circularities prevailing. This is not a new concern, but we suggest that it is its most fundamental. The primary interest here is in social legitimacy of EU law in light of the transformations of EU law that we observe, and a subjects-objects relationship that can no longer rely upon output legitimacy so as to overlook social legitimacy concerns.[77] Social legitimacy is a subjective measure; it is based on the subjects and their acceptance of the political regime on a deeper level than merely the popularity of the institutions etc.[78] It stems from the subject's *belief* that the action, rule or system is morally or legally legitimate. In that sense, it is an elusive task to look for ways in which the legal system can be changed in order to foster its own social legitimacy. We claim, however, that there is an essential prerequisite for the legal system to obtain acceptance from its subjects. It is to recognize the contribution of the subjects' legal understanding rather than rendering the subject's input into the object of legal understanding invisible.[79] We focus upon an inquiry into the relationship of the legitimacy of EU law on the one hand and the plurality of different actors, actions and rules as well as the relationships between them on the other hand. We thus seek to address through methodology the question of legitimacy in a way which deals realistically with coherence. We thus argue that structural normative coherence is possible *between* the subjects and objects of EU law.

[77] Weiler, Joseph HH, 'Europe in Crisis – On "Political Messianism", "Legitimacy" and the "Rule of Law"' (2012) *Singapore Journal of Legal Studies* 248.

[78] See n.77.

[79] Balkin (n.29).

3.2 Looking Beyond a Systemic Understanding of EU Law

We intentionally and consciously seek to side-step a systemic understanding of EU law, which we argue is prevalent in contemporary scholarship. Systemic ordering forms the intellectual basis for the most prominent *re*-engagements in contemporary literature with the development of both transnational legal orders and EU law as discipline.[80] We suggest that systemic understandings of legal orders or ordering offer little to address the social reality and social acceptance problems of contemporary EU law. We argue that systemic understandings of EU law have a particular circularity to them.[81] Systems-based understandings of EU law engage well with its complex multi-level structure and its living components, less so its substantive legitimacy issues.[82] Contemporary theorizations of transnational legal order give systems-based analysis significant precedence. Systemic understandings of EU law appear to reify its chaos, anarchy, unpredictability and irregularity. What has systems theory done for law-making beyond the nation state? We opine that order-based analyses are both over- and under-inclusive. This lack of focus upon the individual is considered in much detail by various case studies in this volume. Systems-based theorizations are striking for their lack of focus upon the individual. Moreover, we contend that the CJEU has rejected a Hartian understanding of EU law in its core case law through its embrace of the subject-object dialectic. This remains its defining characteristic which we argue warrants still further development as a future research agenda.

4. THE SUBJECT-OBJECT RELATIONSHIP AS A PLATFORM FOR EU LAW

We thus argue that the subject-object relationship provides a particularly useful platform in its lexicon for those grappling with key issues of EU

---

[80] See, for example, Halliday, Terence C. and Shaffer, Gregory, *Transnational Legal Orders* (Cambridge University Press, New York 2015) ch.1; Dickson, J, and P Eleftheriadis (eds), *Philosophical Foundations of European Union Law* (Oxford University Press, Oxford 2012), ch.1, both citing inter alia Luhmann and Teubner.

[81] See also de Witte (n.1).

[82] E.g. Teubner, Gunther, *Critical Theory and Legal Autopoiesis: Perspectives of Societal Constitutionalism* (Manchester University Press, Manchester 2016).

law and policy today. We argue that it supports the normative motivations underpinning the project, specifically to include the many omissions from contemporary EU law as set out in this project, and operates as both a powerful framing and reframing tool in this way. It has both a vagueness and flexibility – which we acknowledge and embrace – which is important in so far as it is malleable and broadly applicable across subject streams and sub-disciplines. It accordingly enables us to look *beyond* primary, secondary law and case law so as to look critically at broader developments, through a philosophically-minded lens which acts as a check upon context, real and actual framing and effects. By acting as an enabling device so as to explicitly articulate a broader context, the subjects-objects formulation thus bring transparency to these broader shifts that are charted by various authors. It is both a lexicon and methodology and shifts discourse in its own way and is thus a vivid narrative device. We accept the logic of the simultaneous and symbiotic status of subjects and objects as an integral part of its theoretical structure and contend that it sits on all fours with the theoretical foundations of EU law.

This book attempts to show how the transformational character of EU integration can be accurately captured through the specific study of the transformation of subjects and objects and, vice versa, in a set of particular case studies on its active and dynamic quality. The study of subjects and objects also enables us to consider the internal/external nexus of contemporary EU law with greater precision and transparency. It facilitates our specific study of territory, neighbourhood and the expanding portfolio of those captured by sanctions, regulation and conditionality all under one theoretical 'roof'. Most significantly, we aim to step back holistically and examine the EU project and its unfolding series of crises through the lens of subjects and objects. We can uncover much about exclusions and inclusions, legitimacy and regulatory capture in this period. As a result, we reach the width and depth of EU law. The lexicon of subjects and objects in particular forces a more specific 'take' upon who is most active and passive here, who is left out and the place of markets, risk and uncertainty in our methodological framing.

5. FORMAT OF THIS BOOK

This book is divided into four distinct parts. The first is the most theoretical and seeks to consider the normative motivation and theoretical underpinnings of the subject-object discourse (Part I). The next section considers explicitly the idea of transformations from subjects to objects and objects to subjects, thereby capturing the dynamic character of the subject-object relationship (Part II). The sections thereafter consider the expansive quality of the subjects and objects relationship as to EU law and focus upon the external dimension of EU law and its link to the internal, with respect to the range of actors, entities and subjects that it encompasses, excludes or captures (Part III). This leads to the final section, which seeks to approach methodologically the question of how we understand EU crises. It considers who has been the subject and object of EU measures. Who has been excluded? How do we frame discourse on crises? Who is most active or passive? How can we better capture a legitimacy narrative? (Part IV).

In each section, the authors were asked to address some of the following questions, where possible and applicable to their account. Thus, in Part I, all authors were asked to consider the following:

i. Is the dialectic between subjects and objects useful to capture EU law? Does it provide you with a platform, a means or simply a lexicon to describe your case study?
ii. Does reaching for the lexicon of subjects and objects help not only to present your theoretical contribution or case study, but also to advance your cause or normative claim within your case study?
iii. Do you find the subjects/objects to be more useful as a lexicon with which integration can be described or as a narrative device (with the flexibility to present a narrative holistically)?
iv. Is EU law expansionary in its objects and limiting in its subjects generally? Or expansionary as to both?
v. Are the PIL origins of EU law easily forgotten or practically overlooked?
vi. Do you agree that the lexicon and method of subjects and objects can be a reframing exercise of how we understand EU law?
vii. What is the most powerful motivation to re-orientate or reframe the subjects and objects of EU law?

In Part II, contributing authors were asked to consider the following questions:

i. Articulate if there is a transformation which is central to your case study or a by-product of it. Do you judge this transformation as positive?
ii. Who or what undergoes the transformation in your case study or account? Are there several such active/dynamic elements?

iii. Can the expansion of the scope, reach and relevance of EU law since the milestone in *Van Gend en Loos* be described as a transformation in the position of EU law's subjects and objects? Particularly in your case study?
iv. Is the transformation in your case study best described as a shift from subjects to objects (or objects to subjects) or as a change in the quality/meaning/position of the subject or object?
v. Does the application of the lexicon of subjects and objects to your case study or abstract considerations lead you to identify an omission of EU law? If so, is this omission a legal issue, a socio-political issue or something else?
vi. How, in particular, are individual persons visible in your account of subjects and objects of EU law?
vii. Are citizens both subjects and objects through national and supra-national dichotomies?
viii. Which is more common, shifts from objects to subjects or subjects to objects?
ix. Is a discussion of objects possible without subjects? Could you exclude citizens from your account?
x. Does the transformational quality/active/dynamic quality of subjects and objects assist your case study?
xi. Articulate what the subjects/objects distinction lends to your account.
xii. Is this account partially/wholly/substantially transformational?

Authors in Part III were asked to consider the following questions:

i. Can you articulate the internal/external nexus of EU law in your case study?
ii. How does subject/object align to the internal/external?
iii. Are objects 'external' only?
iv. How do objects become subjects in EU external relations law? Who is involved? Who is most active or instrumental?
v. What is the role of fundamental rights in the shift between subjects and objects here? How do you frame fundamental rights?
vi. Do exclusions from rights to fair procedures/legitimate explanations cause greater challenges for objects or subjects? What makes you form this judgement? Do primary or secondary sources assist you most? What hierarchical structure of norms assist you in your analysis (please be explicit if possible)?
vii. What is external about your case study? Is this well understood or accepted, do you think?

viii. How does the subject/object dynamic change your case study? How would it tell it without it or what added value does it present to you?

And in Part IV, authors were asked the following set of questions:

i. Do the crises need to be understood holistically (e.g. by approaching the different crises in the EU – financial, migrant, Brexit – in order with a common understanding of a crisis) to describe the transformational shift from subject to object? Is a discrete case study, e.g. migration or the euro crisis, sufficient?
ii. Have crises generally changed the subjects and objects of EU law? Why? How?
iii. Does the subjects/objects dialectic capture well/wholly/partly an exclusion from the crises?
iv. What does the subject/object lexicon add to your crises case study?
v. How does the subject/object dialectic assist your case study? Does it develop a legitimacy narrative better?
vi. Are citizens or individual persons the biggest victims of the crisis/crises in your case study? Does the relevance of citizens as subjects diminish in the crisis? Would you describe the citizens as objects as a result of the crisis in your case study?
vii. Is there an external dimension to the crisis that appears in your case study?
viii. If the crisis you develop has seen the multi-level form of the EU change, e.g. EU Executive impinges more upon national politics, is the 'subject' eroded? If so, how do you understand the active quality of erosion?

We next invite the reader to reflect upon these broad areas of inquiry in the sections herein, followed by our Conclusions thereafter.

PART I

Reframing subjects and objects of EU law: normative motivations and theoretical underpinnings

2. The subject and object in the interpretation of EU law

Siniša Rodin*

INTRODUCTION

In this chapter, I will problematize, from the perspective of EU law, roles of different actors, subjects of legal interpretation, and the relationship between them and legal rules as objects being interpreted by them. I will suggest that different temporal and contextual frameworks within which interpretation takes place affect communication between the Court of Justice of the European Union and its critics. I would like to draw attention to the subject-object relationship in legal interpretation and to offer an alternative angle for reflection about judicial work and legal interpretation in general.

Following this introduction, Part 1 will set the methodological framework of my analysis. In Part 2, I will address criticism targeting the problem of coherence of the case law of the Court of Justice of the European Union (CJEU), alleged inability to control its own docket, lack of dissenting opinions, cryptic language of its judgments and legitimacy of its rulings. I will argue that critique of adjudication sometimes fails to identify functional comparators on which the very critique is based and claim that the Court of Justice delivers similar goods to other model courts, just in a different guise. Finally, in Part 3, I will suggest that immediate impact of judicial decisions dramatically differs from their transcendental impact, partly due to the change of context and utterer and partly due to the change of audience targeted by a decision.

---

* Positions expressed in this text are the author's personal opinions and do not represent opinions or positions of the Court of Justice of the European Union.

1. BY MEDIUM OF POSTERITY

In the famous novel by Robert Graves,[1] Claudius, the Roman emperor who suffered from a speech impairment, received a prophecy that was by no means self-explanatory. The relevant part of the prophecy reads: "But when he's dumb and no more here, Nineteen hundred years or near, Clau-Clau-Claudius shall speak clear."

According to Clayton Koelb,[2] in order to understand the prophecy, and to find out how a dumb and absent person can possibly speak clearly, one has to have recourse to two shifts: temporal and personal. First, the speech has to be addressed not to the present audience but to the future one. And, second, there has to be some divine intervention that, according to Koelb, entails the change of the utterer. It is not Claudius himself speaking, not even by means of his writing that, as a matter of fact, was lost, but the future author – Robert Graves – who resurrected the life and times of the long-dead emperor. Thus it is Graves, not Claudius, who tells the narrative. Claudius, being unable to speak clearly to his contemporaries, addresses, by divine intervention of Apollo, the future audience, but this time with clarity, through the medium of history and by the pen of a modern writer. So it is, I would suggest, with the Court of Justice. Ultimately, the original meaning of the Court's judgments is transformed and posterity comes to understand them through the interpretation of a future and contemporary subject.

As a consequence, one has to address the problem of contextual immersion. In order to judge Claudius' actions, or to present a critique of a given social phenomenon such as adjudication or administration of justice, one needs to be immersed in the original, not the contemporary context. One needs to address the critique to Claudius and not to Graves. One needs to realize the difference between the original and transcendental source of the narrative and recognize that a reasonable critique of the original subject entails temporal synchronicity with the original subject itself.

The process in which the unclear speech of the original utterer becomes clear comprises the following elements:

---

1 Graves, Robert, *I, Claudius* (Arthur Barker, London 1934).

2 Koelb, Clayton, 'The Medium of History: Robert Graves and the Ancient Past, in Comparative Literary Dimensions' in Halio, JL, and B Siegel (eds), *Essays in Honor of Melvin J. Friedman* (Associated University Press Inc, London 2000) 39.

- utterances of the original subject;
- temporal change from then to now;
- emergence of the contemporary subject;
- objectification of utterances of the original subject by agency of the contemporary subject; and
- transformation of the original utterances from unclear to clear.

2. THE ORIGINAL SUBJECT: FUNCTIONAL EQUIVALENTS AND JUDICIAL SYMBOLISM

In the case at hand the original subject of legal interpretation is a court, notably the CJEU. At the same time, it is an object of critique. Here the question arises, to what extent is it possible to apply the standards applicable to a court of one jurisdiction in order to criticize another? It would be too banal to claim that one court is similar to another just by the coincidence of the word 'court' or because of the similarity of their principal function, which is to settle disputes between parties.[3] Nevertheless, in many respects, courts of different jurisdictions *are* often similar. They settle disputes, interpret and apply rules of law, exercise authority, aspire to be independent, to speak clearly and reasonably, and be transparent in what they do. In that respect, a critique can take into account any of the above mentioned parameters and put them on a scale. Court A is more independent than court B. Judgments of court C are better reasoned than those of court D. Nevertheless, there is something deeply disturbing in this approach; namely, the critique addressed to a specific court in its institutional capacity seems to be directed to the wrong address.

There are at least three methodological problems. First, there is a problem in how to define the object of a critique. Typically, a critique understands courts – in our case the CJEU – as monolith, personified, subject-entities. There is some confusion here. From the perspective of a critic, a court, as a subject, decides, reasons (or does not), errs and speaks. On the other hand, a court as an object is (non)transparent, (in)coherent, and (un)clear. All this confusion of subject and object is at the core of the plot – the objectification of the original subject (a court) by agency of the contemporary subject (the critic). Thus, the first methodological problem is how to resolve the subject-object anxiety.

[3] To take another example of similarity, a table and a cow are similar in that both stand on four legs.

When in action, a court is a living subject that has a will of its own, that speaks (clearly or cryptically), that reasons, or settles disputes. Once a case is decided, its subjectivity disappears. It is no longer a subject. Interpretation of the results of adjudication depends entirely on the contemporary subject/observer/commentator.

The second methodological problem that is inherent in critique of adjudication is that referential frameworks of the original and contemporary subject do not seem to be commensurable. Single elements of judicial operation, such as independence, reasoning, dissent, transparency, clarity or coherence present themselves differently in different space-time contexts. Expressions like "judgment", "better", "transparent", "dissent" or "reasoned" are necessarily embedded in concrete social and legal contexts, and it can be assumed that a contemporary subject, an observer, belonging to a specific legal and political culture, can speak only from her own experience and tradition, that is, from a tradition which may be dramatically different from the one in which the result of adjudication was produced.[4]

The third methodological problem concerns the identity of the original subject. Regardless of the subject-object confusion, the monolith image of courts, or indeed other institutions, does not correspond to reality. There are always real men and women behind the scenes – judges, law clerks, administrators and other individuals – who operate within a certain social and legal context. A court itself, like any other institution, has no will of its own. And when an individual judge is set to work on a case, there are a number of contextual elements that direct her work. As human beings, judges have their personal beliefs and preferences. They have different social and educational backgrounds and a different understanding of the world. This is not to say that it is not reasonable to impose any social expectations on their work, such as expectations of reasonableness, impartiality, clearness or coherence. This is only to say that the problem is much more complex than it looked at the beginning. I am not trying to say that there are not and cannot be functional comparisons of courts and judges. The fact is simply that they operate in contexts so different that functional comparators are not obvious. With these methodological remarks in mind, I will now turn to the Court of Justice of the European Union.

---

[4] The insight that participants of a tradition speak from within their tradition comes from Feyerabend. See Paul Feyerabend, *Science in a Free Society* (NLB 1978).

Symbolic Language of the Court

One string of critique suggests interrelationship of appointment procedure and lack of clarity and dissenting opinions. In the absence of irrevocable mandate, it is suggested, judges refrain from speaking clearly, while anonymity of deliberation serves to protect judges from national political whim.

While the CJEU is, indeed, based on the somewhat cryptic French judicial culture, we have already learned that lack of transparency does not necessarily mean absence of reasoning. Writing about the French judicial system, Mitchell Lasser has revealed the rich internal debate within the Cour de Cassation as contrasted with the sparse language of its decisions.[5] Bruno Latour, on the other hand, disclosed the working methods of the Conseil d'Etat.[6] My argument here is different from Lasser's. Instead of contrasting internal and external life of the Court, I claim that the CJEU, even in the absence of dissent, and in spite of the sparse reasoning, speaks its own language. The language is symbolic and its grammar is procedure. It is precisely that symbolic language that a critic has to be aware of when scrutinizing the work of the Court.

An incoming case is first allocated to a reporting judge by the president of the Court. The reporting judge is required to write a preliminary report and, in agreement with an Advocate General allocated to the case by the First Advocate General, present it to the *Réunion Générale* (RG) – the plenum of the Court comprising all judges and Advocates General. In the report, the reporting judge must briefly present the case and make several proposals to the RG. While the report remains confidential and is disclosed only to judges and Advocates General, the decisions of the RG are communicated to the parties, Member States and the Institutions of the EU, depending on the situation.

The particulars of the preliminary report are the alphabet of the Court's symbolic speech. First, a formation of the Court needs to be decided. It can be a chamber of three, five, a grand chamber of 15 judges, or the full court. Second, the report will propose whether a judgment is needed or whether the case can be decided in a summary way by an *ordonnance*. Third, a judge rapporteur may propose that a hearing be held, as well as specifying the issues of law and fact which need to be addressed in a

---

[5] Lasser, Mitchel, *Judicial Deliberations: A Comparative Analysis of Judicial Transparency and Legitimacy* (Oxford University Press, New York and Oxford 2004).

[6] Latour, Bruno, *La Fabrique du droit. Une ethnographie du Conseil d'Etat* (La Découverte, Paris 2002).

hearing, in order to restrict the scope of the pleadings to certain points only. Fourth, there will be a proposal whether or not an opinion of the Advocate General is indicated, and if it is, as to which legal issues. Finally, a report will mention the agreement (or absence of it) between the reporting judge and the Advocate General, on all mentioned points.

Before the RG, the report is circulated to 28 judges and all Advocates General. While the procedure is one of tacit approval, each judge or Advocate General can submit a note, in which case the preliminary report will be automatically placed at list A and discussed by the RG. There is a variety of possible outcomes.

Allocation of a case to a chamber of three judges indicates that the law governing the case is clear and that the case will be handled according to the existing case law. Nevertheless, a hearing may be convened if the facts of the case are complex, if the Court does not feel sufficiently informed, or if it considers that it may be otherwise useful to resolve a contradiction existing between the parties. Conversely, there will be no hearing if the facts and legal positions of the parties have been sufficiently clarified during the written procedure. In a chamber of three, there will normally be no need for an opinion of an Advocate General, although, in the newer practice, it is not excluded. If a case is manifestly inadmissible or manifestly unfounded, instead delivering a judgment a chamber may decide by an *ordonnance*.

Chambers of five judges decide cases that require more reflection, either on grounds of complexity of facts, or on grounds of complex legal issues. It can be said that five-judge chambers are a default formation of the Court. A chamber of five can follow existing law and extend the scope of the existing case law to new situations. It can clarify previously decided cases, harmonize case law decided by the General Court or, sometimes, by chambers of three judges. Hearings are the rule rather than an exception, since complexity of facts and law may require oral explanations by the parties. Indeed, the parties themselves will often request a hearing but such requests are not binding on the Court. While the reporting judge has the privilege of proposing whether or not a hearing is indicated, the RG will have the final say. Indeed, the decision whether or not a hearing is indicated will often bring a case to list A and make it subject to discussion at the RG. The same holds for the decision whether to ask for an opinion of the Advocate General, although his or her position on its necessity has a strong persuasive force. Nevertheless, a chamber of five judges can also decide by an *ordonnance*, without a hearing and without an opinion.

A grand chamber of 15 judges is convened to decide on major legal issues that require intervention into existing law, in order to develop new case law, to overrule the existing case law, or to extend its scope to new areas. It will also be indicated where the Court has not previously expressed itself on a certain legal rule or a point of law.[7] According to the Rules of Procedure a Grand Chamber will have to decide upon a request by a Member State or in disputes between institutions of the EU. A Grand Chamber can also decide with or without an opinion of the Advocate General and with or without a hearing. In this respect all considerations previously mentioned in respect of a chamber of five apply. However, decisions of the Grand Chamber without a hearing and an opinion are not frequent. The possibility of deciding a case by an *ordonnance* is also not excluded. However, this is exceptional and usually bears certain symbolic meaning.

The full court decides only in exceptional situations. According to the Statute, the Court shall sit as a full court where it decides on dismissal of the Ombudsman,[8] compulsory retirement of a member of the European Commission[9] or of a member of the Court of Auditors,[10] or where it considers that a case before it is of exceptional importance.[11] What represents exceptional importance can be inferred from recent cases, notably *Pringle*.[12] Usual suspects for full court judgments are also requests for Opinions pursuant to Article 218(11) TFEU where the Court is called to rule on whether an international treaty to which EU plans to commit is compatible with the Treaties.[13]

While, undeniably, the procedure before the Court serves its own functional rationality which is the backbone of what the president of the

---

[7] E.g. *Pringle* (Case C-370/12) EU:C:2012:756.

[8] Consolidated Version of the Treaty on the Functioning of the European Union [2012] OJ C326/47 (TFEU), Art.228(2).

[9] TFEU, Arts 245(2) and 247.

[10] TFEU, Art.286(6).

[11] Protocol (No. 3) on the Statute of the Court of Justice of the European Union [2010] OJ C83/210 (Statute), Art.16 and Rules of Procedure of the Court of Justice [2012] OJ L265/1 as amended [2013] OJ L173/65 and [2016] OJ L217/69 (Rules of Procedure), Art.60.

[12] Case C-370/12 (n.7).

[13] An instance of a full court Opinion was on the occasion of the request for Opinion 2/13 concerning accession of the EU to the European Convention for Protection of Human Rights and Fundamental Freedoms, EU:C:2014:2454. More recently, the full court was seised in Opinion 2/15 Request for an opinion submitted by the European Commission pursuant to Art.218(11) TFEU, still pending.

Court, president Koen Lenaerts, calls 'internal legitimacy',[14] it also emits messages to other actors, such as the Member States, national courts, parties and, ultimately, everyone capable of understanding them. However, it must not be underestimated that the procedure is structured in such a way as to generate information scarcity. Among the multiplicity of actors, starting from the reporting judge, the Advocate General, to the RG, the chamber deciding a case, a national court, parties to the original dispute, Member States, and so on, each one of them, except the formation deciding the case, will be in possession of only some information. The remaining part will have to be reconstructed from the symbolic language of the Court. In other words, the fact that the Court, the original subject, is not 'speaking clear' to the contemporaries is a logical and, most likely, inevitable consequence of the role-playing and information scarcity.

For example, in a preliminary reference procedure, neither a referring national court nor the parties in the dispute before it will have any information about the proposal of the reporting judge to the RG and the discussions within the RG are protected by secrecy. However, once the case is allocated to, say, a Grand Chamber, and an advocate general has been seised to write an opinion, it will become clear that there is a major legal issue at stake and that the intention of the Court was to decide the case accordingly. It will be a signal to the parties to the original dispute to dig deep into their arguments, to reassess the law that governs the case and to be prepared to develop their arguments beyond the existing case law. They will have no clue about the directions the Court is considering to explore, but they will know that a window of opportunity has opened.

Communication between the Court and other actors is not a one-way street.[15] A thoughtful party to a national dispute will try to convince a national judge to formulate a preliminary reference in a way that will resonate at the Court. It will try to identify loose ends in the existing case law and to provoke the desired formation to decide the case. Again, available information will depend to the circumstances of each individual case, will be restricted to the relevant actors and to relevant issues of law and fact and will, due to scarcity of information, remain unclear to the

---

[14] Lenaerts, Koen, 'The Court's Outer and Inner Selves: Exploring the External and Internal Legitimacy of the European Court of Justice' in Adams, M, H de Waele, J Meeusen and G Straetmans (eds), *Judging Europe's Judges – The Legitimacy of the Case Law of the European Court of Justice* (Hart, Oxford 2013) 13.

[15] Bonichot, Jean-Claude, 'Le Rôle des parties au principal dans le traitement des questions préjudicielles' [2013] 277 *Gazette du Palais* 16.

wider audience. While for the parties and other actors to the proceedings information will be sufficient to avoid a situation where 'ignorant armies clash by night',[16] an outside observer might have had the impression that the Court did not speak clear. The Court's answer will typically be restricted to interpreting what is necessary for the referring court to solve the case that gave rise to the preliminary reference.

This process of rationalization is very well explained by President Lenaerts speaking about how the Court deals with political issues and comparing its approach to the US political questions doctrine.[17] The Court is strictly bound by the question asked by a referring court and needs to arrive at a legally binding decision that will help the national court to solve the case at hand. What may appear, to the outside, as a big political and social problem, internally becomes de-emotionalized and rationalized into a juridical conflict that the Court ultimately resolves. Certainly, the question can be asked what happens after the Court has resolved the problem in a rational and legal way and whether the decision, once published, will not be re-rationalized in political terms by the observers.

Sound of Silence

Absence of dissenting opinions at the CJEU appears to be a consequence of its general design. It is not my intention to discuss possible explanations, such as, for example, the need to insulate the work of the Court from the Member States who remain the appointing authority, or the need to speak with one voice in order to give an authoritative statement of law. In the same line, one can also mention the French legal tradition that is said to be at the origin of the Court's design. I will simply start from the existing design and suggest that, despite the absence of dissenting opinions, it is not impossible for an outside observer to identify the diverging legal positions. The process of detection is somewhat similar to detection of exoplanets that cannot be seen by a telescope but have to be imagined on grounds of oscillations of stellar gravity centres. So the differences in reasoning can be detected on grounds of opinions of

---

16 Arnold, Matthew, 'Dover Beach' (New Poems, 1867).

17 See 'Interview du Président Koen Lenaerts Part.3: Le président répond aux principales critiques faites à la Cour; La CJUE est-elle trop autonome, trop introvertie?' (*blogdroiteuropéen*, 8 April 2016) accessed 28 January 2017 at *blogdroiteuropeen.com/2016/04/08/interview-du-president-koen-lenaerts-part-3-le-president-repond-aux-principales-critiques-faites-a-la-cour/*.

Advocates General, formation of the Court and absence of certain elements of reasoning.

It has often been suggested that the role of Advocates General is remedial to the lack of clear reasoning of the Court and absence of dissent. According to the argument, an Advocate General can go beyond the immediate legal controversy and her opinion can shed light on considerations that have not been openly disclosed in the published judgment. While this explanation is certainly plausible, reality is more complex and has to be revealed by a contemporary subject. The easy situation is when the Court decides to follow an opinion and explicitly says so. However, the Court does not always follow the AG's opinions. When it chooses not to follow one, the judgment usually ignores the argument.[18] In such situations it can be inferred that prevailing arguments went against the position of the AG, or at least that a different line of reasoning was chosen.

Second, as already explained, the choice of formation deciding a case is also telling. Allocation to a chamber of three judges already indicates that existing case law will be followed. Such an allocation performs a similar role to a writ of certiorari in the legal system of the United States. On the one hand it allows a certain degree of docket control, since the case will be decided in an expedient way, and on the other hand it communicates the agreement of the majority of the Court that a certain legal issue does or does not deserve more substantial discussion. Admittedly, this will rarely reveal why the Court has undertaken a particular course of action, but, in the context of earlier 'well established' case law, can be telling why it has not. For example, the Court has always been reluctant to recognize the horizontal direct effect of directives but has, on the other hand, developed remedial causes of action for injured parties.[19]

Third, there is always a temporal dimension that contributes to clarity of reasoning. For an outside observer it is often not enough to look into a single judgment to discover what the Court is saying. It is possible that, for a variety of reasons, usually because of disagreement between judges within a chamber, certain legal issues are omitted from the final text. In such a case, where there is pre-existing case law on the point, it is reasonable to assume that the silence of the Court on the point is a symbolic recognition that the earlier case law remains valid. On the other hand, where there is no earlier case law on the point, the omission of the

---

18 See e.g. *Elchinov* Case C-173/09 EU:C:2010:336, Opinion of AG Cruz Villalon.

19 See joined *Francovich and Bonifaci v Italy* (Cases C-6/90 and C-9/90) EU:C:1991:428.

Court to address a legal issue can be interpreted as an act of tacit deference to either political branch or to national judiciary. The full significance of such deference will become obvious only in future judgments. It is also possible that the lack of agreement within a chamber reflects the differences among the sitting judges and that they will be settled by a larger formation of the Court at a later date and with a different majority. In such a way a minority opinion that was invisible in an earlier case may become visible in a later Grand Chamber case. Sometimes, referring courts themselves provoke reinterpretation of law already settled by a smaller formation of the Court. For example, in the Grand Chamber *Nelson and Others v Deutsche Lufthansa*[20] case the referring court asked the Court of Justice to answer whether certain provisions of a Regulation, as interpreted by the five-judge Fourth Chamber in the earlier *Sturgeon and Others* case,[21] are valid in the light of the principle of legal certainty. In such cases comparison of answers to the same legal issues may provide additional clues about motivation of respective chambers.

3. THE CONTEMPORARY SUBJECT

Due to the change of context, of the utterer and of the audience affected by a decision, the immediate meaning of judicial decisions has to be distinguished from their future meaning.

From a perspective of actors to the proceedings and, more importantly, from a perspective of the Court itself, judicial interactions take place in the present, during the proceedings, and not after. The Court speaks as the original subject and the critique of its work is *synchronous*, that is, takes place in real time, within the procedure. From a perspective of a critic, judicial work is a matter of the past. Critique of adjudication is an ex post critique devised by a contemporary subject in a process where the Court and outcomes of its work become objectified. It is only natural that the problems of adjudication and judicial legitimacy are perceived differently, depending on the subject, time and context.

Speaking about traditions, Paul Feyerabend suggests that their interactions and results raise two kinds of question: observer questions and

[20] *Nelson and Others* (Joined Cases C-581/10 and C-629/1) EU:C:2012:657, para.61.

[21] *Sturgeon and Others* (Joined Cases C-402/07 and C-432/07) EU:C:2009:716.

participant questions.[22] "Observer asks: what happens and what is going to happen? Participant asks: what shall I do?"[23] This distinction is clearly relevant for the present analysis. The original subject is in the position of Feyerabend's participant while the contemporary subject takes the place of an observer. As I have explained above, their understanding will be affected by their identity, time and context.

What is more interesting, it is possible that participants and observers, that is original and contemporary subjects, will have belonged to different traditions and will have maintained competing claims according to which it is precisely their respective demands which are objective and tradition-independent and, that, as a consequence, one set of criteria should be preferred to another. This is, as Feyerabend explains, due to the fact that "critics of a practice take an observer's position with respect to it but remain participants of the practice that provides them with their objections", while, in reality, the two practices simply "don't fit each other".[24]

Translated to my own distinction between the original and contemporary subject, critique of the former by the latter is not only undergoing a double distortion – temporal and personal, but it is the double distortion itself that generates a divergence of traditions: institutional tradition of participants and external tradition of observers. It is due to the double shift that the divergence of traditions within which original and contemporary subjects operate is inevitable. Just as Claudius and Graves speak from different traditions, so do judges and their observers/interpreters/critics.

As I have already mentioned, the usual targets of the critique of performance of the Court of Justice are transparency, clarity, coherence, (lack of) dissent, and docket control. Clearly, the obvious question to be asked is whether these concepts can be understood as objective and tradition-free, or whether they are tradition-dependent. The question here is not whether traditions within which the original subject and the contemporary subject operate are different. My claim is that they necessarily are. The real question is how the mentioned differences emerge in the course of temporal and personal shift.

Apparently, the double shift highlights the different roles that the original and the contemporary subject play. As a participant, the original subject has to respond to the question "what shall I do?" In the context of

---

[22] In Feyerabend's analysis, traditions are neither good or bad, they simply are, and a tradition assumes desireable or undesireable properties only in comparison with some other tradition. Feyerabend (n.4), 27 et seq.

[23] Feyerabend (n.4), [18].

[24] Feyerabend (n.4), [22].

adjudication, the question is "how shall I decide?" or "how shall I respond to claims of other actors to the judicial proceedings?" Judges confront such questions all the time. On the other hand, an observer/contemporary subject/critic seeks answers to questions such as "what happened?" or "what does it mean?" The original subject is concerned with claims and counterclaims of participants to the proceedings. The contemporary subject is concerned with the result of proceedings and its interpretation. Responses to the two sets of questions necessarily take place within different traditions.

Feyerabend further claims that traditions are neither good nor bad, but simply are.[25] From that point on, it does not appear controversial to suggest that claims for transparency, clarity and coherence, presence of dissent and ability of a court to control its list of cases pending are context-sensitive and ultimately depend on time and the subject of critique.

The difference between immediate (unclear) and contemporary (clear) meaning of judicial decisions becomes relevant once the Court has spoken and a judgment is published. This is because the context of judicial deliberations is dramatically different from the context in which the future audience operates. Due to the allocation of information described in Point 2, the *synchronous* audience (other than direct actors taking part in the proceedings) is barely capable of seeing the subtleties of ongoing judicial work. It is not at all surprising that, in eyes of a direct observer, the picture can be blurred and the voice of the Court can be stammering. The prophecy will be fulfilled only by agency of some future actor, historically distanced and alien to the source. It will be Graves and not Claudius who will speak clear.

Admittedly, as a minimum requirement of clarity, a judgment should make sense to those to whom it is addressed. And it is not sufficient that a party[26] winning an argument is comfortable with the decision since the winning party will be satisfied by the very fact of winning. The reasoning should be equally clear to the losing party. But, save in the case of strategic litigation and repeat players,[27] there is no easy way to know whether the parties are happy. It is quite possible that a party losing on

---

[25] Feyerabend (n.4), [27].

[26] To the extent that one can speak about 'parties' before the Court of Justice, having in mind that the list of 'actors' before the Court is much wider and includes national courts, parties to the original dispute, EU institutions, intervening Member States and other participants.

[27] Galanter, Marc, 'Why the "Haves" Come Out Ahead: Speculations on the Limits of Legal Change' [1974] 9 *Law and Society Review* 165.

the merits will still be comfortable or even happy with the reasoning of the Court on a select point of law and will have achieved the desired statement of law that may become relevant for future litigation. However, it must not be forgotten that in all future situations, the original statement of law, the utterance of the Court as the original subject will be objectified and reinterpreted by future contemporary subjects and that any future application will take place in a different factual and legal interpretative context. The Court cannot envisage what is going to happen in the future even if it were its task to do so.[28] What a court can do, at best, is to try to rationalize the complexity of a present case in order to minimize need for future litigation.[29]

It is not only the Court that generates the symbolic speech. This is a two-way process in which '[t]he parties are compelled to "translate" their stories and claims in the idioms of law. They are compelled to adopt law's ontology, its categories, its networks of causality and symbolic associations'.[30] Indeed, active cooperation of participants to the proceedings significantly determines the shape of judgments to come. Preliminary references are provoked by the parties, formulated by a referring judge, defended before the Court by legal representatives, and all of their interventions are translated in legal idioms that ultimately crystalize as the symbolic language of the Court. But, as I have already said, that language will be interpreted by posterity in a dramatically different context from the one in which the case was originally presented and decided.

[28] Ehrlich made a similar argument about parliamentary regulation. 'The law-giver can, by means of his statutes render decisions only in those types of legal cases which come to his attention. Therefore no decisions can be derived from a statute as to legal cases of which the legislator has never thought or been able to think.' Pound, Roscoe, 'An Appreciation of Eugen Ehrlich' [1922] 36 Harv LR 140.

[29] For example, judgment of the Court of Justice in *Laval un Partneri* (Case C-341/05) EU:C:2007:809 caused the parties to settle in the *International Transport Workers' Federation and The Finnish Seamen's Union* (Case C-438/05) EU:EC:2007:772.

[30] Schlag, Pierre, 'Spam Jurisprudence, Air Law, and the Rank Anxiety of Nothing Happening (A Report on the State of the Art)' [2009] 97 Geo LJ 803, 809, 817.

3. Subject-object dialectics and social change

Damjan Kukovec

INTRODUCTION

One of the European Union's key features is bestowing rights on its citizens, creating subjects of law with ever more endowments. With increasing political capacity, avenues of participation, litigation and more, and an inflation of formal documents enacting citizens' rights, Europeans are enjoying more rights than ever before in history. Yet, people across Europe are in revolt against the Union.

Eurosceptisicm, rebellion against austerity brought about by the euro crisis, Brexit and the general malaise about the European Union are often attributed to nationalism, right- or left-wing extremism, democracy/political deficit or to misinformation. But these phenomena cannot fully account for the scepticism or revolt against the Union. To better understand this revolt, the utopianism behind the fundamental ideals and the underlying governance structures of the Union, such as the constant bestowing of rights and subject creation, needs to be addressed.

This chapter addresses the ignorance of the fact that the constant subject creation and building of their political capacity also breeds bureaucracy and alienates the subject from the system. Furthermore, it addresses the utopianism of the relationship between an abstract subject and the 'public' sphere. Finally, it challenges the idea of people's political incapacity. It proposes a hierarchical reconstruction of the already politically capable subject by creation of new objects. Such an alternative construction of the subject can assist us in seizing the transformative possibilities of the European Union.

1. CONSTITUTING THE SUBJECT

The conventional story on subjects and objects of law is that people are not subjects unless the law creates them as subjects. Today, one of the principal legal puzzles is the exact time a 'person' becomes a subject of law with his/her own rights – at conception, at birth or at some time in between. But there is no question that it happens at around that time. But becoming a subject of law does not end there. It is a constant evolutionary process of any human being in a legal system. One gains legal capacity, the right to vote, the right to contract and may start losing these entitlements towards one's death. The legal system and the legal profession are preoccupied with endowing people between birth and death with entitlements, with creating the subjects as fully participating in the legal order.

Creation of full subjects of law was historically a potent tool of resistance against unjust authority. With the abolition of slavery, slaves became subjects of law; when colonial relationships were dismantled, colonial peoples became full subjects of national and international law; women's emancipation led to their becoming full subjects of legal systems. These developments, including bourgeois revolutions, enlightenment, the civil rights movement in the United States, post-Cold War Central and Eastern European revolutions, are to be cherished as fundamental historic precedents of liberation.

The common line of these developments is either a creation or a perfection of the legal order, that breaks time into a Before and an After. Before the break of one or another type, there was war of all against all or at least some regressive type of social system. Such thinking sets us on the progressive trajectory of giving people ever more rights, standing and ability to contest and participate in the political process. This trajectory opens new institutional avenues and creates proper subjects of law, launching them from the private sphere into the public. Objects of law thus become subjects.

The sole alternative to social development and change on a trajectory of giving people ever more rights, standing and ability to contest and participate in the political process is often understood to be a revolution. Yet, revolution shares the utopianism of liberalism inasmuch as it depends on the idea of sudden change bringing a genuinely new legal order into the world – a truth that breaks time into a Before and an After. Such a revolution requires all true believers to revolutionize their pre-existing beliefs and practices. Just as the utopianism of liberal political theory sets out a break between the state of nature and state of law, a revolutionary break in time heralds a new beginning for mankind.[1] The common basic assumption between the idea of a transcendence of a pre-political state of 'nature' and the described revolutionary impulse is that a state of justice can be found in the underlying premises of the social order. Thus, the (moral) order needs constant polishing, reshaping or overthrowing.

Rights have played a special historical role in the endowment of entitlements, assisting in liberation from authoritarian regimes and relationships. Rights can be understood as entitlements that entail duties on others[2] or as moral guarantees.[3] According to Ronald Dworkin, rights are trumps. Dworkin's metaphor suggests that rights trump non-right objectives, such as utilitarian or wealth-maximizing goals. That is, those in a position to provide rights cannot justifiably refuse them on the ground that not providing them would on the whole lead to results that better serve the full range of legitimate interests in or of the community and its members.[4] In this sense, the more rights as trumps are endowed on the population, the more they can protect themselves against public power and others who may not want to respect the appropriate moral standards.

An increased endowment of rights as trumps would thus signal very positive development of the European Union. Europeans have never in history had more avenues for participation and for voicing their concerns in the system as today. Europeans have never had more rights.

Although fundamental rights had already been discovered and recognized by the ECJ as general principles of Community law as long ago as the 1960s with cases like *Stauder*[5] and *Internationale Handelsgesellschaft*,[6] it is the Lisbon Treaty that brought the expansion of the protection of fundamental rights at the level of the European Union to a climax. First, human rights are now more deeply enshrined in the Treaty as basic and foundational values of the EU. Second, Article 6(2) of the Treaty on European Union (TEU) provides for the accession of the EU to

---

1 Ackermann, Bruce, 'Revolution on a Human Scale' (1999) 108.8 Yale LJ 2279.

2 Hohfeld, Wesley, 'Fundamental Legal Conceptions as Applied in Judicial Reasoning' (1917) 26 Yale LJ 710.

3 See e.g. Nickel, James, *Making Sense of Human Rights: Philosophical Reflections on the Universal Declaration of Human Rights* (University of California Press, Berkeley 1987) 561–2.

4 Dworkin, Ronald, 'Rights as Trumps' in Jeremy Waldron (ed.), *Theories of Rights* (Oxford University Press, Oxford 1984) 153.

5 *Stauder v City of Ulm* (Case 29/69) [1969] ECR 419.

6 *Internationale Handelsgesellschaft* (Case 11/70) [1970] ECR 1125.

the European Convention on the Protection of Human Rights and Fundamental Freedoms (ECHR); and third, the Charter of Fundamental Rights and Freedoms attached to the Lisbon Treaty has been given binding status, according to Article 6(3) TEU. With the upcoming accession of the European Union to the ECHR a new and possibly final stage in the remarkable development of fundamental rights in EU law has begun. According to the joint communication from Presidents Costa (the European Court of Human Rights, ECtHR) and Skouris (the Court of Justice of the European Union, CJEU) '[t]he accession of the EU to the Convention constitutes a major step in the development of the protection of fundamental rights in Europe'.[7] The European Union is thus giving people more and more rights and better and better institutional avenues to enforce them. People are thus subjects, not objects of European law.

Yet, people across Europe are in revolt, not perceiving themselves as subjects of the system. In order to understand the reasons for peoples' disillusionment with the Union, we need to explore the role of the underlying structures of governance, including of the over-emphasis on the process of bestowing of rights and a constant creation of an abstract subject who is expected to avail himself of these rights. In other words, the preoccupation with creating subjects out of objects might be contributing to the malaise about the Union rather than helping to address it. To understand more fully people's revolt against the Union, the utopianism in the fundamental ideas behind the subject creation needs to be addressed.

2. UTOPIANISM OF THE SUBJECT CREATION

Endowing people with tools enabling them to voice their concerns and injuries is a noble and essential project of general social development and of the legal profession. Yet, it may give the false impression that the governance model based on creation of subjects of law takes us away from the original state of nature, is inherently progressive, necessarily produces a better society and alleviates social struggle.

Dworkin has argued that the great classics of political philosophy are utopian. They study social justice from the point of view of people committed in advance to no government or constitution, who are free to create the ideal state from first principles. So they imagine people living

[7] Joint Communication from Presidents Costa and Skouris, accessed 29 January 2017 at *www.echr.coe.int/Documents/UE_Communication_Costa_Skouris_ENG.pdf.*

in a pre-political state of 'nature' writing social contracts on blank slates. But real people in ordinary politics act within the political structure as well as on it. Politics is evolutionary rather than axiomatic; we recognize, in working toward a perfectly just state, that we already belong to a different one.[8]

The utopianism of the underlying ideals of bestowing ever more rights and creating ever stronger subjects needs to be addressed if the current ills of the Union are to be more fully understood. The idea of a constitutive moment when people become subjects of law and the state of nature is left behind is reproduced in every argument of an expansion of rights and building of abstract political capacity. It is reproduced in the perception that people are not politically capable and that enhancing people's abstract political capacity should be the central aim of social change. It is also reflected in the perception that the bureaucratic daily life of the European Union is an aberration, rather than a realization of the core ideals of the Union and of the liberal political theory.

3. BUREAUCRATIZATION OF SOCIETY BY BESTOWING RIGHTS AND SUBJECT CREATION

There is a growing perception that today in the European Union the grand ideas are replaced by bureaucracy. Eurosceptics call the European Union a 'bureaucratic monster, sharing the features of all out of control bureaucracies, where its sole purpose appears to be for continual expansion and power'.[9] In their view, the EU and its myriad of regulations has long lost sight of the fact that it does not create business but puts ever-increasing obstacles in the way of companies to create wealth.[10] Europhiles similarly complain about its democratic deficit, political deficit and over-bureaucratization.[11] Even the Pope has argued that Europe's era of philosophy and 'great ideas' has been replaced by the

---

[8] Dworkin, Ronald, *Law's Empire* (Harvard University Press, Cambridge MA 1988) 164–7. According to Dworkin, ordinary politics adds a principle that has no distinct place in utopian axiomatic theory – the principle of treating like cases alike.

[9] See e.g. 'EU Bureaucracy Kills UK Business', accessed 29 January 2017 at *www.dluk.info/european-union-eu-bureaucracy-kills-uk-business.html.*

[10] See n.9 above.

[11] See e.g. Page, Edward C, 'Bureaucracy and the European Union', accessed 29 January 2017 at *www.oxfordscholarship.com/view/10.1093/acprof:oso/9780198280798.001.0001/acprof-9780198280798-chapter-1.*

'bureaucratic technicalities of European Union institutions'.[12] While the late Pope Paul II called the EU 'a beacon of civilization', the current Pope, probably reflecting the sensibility of a large proportion of the population, shares the following opinion: 'In recent years, as the EU has expanded, there has been growing mistrust on the part of citizens towards institutions considered to be aloof, engaged in laying down rules perceived as insensitive to individual peoples, if not downright harmful.'[13]

The distance that the population feels vis-à-vis the Union should not be understood as an aberration, but as a consequence of its governance structures and, specifically, of the demands of protection of rights, of creation of the abstract subject and generally of demands of rule of law and democracy. Bureaucracy is not a negation of the aspirational ideals. On the contrary, the EU is a structural and inevitable victim of the success of rule of law, democracy and of subject creation.

The European Union prides itself in its protection of rights.[14] Acts of the Union are conceived in a sense that everyone participates in the creation of law and that legal challenge is generally open to as many as possible. That this has developed into a system that is difficult to oversee should not come as a surprise. In order to increase both the legitimacy and effectiveness of its action, the European Commission, over the past decade, has continuously stepped up its efforts to integrate stakeholders and concerned citizens in the preparation of new legislation. This practice goes back to its White Paper on European Governance published in July 2001.[15] Concurrently, the European Parliament has, from its side, built up several instruments to scrutinize the Commission's activities, using its own independent sources of evidence and expertise.

Bestowing rights on everyone, on opening numerous channels of affecting and challenging decision-making, on expanding on the number of documents one can rely on in litigation or in other channels of contesting of EU governance, all lead to the existing immense complexity of the system which is perceived as over-bureaucratization of the European Union.

---

[12] See *www.telegraph.co.uk/news/worldnews/the-pope/11252345/Pope-Francis-warns-European-ideal-replaced-by-bureaucratic-technicalities-of-EU.html*, accessed 29 January 2017.

[13] See n.12 above.

[14] See e.g. Moussis, Nicholas, *Guide to European Policies* (European Studies Service, Rixensart 2005).

[15] For a comment and critique of the Commission's White Paper see e.g. Scott, Joanne, 'Mind the Gap: Law and New Approaches to Governance in the European Union' (2002) Eur. LJ 1–18.

The complexity of the system that the rule of law and the subjectivization of the 'object' necessitate, breeds bureaucracy. The rule of law is the legal principle that law should govern a nation, as opposed to the nation's being governed by arbitrary decisions of individual government officials. When government and its officials and agents, as well as individuals and private entities, are accountable under the law, appropriate mechanisms of accountability need to be put in place. These mechanisms of accountability, imperfect as they may be, are even more complex in the context of European Union institutions, as they lack the traditional system of separation of powers.[16]

Furthermore, when the legal system foresees several avenues for litigation and complaints, the complex mechanisms to administer them need to be put in place. If the laws are to be clear, publicized, stable and just, applied evenly and protect fundamental rights, including the security of persons and property and certain human rights, large numbers of people are needed to draft and check the complex laws, take care of the legal basis, ensure that the institutional mechanism of the Union is respected, that substance is in line with expert opinions, that the impact of those laws has been studied, that the laws adhere to the complex drafting rules, that the process by which laws are enacted and enforced is accessible and fair, and so on. If the democratic principle of equality of languages is adhered to, large translation services are needed. If justice is to be delivered in a timely manner by competent, ethical and independent representatives and neutrals who are of sufficient number and reflect the make-up of the communities they serve, this takes time and resources.

Thus, the operationalization of great ideas, including of the rule of law and the idea of rights and subject creation, when administered when rubber meets the road, *inevitably culminates* in the bureaucratic technicalities.

The extreme complexity of the system is a result of enabling citizens to participate in the system and ensuring citizens' procedural and substantive rights. Inclusiveness breeds complexity and, paradoxically, a sense of alienation. It leads to people's sense of being small cogs in a system that is difficult to oversee or to impact meaningfully. Every layer of democratic governance, committee, requirement of a report, and inclusion of stakeholders we add to European government risks adding to

---

16 See Craig, Paul, and Grainne de Burca, *EU Law: Cases, Texts, Materials* (Oxford University Press, Oxford 2011).

a citizen's sentiment that he does not know where to turn and that every move he makes is a wrong one.[17]

The European Union is a democracy;[18] however, the EU legal structure is struggling with internal contradictions of constitutional and democratic theory. The institutional law-making and decision-making is so democratic and so balanced between so many European institutions and actors and services within them and with the involvement of so many European and national actors that accountability, as understood within Member States, inevitably suffers. The European Union is so inclusive of everyone's opinion in its law-making and decision-making and generally aims at such transparency that this visibly complex system feels distant and oppressive. Bureaucratization and complexity of the system are not an aberration, a result of a failure to implement the grand ideas of liberal political theory, but an inevitable part of the (utopian) rule of law, democracy and subject creation.

4. ESTABLISHING POLITICAL CAPACITY OF AN ABSTRACT SUBJECT

The conventional understanding of the subject-object relationship is the creation of an abstract subject out of the object by bestowing citizens with political capacity. Building people's 'political capacity' is a continuation of the project of constituting an abstract subject of law. Political freedom is the central ideal of a liberal society. The concern about political incapacity and remaking the possibilities for global political life, the liberal goal of political freedom,[19] is indeed a central concern of many lawyers in contemporary legal thought, throughout the political and legal intellectual spectrum.[20] Several scholars reduce social problems to

---

17 Kukovec, Damjan, 'Hierarchies as Law' (2014) 21 Colum J Eur L 131.

18 See n.17.

19 Michelman, Frank, 'Law's Republic' (1988) 97 Yale LJ 1493, 1495.

20 This is not surprising, given that, according to Duncan Kennedy, the relationship between law and politics is paradigmatic in contemporary legal thought. See Kennedy, Duncan, 'Three Globalizations of Law and Legal Thought: 1850–2000', in David M Trubek and Alvaro Santos (eds), *The New Law and Economic Development* (Cambridge University Press, Cambridge 2006) at 19. The variety of the argument against political incapacity is particularly frequent in the sense of the need to place politics above economic freedom. See Howse, Robert and Kalypso Nicolaidis, 'Enhancing WTO Legitimacy: Constitutionalization or Global Subsidiarity' (2003) 16 *Governance* 1, 73.

the goal of political capacity and contestation.[21] It is understood as the redemption or achievement of personal freedom from or through institutionalized social power, opening oneself to the experience of 'dilemma' and dialogic engagement.[22]

According to Joseph Weiler, the constitutive moment of creating the subject of EU law has been the *Van Gend en Loos* decision. This is the European moment that marks the Before and After – a moment between the pre-political state and the state of political capacity of the individual in EU law. In this moment, the story goes, individuals became (full) subjects of the legal system. According to Weiler, *Van Gend en Loos* not only shaped the legal order, it played a huge role in constituting that order.[23] As a socio-legal phenomenon, direct effect harnesses the *private* economic, political and social interests of the individual in vindicating those rights to the public interest of ensuring the rule of law at the transnational level. With each individual effectively becoming in that way a 'legal vigilante' of the public rule of law, an effective civil society monitoring system is put in place.

The subject, however, in this vision can slip back into the status of the object. In liberal political theory, the realization of basic rights is a process that secures the private autonomy of equally entitled citizens only in step with the activation of their political autonomy.[24] Ensuring procedures and practices that give all citizens more or less equal influence in the decisions that govern them is thus of primordial importance. However, there is simply no moment in the civic calendar of Europe, argues Weiler, when the citizen can influence directly the outcome of any policy choice facing the Community and Union in the way that citizens can when choosing between parties which offer sharply distinct programmes at the national level. The political colour of the European Parliament only very weakly gets translated into the legislative and administrative output of the Union.

Thus, according to Weiler, direct effect in the context of European governance, objectifies the individual or re-objectifies him or her. In the Member States with imperfect but functional democracies the individual is 'the' political subject. In the European Union, with its defective democratic machinery where the individual has far less control over norm

---

21 See further Kukovec, Damjan, 'Hierarchies as Law', n.17 above.

22 Michelman, n.19 above, at 1541.

23 Weiler, Joseph HH, 'Van Gend en Loos: The Individual as Subject and Object and the Dilemma of European legitimacy' (2014) 12.1 Int'L J Const. L 94–103.

24 Habermas, Juergen, 'Paradigms of Law' (1996) 17.4 Cardozo L Rev 771, 784.

creation, direct effect has the paradoxical effect of objectifying him or her – an object of laws over which one has no effective democratic control.

In Weiler's portrayal, the individual is abstract and equal to other individuals, he is interested in affecting the legal process and, specifically, the outcome of the legislative process. However, pitting the interest of an abstract individual against the public rule-making institutions reproduces the public/private distinction in governance, suffers from a misrepresentation of power relationships and leads us into a deadlocked debate about Europe's future.

First, Weiler's description of the problem of accountability relies on the conventional vision of governance in which 'government' is composed of entities created through authoritative legal instruments. It makes and enforces policy through authoritative announcements ('law') and through provision of goods and services. Individuals and non-state associations participate in various ways, some of which may be unwholesome, but actions of government are ultimately institutionally distinct from outside influence.[25]

This vision of governance misses the fact that acting along with government in the heterarchical range are a near-limitless range of human associations and institutions, which exist along a continuum from the unorganized and even unconscious to the highly organized and government-like.[26] It misses the fact that governance is far more complex and structured by asymmetric power relationships than the conventional account of governance would acknowledge. By distinguishing between an individual's private interest and a public interest and by limiting the legal process to the legislative process of the Union institutions, this account of governance reproduces the public-private distinction, misrepresents power relationships and fails to address the stifling power asymmetries in society.

Social struggle always takes place between differently positioned individuals, not between (imaginary) public and private interests. It is a hierarchical struggle – between people in varied hierarchical positions in society. This switches the focus of social change to daily reality – to the law in action – the constantly shifting global hierarchical structure.

Second, there are vast differences between people in terms of how they can affect the legal process, even if we reduce it to the legislative process

---

25 Kukovec, 'Hierarchies as Law', n.17 above.

26 Sagers, Chris, 'Myth of Privatization' (2005) accessed 29 January 2017 at *papers.ssrn.com/sol3/papers.cfm?abstract_id=839386.*

of the Union institutions, as in Weiler's portrayal. Formal 'rights' and 'duties' are in practice vessels to be filled with the substance of prior endowments – endowments of skill, social position, wealth, or other phenomena that give substantive value (or lack thereof) to their holders.[27] 'Private' individuals are a far from homogenous group. Mark Galanter divides actors into those claimants who have only occasional recourse to the courts, one-shooters, and repeat players who are engaged in many similar litigations over time. An analogous analysis might be applied to the regulatory and rule-making phases of legal process. In both scenarios, repeat players enjoy several prior advantages over one-shooters.

Yet, these prior endowments are missed in the discussion of the abstract individual in need of political capacity to influence the content of laws. Anatole France's observation: 'The law, in its majestic equality, forbids the rich as well as the poor to sleep under bridges …' could be restated for the purposes of the current discussion in the sense of 'The law, in its majestic equality, permits the rich as well as the poor to influence the legislative process'. In other words, the imaginary individual who actually actively pursues his interest in litigation or in the legislative or administrative process is often a repeat player, a 'have', rather than 'have not', despite the fact that 'have-nots' have the right to vote or to otherwise participate in the formal processes just as well. This is just one example of the problem of hierarchical power imbalances that are missed in the contrast of a clash between the interest of an abstract private individual and the public interest.

Last but not least, the debate about accountability of European institutions and about avenues of citizens' direct influence over the outcome of any policy choice facing the Community and Union becomes gridlocked in a discussion between increasing complexity of EU governance[28] and the creation of the European superstate,[29] with both options bound to distance the population even further from the European Union.

5. A TURN TO A RECONSTRUCTION OF A HIERARCHICALLY CONSTRUCTED SUBJECT

The European Union needs a shift in legal thought. The population has begun to realize the impossibility of the professed ideals of universal

---

27 See n.26 above.

28 See below, Section III.

29 Mancini, Federico, 'Europe: The Case for Statehood' (1998) 4 *European Law Journal* 1, 29.

inclusion within the European Union.[30] In everyday life, the lofty ideals are felt as a hierarchical struggle determined by irreducible exclusion. The claimed ethos of society has a tendency to fade in the wake of the daily hierarchical reality that people find stifling and unjust. Instead of focusing on rights of abstract individuals who are subordinate to the 'public' sphere, social change should be sought in the particular injury of a particularly situated individual who is already politically capable, but is structurally subordinate to those who are hierarchically privileged.

In this portrayal, every subject is already politically capable. The subject does not need a right bestowed on him to be an actor in the legal system. The proposition that people are not politically capable or that they are not deciding is a misrepresentation of power, authority, law and governance. When we see law as hierarchies between people in every moment in time rather than as legal doctrines and concepts, it becomes clear that law is not just what lawyers do,[31] but what all of us do all the time. We are too often used to thinking that we have conferred regulatory power on either political institutions or on legal expertise.[32] We lawyers and advocates are powerful, but an emphasis on the power of legal expertise could suffer from under-inclusion and over-inclusion at the same time. First, lawyers across the globe find themselves in radically different structural situations, with immense power differences. Second, we are all deciding. Each of us forms and conforms to authority all the time. Constant authoritative syntheses are not made by institutions, nor only by legal experts, but by all people, all the time.

Thus, we should explore how not just we, lawyers, but every person, no matter in what institutional, vocational and daily setting they find themselves, acts legally and politically. In this sense, all of us – people from every domain in every social setting – are legal actors. We are not led by the invisible hand of expertise, but by the invisible hand of the ideology of all of us. All of us already have 'regulatory power'. People are not passively constituted by abstract legal entitlements, but themselves impose injuries on themselves and others all the time and in every social setting. The decision-making power of each of us goes far beyond

---

[30] Kukovec, 'Hierarchies as Law', n.17, 170–4.

[31] Weber, Max, *Economy and Society* (Harvard University Press, Cambridge MA 1954).

[32] David Kennedy, for example, has argued, 'We have substituted the forms of politics for the experience of political life. Too often we have opted for electoral form over participation and popular engagement.' Kennedy, David, *The Dark Sides of Virtue* (Princeton University Press, Princeton NJ 2004) 350.

voting, representation, litigation and what is usually understood as participation in or exercise of governance.

The idea that there is no space for political contestation is contradicted by the fact that every day all of us contest, or fail to contest, countless hierarchies. We are all constantly deciding and creating our social and legal life in every social setting. All of us in our daily work and lives respond to or do not respond to the concerns of others. All of us keep making or not making a difference in the normative situation of others.

Thus, it is not just lawyers, but each of us constantly performing legal acts. In this sense, each person already has 'regulatory' and political power. The problem is not that we do not have the power and need to claim it from 'the market' or that people are only informed, consulted, our polling data serving as base line for expert management and that citizens are not actually deciding. Nor is it that people are not participating in global governance and that the possibility for global political life needs to be remade. Global governance, just like authority, does not need to be 'claimed'.[33] It is already here. Citizens already have political power and are already deciding. We are governing all the time. We are already politically capable.

The claim of political incapacity reproduces the public/private distinction of liberal political theory, which, while challenged in legal thought,[34] nonetheless persists to this day. Karl Marx maintained that the universal, abstract categories of the public or private sphere are not adequately grounded in social conditions and the forms through which social life is conducted. The public/private distinction tends to legitimate and mystify

---

[33] Kennedy, David, 'Law and the Political Economy of the World' (2013) 26 Leiden J Int'l L 7, 40.

[34] See Hale, Robert, 'Coercion and Distribution in a Supposedly Non-coercive State' (1923) 38 *Political Science Quarterly* 470. Duncan Kennedy's critique of the public/private dichotomy is based on the view that the range of distinctions that characterize liberal legality, 'state/society, individual/group, right/power, contract/tort, law/policy, legislative/judiciary, objective/subjective, reason/fiat, freedom/coercion' are all going through 'similar processes of decline'. He argues that the public/private distinction has increasingly lost its capacity to plausibly capture features of reality and specify differences that are consistent and relevant for legal decision-making. Duncan Kennedy provides a critique of the public/private distinction that is 'localized' to legal categories, legal consciousness, and the sphere of legal social relations. See Kennedy, Duncan, 'The Stages of the Decline of the Public/Private Distinction' (1982) 130 U Pa. L Rev. 1349.

structures of power through which individual autonomy, social institutions and legal action are accomplished.[35]

The liberal ideal of people as political beings pursuing political freedom can be traced at least as far back as Aristotle. Political society and political capacity in the liberal tradition are seen as something outside our daily existence, something that needs to be achieved. In the words of Aristotle, people are 'zoon politicon', social and political beings, and a political society is necessary for the full perfection of our existence. The recipe of the good life lies in our self-realization that we can achieve in a public entity such as a polis.[36] Virtue in this sense consists partly of a willingness to subordinate one's private desires and interests to the common good. Only through active participation in the deliberative politics of a republic can a person fully realize himself. Similarly, according to social contract theorists, political community is achieved by human ingenuity – by a social contract.[37]

While a particular form of political society certainly needs a human creating hand, society is never outside our daily existence. We do not need to create a public hand, a polis, an institution, a political contestation, or any other entity or activity to create society or our political capacity. Only if we see politics as divine, something we cannot attain until some 'public' intervention or 'public hand' actually occurs, can we think that we are politically incapable. In such a picture, politics is divided from the quotidian, separate from our daily existence. There is a need for the creation of something – a lever, institution or contestation – that will make us politically capable. Reproduction of the public/private distinction is thus reproduced in thinking about governance.

The search for political capacity seeks governance outside of the already existing quotidian or institutional form. Waiting for 'an adequate political process',[38] or for 'a perfect transnational political space', resembles waiting for Godot. Global governance is not a construction of

---

[35] See Turkel, Gerald, 'The Public/Private Distinction: Approaches to the Critique of Legal Ideology' (1988) 22 Law & Soc'y Rev. 801, 802; Marx, Karl, 'On the Jewish Question' in Robert C Tucker (ed.), *The Marx-Engels Reader*, 2nd edn (Norton, New York NY 1978).

[36] Aristotle, *Politics* trans. Benjamin Jowett (Clarendon, Oxford 1885).

[37] See John Locke, *Second Treatise of Government* (1689); Thomas Hobbes, *Leviathan* (1651); Jean Jacques Rousseau, *The Social Contract* (1762).

[38] Somek, Alexander, 'From Workers to Migrants, from Distributive Justice to Inclusion: Exploring the Changing Social Democratic Imagination' (2012) 18(5) *European Law Journal* 716–7.

mental maps. Rather, governance is a constant, ontological hierarchical struggle between people in which each of us is politically capable.

The British people will remain subjects of the EU legal structure in countless instances even after the United Kingdom actually leaves the Union. They will be in a hierarchical relationship with the population of Europe, despite the fact that the UK and its citizens will not formally participate in the governance through European institutions. Thus, they will remain subjects of EU law. They will just be able to use the EU legal order in a different way from before. Likewise, people of Eastern Europe did not obtain general political or legal capacity by joining the Union. They were only able to use a very limited set of tools differently and in different social settings. But political and legal capacity was always there.

The problem is rather that they were constantly hierarchically unprivileged. Being inside or outside the Union might be very important to some specific hierarchical situations. However, a detailed evaluation of the existing set of hierarchical relationships that structure the position of various actors and our ideology could thus reveal that the current legal position of many actors in the United Kingdom, Switzerland or Norway is more similar in the legal structure of the European continent than the position of many of the insiders in the Union from the disadvantaged European periphery,[39] despite the fact that all insiders are European citizens, that they are fully represented at every level of EU decision-making and seemingly have all the institutional avenues for the realization of their interest at their disposal. Hence the need for a turn from abstract political capacity to the reconstruction of the hierarchically constructed subject.

6. LAW UNDERSTOOD AS A STRUCTURE OF HIERARCHICALLY CONSTITUTED SUBJECTS

When we consider the subjects of the legal system, our understanding of the legal system needs to be considered too. The idea of constructing the legal system with a view to aiding an abstract individual and the idea of subject's political incapacity misrepresents the subject-object dialectic. What is the law that needs to be changed and how does the subject and object dialectic fit into our understanding of law?

---

[39] Kukovec, Damjan, 'Law and the Periphery' (2015) 21(3) *European Law Journal* 406.

According to Michel Foucault, we are constituted subjects. There is no sovereign, founding subject, a universal form of subject to be found everywhere. On the contrary, he believed, the subject is constituted through practices of subjection, or, in a more autonomous way, through practices of liberation, of liberty, as in Antiquity, on the basis of a number of rules, styles and inventions to be found in the cultural environment. According to Gilles Deleuze, a subject is neither pre-existent nor stable, but always in the process of becoming other.

We are already subjects with political capacity. There is no beginning of the legal system, no Before and After in this picture, only hierarchically constructed subjects. In order to understand how subjects are legally constituted, a reinterpretation of Hohfeld's legal entitlements is needed. Hohfeld argued for a reconceptualization of private law rules as products of interplay between 'justice and policy', rather than as conceptual derivations. Hohfeldian analysis led to a decomposition of the notion of property and contract into bundles of rights, privileges, power and immunities – together, legal entitlements – without a common conceptual core. The focus of such analysis is not abstract concepts, such as property, contract, restitution, money or sovereignty, but rather any legal doctrine as a set of freedoms and prohibitions, as juridical composites that enable us to imagine their reshuffling. This focus is a staple of realist and post-realist analysis in contemporary legal thought, but is nonetheless deficient. Legal doctrines can be reimagined as a bundle of freedoms and prohibitions, but such analysis of the legal system is inapposite to explaining hierarchies and the global hierarchical structure.

Instead of Hohfeld's decomposition of property and contract law, every person should be understood as representing a set of freedoms and prohibitions or of injuries and recognitions in every moment in time. Each of us is a constantly fluid bundle of injuries and recognitions that set us into a particular situation in the global hierarchical structure. Ineradicable hierarchical relationships constitute us as subjects and hierarchies are constituted by injuries – decisions that we take in each moment.

In order to understand law and subject-object dialectic, law and governance need to be articulated as a constant (hierarchical) struggle. The three elements of the phenomenon of law here distinguished are not intrinsically separate elements. They are three aspects of a single phenomenon.

I. Hierarchies: Injuries Law is an assemblage of all hierarchies, injuries and recognitions as set up in every moment. The constantly fluid patchwork of hierarchies forms our global social system. Our decision-making in every moment in time implies a hierarchy, formed by injury and recognition.

II. Ideology: Memory of Past Hierarchies. The second aspect of the legal system is our ideology, which is memory – our synthesized past experience. This aspect of law explains where our sense of right and wrong comes from. It stems from our select memories of our past experience, from our memories of past injuries and hierarchies that are shared or contested by others. The legal constellation is a constantly shifting assemblage of hierarchies in every moment in time and this is constantly brought into the present. We synthesize the hierarchies and injuries of yesterday in our memory as the justice of today.

III. Tools: Tools are the objects. This is the World of Ideas, Concepts and Theories. Tools are disjointed, fragmented and contradictory elements that we have at our disposal in arguing for the reallocation of injuries and recognitions. Legal rules, national laws, international laws, policies, purposes, principles, doctrines, human rights, economic and social theories, statistics, efficiency, left-right and identity politics, critique, legal orders, institutions, capitalism and social theories are tools to be invoked and deployed for reproduction or transformation of reality. Legal thought has often focused on the inherent quality of tools. For example, critique is perceived as inherently benevolent, and has been suggested as a goal of our work. Efficiency or economics, on the other hand, is sometimes considered a bad idea. However, every tool can be used to portray injury, and an a priori rejection of a tool because of its alleged inherent quality is to be considered with caution. Tools from every domain of our social life – economics, law, politics, and sociology – and from any intellectual tradition can be used for authoritarian and liberating purposes. Doctrines, theories or any other tools cannot be applied equally to those who are differently situated hierarchically. As each of us is thrown into a different position in the global hierarchical structure at any moment in time, any legal rule or other tool applies differently to each of us. 'Efficiency', 'the market', 'transnational solidarity', 'social question', 'public interest', social dumping, the principle of equality, and critique are all tools that tell us relatively little about themselves before they are deployed in reality. The central questions are always who will be injured, and how, by usage of a tool, and whose hierarchical position will be reaffirmed.

In this understanding of law, there is no Before and After, no pre-legal state and no starting point of the legal system. There is thus no constitutive moment such as *Van Gend en Loos*. The idea of an abstract individual pursuing his abstract interests in the legal order is not central to legal analysis. Rather, law is the hierarchy of the past moment, the injuries that are imposed on the hierarchically subordinate.

When thinking about subject-object analytics and social change, the question we should be asking is whose ideology, reflecting a particular structural position of a subject, is guiding decision-making, whose injuries we take seriously and which subject's position is reinforced by our daily actions. In this approach, injury, ideology and tools should be understood as building blocks of social change. In the context of the relationship between the European Union's centre and its periphery, I have argued for an articulation of a new tool, a doctrine of dumping the European Centre, to contest the existing hierarchical reality.[40] Tools, objects in the subject-object dialectic, need to be developed that reflect hierarchical injury, rather than merely reflecting the (utopian) ideals of a just society. Ideals of society are to be pursued, but injury is to be articulated and contested.

CONCLUSION

Brexit[41] and the general population's malaise about the European Union signal the demise of the belief in the current practices of EU governance. Rather than simply understanding the opposition to the Union as based on forces of nationalism, it is important that the current ills of the Union are understood as a structural result of its successes. In other words, they result from the Union's deep structure, including from the constant creation of political capacity, rule of law and bestowing of rights and creating subjects from objects.

There should certainly be an element of utopianism, an ideal, an inspirational element in governance. Yet, ignoring the utopian and the conflicting nature of existing structures of governance can lead to disillusionment and reproduction of existing injustices. It would also prevent us from exploring other opportunities for social change and from

---

[40] Kukovec, Damjan, 'Economic Law, Inequality and Hidden Hierarchies on the EU Internal Market' (2016) 38(1) Mich J Int'L L.

[41] For a discussion on Brexit, see e.g. Kukovec, Damjan, 'Brexit – A Tragic Continuity of Europe's Daily Operation', accessed 29 January 2017 at *verfassungsblog.de/brexit-a-tragic-continuity-of-europes-daily-operation/*.

rebooting the European project. The subject that needs to be reconstructed is to be understood as politically capable, but hierarchically privileged or subordinate. New tools reflecting hitherto invisible injuries need to be developed for the reconstruction of (hierarchically) constituted subjects, for the reconstruction of the existing hierarchical reality.

4. Subjects and technologies of European governance: reflections on suspect crossings

Emilios Christodoulidis

THE ELUSIVE SUBJECT OF EUROPEAN INTEGRATION

The project invites us to consider how the interface between subjects and objects of EU law can be thematised; what its facets might be and how one might make sense of what appears as an increasingly blurred line separating subjects from objects. With some caveats customarily inserted, this blurring is often welcomed as the invitation to deconstruct fixed binarisms and to release the democratic energies of European integration, whatever those were, and however tightly coupled they were envisaged with market dynamics. In the context of the current project, too, the questioning of the organising distinction of subjects and objects is taken as a marker of democratic experimentation. The editors refer variously to the importance of the recognition of the 'richness of different legal subjects' where EU law offers particularly fertile grounds; 'a different understanding of the term subject', it is suggested, 'is liberating … [by] allow[ing] us to use the lexicon of subjects to think of law beyond rights and entitlements of the subjects in order to observe and describe a wide spectrum thereof.' Now 'liberating' may be overstating our capacity today to reimagine the European citizen at the difficult conjuncture of market fanaticism with the various (imminent and prospective) 'exits' (Brexit, Grexit) and widespread xenophobic contraction of public space – the space that affords appearance to political subjects. In other words, in a Europe where the pursuit of market utopia[1] is forcing the shrinkage of

[1] For 'market utopia' see Polanyi, Karl, *The Great Transformation: The Political and Economic Origins of Our Time* (Farar and Rinehart, New York 1944).

the idea of collective peoplehood back to the depleted and largely abhorrent identifications with defensive nationalisms, the European challenge to think of the many sites of subjecthood and the variety of subject-positions becomes both more urgent and more improbable, in this twilight of European constitutionalism.[2]

Let us nevertheless begin to unpack the 'subject' pole of the distinction under scrutiny. We can say, quite uncontroversially I think, that 'peoplehood' (the demos, the 'we') has become an increasingly problematic category in European constitutional thinking. The expressions of the difficulty can be traced along two different trajectories. The first, more straightforward one, typically rehearses the problem in terms of democratic deficits and varieties of the 'no demos' thesis, where under conditions of the acceleration of European integration, subsidiarity has become increasingly hollowed out and competences have been transferred wholesale to supranational institutions. The deficit was expressed in the asymmetry between national and European Parliament(s), the differential between the robustness of the former and the toothlessness of the latter, with popular sovereignty as the crucial stake in a more or less zero-sum game between them. This course has, of course, only accelerated under conditions of austerity, deepened to the point that constitutionalism begins to falter on its 'social' axis, as it must (falter), in those situations when the key 'democratic' decisions are over the handing over of budgetary sovereignty to a country's debtors.

The case of Greece in instructive. The Greek Court of Cassation had the opportunity to reflect on the constitutionality of the first memorandum and the 'conditionalities' it contained in its decision 668/2012.[3] The case was brought before the Court by the Athens Bar together with the civil servants' trade union and others. The appellants asked that the government's decisions to cut wages and pensions in line with the Troika's prescriptions be struck down as violating key constitutional provisions of the Greek Constitution. The provisions in question were those of Article 28 which establishes the relation between national and

---

2 The reference is to Dobner, Petra, and Martin Loughlin (eds), *The Twilight of Constitutionalism?* (Oxford University Press, Oxford 2012).

3 The law appealed was 3845/2010, entitled 'Measures for the implementation of the Mechanism in support of the Greek Economy from the Member-States of the Eurozone and the IMF'. For an analysis of the case see also Contiades, Xenophon and Ioannis A Tassopoulos, 'The Impact of the Financial Crisis on the Greek Constitution' in Contiades, Xenophon (ed.), *Constitutions in the Global Financial Crisis: A Comparative Analysis* (Ashgate, Farnham 2013), 202.

supranational law. In effect what the appellants were arguing was that the Memorandum of Understanding (MoU), as incorporated in the legislation, compromised budgetary sovereignty because it transferred national competences to international bodies. In this case, as in a number of cases in courts across the continent, the court rejected the appeal (as in most of the cases) under the increasingly fraught imperative of the preservation of monetary union at all costs.

THE SHIFT TO GOVERNANCE

That first trajectory of European collective subjecthood tracks the changes along the more familiar oscillation between national and 'post'-national identifications. But alongside it has emerged a second, rather less visible process, of a significant shift from government to *governance*, whose function has been to displace the first process. With the shift come significant changes in the forms of analysis and explanation and the structures of legitimation. Regarding the former, *formal* modes of analysis come to pervade. This development will be tracked in a more systematic way below; suffice it to say that governance is constitutively coupled with forms of analysis and knowledge production that, by centring it on outcomes and effects, seek solutions in terms of synchronic models of functional equivalence and bracket historical-causal forms of explanation. Regarding the latter, with the clear impasses into which the macro-supervisory role of the state had entered, and with public officials no longer seen as capable of guaranteeing procedures or supervising expertise in any realistic sense – political accountability needed to be rethought. It was rethought in terms of a shift from *input to output legitimation*,[4] from overseeing procedure to auditing performance. The 'audit explosion' introduces indicator-based policy-production and implementation, the use of *performance measures* – the whole array of targets, standards and benchmarks – to audit outputs and relate them to budgets. The idiom of 'good governance' spreads across an increasing range and to new levels as it is adopted by both regional blocs (for example the European Union) and international bodies (for example the World Bank).

Now, if our concern in all this is with the *fixity* of the boundary between subjects and objects of EU law, the shift to governance achieves

[4] For a very good account of the distinction in this context, see Scharpf, Fritz W, 'Problem-solving Effectiveness and Democratic Accountability in the EU' No. 03/1 Max Planck Institute for the Study of Societies, February 2003.

the most comprehensive dissolution of that boundary, the full collapse of the first pole of the distinction (subjects) into the second (objects). The shift away from democratic decision-making – the abandonment of the deciding subject of the European polity – and toward 'governing through numbers' (to borrow Alain Supiot's recent title[5]), is played out in the field of legitimation as the shift from input to output legitimation. It is the fundamental, insidious and, worryingly, unaddressable shift that confronts us with the mutation from subjects to objects of EU Law. In the next Section we will look at one key area in which this is effected through the use of indicators in European policy.

But, in the meantime, we must confront the following quandary: if ambiguity or porosity at borders is often welcomed as a sign of a promising yielding of strict binarisms, in the case of EU governance it undoubtedly marks *a loss on the register of democracy*. It is a loss because the yielding is a movement away from democratic categories that require and pivot on collective-*subject* positions and toward *objective* – 'scientific' – considerations. The substitution sacrifices *decision* to the supposed warrant of *impartial or scientific assessment.* The consequent loss is staggering.

The most direct path to substantiate the claim borrows insights from Actor-Network Theory (ANT) to examine the suspect crossing from democratic decision to technology of governance. Admittedly what I draw from ANT is highly selective. ANT invites as its very inaugurating gesture the collapse of the binary subjects/objects and in the direction of hybrid *actants* that ascribes agency across the divide.[6] For Bruno Latour, who is the towering figure in this tradition, agency is read into the mutual constitution, engagement and reciprocal co-development of humans and non-humans in the unfolding of the 'actor-network' in which capacity – to reach decisions and to act – is not the prerogative of human agency but is to be found in the materiality of what part-determines, inflects or shifts it. As Alain Pottage puts it in his excellent (and highly critical) paper, *The materiality of What?*, a key objective of Latour's is to get away from the assumption of 'society' as a 'pre-existing frame or landscape of social action' and to 'open up instead the idea of a sociality of association, in which networks are an emergent property of the association between

[5] Supiot, Alain, *La gouvernance par les nombres* (Fayard, Paris 2015).

[6] McGee, Kyle, *Bruno Latour: The Normativity of Networks* (Routledge, Abingdon 2014).

actors whose competences are themselves emergent effects of association'.[7] It is this fundamental co-implication that defines the field of association, and to *begin with the subject* as methodological departure becomes at best an analytical exercise of little value.

The elevation of *the network* as key concept, of course, predates ANT. If the late '70s and '80s in the political systems of the US and the UK were fundamentally relaunched on the dictates of the radical agenda of the New Right with the decisive shift toward the individualistic creed and the privatisation of social resources, a second stage, in the 1990s, generalised it across Western economies and relaunched it in terms of network and joined-up governance.[8] Governance shifts policy-making away from hierarchies and toward networks in the move of decentralisation and fragmentation that characterised the first wave but now harnessed to networks. The discovery of networks as a new organising basis for society, as new points of entry of new actors in policy processes, and as organising structures to co-ordinate activities and allocate resources comes with an emancipatory idiom that changes the political imaginary: new spaces of participation, new understandings of 'stake-holding', the mobilisation of fragmented, cross-cutting, plural, mutually re-enforcing and cross-fertilising identities, the whole set of 'multi-perspectival' politics is hailed in to inform the processes of joined-up governance. A new concern with the appropriateness of solutions to the complexity of the receiving field, and an emphasis on flexibility and responsiveness: the discovery that problems can be 'wicked', the moulding of partnership structures to confront them and democratic experimentalism to innovate. The use of this idiom is for the most part a legitimatory cover for the brutality of the extraction of surplus value from an increasing range of social resources. In the important work of Manuel Castells, the global network enables the processes of extracting profit: 'Networks converge toward the meta-network of capital that integrates capitalists' interests at a global level and across sectors and realms of activity ... Thus global financial markets, and their networks of management, are the actual collective capitalist', directing the flows of capital 'toward this *mother of all accumulations* that is the global financial network'.[9]

---

7 Pottage, Alain, 'The Materiality of What?' (2012) 39(1) *Journal of Law and Society* 167–83 at 171.

8 For a useful account see Bevir, Mark, *Democratic Governance* (Princeton University Press, Princeton NJ 2010).

9 Castells, Manuel, *The Rise of the Network Society: The Information Age: Economy, Society, and Culture*, Vol. 1 (John Wiley, London 2011) 171. See also

This is moving too fast, perhaps, and our concern here is only indirectly with the facilitation of the flows of capital. We are concerned more precisely with how the 'network' element of the 'actor-network-theory' enables a rethinking and configuration of the subject/object divide. So let us undertake a 'deconstruction' of a more familiar constitutional category: that of 'the people' and the inscription of its constitutive democratic capacity in the Constitution as popular sovereignty. And let us look at how the 'actor' of democratic self-determination increasingly yields to the 'network' of 'democratic' governance.

INDICATORS AND THE ECLIPSE OF THE DEMOCRATIC SUBJECT

One of the key ways in which the operation of statistical information is mobilised is through benchmarking and the use of indicators. Principally associated with scholarship emerging from New York University (key figures include Benedict Kingsbury, Sally Engle Merry and Kevin Davis) the theorisation of indicators as a technique of global governance has been at the centre of literature both facilitative and critical of policy-making. The 'critical' take includes the following questions: How does the increasing use of indicators in global governance affect the distribution of power, and the power of the governed? How does it affect the nature of decision-making about the allocation of resources and efforts to monitor compliance with global standards? Spanning an extraordinary range from public actors such as the World Bank or the US State Department, to NGOs such as Freedom House, to hybrid entities such as the Global Fund, to private sector political risk rating agencies, indicators are used to compare and rank states for purposes as varied as deciding how to allocate foreign aid or investment and whether states have complied with their treaty obligations. According to a broadly accepted definition:

> 'An indicator is a named collection of rank-ordered data that purports to represent the past or projected performance of different units. The data are generated through a process that simplifies raw data about a complex social phenomenon. The data, in this simplified and processed form, are capable of being used to compare particular units of analysis (such as countries or

---

'A Network Theory of Power' (2011) 5 *International Journal of Communication* 773–787 at 784.

institutions or corporations), synchronically or over time, and to evaluate their performance by reference to one or more standards.'[10]

The key elements in this definition are simplification and comparability: simplification is based on reductions of complex situations on the basis of criteria of salience. 'Indicators simplify "raw" data and then name the resulting product take the form of, or can readily be transformed into, numerical data.' Indicators 'measure', for example, the level of respect for the rule of law in a given country in a given year in a way that may be represented by an indicator such as the 'rule of law index'. That simplification can involve aggregation of data from multiple sources and it will certainly involve filtering that excludes certain data. The criteria are used to abstract key features and keep them constant across situations, which in turn allows the comparability of the situations; comparisons then produce data which are fed into processes of decision-making. Governance comprises the means used to influence behaviour, and the production and the distribution of resources.

To understand indicators as technologies of governance is to look at the ways in which they are capable of delimiting and altering the topology and dynamics of European governance across the board: at the level of processes of standard-setting, decision-making and, for those of a more radical bent, contestation.

Regarding 'contestation', the 'critical' take on indicators is alert to built-in biases and is alert to the need of revisability even, or especially, where the structuring assumptions are tacit. There is also an acknowledgement that a significant degree of selectivity is exercised by the compiler of the information in terms of the choice of indicators, the relative weight ascribed to them, the margins available regarding (smoothing over) data unavailability, a selectivity in turn significantly magnified when it comes to composites which aggregate a variety of indicators or cross-cutting compilations. Across the spectrum of this selectivity the critical theorising of indicators invites qualifications and revision opportunities: 'The theory or idea embedded in an indicator may be developed or reframed by its users or by other actors in ways that differ from anything intended by the producers.'[11] And further: 'The use of indicators as a technology of global governance can be expected to affect where, by whom, and in relation to whom governance takes place;

[10] Davis, Kevin E, Benedict Kingsbury and Sally Engle Merry, 'Indicators as a Technology of Global Governance' (2012) 46(1) *Law & Society Review*, 71–104 at 73.

[11] See n.10.

the processes through which standards are set; the processes through which decisions are made about the application of standards to particular cases; and the means and the dynamics of contesting and regulating exercises of power in global governance.'[12]

But how seriously is one to take this reflexivity? Surely not seriously enough to undo what is their specific achievement: the function of indicators is constitutively that of simplification, quantification, comparability, and it is only *by means of* and not *over* these functions that revisability can be invited. Their achievement is that they invite transparency in that very form, and their 'blindspot' consists in the fact that the form in which they establish transparency and enable observation cannot at once be deployed and queried. It is thus of the very essence and functionality of indicators that they abstract, suppress and generalize. To say that the 'transformation of particularistic knowledge into numerical representations that are readily comparable *strips* meaning and context from the phenomenon', and to treat that as a *concession* is meaningless because it allows no redress. When it comes to indicators, 'numerical' reduction is their epistemological achievement and the source of their authority. 'In this numerical form, such knowledge carries a distinctive authority,' we are reminded.[13] It is this authority that explains why they are produced as, and used as, markers for larger policy ideas, displacing democratic practice and the contingency and consequent risk that political choices carry, as expressions of collective subject positions.

It is thus at the level of *the normativity of indicators* that the critique of governance needs to be understood and undertaken, confronting the obvious ways in which *political* choices have been made to yield to the new understanding of social policy that travels as governance, in the latter's soft forms of co-ordination, the new flexibilities, the benchmarking and the designation of the practice as 'good', on allegedly objective standards and against highly questionable distributions of utility and rationality.

---

[12] See n.10, at 75.
[13] See n.10.

5. Who, then, in [European] law, is my neighbour? Limiting the argument from external effects

Joseph Corkin

POLITICAL SELF-DETERMINATION – FACTUAL INTERDEPENDENCE – COSMOPOLITANISM – COMMUNITARIANISM

> 'The common man who for generations has been the tool of insane politicians and governments, who has suffered privations and sorrow in wars that were of profit to tiny privileged groups, is today rising from being the object of history [to] becoming the subject of history. For the ordinary men and women in the world, the oppressed all over the world are becoming the conscious creators of their own history.'
>
> (Nelson Mandela, speech to the African National Congress Youth League Conference, 1951)

> 'People say we have to stop and debate globalisation. You might as well debate whether autumn should follow summer. The character of this changing world is indifferent to tradition. Unforgiving of frailty. No respecter of past reputations. It has no custom and practice. It is replete with opportunities, but they only go to those swift to adapt, slow to complain, open, willing and able to change.'
>
> (Tony Blair, speech to the Labour Party Conference, 2005)

Half a century separates these two conference speeches, one made at the height of South African apartheid oppression, setting out the Leninist creed of history as a struggle over who gets to be the 'who' or subject of history, and who merely the 'whom' or object of history; the other, setting out the globalisation creed, was made when the Liberal World Order was in full pomp, before the global financial crash and a wave of illiberal nationalism challenged its inevitability. Growing assaults on the

Liberal World Order, from an anti-globalisation left and, more significantly, from an illiberal nationalist right are primarily about reclaiming a diminishing subject-hood. They appeal precisely to those whom Tony Blair's speech disregards: those whose identities *are* bound up in local traditions, who *are* vulnerable, less nimble and more parochial in their outlook and who *are* neither willing nor able to adapt to globalisation. They are the 'whom' or objects of globalisation and their challenge to the Liberal World Order has made it look, for once, vulnerable. The End of History, read as a struggle to determine the proper ideology that was supposedly at an end because there were no plausible alternatives, looks itself to be at an end.

But class politics never disappeared just because global political elites decided that an economically and socially liberal model that embraced globalisation was not up for debate, which had instead to be conducted in shades of grey around this centrist consensus, even as its contradictions accumulated. The Liberal World Order was premised on a post-war settlement that promised, but is now clearly failing to deliver, security, stability and prosperity for all. And those who benefit least are now rebelling. Rejecting liberal internationalism in favour of local identities (national, ethnic and religious), they assert local interests more forcefully (economic nationalism etc.), repudiate global commitments and obligations towards outsiders, and take refuge in local symbols, cultural values and traditions. However inchoate their identity-driven politics and however cynically and opportunistically it is manipulated by a new breed of demagogues, their complaint is simple: that without unravelling globalization, they cannot be what Nelson Mandela calls 'the conscious creators of their own history'. Yet they direct their frustration at, or it is directed towards, the very international institutions that might, at least potentially, have restored their diminished subject-hood, to enable some collective mastery of a globalisation, which is increasingly turning them into the objects of others' law and power. The dismantling of these institutions will, far from unravelling globalisation (which will continue regardless) only bring, in Mandela's words, 'profit to tiny privileged groups' that can master it to their own narrow ends.

We are caught then between the *liberal internationalism* of a now precarious Liberal World Order that diminishes the meaning of national borders, citizenship and political self-determination and an *illiberal nationalism* that exaggerates the meaning of those borders and national citizenship, and particularly our capacity for political self-determination within and through them, and that simultaneously undermines the very institutions through which we might really achieve political self-determination in an interdependent world, albeit multilaterally. But if we do just about hold on to these institutions, this still leaves us with the great challenge of how to reconfigure ideas of political self-determination, citizenship, communities and borders around them, given the interdependence that connects all our fates to one another through complex global systems: economic, technological, cultural and ecological. Indeed, the failure to do so has contributed significantly to the malaise that encourages this illiberal nationalism. The increasing power of these institutions, not least the EU, and the impact on our subjecthood, demands some form of constitutionalisation to protect our capacity for political self-determination. More difficult is to determine precisely what form this should take. Moreover, our factual interdependence also has profound implications for political self-determination within the nation state and how it is to be reconciled with the political self-determination of others beyond its borders; non-constituents who are consequently the objects of law made elsewhere, the effects of which spill over national borders.

This chapter considers a popular theory among EU scholars that the EU's legitimating mission is an effort to manage our factual interdependence democratically; ensuring that individuals who are the objects of law made in neighbouring states are represented as quasi-subjects of that law, compensating for what Joerges calls 'the structural democratic deficits of nation-statehood' by which he refers to their tendency to make law without regard to the impact on non-constituents.[1] On this reading, the market freedoms, and especially the doctrine of mutual recognition, oblige states to acknowledge the concerns and interests of non-constituents when making and applying their law, justifying any refusal to recognise the substantive equivalence of a neighbour's law if this ends up hindering free movement. It is an 'argument from external effects'[2] that views EU law as imposing a democratically justified check on *formally independent* but *factually interdependent* national legal systems, each forced to take seriously the others' justified claims for recognition. But that check is also necessarily limited because, taken too far, it would undermine the national claim to exist as a political community whose

[1] Joerges, C, '"Brother, can you Paradigm"' (2014) 12 I. Con. 769, 782; Joerges, C, 'Europe's Economic Constitution in Crisis and the Emergence of a New Constitutional Constellation' (2014) 15 *German Law Journal* 985, 1026; Dawson, M, *New Governance and the Transformation of EU Law: Coordinating EU Social Law and Policy* (Cambridge University Press, Cambridge 2011) 151.

[2] Somek, A, 'The Argument from Transnational Effects I: Representing Outsiders Through Freedom of Movement' (2010) 16 *European Law Journal* 315.

members collectively determine their own law *for themselves*. National citizens must then remain the *primary* subjects and objects of national law, even if EU law makes non-constituents *quasi*-subjects of that law, precisely because factual interdependence renders them also its objects. Ultimately, the EU demands a degree of good neighbourliness, which is difficult to tie down because what this requires depends on how extensive our obligations are to those beyond our own immediate community, which can be seen from multiple perspectives: moral, democratic and ultimately legal.

The argument from external effects – that EU law serves to internalise the externalities of national law – reconstructs Europe's integration project as fulfilling something akin to the function that Kant ascribed to the *ius cosmopoliticum*, obliging otherwise sovereign states to treat one another's citizens with *Hospitalität* by committing them to behave as good republics that co-exist peacefully with one another.[3] It understands democracy in a deeper sense than merely as a set of formal institutions; more universal than nationalism, which is about individuals seeking recognition as citizens of a *particular* national community, democracy is about individuals seeking recognition *as human beings* whose dignity demands they be treated as more than the mere objects of another's law and power. From this more universal perspective, if each national legal system can assert an equally strong claim to the democratic pedigree of its own law by reference to the national institutions that make and apply it, then its external effects – the extraterritorial reach of what is supposedly territorially bound – on the equally legitimate national legal systems of its neighbours ought to make their respective constitutional claims self-limiting. They ought, as far as possible, to recognise one another's law. For many EU scholars, this is the purpose of the EU's mutual recognition regime, which operationalises the argument from external effects by settling conflicts between national legal systems in a way that, on the one hand, respects national political self-determination and, on the other, controls its parochial tendency to ignore how this interferes with the right of others to *their* political self-determination. So, for Joerges, the internalization of externalities establishes the conditions under which national claims to legitimate authority are constitutionally justified, thereby correcting a systemic failing in the nation state, or even

[3] Kant, I, 'Perpetual Peace: A Philosophical Sketch', in Reiss, H (ed.), *Kant: Political Writings*, 2nd edn, trans. H Nisbet (Cambridge University Press, Cambridge 1991) 93.

its very own 'democratic deficit'.[4] Operating under the motto 'Unity in Diversity', which he borrows from the ill-fated Constitutional Treaty, his private international law-inspired theory of conflicts-law constitutionalism depicts the EU as 'taming' or 'civilizing' the nation state by 'completing' or 'perfecting' its constitutionality.

The idea was always provocative, given the EU's own well-documented democratic deficits, and this chapter considers at length one particular critique: Somek dismisses the argument from external effects as a facile, politically-correct conventional wisdom that has somehow become a shibboleth of admission – a 'Darling Dogma' – for an elite club of EU scholars whom he dubs the 'Bourgeois Europeanists'; intellectually comparable, he suggests, to another of their articles of faith: that Europe is peaceful because it integrated, and not the other way around.[5] The EU has been such a prominent feature of our constitutional landscape for so long that it is now legitimate to ask whether those who defend it are today's reactionaries. Ultimately the answer depends on what they defend it against: those who, like Somek, argue its prioritization of open markets, competition, liberalization, privatization, prohibitions on state aid, free trade deals, austerity, and an economic framing of matters that a European social market tradition deems instead to be about social provision and redistributive justice, undermine our political self-determination and aspirations to social justice. Or against an illiberal nationalism, and then, less for the EU's record than its potential, over time and suitably reformed, to promote political self-determination and social justice *across borders*, that might then lead to us embedding European markets in a *democratic* European society.

A list of those who assert some version of the argument from external effects, and who would then seemingly qualify as Bourgeois Europeanists, reads like a *Who's Who* of EU scholars because the argument not only finds frequent direct expression but also underlies ideas of constitutional pluralism, conflicts-law constitutionalism and the EU as a *demoi-cracy*, or as ensuring constitutional tolerance.[6] The purpose of this

---

[4] Joerges, C, 'Unity in Diversity as Europe's Vocation and Conflicts Law as Europe's Constitutional Form', *LEQS Paper* No. 28/2010, accessed 30 January 2017 at *www.lse.ac.uk/europeanInstitute/LEQS/LEQSPaper28.pdf.*

[5] Somek, A, 'The Darling Dogma of Bourgeois Europeanists' (2014) 20 *European Law Journal* 688.

[6] See e.g. Whelan, F, 'Prologue: Democratic Theory and the Boundary Problem', in Pennock, J and J Chapman (eds), *Nomos XXV: Liberal Democracy* (NYU Press, New York NY 1983); Maduro, M, 'Reforming the Market or the State? Article 30 and the European Constitution: Economic Freedom and

chapter is not primarily to defend these theories, but more specifically to understand how they and Somek's critique speak to the liberal internationalism versus illiberal nationalism divide that is opening up in Europe (and beyond) and the implications for our subject-hood. The chapter begins by grounding the argument from external effects more thoroughly. It then turns to Somek's critique of the argument, which it concludes has some merit but is ultimately exaggerated, before explaining how his valid criticisms might be met.

THE ARGUMENT FROM EXTERNAL EFFECTS

The idea of reconciling the impulse for national political self-determination with our factual interdependence is not new. Kant's Perpetual Peace project was also a quest for an international rule of law that subjected the state to external constitutional discipline; a theory that he set out in the headiest days of the Enlightenment, when a rationally derived universal constitutional order seemed possible. But progress towards this supposed goal has been slow and the international institutions that are its legacy are now faltering, especially an EU that has travelled further down the path than any, cajoled along by a court whose

---

Political Rights' (1997) 3 *European Law Journal* 55; Weiler, J, *The Constitution of Europe: 'Do the New Clothes Have an Emperor?' and Other Essays on European Integration* (Cambridge University Press, Cambridge 1999) 221; Eleftheriadis, P, 'Cosmopolitan Law' (2003) 9 *European Law Journal* 241; Nicolaïdis, K, and G Shaffer, 'Transnational Mutual Recognition Regimes: Governance Without Global Government' (2005) 68 *Law and Contemporary Problems* 263, 300; Goodin, R, 'Enfranchising All Affected Interests, and its Alternatives' (2007) 35 *Philosophy and Public Affairs* 40; Menon, A, and S Weatherill, 'Transnational Legitimacy in a Globalising World: How the European Union Rescues its States' (2008) 31 *Western European Politics* 397; Menéndez, A, 'The European Democratic Challenge: The Forging of a Supranational volonté générale' (2009) 15 *European Law Journal* 277; Miller, D, 'Democracy's Domain' (2009) 37 *Philosophy and Public Affairs* 201; Neyer, J, *The Justification of Europe: A Political Theory of Supranational Integration* (Oxford University Press, Oxford 2012); Nicolaïdis, K, 'European Democracy and Its Crisis' (2012) 51 JCMS 351, 356 and 361; Benvenisti, E, and G Downs, 'The Premises, Assumptions, and Implications of Van Gend en Loos: Viewed from the Perspectives of Democracy and Legitimacy of International Institutions' (2014) 25 EJIL 85; Lindseth, P, 'Equilibrium, Demoi-cracy, and Delegation in the Crisis of European Integration' (2014) 15 *German Law Journal* 529, 536 and 566; Innerarity, D, 'Transnational Self-Determination: Resetting Self-Government in the Age of Interdependence' (2015) 53 JCMS 1061.

direct effect and supremacy jurisprudence has done so much to subject its members to a strong European rule of law.

Various reconstructions of the integration project, including constitutional pluralism, conflicts-law constitutionalism and the EU as a *demoicracy*, acknowledge our real commitments to the nation state as well as some obligation to limit its external effects, tempering our national political self-determination accordingly. Importantly, these theories do not work simply from what ought to be, as per an abstract Kantian moral and political philosophy, but deploy its universalism as an ideal, against which to assess what is practicable in the real world and our real (felt) connections to our national political communities, just as economists invoke a perfect market to understand existing imperfectly-functioning markets that fall short of the ideal.[7] For them the EU serves to manage conflicts between necessarily independent, but factually interdependent, national legal systems that affect and are affected by their neighbours, thereby ensuring the civilised legally-mediated settlement of those conflicts in a way that leaves plenty of room for political self-determination at the national level (and the ongoing legal differences that generate the conflicts in the first place). They accept that we cannot reconceptualize the nation state for, nor subordinate it to, a unified, hierarchically-arranged, supranational legal order – some sort of United States of Europe – but that this does not exclude the idea that we have obligations towards our neighbours, nor that these obligations might be managed by EU law. For them, the EU and its members *together* comprise a constitutional order whose outputs we can understand as a combination of the national and the supranational, each operating in their constitutionally justifiable spheres to manage the conflicts that arise between their formally independent but factually interdependent legal systems. While the EU magnifies the democratic pathologies of nation states by opening them up (further) to one another, thereby increasing their external effects on one another, it also provides the means to deal with that factual interdependence through a supranational law that requires them to consider their effects upon one another. Additionally, it facilitates their co-operation on other interdependencies to achieve collectively that which they could not unilaterally.[8]

---

[7] Rosenfeld, M, 'Is Global Constitutionalism Meaningful or Desirable? (2014) 25 EJIL 177.

[8] Joerges, C, 'Europe's Economic Constitution in Crisis and the Emergence of a New Constitutional Constellation' (2014) 15 *German Law Journal* 985, 1026.

These constitutional reconstructions of the integration project, as enabling the peaceable co-existence and even beneficial interaction of its members, follow in the Kantian cosmopolitan tradition that recognizes that moral and political obligations extend across borders. However, they tone down its universalism to acknowledge Europeans' deep commitments to their nation states, which demand respect for national law and institutions that have developed over time to contribute to a certain texture of society – an identity and feeling of solidity that furthers a sense of community and reinforces its values.[9] For as long as we remain politically, culturally and emotionally attached to our national political communities, we will experience any emasculation of their law and institutions as deeply undemocratic, particularly when this is only to further a largely economic form of integration.[10] At the very least, any European rescue-cum-civilization of the nation state must avoid imposing a totalising, socially-disembodied and ultimately alienating economic rationality – a neoliberal homogenization that hollows our national politics by flattening out national legal differences – especially if this intrudes on socially and culturally-sensitive fields.[11]

Theories that recognise our commitment to the nation state while acknowledging its external effects and the obligation to temper national political self-determination accordingly, reject the idea that the failure of the EU to subject its members to stricter supranational constitutional discipline leaves it in the 'institutional limbo of multilevel governance'.[12] For them, multilevel governance, accompanied by a multilateral or pluralistic constitutionalism, is necessary to enable dynamic, non-hierarchical co-operation between the levels,[13] avoiding the dilemma of

---

[9] Simons, J, 'Democratic Aesthetics' (2009) 50 *Culture, Theory and Critique* 1; de Witte, F, 'Sex, Drugs & EU Law: The recognition of moral and ethical diversity in EU law' (2013) 50 CMLR 1545.

[10] Davies, G, 'Democracy and Legitimacy in the Shadow of Purposive Competence' (2015) 21 *European Law Journal* 2, 19.

[11] Haltern, U, 'Pathos and Patina: The Failure and Promise of Constitutionalism in the European Imagination' (2003) 9 *European Law Journal* 14; Everson, M, 'European Citizenship and the Disillusion of the Common Man' in Nickel, R (ed.), 'Conflict of Laws and Laws of Conflict in Europe and Beyond' (ARENA Report 01, Oslo 2009); Davies, G, 'Democracy and Legitimacy in the Shadow of Purposive Competence' (2015) 21 *European Law Journal* 2, 16.

[12] Picciotto, S, 'Constitutionalizing Multilevel Governance?' (2008) 6 *Int J Constitutional Law* 457, 472.

[13] Carrozza, P, 'Constitutionalism's Post-Modern Opening' in Loughlin, M, and N Walker (eds), *The Paradox of Constitutionalism: Constituent Power and Constitutional Form* (Oxford University Press, Oxford 2007) 169 at 186.

having to choose between a normatively unappealing (and practically unrealistic) national isolationism and the limited legitimacy of supranational institutions, neither of which offers a self-contained framework for legitimate political self-determination. They instead consider that national and supranational constitutional orders ought to be read together, as somehow completing the constitutionality of one another. In these terms, national constitutional orders do not draw their legitimacy exclusively from their relationship to *a* national people, but from how they relate to those beyond their borders as well, which obliges them to support, develop and subject themselves to an appropriately structured system of international law that sets the boundaries of their legitimate sovereign authority. As Kumm puts it:

> 'A state would overstretch its claim to legitimate authority and, in effect, insist on a relationship of domination with regard to those who are externally affected, if it does not accept the restriction of its authority and help support a constitutional system of international law that is adequately equipped to address these issues.[14]
>
> Seen in this way, EU law is neither derivative nor autonomous, but forms an integrative whole with national law, with which it is locked together in a relationship of mutual dependence and co-constitution, their standards of constitutional legitimacy deriving from what he calls 'an integrative conception of public law that spans the national-international divide.'[15]

On this basis, far from completing ambitious post-war projects to constitutionalise the international order, subsuming national legal orders into some sort of overarching hierarchically-structured global constitutional system, national and supranational constitutional orders co-exist heterarchically (the doctrine of supremacy being no more than an organising principle, not the expression of some fundamental relationship). The EU demonstrates that we need not choose between a global constitutionalism based on a clear hierarchy of norms – cosmopolitan principles at the top, national legal orders at the bottom – and a disorderly global legal pluralism that rejects any attempt to create an 'order of orders', or even just principled modes of interaction.[16] All we need, and what the EU (at least ideally) offers, is a means to manage the

---

[14] Kumm, M, 'The Cosmopolitan Turn in Constitutionalism: An Integrated Conception of Public Law' (2013) 20 *Indiana Journal of Global Legal Studies* 605, 612–4.

[15] Kumm, n.14 above, 612.

[16] Cohen, J, 'Constitutionalism Beyond the State: Myth or Necessity? (A pluralist approach)' (2011) 2 *Humanity* 127.

coexistence of proliferating constitutional orders, as independent sites of norm creation and power, each with its own autonomous legal order and constitutional quality, so that all relate to one another within an overarching and non-hierarchical political 'community of communities' that can handle the collisions and tensions that arise between them under conditions of factual interdependence; conflicts that are as inevitable as they are intractable.

This constitutional pluralism accepts conflicting claims to ultimate authority, denying the possibility of any ultimate authority that could settle the relationship between different layers of law by applying what Krisch calls 'overarching conflict rules'.[17] They are locked instead in dynamic processes of conflict and contestation (the pluralist dimension referred to here simply as factual interdependence). At the same time, constitutional pluralists suggest we can avoid fragmentation and achieve reflexivity and co-operation through dialogue that fosters reciprocity and legal resolution if we draw on shared cultures of mutual accommodation, recognition and compromise, and especially commitments to that holy constitutional trinity of democracy, the rule of law and human rights.[18] Neither a commitment to abstract principles nor to disembodied universalism is required, only recognition of a common political culture and of shared values, which avoids framing politics around a crude communitarianism of identity, nationalism and xenophobia.[19] Each legal order simply agrees to operate within an overarching regime of what Weiler calls 'constitutional tolerance',[20] which respects the deeply unequal distribution of legitimacy resources between national and supranational constitutional levels and so excludes the subordination of national constitutional orders in which we are most comfortable exercising our political self-determination to realise our subject-hood.[21]

---

17 Krisch, N, *Beyond Constitutionalism: The Pluralist Structure of Postnational Law* (Oxford University Press, Oxford 2010) 70, 103, 275 and 296.

18 Cohen, n.16 above, 127.

19 Habermas, J, 'Struggles for Recognition in the Democratic Constitutional State' in Gutmann, A (ed.), *Multiculturalism* (Princeton University Press, Princeton NJ 1994) 106–48 at 134.

20 Weiler, J, 'Federalism and Constitutionalism: Europe's Sonderweg' in Nicolaïdis, K and R Howse (eds), *The Federal Vision: Legitimacy and Levels of Governance in United States and the European Union* (Oxford University Press, Oxford 2001); Weiler, J, 'In Defence of the Status Quo: Europe's Constitutional *Sonderweg*' in Weiler and M Wind (eds), *European Constitutionalism Beyond the State* (Oxford University Press, Oxford 2003) 7.

21 Nicolaïdis, K, 'The Idea of European Demoicracy' in Dickson, J, and P Eleftheriadis (eds), *Philosophical Foundations of European Union Law* (Oxford

We have then 'progressively left the shores of state sovereignty under anarchy', as Nicolaïdis puts it, to enter 'a realm of ambiguity where state-bound *demoi* can no longer do their thing separately', nor organise their co-operation by drawing on traditional constitutional ideas based on the (constructed) existence of *a* people.[22] But to remain committed to the nation state despite our factual interdependence does not mean having to choose isolationism over a United States of Europe, which is not the only alternative. At the same time, anything in between leaves us, as she puts it, on a Rubicon that is 'never clear of a tempest', so that although 'many yearn to land on one shore or the other',[23] this is precisely where we are and must (for the foreseeable future) stay. It is precisely this 'in between' state that constitutional pluralists, conflicts-law constitutionalists, demoicratists etc. seek to explain (and to justify). But controversy is inevitable because, in the words of Gramsci:

> 'The crisis consists precisely in the fact that the old is dying and the new cannot be born; in this *interregnum* a great variety of morbid symptoms appear.'[24]

And right now we are experiencing a very strong kick-back against the idea that the nation state ought to be subject to any supranational constitutional discipline at all, no matter how pluralistic. The supranational law and institutions that make for this disciplining are fragile and not established overnight. The danger is that we will destroy in a day that which took decades to build. Gramsci wrote the above in prison, a victim of the last wave of illiberal nationalism to crash through Europe. While we should be careful to avoid drawing overly-simplistic historical parallels, some are undeniable: the League of Nations never survived the rise of fascism in Europe precipitated by the Great Depression, and now the EU, having quietly expanded through decades of permissive consensus, reaping the dividend of peaceful prosperity, looks as exposed to an

---

University Press, Oxford 2012) 247; Nicolaïdis, K, 'European Demoicracy and Its Crisis' (2013) 51 JCMS 351; Nicolaïdis, K, 'The New Constitution as European "Demoi-cracy"?' (2004) 7 *Critical Review of International Social and Political Philosophy* 76, 85; Nicolaïdis, K, 'We, the Peoples of Europe …' (2004) 83 *Foreign Affairs* 97, 104.

22 Nicolaïdis, K, 'European Democracy and Its Crisis' (2012) 51 JCMS 351, 366.

23 Nicolaïdis, n.22 above, 366.

24 Gramsci, A, *Selections from the Prison Notebooks*, ed. and trans. by Q Hoare and G Nowell-Smith (International Publishers, New York NY 1971) 275–6.

equally severe economic crisis and the illiberal nationalism it too has awoken. There was always local resistance to liberal internationalist Utopias, but these sentiments are now so widespread that grandiose schemes to constitutionalise the continent, let alone the world, look hopelessly out of reach. Any appetite that there may have once been for a comprehensive body of substantive (harmonized) European law that would have subjected states to an external rule of law by locking them into a unified, hierarchically arranged and supranational legal order, let alone a matching institutional architecture that would enact, administer, implement and enforce that law – a true United States of Europe – has long since disappeared. But just because a federal Europe looks out of reach, does not mean a more pluralistic ordering is too.

The important divide is now between those who hold out hope that we might still *manage* globalisation through international law and institutions, the EU being the most ambitious attempt to do so, and those who oppose such intervention, either because they espouse a laissez-faire free trade fundamentalism, with little concern for achieving social justice through *political* self-determination, or because they are resigned to the idea that globalisation is irredeemable and consider that the only way to protect jobs, public services, the economy and our distinct national ways of life is to erect barriers to the world. The latter place a rather vainglorious faith in national sovereignty (anyway a misleading term under conditions of factual interdependence) and so offer only a simplistic non-solution to complex global challenges. But Brexit demonstrates how the former will often use them as political cover to pursue their diametrically opposed agenda, in the same way as culture wars have been used to gain electoral support for neoliberal economic programmes that in no way benefit those who vote for them.

Those who embrace an open world, for whom interdependence is an opportunity not a threat, may comfort themselves (rather conveniently) that it coincides with the common good, perhaps relying on that hackneyed slogan 'a rising tide lifts all boats'. But globalisation is not working out so well for many others, to whom it appears as little more than a profound source of cultural dislocation and a growing threat to employment prospects that exerts relentless downward pressure on their pay and conditions. For those more embedded in their community and whose identities are more dependent on that embedding, the cultural dislocations and economic inequalities of a Liberal World Order that is apparently indifferent to their plight represents a direct attack on their subject-hood and therefore their dignity. There is, then, no contradiction in their turning inwards, choosing a closed world of inward-looking communities – of resurgent nationalism, xenophobia and isolationism –

even as we become increasingly aware of how interdependent our world is. While they may be looking for answers in the wrong places, encouraged to do so by illiberal nationalists, their social conservativism, preoccupation with immigration, rejection of multiculturalism and pessimism about their economic futures under globalisation represent a bunkering down; a yearning for subject-hood in the face of deep insecurity and alienation, prompted by exposure to global forces far beyond their capacity to control. Yet the political establishment – Blair's speech a classic of the type – too often treats them contemptuously, as architects of their own misfortune; too inflexible to adapt to an open, fast-changing world and seeking only a return to the sterile comforts of a closed, unchanging world that are no longer available.

And so the growing interdependence *between* national communities is matched by a growing separation *within* them; between those who benefit from that interdependence and those who are more embedded in their particular communities. Metropolitan professionals often have more affinity with one another, regardless of where they are in the world, than with those who are embedded in their (nominally) shared national communities; a separation that is both economic and cultural. But these groups have urgently to become reacquainted because if the beneficiaries of the Liberal World Order cannot show how nations can remain open to one another while still allowing for social justice and political self-determination within them, including due respect for the concerns and interests of those who are more embedded, the clamour for isolationism and protectionism will grow and politics will increasingly revolve around nationality and identity, often in distinctly illiberal forms.

When people feel insecure, worrying about others becomes a distraction that leaves them receptive to the argument that there is not enough to go around and we ought to focus on those closest to us. Those who want to retain and even to extend the achievements of the Liberal World Order – its open, connected markets and societies and the free and productive flow of ideas, people, goods and information – have to demonstrate to those who are increasingly resentful that few of the benefits accrue to them, how it can indeed be managed through international law and institutions to this end; how open borders, markets and societies, and the resulting cross-border spaces, might be made to benefit more than just those with particular skills to exploit them. If they cannot, then those losing out will (quite justifiably) seek to deny others the chance to go on winning at the globalisation game, taking every rare opportunity they get to knock the international institutions they blame, or are encouraged to blame, for their predicament, which will do little more than ensure the resentment is reciprocated. Brexit was the perfect example; a howl of rage against exclusion, alienation and remote authority that has left cosmopolitans across Europe reeling and panicked.

And as the knocks accumulate, the confidence of the political establishment that supported the Liberal World Order and that had, until now, successfully defended the institutions that sustained and managed it, dwindles, cowed by a new breed of demagogues who require no brilliant strategy to mobilize communities against these institutions. They present an easy target, far less ephemeral than globalization or modernity, even more so when politicians are prepared to debase the political culture with a post-truth politics that asserts without basis in fact and that coarsens debate by exploiting the very ugliest of identity politics. A generalized malaise is then channelled towards narrow, protective and intolerant instincts, with the political establishment reluctant to defend the international law and institutions in the firing line (more for what they symbolize than anything specific that they have done) for fear of appearing out of touch.

SOMEK'S CRITIQUE

This is the unpromising political backdrop in which the argument from external effects must operate. But Somek's powerful critique of the argument, to which the chapter now turns, is more refined than any knee-jerk nationalism, going to the very normative core of the theory. He asks rhetorically, how can democracies be undemocratic by virtue of a condition (boundedness) that makes them possible in the first place and interrogates the supposedly democratic justification for obliging states to justify their refusal to recognise the substantive equivalence of a neighbour's different legal solution to a common problem if this hinders free movement between them. That obligation supposedly balances respect for national political self-determination with avoidance of its external effects, thereby protecting the political self-determination of others. But Somek argues that requiring states to recognise their neighbours' different laws and so denying them the right to insist on applying their own (unless they can justify doing otherwise in a manner that complies with the EU's mutual recognition regime and to the satisfaction of the Court of Justice) may open them up to one another, to realise political self-determination *between* them, but it does so only at the cost of political self-determination *within* them.

For Somek, extending accountability for national law to an enlarged public that includes non-constituents may increase competition and consumer choice but, like other forms of liberalization, it fails to compensate for the loss of political self-determination in the downgrading of national law through its increased exposure to supposed equivalents in neighbouring states.[25] By restricting what states can do internally, the regime diminishes the meaning of borders and citizenship, which are inherent to the idea of a state as a *self-governing* community: if everyone is effectively a member, their concerns and interests to be taken into account, it is in fact no longer truly a self-determining political community at all because the relevant constituency has become infinite. Based on the Kantian moral ideal of pure impartiality, the argument from external effects is, suggests Somek, difficult to limit because all who are affected by a law, regardless of citizenship, seemingly have an equal claim to the lawmaker's attention. But, says Somek, a self-governing political community cannot be held responsible for every external effect of its law and ought to be able to limit the causal horizon of its responsibilities by, at some point, ignoring the remote and/or aggregate effects of its law on those beyond its borders. It must be able to dismiss some effects as no more than the *incidental* consequences of its factual interdependence with other states and their law; an 'othering' that is normally effected through borders, and citizenship, within which a state is free to determine its own laws, to establish its own systems of mutual solidarity and to protect itself from external threat.

Somek also suggests that the regime embeds neoliberalism because the 'context of justification' – when a state wishes to insist on its national law despite external effects – excludes 'symmetrical democratic debate' because 'non-commercial interests have to be strong enough to outweigh the interest in the free flow of goods'.[26] This was tolerable as long as the regime was genuinely limited to enabling the free movement of goods (and so only increased regulatory competition) but, extended to service provision and even the establishment of companies,[27] it has stripped

---

25 See also Nicolaïdis, K, and G Shaffer, 'Transnational Mutual Recognition Regimes: Governance Without Global Government' (2005) 68 *Law and Contemporary Problems* 263, 284, and how the same problem arises with the Transatlantic Trade and Investment Partnership, which proposes to align EU and US standards through mutual recognition.

26 Somek, A, 'The Argument from Transnational Effects I: Representing Outsiders Through Freedom of Movement' (2010) 16 *European Law Journal* 315, 342.

27 E.g. *Centros Ltd v Erhvervs- og Selskabsstyrelsen* (Case C-212/97) [1999] ECR I-1459, [27].

states of the means to organize capitalist production and exchange.[28] The regime imposes an exclusively negative form of integration that opens up national markets to one another by *removing* obstacles to free movement that a state cannot justify to the satisfaction of the Court of Justice. But this has the potential to disrupt the coherence of complex areas of national law, disturbing serious efforts to control the power of capital, as happened (infamously) with the Court's strict scrutiny of acts of international trade unions solidarity that reinforced a structural bias in favour of individual (as opposed to collective) forms of self-determination.[29]

Finally, Somek argues that the EU fosters a transnational social space with a very particular 'cosmopolitan attitude': one that is essentially negative, when compared to the ennobling Kantian cosmopolitanism that conceives of humanity as a single community. Those whom he calls 'accidental cosmopolitans' experience themselves as neither tied to a particular place, where they live in communion with others, whose lives give rise to legitimate demands upon them, nor as 'citizens of the world'.[30] They interact instead exclusively as market actors, through contingent exchanges, organized by private law. It is self-determination of a type, but of a purely individual (market) form that is dismissive of collective (political) forms that they anyway consider almost pointless, and certainly too much fuss, in a borderless age of global interdependence. EU economic law is their kind of law; that of a post-ideological 'regulatory state' whose institutions manage the apolitical delivery of bourgeois comforts and intellectual certainties, including 'interaction-facilitating regulation'[31] that is little more than an 'administrative service' for tackling calculable and discrete instances of harm and for stabilising, facilitating, or even optimising self-interested private exchanges.[32]

---

[28] Somek, A, 'Europe: Political, not Cosmopolitan' (2014) 20 *European Law Journal* 142, 156.

[29] Joerges, C, and F Roedl, 'Informal Politics, Formalised Law and the Social Deficit of European Integration: Reflections from the Judgments of the ECJ in *Viking* and *Laval*' (2009) 15 *European Law Journal* 1.

[30] Somek, n.28, 142.

[31] Mair, P, 'Ruling the Void: The Hollowing of Western Democracy' (2006) 42 *New Left Review* 25.

[32] See Majone's theory of the 'regulatory state' as achieving Paraeto optimality (Majone, G, *Regulating Europe* (Routledge, Abingdon and New York NY 1996)).

Critique of the Critique

There is a great deal in Somek's critique, but also a great deal of exaggeration. First, it fails to recognize that although the argument from external effects is grounded in a Kantian universalism, the argument also makes considerable allowance for our deep commitments to the nation state and the special obligations that we owe (or feel we owe) our fellow national citizens. Second, the EU's mutual recognition regime does not reinforce neoliberalism by conferring a generalized right on individuals or corporations to be subject to the least onerous national legal standard, simply by reconstructing laws that they do not like as unjustifiable hindrances to free movement. Third, the Bourgeois Europeanists are fully aware of the deregulatory potential of the regime and the need to accompany it with a compensatory re-regulatory (harmonization) programme that avoids its 'social deficits'.[33] The regime implements an exclusively negative form of European integration and must *always* be read alongside the EU's powers to implement a positive form of integration (whether this is sufficiently compensatory is obviously another question[34]).

The regime obliges a state to justify any refusal to recognise the equivalence of its neighbour's law when it insists on applying a more onerous legal standard than its neighbour deems necessary, which has the effect of hindering the entry of a non-compliant good or service, produced or marketed under its neighbour's less stringent standard. But the opportunity to justify the hindrance remains nonetheless. Everything then turns on how closely the Court of Justice scrutinizes the justification the state puts forward. At times, the Court's scrutiny is too exacting, thereby reinforcing the power of capital and weakening political processes that were already struggling to control it. But it is an exaggeration to suggest that the Court has turned the regime into a 'neoliberal charter' – a means for those seeking liberalization, deregulation and the erosion of national welfare traditions to prise open national legal orders – that leaves democracy a casualty in the process of its supposed supranational reinforcement. And, even if the Court comes close to doing so on occasions, Somek's criticism goes to the judicial implementation of the theory, not to the theory per se. The regime need not be applied

---

33 Scharpf, F, *Governing in Europe: Effective and Democratic?* (Oxford University Press, Oxford and New York NY 1999).

34 Scharpf, F, 'The Joint-Decision Trap Revisited' (2006) 44 *Journal of Common Market Studies* 845.

ahistorically to implement some abstract universal Kantian cosmopolitanism that is oblivious to how national political communities were established over time and represent real historical achievements and, even when it strays in this direction, we could easily recalibrate it to acknowledge more thoroughly the achievements of the nation state and the idiosyncrasies of national law. The regime in fact only puts states under pressure to *justify* their refusals to recognize their neighbours' laws, which neither prohibits all external effects, nor the showing of special consideration towards national citizens. The Court might perfectly well test a state's justification for why it insists on applying its own legal standard with proper regard for the democratic pedigree of that standard, thereby lending states a wider margin of appreciation (and often it does just this, diminishing the potency of Somek's critique).

Somek can depict the regime as 'bourgeois' only in the narrow sense that it deems obstacles to a *particular* form of economic activity (free movement across national borders) as an imposition that hinders a *particular* form of private ambition, prima facie wrong unless justified. This does indeed work from the negative (bourgeois) idea of liberty, understood as *freedom from* interference,[35] but only at a high level of abstraction. Practically speaking, the obligation to justify the interference does not disrespect the only ever partially compromised democratic pedigree of national law as the democratic expression of a national political community, and so worthy of considerable deference despite the structural tendency of the political processes enacting it, or overseeing its enactment, to ignore or heavily discount the concerns and interests of non-constituents. This is because there is a margin of appreciation built into the regime's enforcement (for example, its proportionality test that requires states to demonstrate that hindrances to free movement were proportionate to their policy objectives). This margin is calibrated to respect the democratic pedigree of national law. When the Court considers whether national law unjustifiably hinders the entry of goods and services legally produced in a neighbouring state, it tests the justification for applying that law (and for rejecting the substantive equivalence of a neighbour's less onerous law) with considerable deference, intervening only when the state discounted the concerns and interests of non-constituents *too* heavily.

The regime demands only that national political processes *consider* the effects of their law beyond their borders, placing the concerns and

---

[35] Berlin, I, 'Two Concepts of Liberty', in Berlin, I, *Four Essays on Liberty* (Oxford University Press, Oxford 1969).

interests of non-constituents into the balance, not that they must carry equal weight, which acknowledges the special consideration states are entitled to show their own citizens. The regime is then only a *check* on national law to prevent *excessive* (but by no means all) national parochialism, thereby managing conflicts between national legal systems, without impinging on the core legitimacy of the nation state. Certain ongoing legal differences, and therefore hindrances to free movement, have to be tolerated to respect the deep commitment of Europeans to their nation states and their laws and institutions.

The argument from external effects is perhaps at fault, however, for failing to furnish the Court with sufficient constitutionally-informed guidance as to how it ought to apply the regime to test a state's justifications for refusing to recognize the substantive equivalence of a neighbour's law. This is an important criticism, but one that is surmountable if we not only ground the claim non-constituents justifiably assert over a neighbouring legal order (to have their concerns and interests considered) theoretically, but also translate that claim into detailed rules for the Court to apply, to render it workable in practice. Somek complains that the Bourgeois Europeanists fail to provide that grounding, let alone any detailed rules, and only sketch out their 'Darling Dogma' as a rather indeterminate *political* right. In one sense, his criticism is semantic because all they claim by reconstructing the EU's mutual recognition regime as implementing a democratic ideal is that the award of certain economic rights, in the form of directly effective market freedoms, can serve a democratic purpose. Relabelling those rights as 'political' to reflect that purpose is little more than a rhetorical flourish, not categorically different from Somek's own claim that prohibiting direct forms of discrimination against non-constituents suffices to secure a *virtual* form of representation in neighbouring political processes. But in another sense, his criticism is more profound because it is surely incumbent on those who claim judicially-enforced *economic* rights serve a *democratic* purpose to set out precisely which external effects non-constituents ought to be protected against to serve that purpose and, conversely, which external effects ought to be tolerated to respect the democratic pedigree of national law that is only ever *partially* compromised by its external effects.

Limiting the Argument from External Effects

Falling ultimately to the Court to implement, no matter how sensitively it tests a state's justification for refusing to recognize the substantive equivalence of a neighbour's law, and even showing considerable regard for the democratic pedigree of the national law in question, it will always struggle to grasp the underlying reasons for certain legal differences and why a state might wish to maintain them. Differences between different states' legal solutions are rarely the result of a blithe disregard for the effects on one another's citizens. For a state to be meaningfully self-governing, the nuanced balances, compromises and trade-offs struck between the competing concerns and interests of various domestic constituencies, as effected through its political process and manifested in its law, deserve considerable respect.[36] The Court ought only then to test for the *excessive* discounting of non-constituents' concerns and interests, while generally deferring.

Determining which external effects can be justified and which not – or where to locate the threshold at which a state must accept a neighbour's different legal solution because its cannot justify insisting upon its own – requires a foray into constitutional theory, if not moral philosophy because it turns on the moral obligations we owe strangers or, in this case, those outside our political community. The Bourgeois Europeanists largely avoid this, but then so too does Somek. He stops at the idea that, unless Europeans proceed towards full political integration, and so start to construct a larger polity that internalizes their externalities in quite a different way, national political communities must be left to regulate their own affairs regardless of the consequences for non-constituents, provided they do not discriminate directly. This is a rather isolationist idea of national sovereignty, or at least an unambitious idea of what political self-determination demands, which reifies the idea of a *bordered* political community that looks after its own citizens through its own law (until they begin to show more cosmopolitan inclinations). The nation state remains the *only* relevant political community, entitled to assert its jurisdiction and apply its law in pursuit of its interests, almost regardless of the effects on those beyond. But such standoffishness fails to correct the genuine constitutional lacuna in the nation state under conditions of factual interdependence, as identified by the Bourgeois Europeanists.

Ultimately, there are no viable absolute positions here, only a balance to be struck: between respect for the nation state as a self-governing political community in which we are comfortable governing ourselves,

[36] Corkin, J, 'Reconciling European Integration and National Sovereignty with a Conflict of Laws Method: Conceptually Compelling, Practically Problematical?' in Nickel, R (ed.), *Conflict of Laws and Laws of Conflict in Europe and Beyond: Patterns of Supranational and Transnational Juridification* (ARENA, Oslo 2009) 361.

and the management of conflicts that stem from its factual interdependence with other self-governing political communities. This raises both moral and practical (legal) issues. A nice way into the problem is to re-ask the famous question Lord Atkin posed in *Donoghue v Stevenson* – 'Who, then, in law, is my neighbour?' – on his way to establishing a general duty in British law to:

> 'take reasonable care to avoid acts or omissions which you can reasonably foresee would be likely to injure ... persons who are so closely and directly affected by [your] act that [you] ought reasonably to have them in contemplation as being so affected'.

Lord Atkin alluded to the Parable of the Good Samaritan, but he recognized that a *morally framed* 'neighbourhood principle' would be *legally workable* only if it incorporated some careful checks on how far the legal duties we owe strangers extend, thereby limiting our legal (if not our moral) obligations to something manageable. His reasonable foreseeability of injury test was then subjected to decades of judicial refining.

What underlying considerations ought to inform the judicial refinement of a mutual recognition regime that has, essentially, to do the same thing? What is the extent of our obligations towards our neighbours or, from the other direction, how far are we justified in favouring our community at our neighbour's expense? The next two sections consider this from a moral perspective, without application to the EU, concluding that we might morally expect a degree of other-regardingness (or neighbourliness) in how we govern ourselves within a national political community, but that it would be unreasonable to require a national political community to show the same concern for non-constituents as it does for its own citizens. On this basis, the penultimate section develops the idea of a communitarian inflection on our universal moral obligations, graduated between insiders (citizens) and outsiders (non-constituents). The EU then reappears in the final section as achieving just such a graduated recognition for those beyond our primary (national) political communities. Furthermore, grounding the universal in the real allows for moral and political obligations to change over time and can then accommodate the possibility of our changing identities as members of this secondary (European) political community, as the obligations that we feel towards one another within it strengthen. The slope on this graduated recognition may become gentler over time. The chapter concludes that this can only happen through a virtuous circle and cannot be forced.

HOW FAR ARE WE JUSTIFIED IN FAVOURING OUR OWN COMMUNITY?

Viewed sociologically, we are apparently only capable of transcending our self-interest within communities in which we share (admittedly heavily constructed) histories, purposes and cultures, whereas from the point of view of universal moral philosophy this can be dismissed as no more than a quirk of human nature, to be risen above. The implications for political theory are profound. While Kantian theories are more unworldly, building up from the ideal, communitarian theories incorporate these sociological observations, building up from communities and emphasizing the connections between individuals and *their* community and the special obligations *its* members owe (or feel they owe) one another. For them, we only achieve individual autonomy within a network of social attachments through which we pursue the ideal of public reason giving,[37] as well as developing bonds of mutual trust that teach us the virtues of self-restraint and -sacrifice. So, for Putnam, society depends on relationships of reciprocity, trust and loyalty of the kind that bind community associations and groups, civic organizations, clubs, societies and other kinds of voluntary activity.[38] This social glue, or what Aristotle called civic friendship or concord,[39] is what enables citizens to enter sympathetically into one another's concerns, so that they are willing to exert themselves on behalf of their community, not just for their own benefit but because they feel genuine goodwill and affection towards one another, which grounds their commitment to social justice and without which political self-determination is impossible.[40] Not only that, but a community also makes us *who* we are: our identity, our beliefs, our needs, our desires, our characters and so on. It is in, and thanks to, relationships of mutual recognition that we develop our capabilities and flourish (as the social animals we naturally are) in spheres of primary sociability, legal institutions and moral norms, and in

---

37 Rawls, J, *Political Liberalism* (Columbia University Press, New York NY 1993).

38 Putnam, R, *Making Democracy Work* (Princeton University Press, Princeton NJ 1993).

39 Aristotle, *Nicomachean Ethics*, Book 8.

40 Kymlicka, W, *Politics in the Vernacular* (Oxford University Press, Oxford and Ontario 2001), 224–9; Walzer, M, *Spheres of Justice* (Basic Books, New York NY 1983) 31; Miller, R, 'Cosmopolitan Respect and Patriotic Concern' (1998) 27 *Philosophy and Public Affairs* 202.

networks of solidarity and shared values.[41] This demands a sense of belonging that is found only in a *bounded* community in which we can pursue our social potential and gain mutual respect, recognition and dignity by participating in its public spaces,[42] especially in exercising our political self-determination (subject-hood) to collectively shape its laws.

What social justice requires is not then established in the abstract, through philosophical inquiry, but exists in those principles established in practice and rendered legitimate by the *actual* support of a self-governing political community whose members (citizens) deliberate with one another, exchanging reasons aimed at establishing what makes sense to them *as a community*, and not the discovery of some transcendental, a priori normative truth.[43] In this way, communities tackle social injustices that their members deem collective failings that demand collective solutions, and especially the regulation of markets, which makes capitalism, too, culturally rooted and socially embedded, continually reorganized *within* bordered communities, where our human needs, beliefs and characters (as citizens, as workers, as business partners and as friends and relations) are formed through social interaction.[44] In political communities, we challenge and avert the potentially crushing effects of an unregulated ordering on those without access to capitalistic means of production and we do so in ways that differ from one community to the next, through social counter-movements that are channelled through political processes into law, thereby socially embedding (regulating) market forces and especially the destructive effects of labour commodification.[45] So every community develops *distinct* strategies, manifested in *its* law, for coping with the social risks constitutive of capitalism's operation.

Those who build their political theories up from individuals and would organize political authority exclusively to maximize individual autonomy suggest we owe no *special* obligations to members of our own communities, but only *universal* obligations to all. But the idea that moral

---

[41] Honneth, A, *The I in We: Studies in the Theory of Recognition* (Polity, Cambridge 2012).

[42] Tamir, Y, *Liberal Nationalism: Studies in Moral, Political, and Legal Philosophy* (Princeton University Press, Princeton NJ 1993) 73.

[43] Habermas, J, *Between Facts and Norms*, trans. W Rehg (MIT Press, Cambridge MA 1994).

[44] Polanyi, K, *The Great Transformation: The Political and Economic Origins of Our Time* (Beacon Press, Boston MA 2002, first published 1944).

[45] Block, F, and M Somers, *The Power of Market Fundamentalism: Karl Polanyi's Critique* (Harvard University Press, Cambridge MA 2014).

and political principles (fairness, equality, justice etc.) apply to everyone equally, so that we ought to love our neighbour truly as we do ourselves, runs up against the reality that we seem only capable of transcending the pursuit of self-interest within bounded communities. Abstract, universal theories tend to be based on a more atomistic understanding of individuals, as less embedded in *their* community, so that while the obligations they owe, they owe to all, in fact they owe few obligations to anyone, other than those they have voluntarily assumed in private law. But does this confuse cosmopolitanism with libertarianism, thereby exaggerating its break with communitarianism, or might we just owe a richer set of obligations to members of our own community, which in no way negates the idea that we owe at least some obligations to those beyond?

The gap between communitarianism and milder forms of cosmopolitanism is more bridgeable than the cleavage between communitarianism and stronger forms of liberalism, including libertarianism, which prioritizes individual freedom, rights and self-fulfilment and fetishizes self-authoring and individual autonomy in ways that jar with real lives framed by care, nurture and dependence. Absent from the 'there's no such thing as society' narrative is any notion of solidarity or recognition that interdependence is inescapable. We supposedly flourish as human beings when trading money for other commodities as atomistic consumers, or our labour-power as workers when competing with one another over who is prepared to work for the least money and to tolerate the worst conditions. This is surely an abasement of the human condition. The exclusive focus on individual freedom, constrained only in so far as is necessary to promote the individual freedom of others – the sole metric for optimization – neglects our dependence on other external determinations. A society structured along such lines ignores how identities and individual life projects are formed within communities and fails to establish and renew the moral and social resources necessary to maintain a civilized order (collective institutions, civic responsibility, mutual trust etc.) in which those identities and projects flourish. A political community must not only safeguard the margins of liberty necessary for individual self-determination and chosen relationships, but simultaneously set the background conditions for those relations to promote justice and stability, which is more than just a glib triangulation of communitarianism and liberalism.

COMBINING REAL COMMUNITIES AND UNIVERSAL THEORY

Grounding cosmopolitanism in a universal moral theory can look rather thin or unworldly, more suited to the unencumbered individual, or Somek's 'accidental cosmopolitan', than to real flesh-and-blood humans, whose struggle for recognition within, and sense of belonging to, real (bordered) communities better captures a swathe of diffuse and less abstract forms of human longing and suffering. A better place to ground political theory is in the *interaction* between real communities that comprise real people and universal moral theory; an interaction that is located here between our emotional attachment to the nation state (its law, its institutions, our fellow citizens and the significance we attach to governing ourselves within it) and universal theories that suggest we ought to consider effects on those beyond its borders and their similar attachments to their own communities.

Schopenhauer also suggested we move away from universal theories to trace motives back to something more real.[46] For him, that lay in the biological imperative of our will to live, which he considered the fundamental drive of our nature: what could be more real than the physical object we know more intimately than any that we perceive, our own body, and what feeling more poignant than our unremitting desire to perpetuate ourselves? He suggested that we are thereby imbued with something we take to be love and that allows us to put the well-being of those closest to us before our own, even to the point of overriding our will to live, so that we sacrifice our lives willingly for them (nowadays, we would call this evolutionary psychology or socio-biology).[47] He was influenced by a Confucian understanding of humans, as naturally endowed with empathy or humanity (*ren*), so that we feel more strongly towards those closer to us than towards those further removed; a graded compassion, or partiality, that contrasts with the universal idea of an indiscriminating, contiguous or universal love (*jain ai*).[48] This graduated notion of obligation, he argued, was not a human frailty or psychological limitation, but was rather a morally justified aspect of living among those

---

46 Schopenhauer, A, *The World as Will and Representation*, trans. EFJ Payne from the original *Die Welt als Wille und Vorstellung*, 1818 (Dover Publications, New York NY 1969).

47 See e.g. Dawkin, R, *The Selfish Gene* (Oxford University Press, Oxford and New York 1976).

48 See Allan, S, *Buried Ideas: Legends of Abdication and Ideal Government in Early Chinese* (State University of New York Press, Albany NY 2015) 101.

with whom we share special connections. He derived from it a morality, grounded not in the abstraction of universal moral theory, but in the mutual compassion or empathy we feel towards fellow sufferers of the human condition that we affirm, consciously or unconsciously, in our parenting, in our relations with those closest to us and in our participation in building communities based on reciprocity; an unselfish gesture here, a personal sacrifice there.

For Schopenhauer, only in the unceasing misery of our common predicament – profound existential despair at our own mortality – are we aware of our fundamental commonality with those around us and can then break through to an eternal world (he called this 'the will') that exists beyond the world of appearances (mere representations in our mind) to gain direct knowledge of the nature of our metaphysical reality and our unity with all life. It is, however, unnecessary to buy into his metaphysics or his Buddhist-inspired thinking – that we are all aspects of one life, and that our apparent separateness is only an effect of how we experience forms under conditions of space and time – to appreciate our profound connection to those around us, which, if claimed as the truth of our lives and lived as if it were so, weaves us into history and the very fabric of civilization; the solace of belonging to something eternal. This goes to the very core of what it means to belong to a community that governs itself over time, as a never-ending project of collective self-determination; a subject-hood through time. For these purposes, a theoretical destination in a completed Liberal World Order or, for example, Kojève's 'universal and homogenous state' that supposedly emerges at the end of history,[49] scarcely seems important.

Nor is this communitarian inflection on our moral obligations, graduated between those within and those beyond our community, antithetical to a cosmopolitan point of view. But it does demand that the move towards cosmopolitanism – the effort to expand our moral horizons, to show concern for an ever-larger community – is *lived* rather than *prescribed*. The cosmopolitan ideal must then be a journey, undertaken by individuals and communities, not a destination determined by universal moral and political theory capable of constitutional embedding, and especially not by the EU. Attempts to cajole us in this direction before we are ready will only be counterproductive, undermining the very democratic arenas (currently national constitutional democracies) in which we most effectively expand our moral horizons to strive for a

[49] Kojève, A, *Introduction to the Reading of Hegel: Lectures on the Phenomenology of Spirit* (Cornell University Press, Ithaca NY and London 1969) 58.

better world, or even driving us back towards more parochial national or even sub-national (racial, religious etc.) identities.[50] To that end, Habermas's democratic-federal vision for Europe is seductive, beautiful even, but must remain, for the time being at least, only a vision;[51] something that committed cosmopolitans might try to persuade others of, by encouraging them to expand their moral horizons, but ultimately something those others will have to accept personally. While more political, cultural and emotional unity across national borders would enable us to embed a European economy within a democratic European society, we are certainly not there yet and nor can the idea be forced upon us. Indeed, for as long as our historically-constituted national institutions remain, as a matter of sociological fact, our principal means of political self-determination, they must also remain the locus of legitimacy for any realistic constitutional theory that seeks to encompass the state and its relations towards other states.

APPLIED TO THE EU

If the EU were suitably respectful towards national legal differences and its *formal* institutions of democracy were more procedurally perfect, it might encourage Europeans to identify more with it as *their* (secondary) political order. This would pave the way (legitimately) towards further integration, but crucially not by dint of those institutions alone, rather in how they encourage the development of deeper *informal* institutions of democracy at the European level – emotional, social and cultural[52] – that might sustain a virtuous circle. Integration would then proceed at the speed that those informal institutions of democracy developed to support the formal institutions, each encouraging the other to gradually strengthen Europeans' identification with the EU as *their* 'Union' in the fullest sense of that word. There is nothing especially radical in the idea of such a virtuous circle. National identities, including the characteristics

---

[50] Kymlicka, W, 'Citizenship in an Era of Globalization: Commentary on Held' in Shapiro, I and C Hacker-Cordon (eds), *Democracy's Edges* (Cambridge University Press, Cambridge 1999) 112.

[51] Habermas, J, 'The Crisis of the European Union in the Light of a Constitutionalization of International Law' (2012) 23 *European Journal of International Law* 335.

[52] Rummens, S, and S Sottiaux, 'Democratic Legitimacy in the Bund or "Federation of States": The Cases of Belgium and the EU' (2014) 20 *European Law Journal* 568, 585.

we attribute to them retrospectively, are not primordial, but were developed in the same way, as individuals transferred allegiances to newer, larger political communities *because* they came to recognize themselves as the subjects of those communities, able to govern themselves through their institutions, rather than merely objects who had been colonized by another. In this way, Habermas describes how national identities were the result of an organized form of *political* integration, mobilized over the course of the nineteenth century through:

> 'a circular, either mutually reinforcing or mutually inhibiting, interaction between political processes and constitutional norms, on the one side, and the networking of shared political and cultural attitudes and convictions, on the other side. Old loyalties fade, new loyalties develop, traditions change and nations, like all other comparable referents, are not natural givens'.[53]

In the evolution from city state to nation state, political self-determination (or subject-hood) played a fundamental part in defining new national peoples, their (political) identities developing through participation in processes in which rival options could be expressed, confronted and decided upon, so that, as these contests were accepted as legitimate, so too were the communities in which they took place. Quite simply, national identities were formed through participation in political processes. Applied to the EU that means, as Hix so nicely puts it:[54] 'No EU democracy without a European demos!' becomes 'No European demos without EU democracy!' Although formal institutions of democracy, unsupported by the informal institutions of democracy of a genuine (felt) political community are no basis for democracy *alone* (offering only empty proceduralism), they are paradoxically a necessary first step to driving a virtuous circle that generates those informal institutions that will eventually ground them. But in democratizing EU procedures to sustain such a virtuous circle, we must not lose sight of the fact that Europeans continue to insist on the normative achievements of their nation states, to which they (justifiably) attribute their freedom, equality and security.

Nation-building has always been marked by struggle; people actively seeking recognition for *their* culture, history, language, and identity, whereas Europe is marked, culturally and even just linguistically, by huge

---

[53] Habermas, n.51, 346; Habermas, J, 'Democracy in Europe: Why the Development of the EU into a Transnational Democracy is Necessary and How it is Possible' (2015) 21 *European Law Journal* 546.

[54] Hix, S, 'The Study of the European Union II: The "New Governance" Agenda and its Rival' (1998) 5 *Journal of European Public Policy* 38, 53.

diversity, so that fostering a national-type identity, based on a common cultural tradition, is not only challenging but inevitably meets fierce opposition, especially against attempts to substitute national identities. A European national-type identity will only form slowly and organically and cannot be forced clumsily with flags and anthems. All the EU can do is cultivate a virtuous circle that encourages its development. But whatever form that identity eventually takes, inevitably *alongside* our national identities, it must be thicker – a genuine *civic* identity – than the *consumer-worker* identity its market focus has hitherto promoted more successfully. The EU cannot be built upon such a thin identity as that of Somek's accidental cosmopolitan who, devoid of community bonds or sense of civic responsibility, scarcely belongs to any community at all: a mere tourist who moves effortlessly between different communities through the anonymity of 'non-places'[55] (online shopping sites, airport-lounges that could be anywhere etc.) whose hyper-commodification – consumption most clearly person-to-commodity rather than person-to-person – abstracts from the social nature of society. This runs against Europe's deepest cultural traditions. The EU must not only then abandon the integration-by-stealth nurtured by political establishments of previous epochs, but also its reliance on the related idea of a 'market citizenship',[56] which depicts citizens primarily as consumer-workers whose rights derive from economic freedoms, which it has used to drive this form of integration thus far. European integration will otherwise become increasingly hollowed out and atomistic, when compared to citizenship traditions centred on the meaning of collective action (social solidarity, justice and the civic ideal).

Perhaps more than ever now, the EU needs what Weiler calls a 'messianic' vision of a better society that appeals to us as humans, not just as economic units.[57] But to get to this, it may have to do something counter-intuitive: go backwards to move forwards; accepting that less may, for the time being, mean more. This would mean abandoning the bicycle theory of integration that assumes the project must keep moving forwards or fall over. Peddling more slowly, or even in reverse, may

---

[55] Augé, M, *Non-places: An Introduction to Supermodernity* (Verso, London and New York NY 1995).

[56] Everson, M, 'The Legacy of the Market Citizen' in Shaw, J, and G More (eds) *New Legal Dynamics of the European Union* (Oxford University Press, Oxford 1996).

[57] Weiler, J, 'In the Face of Crisis: Input Legitimacy, Output Legitimacy and the Political Messianism of European Integration' (2012) 34 *Journal of European Integration* 825.

mean being more careful to accumulate political capital by selecting popular manageable projects and delivering them well, while spending that capital (picking battles) more wisely. Not, for instance, assuming it has built up enough to stick dogmatically to the principle of free movement of persons (a touchstone issue for so many of its citizens) and on which it arguably paid the price with Brexit. On that point: the idea that Brexit will enable a deepening of political integration along federalist lines (when the EU finally loses its most Eurosceptic member) misreads the political mood across a continent in which popular discontent with the EU is far from confined to the UK. The frustration (fair or otherwise) of those who feel they have benefited little from the EU, or are even systematically ignored, is continent-wide and will not be contained by fear (again, as Brexit amply demonstrated). Indeed, a harsh deal with the UK *pour décourager les autres* may only reinforce the idea of the EU as out of touch and concerned solely with maintaining the status quo. Too many Europeans feel they have nothing to lose by throwing everything up in the air to see how the pieces land. And if the EU proves unwilling or unable to bend, it may break. It also means recognizing more thoroughly how much its citizens cherish the normative achievements of their nation states, both substantive (regulatory and welfare) and procedural (their democratic constitutional organization). Europeans have a well-founded interest in maintaining those achievements and in resisting the encroachment of an EU whose power is, as Harlow puts it, 'diffused to networks of private and public actors' that frequently escape 'the painfully established controls of democratic government and public law' that we are accustomed to at the national level.[58] The rub is that these achievements are increasingly fragile and precarious without its encroachment. But on this, the EU must make its case more carefully, demonstrating how it complements, or even reinforces, national political self-determination, rather than appearing to undermine it.

Established to enable co-operation and to inoculate Europeans against chauvinistic illiberal nationalism, the EU has taken this purpose to such a length that it is now encouraging the very monster it was supposed to slay. The greatest risk is that it fails to read the way the wind is blowing and pushes on regardless, towards its vision of a liberal internationalist Utopia, without taking its citizens with it. It ought instead to reaffirm what makes it unique: that the integration project proceeds through a

---

[58] Harlow, C, 'Global Administrative Law: The Quest for Principles and Values' (2006) 17 *European Journal of International Law* 187, 212.

dynamic, constantly changing body of law in relation to which individuals (alongside their nation states) are both the objects and the subjects, which is far removed from the classical idea of international law as a static body of rules made by states, as the givers of that law, acting upon individuals, as the takers of that law who are merely acted upon. An expanding EU has rubbed up against the limits of integration and must recognize the resistance of its citizens because this is also to recognize their subject-hood. Otherwise, its tendency to regard even a standstill as a step backwards will fuel the very illiberal nationalist sentiments it was supposed to overcome. By respecting different national traditions of organizing and embedding capitalism, and even assisting states to maintain them in the face of global pressures, it might genuinely emancipate Europeans from 'the oppressive omnipresence of markets' and even sustain 'the ways of life associated with Europe's social legacy'.[59] It would then truly put European integration back into the hands of its citizens, whose political self-determination it would enable rather than undermine.

[59] Somek, A, 'What is Political Union?' (2013) 14 *German Law Journal* 561, 579.

PART II

Transformations: from subjects to objects, from objects to subjects

6. Subjects and objects of EU human rights law

Sionaidh Douglas-Scott

1. A PRELIMINARY QUESTION

On 23 June 2016, 51.9 per cent of those voting in a Referendum on the UK's continued EU membership voted to leave the EU. However, in the course of the Referendum campaign, and in the aftermath, it became clear that many people, among both those voting to leave and those voting to stay, were uncertain about what the EU does, and where it might be headed. The EU is of course a market, it is concerned with free trade. But the EU was always about more than this, as the Preamble to, and list of objectives in, the original Treaty of Rome made clear. It was not concerned just with free trade but also aspired to 'ever closer union', and also possessed a social dimension (for example, the former Article 2 EEC reference to 'an accelerated raising of the standard of living', and the provisions in the original Article 119 EEC, now Article 157 of the Treaty on the Functioning of the European Union (TFEU), concerning equal pay for equal work for men and women). Such provisions were included at the very start, they were not latecomers to the party. Since then, the EU has expanded its competences and arena of action to include a myriad of other matters – including the environment, EU citizenship, justice and home affairs, criminal law, and co-operation in foreign policy.

This expansive remit does present a problem for analysis of the subjects and objects of EU law. How should we understand them if we are not clear what they are subjects and objects of? The EU is an ambiguous and many-faceted polity, and has been interpreted in many, sometimes inconsistent, ways. How do we interpret this vast polity: as an (almost) neo-liberal or a 'complete market' phenomenon,[1] or do we interpret it as a something else, which takes account of social justice,

[1] See e.g. Carfuny, A, and M Ryner (eds), *Neoliberal Hegemony and Transformation in Europe* (Rowman & Littlefield, Lanham, Boulder, New York,

political participation, individual rights, environment, not just as epiphenomena to market building but as goals in their own right? Can the EU be both of these things? And yet it often aspires to be so.

This chapter pursues these reflections about the contested nature of the EU in the context of EU human rights law, focusing in particular on some case law of the European Court of Justice (CJEU). It investigates how the subjects and objects of EU human rights law can be understood, given the problematic contested identities of both human rights themselves and the very nature of the EU itself.

2. OBJECTS AND SUBJECTS OF EU LAW

However, the very theme of this collection presents a further problem: how to understand the terms 'subjects' and 'objects' of EU law. Given that the EU itself appears to be riven with tensions just described, it may not be surprising to encounter difficulty in identifying its subjects and objects. Yet, however the EU is interpreted, its subjects and objects do not appear very clear. For if we scan the vast bodies of EU treaties, secondary law and case law, we find a multitude of different interests, actors, objects and subjects, dispersed in diffuse manner. Neither 'subject' nor 'object' is a particularly well-defined concept in EU law, nor in international law, nor even in legal, social or philosophical theory. As a result, EU scholarship has tended to eschew research into how its subjects and objects are conceived, sometimes preferring more pragmatic (but ultimately more vague) terms such as 'actors'.[2] In what follows, I set out a few simple remarks on the subject/object distinction in order to set up the rest of the discussion.

'Subject'

The term 'subject' is a word of many different definitions and usages. The *Oxford Dictionary of English* (ODE) lists at least 5 different senses of the word 'subject' when used as a noun.[3] Perhaps most notably, some

---

Toronto and Oxford 2003); Grahl, J, and P Teague, 'The Cost of Neo-Liberal Europe' (1989) *New Left Review* 174.

[2] See e.g. use of the term 'actors' in this note for guidance published by EU Commission DG Competition: accessed 30 January 2017 at *ec.europa.eu/competition/antitrust/key_actors_en.pdf.*

[3] *Oxford Dictionary of English* (Oxford University Press, Oxford 2010) 1773.

of these senses seem almost contradictory. On the one hand, the ODE notes its usage as the main component of a clause, 'the element about which the rest of the clause is predicated'. This suggests an element *working upon* other things. 'Subject' is often used to refer to, or imply, an active conscious individual or social group or institution, with consciousness and/or will (see ODE fifth sense of 'subject'). This growing importance of the individual as subject has affected law. In international law, for example, it used to be thought that only states could be subjects, but this broadened over time to include other actors such as individuals, or non-government organizations (NGOs), etc.[4] The notion of those whom the law treats as subjects varies over time, and is often a product of the legal consciousness of the epoch. There may be requirements for individuals to be citizens, to have the vote, to own private property, possess 'will', to be treated as legal subjects. To have 'legal personality', or to be a legal subject, need not, however, mean that you are a human being (a feature that perplexes some in the case of 'human' rights) – for legal subjects may be juristic persons, corporations, public authorities or NGOs. On the other hand, some human beings may not be legal persons, or legal subjects: for example, if they are not adults, or they have a mental incapacity, or (if we look to other times and places) are women, or people of colour. Throughout history there have been human beings who have been invisible as subjects of the law.

However, in contrast to the sense of subject just defined, the subject has also been understood in a confusingly different sense. The ODE also defines 'subject' as 'a person or thing that is being … dealt with'. This is the notion of subject, not as active, conscious expresser of will, but rather a concept of subject as one who is not acting on others, but acted upon. Related to this is the concept of subject as under the authority of a ruler, as in 'the Queen's subjects', 'subjected to' certain actions. Until the 1948 British Nationality Act, there was no formal legal category of British citizen – merely subjects of the Crown. According to the ODE, the fourth sense of subject is someone 'owing allegiance to a monarch or other supreme ruler'. Blackstone wrote that 'allegiance is the tie which binds the subject to the king, in return for that protection which the king affords the subject'.[5] Foucault also took a related view, believing the subject to be a prime effect of power: 'The individual is not to be

---

[4] For discussion of this see e.g. Cassese, A, *International Law* (Oxford University Press, Oxford 2004) ch.4.

[5] Blackstone, W, 'Of the People, Whether Aliens, Denizens, or Natives' in *Commentaries* (University of Chicago Press, Chicago 1979, first published 1765–9) Book 1, ch.10.

conceived as a sort of elementary nucleus, a primitive atom, a multiple and inert material ... In fact, it is already one of the prime effects of power that certain bodies, certain gestures, certain discourses, certain desires come to be identified and constituted as individuals.'[6] These accounts give the subject a far less autonomous, or assertive, role in law, perhaps even annihilating individuality or at least, as the legal realists might suggest, reducing it to a shorthand for our policy goals.[7]

Such a confusing tension between understandings of the term 'subject' cannot but lead to confusion in its usage and application. For the rest of this chapter, I will be working primarily with this first sense of 'subject', as active party working upon other things (partly in order to attempt some differentiation from the term 'object') but noting also that this other understanding of subject as 'being dealt with', 'subjected to', often rises up and undermines the supposed autonomy of the subject.

'Object'

There are also different senses and usages of the word 'object', again some seemingly incompatible with others.[8] Objects are defined as material things that can be perceived by the senses, but also as goals or ends of effort or activity. Another important understanding of 'object' is that of a thing that forms an element of, or constitutes the *subject matter* of, an investigation or science – thus identifying objects and subjects in a confusing way. This again reveals ambiguity and ambivalence in how we understand these concepts.

For the most part, the sense of 'object' I will work with in this chapter is that of object used in contrast to the term 'subject', so as to afford some distinction between the two terms. In this sense, 'object' is often taken to refer to that which the subject's cognitive or other activity observes, or acts upon. It is a very general category. Indeed, Charles Pierce described 'object' as 'anything we can think or talk about'.[9] Perhaps even anything we might be aware of or pay attention to. So it

---

[6] Foucault, M, 'Truth and Power' in Gordon, C (ed.), *Michel Foucault: Power/Knowledge* (Harvester, Brighton, W Sussex 1980) 98.

[7] See further on this, e.g. Cohen, F, 'Transcendental Nonsense and the Functional Approach' (1935) 35 Col L Rev 809.

[8] A variety of dictionary searches – including the *Oxford Dictionary of English*, the *Merriam Webster Online Dictionary* – revealed these usages.

[9] Pierce, CS, 'Reflections on Real and Unreal Objects' (Undated, MS: 966).

need not be a material object.[10] I will work with this very vague usage, and use the category of 'objects of EU law' to encompass many different things.

One further thing to note, however, is that legal categories have developed so as to mirror the confusions and ambiguities in the understandings of the terms 'subject' and 'object'. As international legal actors have diversified, and legitimate topics of legal regulation expanded, the line between subjects and objects has blurred. For much of the time we can be both subjects and objects in the world, and for law. So it would seem that neither category is very clear. This is confusing but the vagueness is also interesting. It suggests an ambiguity, an ambivalence and lack of security in our interactions and relationships with the (legal) world. This ambivalence is especially present in EU human rights case law, as I will seek to demonstrate.

Subjects and Objects of EU Law

The study of EU law, and indeed law more generally, tends to be text-based. Cases, treaties, legislation and academic writings are the legal sources through which those of us working in the field of EU law relate to it. Language is usually our first port of call when we seek out what the law is and how it orders our lives. But if we really want to capture the meaning of law we need to do more than simply look to words and letters. Culture, history, society, religion, economics, all play their part in determining law. Beyond the text, EU law has a rich existence in the physical world. It is often created, transmitted and authorised through objects or images. From the symbolic (the EU flag with its stars, the grand institutional buildings in Brussels, Strasbourg, Luxembourg and elsewhere), to the mundane (the EEC butter mountain or a milk quota), the legal authority of the EU is located in the objects around us. Similarly, the practice of EU law often relies on material objects or images, both as evidence (for example, the composition of products subject to EU free movement laws such as French *Crème de Cassis*, or German *Bier*[11]) and to found authority (for instance, a Schengen border post, or a piece of paper executing a European arrest warrant, or

---

[10] See Crane, T, *The Objects of Thought* (Oxford University Press, Oxford 2013).

[11] Both prominent objects in famous EU litigation, see e.g. *Rewe-Zentral AG v Bundesmonopolverwaltung für Branntwein (Cassis de Dijon)* Case 120/78 [1979] ECR 649; *Commission v Germany (Beer Purity)* Case 178/84 [1987] ECR 1227.

consumer goods marked to demonstrate compliance with EU standards which illustrate complex issues of trade regulation).

In what ways, then, might studying EU law through its subjects and objects enlighten us? How might they reveal, or perhaps mask, particular aims or projects of EU law, and what does this tell us about the reasons why some (physical or material) subjects and objects are foregrounded, and others hidden or ignored? Which, if any, subjects or objects have been written out of EU law? We might take as an example those faceless individuals whose names we associate with important cases, but who have been lost in the depths of history – for example Herr Stauder, who sparked off the EU's fundamental rights jurisprudence with his claim to free butter.[12]

3. HUMAN RIGHTS AND EU LAW

One area of EU law that appears rich for investigation of its subjects and objects is that of human rights. This is because the very doctrine of human rights appears (at least to many) to be premised on a certain affirmative conception of individual subjects capable of possessing dignity and autonomy, and therefore to forge very close links with the first sense of 'subject' noted above. For example, take Griffin's account of human rights: 'Human rights can then be seen as protections of our human standing … or personhood … To be an agent, in the fullest sense of which we are capable, one must (first) choose one's own path through life – that I not be dominated or controlled by someone or something else (call it "autonomy").'[13] Rights-based theories came to the fore when the modern era recognized the individual as a foundation of much legal political and moral discourse. In contrast, international law has for long taken states and international treaties as its dominant elements. Furthermore, in cases such as *van Gend*,[14] the CJEU appeared quite deliberately to turn individuals from objects to subjects of EU law, by vehemently emphasising rights, and distinguishing the EEC from traditional international law. And in a more contemporary context, respect for human rights is listed in Article 2 of the Treaty on the European Union (TEU) as one of the values on which the EU is founded – so it seems the EU is

---

[12] *Stauder v City of Ulm* Case 29/ 69 [1969] ECR 419.

[13] For example see e.g. Griffin, J, *On Human Rights* (Oxford University Press, Oxford 2008) 33.

[14] For further on *van Gend*, and objects and subjects of EU law, see Fahey and Bardutzky, in chapter 1 of this collection.

now staking its identity on their recognition, making this a particularly significant subject for EU law.

However, on closer inspection, the notion of individuals as subjects of EU human rights law may not be so clear at all. To begin with, in its early days the (former) EEC did not accord so much importance to individuals as subjects or objects of its law, nor indeed to human rights. This is clear from the wording of the Treaty of Rome, which in so far as it gives rise to any rights or obligations, tends to accord them to Member States. To be sure, the judgment in *van Gend en Loos* acknowledged the significance of individuals in (EEC) law: 'the subjects of which comprise not only member states but also their nationals', going on to state, '[i]ndependently of the legislation of Member States, Community law […] not only imposes obligations on individuals but is also intended to confer upon them rights which become part of their legal heritage'.[15] Yet, even then, human rights entered EU law only embryonically, for a long time seemingly by-products of a hugely more significant Internal Market interest. After all, a central argument in *van Gend* was that customs duties should not be payable on goods imported into the Netherlands. The history of human rights protection in the EU, particularly through the legal decisions of the CJEU, readily translates into the form of a familiar narrative: that human rights were not concerns of the EU's founders, but instead grudgingly recognized by the CJEU in the face of a threat to the sovereignty of EU law, and European integration more generally, from national constitutional courts which threatened to disapply EU acts that failed to comply with their human rights standards. As a result, the fear is that human rights have become instrumentalized to further European integration.[16] Such an approach has as much of a Marxist teleological flavour, with all roads leading to a functioning capitalist Common Market, as it does a Kantian basis in dignity.

To be sure, Article 6 TEU now accords the EU Charter of Fundamental Rights the same legal value as EU treaties, suggestive that it is no mere spin-off of Internal Market Law. It covers a comprehensive range of rights – civil, political and social, evoking an indivisibility of rights that undermines any conception of the subject of EU rights as only market actor, or market citizen. There now exist decisions – for example *Volker*

---

15 *van Gend en Loos* Case 26/62 [1963] ECR 1.

16 See e.g. Coppell, J, and J O'Neill, 'The European Court of Justice: Taking Rights Seriously?' (1992) 29 CML Rev 689; also Douglas-Scott, S, 'Human Rights in the European Legal Space?' in Walker, N, J Shaw, S Tierney (eds), *Europe's Constitutional Mosaic* (Hart Publishing, Oxford 2011).

and Schecke, *Test-Achats*, *Google Spain*[17] – in which the CJEU has annulled EU measures for incompatibility with Charter rights, something that once looked as if it might never occur. The existence of the Charter may be thought to have legitimized the Court's ability to refer to human rights when deciding cases. No longer is it constrained by having to argue that human rights are general principles of law[18] which are inspired by constitutional traditions and international treaties, especially the European Convention on Human Rights (ECHR).

Yet if we try to identify some of EU law's subjects or objects we can see what may be the problems. Case law from the European Court reveals that individuals are often subsumed to principles of EU law, such as direct effect, autonomy, supremacy, jurisdiction and proportionality, that render the distinction of 'subject/object' highly ambivalent. The next sections examine these points in greater detail, focusing in particular on issues such as the role of corporations/legal persons as subjects; the role of economic integration as a potential subject, the undermining of actual persons as subjects of litigation, in order to highlight where the areas of tension and ambiguity may lie.

4. WHERE CAN WE FIND THE SUBJECTS OR OBJECTS OF EU HUMAN RIGHTS LAW?

This section examines some potential candidates for the subjects and objects of EU fundamental rights law. For reasons of space, only a small sample of cases is examined, although it is submitted that the cases chosen provide relevant, prominent and extremely influential examples of the jurisprudence.

The Earlier Development of EU Law: Ambiguous Subjects and Objects of EU Human Rights Law

First, when we seek out candidates for subjects and objects of rights, we find almost an *embarras de choix*. But it is the objects (conceived not just

---

17 *Volker und Markus Schecke and Eifert* C-92/09 and C-93/09 [2010] ECR I-11063; *Association Belge des Consommateurs Test-Achats v Council* C-236/09 [2011] ECR I-00773; *Google Spain* Case C-131/12 [2014] ECLI:EU:C:2014:317.

18 In the absence of an EU Bill of Rights, human rights were first introduced into EU law as 'general principles of law' in *Internationale Handelsgesellschaft* Case 11/70 [1970] ECR 1125.

in the sense of what it is that the subjects are acting upon, but as things to think about, or of relevance to the case more generally) that are often more prominent than an autonomous rights-bearing subject, and the very notion of rights themselves often only seem to play cameo roles in the EEC's earlier days.

The first cases to raise human rights questions in the (former) EEC context came before the Court in the late 1950s. Not surprisingly, they concerned the common organization of markets. In the *Stork* case,[19] the ECJ refused to annul decisions of the High Authority of the European Coal and Steel Community[20] on the basis of their incompatibility with rights provisions in (then) West German constitutional law. In *Sgarlata*[21] in 1965, which concerned applications by citrus fruit growers for annulment of Commission regulations, argued to be incompatible with fundamental rights under Italian constitutional law, the ECJ declared these applications inadmissible, although, to be sure, the Court soon ceased to adopt this position (that is, of closure to rights claims).

The objects of the next cases were not so different, however. For example, the (perhaps central) object of the first case where the ECJ openly acknowledged the importance of fundamental rights in (then) EEC law, was the 'butter mountain', in the *Stauder* case.[22]

In order to deal with the butter surplus, one of the many unwanted by-products of the Common Agricultural Policy, the Commission had authorized Member States to provide subsidized butter to certain social security recipients, who in return had to provide a coupon issued in their name. Stauder refused to reveal his name on the basis that this violated his dignity, a fundamental right under German law. The European Court held that as it was not necessary to identify a recipient of subsidized butter by name, any possible infringement of human dignity could be avoided by interpreting the measure in this way. Thus, the doctrine of fundamental rights finds its first mention in Community law. And, somewhat ironically, an applicant who did not wish his name to be revealed became famous that very reason. Stauder himself remains faceless however – there are no images to be found of him, as far as I can see.

Stauder was followed by *Internationale Handelsgesellschaft*,[23] a canonical case in EU human rights law. This did not at first appear to be promising human rights material, being another common agricultural

---

[19] *Stork v High Authority* Case 1/ 58 [1959] ECR 17.

[20] Now defunct, but then equivalent of (what was to be) the EU Commission.

[21] *Sgarlata v Commission* Case 40/64 [1965] ECR 215.

[22] *Stauder v City of Ulm* Case 29/69 [1969] ECR 419.

[23] *Internationale Handelsgesellschaft* Case 11/70 [1970] ECR 1125.

policy case, brought by a company which was claiming the return of a deposit which had been confiscated. This forfeiture was required under EEC Council Regulation 120/67 which set up a common market in cereals. The applicants claimed that the forfeiture was a violation of their basic rights under German constitutional law. The European Court, fearing that if Regulations could be invalidated for non-compliance with national fundamental rights, supremacy of EEC law would quickly be sacrificed, found an ingenious solution to the case. It suggested that EEC law itself might protect these very same fundamental rights, holding, 'In fact respect for human rights forms an integral part of the general principles of Community law protected by the Court of Justice.'[24]

This may have been a landmark case; however, it is hard, if not impossible, to find an image of Internationale Handelsgesellschaft. It is a faceless, unpronounceable (for English speakers at least) company. Moreover, human rights themselves appear curiously elided. In describing the European Court's resolution, Joseph Weiler has written: 'the surface language of the Court is … the language of human rights. The deep structure is all about supremacy …'[25] Such a holding did nothing to halt disquiet in Germany and, when the case was submitted to the *Bundesverfassungsgericht* (the German Federal Constitutional Court), that court gave its famous judgment, otherwise known as *Solange I*,[26] where it stated that, so long as effective protection of fundamental rights had not been assured with sufficient certainty within the EEC, it therefore considered itself competent to check whether Community law was compatible with fundamental rights enshrined in the German *Grundgesetz* (the German Basic Law). This tension between the ECJ and *Bundesverfassungsgericht* continues to be a notable feature of EU law to date. Therefore, a primary claim comes from a state insisting on applying its own Bill of Rights and challenging the supremacy of EEC law – we might as well have a picture of the German Constitutional Court in our minds as that of human rights. Who are the subjects and objects of EU human rights law here, where the human rights litigant is a large commercial company, and the dominant theme is that of apex courts battling over the supremacy of 'their' jurisdiction and legal principles?

Therefore, the argument is that cases regarded as important precedents for recognizing rights in EU law are often more important for other

---

[24] *Internationale Handelsgesellschaft* Case 11/70 [1970] ECR 1125, para.4.

[25] Weiler, JHH, 'The Transformation of Europe' (1992) 100 *Yale Law Journal* 2403, 2483.

[26] The *Bundesverfassungsgericht*'s first *Solange* decision is reported at [1974] 2 CMLR 540.

reasons. Just as *Handelsgesellschaft* underlined the supremacy of EU law, so *van Gend*, although including much rights rhetoric, is most remembered for introducing the principle of direct effect: 'The Community constitutes a new legal order of international law for the benefit of which the states have limited their sovereign rights, albeit within limited fields and the subjects of which comprise not only member states but also their nationals', and also that 'It follows from the foregoing considerations that, according to the spirit, the general scheme and the wording of the treaty, Article 12 must be interpreted as producing direct effects and creating individual rights which national courts must protect.'[27] And, in this way, the EEC was transformed from a regional free trade community into a 'new legal order'. Had this not been the case, according to Stein, 'It is safe to say, with the benefit of hindsight, that … Community law would have remained an abstract skeleton, and a great variety and number of Treaty violations would have remained unresolved and unredressed.'[28] The introduction of direct effect in *van Gend* resulted in the creation of lots of citizen enforcers of the treaty, or 'private Attorney Generals'. This transformation of the individual into a European subject occurred many years before the introduction of formal EU Citizenship with the 1992 Maastricht Treaty introduced a significant discourse of subjectivity into EU law. Yet, the lofty characteristics of *van Gend* are belied by its subject matter: tariff classification of urea formaldehyde, a subject which is hardly world shattering, and may explain the 'benign neglect' of the Court's early jurisprudence.[29] And, in any case, whose rights were at issue – those of a very large haulage company, not an individual human being. In conclusion, then, many of these early cases reveal an absence of the traditional 'subjects' of human rights law – individuals – in favour of corporate entities, nonetheless capable of legal subjecthood and personality. The cases are more important perhaps for their objects, the stuff of creation of a common market – agricultural quotas, food mountains, tariff barriers – and the legal tools necessary to make these markets a success: direct effect and supremacy of EU law.

A few years later, another case was decided by the CJEU – equally important for the development of EU human rights law. If we move on to the case of *Defrenne v Sabena*[30] – here we find a human being, Gabrielle Defrenne, as subject and claimant, although we remember the defendant

---

27 *van Gend en Loos* Case 26/62 [1963] ECR 1.

28 Stein, E, 'Lawyers, Judges, and the Making of a Transnational Constitution' (1981) 75 *American Journal of International Law* 1, 6.

29 See n.28.

30 *Defrenne v Sabena* (No 2) Case 43/75 [1976] ECR 455.

airline, Sabena, too (most likely for its discriminatory behaviour). Yet the case is perhaps most remembered by EU lawyers for its assertion of the principle of horizontal direct effect – EU law can be pleaded against private parties, although equal pay was very important. But the inroad to equality was horizontal effect – a procedural device.

We have a subject, but what was her claim? She was a flight attendant (or 'air hostess' in the language of the 1970s) with the Belgian national airline, Sabena. She had suffered an abundance of discrimination at their hands. Originally, the average career of an air hostess was 18 months, because collective agreements had demanded that for this job women be unmarried, widowed or divorced, and childless. Standard contracts prevented women aged over 40 from flying, although male stewards could work until 55 and, after 23 years of service, stewards were entitled to an extra pension. Hostesses were dismissed when they reached 40 and excluded from this system, and Sabena had no obligation to relocate them. So Defrenne brought an action against Sabena, much of it based on the equal pay provisions of (then) Article 119 EEC. Defrenne was the subject of the litigation, but it is very hard to find out much about her. I could find only a blurry old newspaper photograph.

However, *Eliane Vogel-Polsky* is another matter. She was one of the main lawyers in the *Defrenne* case. Vogel-Polsky was a young Belgian advocate, who specialized in social and labour law cases.[31] She was in herself a fascinating subject; the brilliant daughter of Russian Jewish émigrés, who had to go into hiding in a Catholic convent in Belgium during the Nazi occupation. Vogel-Polsky's contribution was essential to the outcome of the case, which might have been lost had it not been for her input, and for this reason we should also approach her as a subject of EU human rights law. Vogel-Polsky was interested in the relationship between international law, EEC law and Belgian collective bargaining. She argued that former Article 119 EEC (now Article 157 TFEU) could be self-executing, that is directly effective in EU language, and she compared Article 119 EEC to former Article 95 EEC (discriminatory taxation on goods, now Article 110 TFEU) which the ECJ had in the

[31] See further, 'Eliane Vogel-Polsky; A Woman of Conviction', accessed 30 January 2017 at the website of the Institute for the Equality of Men and Women, *igvm-iefh.belgium.be/en/publications/eliane_vogel_polsky_a_woman_of_conviction*; also her obituary in *Le Monde* (in French) of 9 December 2015, accessed 30 January 2017 at *www.lemonde.fr/disparitions/article/2015/12/09/eliane-vogel-polsky-juriste-et-militante-feministe-est-morte-a-90-ans_4827591_3382.html.*

Lütticke case[32] found capable of direct effect, giving individuals enforceable rights in their national courts if Member States had not taken implementing measures by the specified deadline. Vogel-Polsky queried whether there was any significant difference between Article 95 and Article 119 EEC. Both were clearly worded, established a principle and set a deadline within which states should act. Surely it could not be determinative that Article 95 dealt with matters considered central to the Common Market (fair competition and free movement of goods) rather than equal pay for men and women? The Court agreed with Vogel-Polsky, who subsequently wrote: 'The Court accepted… that Article 119 had to be applied. It even accepted that this was a fundamental right. So it was a fantastic ruling.'[33] And this 'fantastic ruling' led the way for other important rulings on EU social rights, such as that a refusal to employ, or the dismissal of, a pregnant woman based on her pregnancy or her maternity amounts to direct discrimination on the grounds of sex, contrary to EU law.[34]

I have suggested we categorize Eliane Vogel-Polsky as a subject of EU law. Yet, in some ways, in spite of her crucial contribution to the development of EU law, she seems to have been excised from it, her important role largely forgotten, at least outside of Belgium, and the circle of EU labour lawyers. In terms of steering, or acting upon the raw material of the *Defrenne* case, Vogel-Polsky may be identified as a principal subject. Yet, as individual subjects, she, and the eponymous Gabrielle Defrenne, are obscure, sidelined from principal roles to Pierce's things 'we can think or talk about' – inchoate objects rather than prime subjects.

Latter-day Subjects and Objects

For reasons of space, it is impossible to discuss the many entities that have figured as objects and subjects of the relevant case law. The remainder of this chapter shifts to a focus on recent rulings that raise salient questions for the identification of subjects and objects in EU law. Who are the subjects and objects of EU human rights law in more recent cases, and might a latter-day Vogel-Polsky describe the ECJ as continuing to give 'fantastic rulings'? Of course, whether a ruling is 'fantastic' or not can be a very subjective assessment. The *Viking* and

---

32 *Lütticke* Case 57/65 [1966] ECR 27.

33 'Eliane Vogel-Polsky; A Woman of Conviction', n.31 above, 92.

34 Arts 2(3) and 5(1) of Directive 76/207/EEC (now Art.2(2) of the Recast Directive 2006/54). See also e.g. *Dekker* Case C-177/88 [1990] ECR I-3941.

Laval judgments[35] stand out as highly significant rulings of the 2000s, yet have been subject to much opprobrium, especially from those more likely to assert an affirmative role for social rights in EU law. In both *Viking* and *Laval*, the applicant companies claimed that their market freedoms were restricted by trade union collective action. Although the right to collective action was acknowledged by the European Court as a 'fundamental right', and the Charter cited as a foundation[36] for this, in both cases it was held to be outweighed by the freedom to provide services, as the Court found that the right to strike had not been exercised proportionately. Yet such reasoning is discordant with fundamental rights and has been strongly criticized,[37] especially in its application of a proportionality test to the concept of fundamental rights themselves. The moment collective action is found to be a 'restriction' and thus in breach of EU law, social interests are undermined, having to defend themselves from the economic. Normally, as in the test applied by the European Court of Human Rights (ECtHR), it is the *restrictions* on fundamental rights that must satisfy a proportionality test. And such a style of reasoning tends to lessen the focus on individual litigants in favour of something more like a mathematical balancing equation.

And, in any case, who are the rights-bearers or subjects in the *Viking* and *Laval* litigation? It could be argued that the Viking and Laval companies are simultaneously subjects and objects of EU human rights law. Subjects, in that they asserted their 'fundamental freedoms' or free movements of services, but also objects, because there was an attempt to enforce collective rights against them. And whether we categorize them as subjects or objects, in any case they appear to eclipse the workers at issue, who would more usually be seen as the rights-bearers, and whose claims were demoted from primary claims to restrictions on rights.

Nor is identification of subjects and objects aided by the growth of a ubiquitous proportionality reasoning, which eclipses and effaces the human in this litigation. In the words of a fervent advocate, 'proportionality is a universal criterion of constitutionality'.[38] This translates into a balancing exercise, an investigation of countervailing concerns. And

---

[35] *Laval* Case C-341/05 [2007] ECR I-11767; *ITWF v Viking Line* Case C-438/05 [2007] ECR I-10779.

[36] See Article 28 Charter on the right of collective bargaining and action.

[37] See e.g. Barnard, C, 'Social Dumping or Dumping Socialism' (2008) 67 *Cambridge Law Journal* 262; Nicol, D, 'Europe's Lochner Moment' (2011) *Public Law* 308.

[38] Beatty, D, *The Ultimate Rule of Law* (Oxford University Press, Oxford 2004) 162.

rights litigation shifts away from interpretation of the right itself, and of the subject of the right, and even any objects of litigation, into a relationship and procedural form, an abstract balancing exercise.

One area in which EU human rights law might have great value is in the context of measures taken in response to the eurozone crisis. The provision of financial assistance – 'bailouts' – to eurozone countries in severe financial difficulties resulted in heavy interference by the EU in financial and economic policies of recipient Member States. There have been several references to the ECJ (for example, from Portugal and Romania) on whether reforms to national labour law (required by the Troika – the European Commission, the European Central Bank and the International Monetary Fund) are compatible with the Charter.[39] The Court has usually found these references inadmissible. Partly, this has been because the Court has decided that relevant acts taken were not those of *EU* institutions. Article 51(1) of the Charter provides that it is 'addressed to the institutions ... of the Union ... and to the Member States only when they are implementing Union law'. States have no obligation to comply with the Charter when they are not acting as the EU's agents, that is, when acting on purely domestic matters. One issue of critical importance has been the question whether EU institutions can disregard the Charter if acting *outside* the EU framework, for example in the context of the European Stability Mechanism (ESM) Treaty, which is an international treaty, not EU law, thus denying the possibility that actors may be subjects or objects of *EU* law at all.

Therefore, in both the *Viking* and *Laval* litigation, and in the context of the financial crisis, ambiguity in the terrain of who are the proper subjects and objects of EU law has been used to deter the development of an effective human rights law. In the case of *Viking* and *Laval*, this is because those most obviously possessing rights – employees – found their enforcement attempts subject to proportionality assessment usually not applied in the context of fundamental rights. As rights possessors, they were not treated as subjects, their claims were not centre stage. And

[39] See e.g. *Inspectoratul General al Politiei Romane (IGPR v Corpul National al Politistilor – Biroul Executiv Central* Case C-134/12 [2012] ECR I-000. Also see further, Cases C-462/11, C-369/12). On the Portuguese MoU see Cases C-128/12, C-264/12 and C-665/13; see also Greek cases concerning the Council decision adopted within the framework of the excessive deficit procedure (Cases T-541/10 and T-215/11); see further cases arising from the Cypriot banking crisis (Case T-327/13; opinion in Joined Cases C-8/15 P, C-9/15 P and C-10/15 P; opinion in Joined Cases C-105/15 P to C-109/15 P).

in the case of the financial crisis, rights claims were excluded altogether, as relevant legislation was taken to exist outside of the EU framework.

Overarching all of this, the most prominent subject of EU law, and sometimes even of EU human rights law, appears to be economic integration. The fundamental freedoms of EU law have been highly developed to this end. Likewise, the concept of direct effect, introduced by the ECJ partly, in its own terms, to uphold 'individual rights'. Supremacy of EEC law was at least partly the rationale for the Court's introduction of a fundamental rights jurisprudence in the first place. But these developments have been in the context of general economic integration and do not always sit comfortably with the individual language of rights.

One final example will suffice to pursue this point, and that is the ECJ's *Opinion 2/13* on the compatibility of the Draft Agreement on EU Accession to the ECHR with the EU Treaties.[40] In this Opinion, the ECJ found many ways in which the Draft Agreement violated the autonomy of EU law, and so was deemed invalid. Space prevents any detailed examination of the reasoning of the case here, but as Halberstam comments, 'the [CJEU] is concerned with fundamental rights only as part of that [i.e. EU] order. This means solicitude for international human rights agreements comes with a caveat. The Court will show solicitude for international human rights agreements only in so far as these international agreements do not undermine the legal and … constitutional architecture of the European Union'.[41] Autonomy of EU law leads to thinking about the EU's sovereignty, and identity. Perhaps the true subject of EU human rights law is – autonomous EU law?

Such a stress on autonomy suggests something hermetically sealed, an atom, rather like the states that are the subject of classical international law. This indeed appears to be the attitude of the 2014 *Opinion 2/13* Court, and it is somewhat extraordinary. Surely a commitment to human rights is of little value if it cannot apply even in those cases in which the enforcement of a right may undermine the participant state's constitutional architecture.[42] Would ECHR membership under the terms of the EU Draft Agreement compromise the autonomy of the EU system any

---

40 *Opinion 2/13* on EU Accession to the ECHR ECLI:EU:C:2014:2454.

41 D Halberstam, D, '"It's the Autonomy, Stupid!" A Modest Defense of *Opinion 2/13* on EU Accession to the ECHR, and a Way Forward' (2015) 16 *German Law Journal* 105–46.

42 As the UK has found in the context of its ECHR membership, notably in the 'prisoner voting' cases, to the dismay of many, see e.g. *Hirst v the United Kingdom* (No 2) [2005] ECHR 681.

more than the autonomy of the ECHR's States Parties is presently compromised? This seems unlikely, in which case it is unclear why the EU should expect membership on different terms.

In any case, surely Accession to a human rights treaty should not be primarily about the autonomy of the EU legal order. It should be primarily about how best to protect human rights. As President Dean Spielmann recently stated in the annual report of the ECtHR:

> 'Let us not forget, however, that the principal victims will be those citizens whom this opinion (no. 2/13) deprives of the right to have acts of the European Union subjected to the same external scrutiny as regards respect for human rights as that which applies to each member state.'[43]

5. CONCLUSION

My conclusion is that the subject of EU human rights law is under analyzed and often ignored by the ECJ. We have to search hard to find it. Although in the early days the ECJ used the term 'rights' a great deal, and in *van Gend* talked about the EEC endowing individuals with a heritage of 'rights', at key moments the subject of those rights is missing or undeveloped. Litigants of important cases are forgotten, or faceless. There has often been use of displacement, or transference, whereby important cases become associated with something other than rights – whether it be supremacy, direct effect, transport vehicles, butter mountains, proportionality, autonomy, and so on. In some cases these other things (such as the principles of supremacy, direct effect, autonomy, economic integration) become the true subjects of EU law, propelling it forward. Claimants themselves, the Stauders, the Defrennes, and so on are more likely to become subjects in the subordinate sense, the 'worked upon'. Other components, such as butter mountains or milk quotas (and today, instruments such as European Arrest Warrants), are the objects of EU law, with important roles, often memorable ones, often overshadowing those who were originally conceived as subjects – such as Herr Stauder.

I hasten to add that this conclusion is unlikely to apply only to peculiar failures of the CJEU and EU law. Many, if not most, other courts and legal systems display such displacement activity, although their examination is beyond the scope of this chapter.

[43] 'Foreword', European Court of Human Rights Annual Report 2014.

Nonetheless, at a time when there is much scepticism about the European project, not least when (a slender) majority of British voters rejected the EU, there could be benefits from a more direct engagement with subjects and objects of human rights in the EU, of a sort that provided the EU with greater perceived legitimacy and a more human face. Otherwise it might appear that the 'true' subject of EU human rights law is the autonomy of EU law itself – a self-referential, and unhappy conclusion for the EU.

7. Local governments as subjects and objects of EU law: legitimate limits?

Josephine van Zeben*

The European Union's multi-level governance system allows for the involvement of a broad range of actors, including non-state actors and individuals, which have been excluded from traditional forms of international law.[1] This chapter focuses on a group of actors that, while central to the operation for the EU and its Member States, lacks legal status under EU law. Local governments remain firmly within the exclusive sphere of competence of the Member States, as underlined in the European Treaties,[2] and therefore depend on national law for their place within the EU's legal system.[3] The idea that arrangements pertaining to local government are, and should be, outside the scope of

* I am grateful for constructive comments on earlier versions of this chapter by Christiane Ahlborn, Ana Bobić, Elaine Fahey, Samo Bardutzky, and two anonymous reviewers.

[1] *van Gend en Loos v Nederlandse Administratie der Belastingen* Case 26/62 [1963] ECR 1.

[2] See Art.4(2) Treaty on European Union (TEU) ('The Union shall respect [...] [the Member States'] national identities, inherent in their fundamental structures, political and constitutional, inclusive of regional and local self-government.') This position is comparable to that of the United States, see Frug, G., 'Empowering Cities in a Federal System' 19(3) *The Urban Lawyer* (1987) 553, 554 (referencing *Hunter v Pittsburgh*, 207 U.S. 161 (1907)).

[3] For case law of the EU Court of Justice on the position of local governments, see Nicola, F., 'Invisible Cities in Europe' (2012) 35 *Fordham International Law Journal* 1282. This chapter will highlight the ways in which local government has been marginalized in *legal* analyses of the European Union. Local governments do form part of more inclusive frameworks such as that provided by multi-level governance scholarship, see e.g. Marks, G., L. Hooghe, K. Blank, 'European Integration from the 1980s: State-Centric v. Multi-level Governance' (1996) 34 *Journal of Common Market Studies* 341, and Marks, G. and L. Hooghe, 'Unraveling the Central State, but How? Types of Multi-level Governance' (2003) *American Political Science Review* 233.

EU law has gone largely unquestioned by EU legal scholars,[4] and the European courts.[5]

Notwithstanding this legal vacuum, local governments are routinely affected by, and affect, EU law in their roles as public service providers and conduits for political participation. Some EU involvement pertaining to the service provision by local governments has been overwhelmingly positive, for example through investment in local infrastructure and development.[6] The net effect on the democratic role of local governments is less clear.[7] While some localities have been hugely successful at increasing their influence by bypassing the Member State and forging their own relationship with Europe,[8] others have seen their domestic positions eroded through EU membership and centralization of democratic processes to the national level.[9] The discrepancy between the legal and factual status of local governments under EU law can also be seen to contribute to the disconnect felt between EU citizens and the EU institutions; without awareness of the role played by European policies

---

[4] Those arguing in favour of a more inclusive approach see Weatherill, S., and U. Bernitz (eds), *The Role of Regions and Sub-national Actors in Europe* (Hart, Oxford 2005) 3–6. (It should be noted that their focus is on regions, rather than local governments, which differ with respect to their legislative capacities. Nevertheless, parallels may be drawn as to the normative arguments in favour of their inclusion into the EU's legal order.) See also Scott, J., 'Member States and Regions in Community Law: Convergence and Divergence' in Beaumont, P., C. Lyons and N. Walker (eds), *Convergence and Divergence in European Public Law* (Hart, Oxford 2002).

[5] For the purpose of liability for breaches of EU law for instance, the CJEU has consistently held that the Member State is liable regardless of which body was 'responsible' for the breach according to the internal division of powers of the Member States. See Davis, R., 'Liability in Damages for a Breach of Community Law: Some Reflections on the Question of Who to Sue and the Concept of "the State"' (2006) 31 *European Law Review* 69.

[6] The budget for regional development for 2014–20 is €454 billion. For a complete overview, see *http://ec.europa.eu/contracts_grants/funds_en.htm* (accessed 31 January 2017).

[7] See also Loughlin, J. (ed.), *Subnational Democracy in the European Union: Challenges and Opportunities*, (Oxford University Press, Oxford 2001).

[8] See e.g. the work of REGLEG – the Conference of European Regions with legislative powers – accessed 31 January 2017 at *www.regleg.eu/*.

[9] See Jeffery, C., 'Sub-National Mobilization and European Integration: Does It Make Any Difference?' (2000) 38(1) *Journal of Common Market Studies* 1–23. See also Martinico, G., 'The Impact of the Treaty on Stability, Coordination and Governance on the National Constitutional Structure: The Regional Example' (2013) 1 *MJIL Emerging Scholarship Project* 101.

and/or funding in local initiatives, the impact of the EU on everyday life can be even harder to identify.[10] In addition, the lack of local involvement means that the application of the subsidiarity principle remains limited despite its explicit inclusion of local actors in the Lisbon Treaty's restatement.[11]

Underlining the importance of understanding the EU's effects on local government, and vice versa, does not necessitate the adoption of a normative position as to the 'correct' spheres of influence of the EU and its Member States.[12] Rather, it may be seen as an attempt to create a more complete picture of the EU's legal system by exposing the roles played by these vital actors. Some scholars have concluded that 'writing on European cities is an impossible task',[13] due to the heterogeneity of local government models among the EU Member States;[14] the difficulty of reconciling legal and geographical definitions of place;[15] definitional confusions between the 'regional' and the 'local';[16] and a general lack of – especially legal – data. Questioning the legal position of local

---

[10] Significantly, only 19 per cent of Europeans feel that local governments are sufficiently taken into account in EU level decision-making, see Special Eurobarometer 307, 'The role and impact of local and regional authorities within the European Union' (2009), accessed 31 January 2017 at *ec.europa.eu/COMMFrontOffice/publicopinion/index.cfm/Survey/getSurveyDetail/search/local/surveyKy/939*.

[11] Article 5(2) Treaty on European Union (TEU) reads '[t]he Union shall act only if and in so far as the objectives of the proposed action cannot be sufficiently achieved by the Member States, either at central level or *at regional and local level*'. This marks a change from the previous iterations of the subsidiarity principle, which did not explicitly reference the regional or local dimension of the Member States. See e.g. Art.5 of the Treaty Establishing the European Community (TEC) ('In areas which do not fall within its exclusive competence, the Community shall take action, in accordance with the principle of subsidiarity, only if and insofar as the objectives of the proposed action cannot be sufficiently achieved by the Member States and can therefore, by reason of the scale or effects of the proposed action, be better achieved by the Community.')

[12] See also Panara, C., *The Sub-national Dimension of the EU: A Legal Study of Multilevel Governance* (Springer, Heidelberg 2015) 1–3. For a US perspective, see Frug, G., 'The City as a Legal Concept' (1980) 93 *Harvard Law Review* 1057.

[13] Le Galès, P., *European Cities: Social Conflicts and Governance* (Oxford University Press, Oxford 2002) 18.

[14] Ibid., 5.

[15] See generally, Sassen, S., 'Territory and Territoriality in the Global Economy' (2000) 15(2) *International Sociology* 372–393.

[16] See in detail Section 1.

government within the EU opens a Pandora's box of further inquiry about fundamental issues related to the organizational structures of modern life.[17]

Attempting to answer all these questions within the limited scope of this chapter would preclude any meaningful depth of analysis. In line with the analytical framework underlying this edited volume, this chapter will therefore restrict its analysis to two fundamental questions: First, are local governments *subjects* and/or *objects* of EU law? Second, what are the implications of local governments' 'subjecthood' and 'objecthood' under EU law? Specifically, how does the status of local governments under EU law affect the EU's ability to safeguard core principles of subsidiarity and representative democracy? These questions are answered by providing a categorization of local government models in the EU Member States and a tailored definition of 'subject' and 'object' of EU law (Section I). These two parameters frame our analysis of the legal and factual realities of local governments as subjects and objects of European law (Section II). The concluding section discusses the implications of the legal and factual status of local governments for the development of the EU (Section III).

1. LEGAL PARAMETERS OF EU LOCAL GOVERNMENT

This section provides a working definition of 'local government' followed by a categorization of local government arrangements in the Member States. The resulting non-exhaustive models of local government are fundamental in understanding EU-local government interaction. The final part of this section provides an overview of the ways in which local governments take on the role of subject or object under EU law.

A. Defining European Local Government

This chapter has thus far stubbornly and cumbersomely referred to 'local government' as its subject of analysis. As most local governments are cities (of various shapes and sizes), one may wonder why this easier, and more accessible, shorthand has not been adopted. European (legal) documents typically refer to 'local and regional authorities' as a single

---

[17] For detailed treatment of general normative theories applicable to local government, see King, D., and G. Stoker, *Rethinking Local Democracy* (Palgrave, Basingstoke 1996).

level of government, despite the fact that regions may cross Member State boundaries and often encompass several local governments.[18] The same terminological fluidity can be found in European legal scholarship, which similarly uses the term 'city' interchangeably and inconsistently with 'local government', 'sub-national actor' and 'region/regional government'. As a result, the European 'city' remains legally underspecified and may be both over- and under-exclusive of various forms of local government. Regrettably, the term 'local government' does not itself remedy this lack of specificity. The wide range of institutional arrangements among the Member States is a key challenge in forming a coherent legal understanding of EU local government.

The current EU definition of the 'city' – adopted in 2012 in coordination with the Organization for Economic Co-operation and Development – is based on number of inhabitants and population density in order to facilitate comparisons across European Member States.[19] This quantitative definition leaves out many, harder to quantify, characteristics of local governments, such as their connectivity, historical foundation, service provision, political importance, being a recipient of urban policy funds, or the holding of city rights through a charter. Individual Member States continue to use their own methods of defining local government, particularly cities. The United Kingdom continues to confer city status through the monarch, which means that very small localities, such as St Davids in Wales with fewer than 2,000 inhabitants, can also be 'cities'.[20] This example highlights one of the key distinctions in species of local government, that between cities and towns.

As the focus of this chapter is on the legal rather than demographic and geographical characteristics of local government, 'local government' will here refer to *municipalities* – including both cities and towns – with administrative, rather than legislative, powers.[21] Typically, these municipalities represent the first level of elected government within a

---

[18] See e.g. Art.5(2) TEU, '[t]he Union shall act only if and in so far as the objectives of the proposed action cannot be sufficiently achieved by the Member States, either at central level or *at regional and local level*' (emphasis added).

[19] See Dijkstra, L., and H. Poelman, 'A harmonized definition of cities and rural areas: the new degree of urbanization', Regional Working Paper 2014, 5, accessed 31 January 2017 at *ec.europa.eu/regional_policy/sources/docgener/work/2014_01_new_urban.pdf*. See also Dijkstra and Poelman, 'Cities in Europe: The New OECD/EC Definition', Regional Working Paper RF 01/2012, accessed 31 January 2017 at *ec.europa.eu/regional_policy/sources/docgener/focus/2012_01_city.pdf* (based on population and density threshold).

[20] Dijkstra and Poelman, 'Cities in Europe', n.19 above, 4–5.

[21] See also Panara, n.12 above, 6.

state system but the heterogeneity of sub-national structures in the Member States makes it impossible to posit this as an absolute requirement for their inclusion in this working definition. It would be similarly misleading to make any comment as to the level of autonomy, size or location of these actors as they vary widely. These arrangements will instead be the focus of the next section of this chapter and grouped in dominant models of institutional local government arrangements.

B. Models of European Local Government

The modern-day position of municipalities in the European Member States, and indirectly in the European Union, is heavily influenced by their long and colourful history. The current diversity in central-local arrangements can be traced back to the different ways, and moments, at which the Member States transformed into nation states. Rather than attempting to summarize this rich history,[22] we will focus on systematizing the diverse set of local conditions that emerged from it.

The relationship of the local government with the central government informs almost all other parameters of local government life. These relationships are multi-faceted and vary even within jurisdictions. As a starting point, we may look to the three main models of interaction developed by Clarke and Stewart: the *relative autonomy* model, the *agency* model, and the *interaction* model.[23] The key differences between these models lie in the degree of autonomy of the local government – high in the relative autonomy model, restricted to implementation in the agency model, and shared in the interaction model – and its ability to raise revenue through taxation – direct taxation only being envisaged under the relative autonomy model, while under the other models local government relies mostly on grants or indirect taxation.[24] Autonomy and

---

[22] Patrick Le Galès provides an excellent overview of the transition from medieval Europe of cities to a Europe of nation-states. See in detail Le Galès, n.13 above, 31–75.

[23] Models adapted from Clarke, M., and J. Stewart, *The Future for Local Government: Issues for Discussion* (1989) referenced by Stoker, G., 'Introduction: Trends in European Local Government' in Batley, R., and G. Stoker (eds), *Local Government in Europe: Trends and Developments* (Palgrave, Basingstoke 1991) 1 at 6.

[24] See n.23 above.

finance also feed back into the two key roles played by local governments: conduit for democracy[25] and public service provider.[26]

The legal status of local governments under these models is typically captured in national constitutions or basic laws with defined rights.[27] Legal competence, on the other hand, can be regulated either constitutionally or through statute. Most countries operate under the doctrine of general competence, giving local authorities general power of jurisdiction over issues within their geographical areas and over their inhabitants.[28] These general powers can be limited by statute and influenced by the level of discretion that local governments have over certain policy areas; under an interaction model, the legal competence to take certain action may still be subject to an obligation to confer with the central or regional government regarding what actions to take. In addition, local government actions are typically subject to judicial review by (administrative) courts or/and by regional or state authorities.[29]

Table 7.1 summarizes these features by listing the main characteristics of each model. These models are not meant to be exhaustive as significant variance continues to exist within models. In general terms, federal Member States more frequently adopt a relative autonomy model than unitary Member States. However, this also depends on the historic position of the local government in question;[30] even in a country with historically centralized government such as Britain, London – particularly the City of London – holds a special position with a relatively large measure of autonomy.[31]

---

[25] This was especially important for the Central and Eastern European countries in the period between the end of the Cold War and EU membership. See Coulson, A. (ed.), *Local Government in Eastern Europe: Establishing Democracy at the Grassroots* (Edward Elgar Publishing, Aldershot and Brookfield VT 1995).

[26] Western European countries have traditionally focused heavily on this role as compared to the democratic role, particularly the UK. See Blair, P., 'Trends in Local Autonomy and Democracy: Reflections from a European Perspective' in Batley and Stoker (eds.), n.23 above, 41.

[27] Norton, A., 'Western European Local Government in Comparative Perspective' in Batley and Stoker (eds), n.23 above, 21 at 34.

[28] See n.27 above.

[29] Mouritzen, P., and K. Nielsen, *Handbook of Comparative Fiscal Data* (DDA, Odense 1988) as cited by *Norton*, at 23.

[30] See also Seymour, M., et al., 'Fault lines: Cohesion and Division in Modern Europe' (2014) 60(3) *Australian Journal of Politics & History* 329–333.

[31] See also Travers, T., *London's Boroughs at 50* (Biteback Publishing, London 2015).

Table 7.1 Local government models

Feature *Model*	**Autonomy**	**Finance**	**Legal Competence**	**Judicial Review**
Relative Autonomy	High	Direct taxation	General competence	(Administrative) Courts and/or regional/state authorities
Agency	Limited	Grants or indirect taxation	Only those related to delegated duties	
Interaction	Shared	Grants or indirect taxation	General competence with consultation duty	

C. European Roles for Local Government: Subjects and Objects

This chapter adopts a participatory definition of 'subject' and 'object' under EU law: whether one is a subject or object of EU law depends on the formal ability to participate in the process through which rights and obligations are created.[32]

Local governments will be considered *subjects* of EU law where they are able to directly (at the EU level) or indirectly (through their Member State) influence the legal rights and obligations placed on them by EU law. As a direct subject, local governments are included, through consultation at the EU level,[33] in the legislative process. A local government is an indirect subject of EU law when it influences the Member State's position on the issue under discussion at the EU level through domestic channels. In order for a local government to be a direct subject, provisions would have to be made in EU law, while both direct and indirect participation depends (at least partially) on domestic institutional arrangements.[34]

---

[32] This definition excludes the important role of informal influence through lobbying or soft power, as this chapter focuses on *legal* relationships between the EU and local level. See e.g. Weatherill, n.4 above, 9.

[33] Consultation is the only realistic means of inclusion at this point and in line with the position of the Committee of Regions, which is advisory, see Art.13(4) TEU. See also Arts 100(2), 148(2), 149, 153(2), 164 TFEU.

[34] Cf Panara, n.12 above, 4, arguing that 'sub-national authorities [NB: regional and local actors] are an integral part of the EU atypical multilevel system and have the status of "full subjects" within that system, i.e. they enjoy "rights" and "duties" stemming from the European constitutional composite'. This statement applies primarily to regions rather than local governments and

Local governments are *objects* of EU law when they derive rights and obligations from EU law but do not partake in the creation of these rights and obligations. Objecthood can be passive or active. A local government takes on the role of *passive object* in one of two ways: first, if it is charged with implementing or enforcing rights and obligations on third parties – individuals or other private actors – under its purview. This passive objecthood may transition into indirect subjecthood when significant discretion is given to the local government in its role of implementer or enforcer. As this discretion is the consequence of national rather than EU law, a transition to direct subjecthood is not possible.

Local governments also become passive objects when their own behaviour is regulated by EU law, for example EU state aid law that it must observe when awarding works for which it is responsible under national law.[35] In this case, the local government continues to be a passive rather than active object of EU law, as EU law does not directly address the rights and obligations of local governments but rather regulates an area of law that domestically has been delegated to the local government. As a result, not all local governments may be affected by this EU provision, as some may be awarded different roles domestically. In order for a local government to be an *active object*, the EU law would need to directly address the rights and obligations of local governments. Active objecthood potentially conflicts with Article 4(2) TEU, which places the institutional arrangements concerning local governments within the 'national identity' prerogative of the Member State.[36] Provisions that do not pertain directly to the 'institutional arrangements' referenced in Article 4(2) TEU could be argued to fall outside of the national identity prerogative and may therefore pass a national identity-based review. However, it is difficult to envisage provisions without at least an indirect effect on the status of local governments within the Member State.[37]

side-steps the question whether these actors can meaningfully determine the nature and extent of these rights and duties.

[35] See also Section 2.

[36] Art.4(2) TEU.

[37] See Weatherill, n.4 above, 7 '[EU law's f]ormal lack of regard for domestic constitutional arrangements may be combined with activity that in practice severely disturbs those internal patterns.'

Table 7.2 Subject and object roles of local governments under EU law

Role	Subject		Object	
Process	Direct	Indirect	Active	Passive
Legislation	*Formal right of consultation*	*Representation through the MS*	*EU laws on LG rights and obligations*	*EU laws related to areas within powers of LG*
Implementation and/or enforcement		*Discretion in implementation/ enforcement*		*LG as implementer/ enforcer without discretion*

This participation-centric perception of subject and object differs from some of the definitions adopted in this volume.[38] Samantha Velluti adopts Kruger and Skelton's definition of subject and object which defines a 'legal subject' as an entity – either a natural or a juristic person – recognized or accepted as being capable of holding rights, duties and capacities and a "legal object" as something or someone in respect of which a legal subject may hold rights, duties and capacities.[39] Under this definition, the position of local governments would be very similar to that of individuals under EU law due to the Member States' exclusive sphere of influence over their internal institutional arrangements. Conversely, Article 5(3) TEU explicitly includes the local level into the subsidiarity principle by stating that '[t]he Union shall act only if and in so far as the objectives of the proposed action cannot be sufficiently achieved by the Member States, either at central level or *at regional and local level*'. A participatory definition better captures these complexities of the situation of local governments and provides the framework for detailed discussion of local government as subjects and objects of EU law in the next section.

---

[38] For a similar approach as the one taken in this chapter, see Korkea-aho, Chapter 11 of this volume.

[39] Kruger, H., and A. Skelton (eds), *The Law of Persons in South Africa* (Oxford University Press, Oxford 2010), 11–13, applied by Velluti, Chapter 13 of this volume. See also e.g. Fahey and Bardutzky, Chapter 1 of this volume (on the duality of the concept of the subject, consisting of the individual's 'authorship and position of responsibility within the system' and the individual as 'legal vigilante' with a central role in the enforcement of the EU's 'new legal order').

2. LOCAL GOVERNMENTS AS SUBJECTS AND OBJECTS

While analytically distinct, there are functional overlaps between the subject and object roles of local governments under EU law. This section therefore discusses the four different positions in turn to show how they combine to cover the formal (i.e., based on EU and domestic law) positions of local governments within the EU.

A. Local Subjecthood

As direct subjects of EU law, local governments would play a formal role in the EU's legislative process. At present, there are no provisions within the EU Treaties that give these actors such a role. The only direct representation of local interests is through the Committee of the Regions (CoR), whose mandate is exclusively advisory.[40] Any changes to the current position would affect, at least indirectly, the domestic position of (most) local governments, triggering Article 4(2) TEU concerns and the need for active Member State support. The sheer number of local governments in the EU would furthermore necessitate the appointment of a body that could act as a conduit for the heterogeneous interests of sub-national actors, particularly regions and local governments.[41] The CoR would be an obvious candidate for this role but is widely perceived as ineffective and is unlikely to be able to effectively address this challenge in its current form.[42]

---

[40] Art.13(4) TEU. For examples of opinions issued by the CoR, see Opinion of the Committee of the Regions, The Seventh Environment Action Program and the Sustainable City, 19 August 2014; Opinion of the Committee of the Regions, Towards an Integrated Urban Agenda for the EU, 19 August 2014; Resolution of the Committee of the Regions on the 20th Anniversary of the Committee of the Regions, 'Empowering regional and local authorities in the European Union', 19 August 2014; Opinion of the Committee of the Regions on 'Energy efficiency in cities and regions – a focus on the differences between rural districts and cities', 27 July 2012.

[41] Domestically, regions are more likely to hold legislative powers and may even act as supervisors of local governments (see Mouritzen and Nielsen, n.29 above).

[42] Many sub-national actors have created separate lobbying groups that represent their specific interests. A key example is REGLEG, which represents 72 regions with legislative powers, see n.8 above. Their success further undermines the efforts of the CoR and has created a division between sub-national

Local governments assume the role of indirect subjects when exercising formal rights of indirect representation through their national representatives in the EU's legislative process, and when exercising significant discretion in their (domestic) implementation or enforcement of EU law. The locus of indirect subjecthood can be European or national – local governments are either represented in the EU legislative process or responsible for domestic implementation/enforcement of EU law – but depend primarily on domestic institutional arrangements. The diversity in domestic arrangements makes detailed discussion of 28 Member States impossible within the scope of this chapter.[43] We will therefore refer back to our relative autonomy, agency and interaction models to provide an overview of most common interactions.

Indirect subjecthood in the legislative process can be achieved through representation in the Council. Each EU Member State is entitled to send a 'representative at ministerial level'[44] to the Council – typically a national minister. Federal Member States with a *relative autonomy* model have been seen to opt for representation by a regional minister when the matter under debate is one that belongs to the (exclusive) competence of the state government, for example in Austria, Belgium and Spain.[45] Germany's federal system, while usually in line with *a relative autonomy* model, is closer to the *interaction* model with respect to Council representation. In cases concerning exclusive *Länder* competence, a regional minister may represent Germany in the Council,[46] and can bind the federal government. Regional representation must therefore act 'with the participation of and in coordination with' the federal government, which has been construed as deferential to the position of the federal government.[47]

Portugal, conversely, allows for the participation of regional representatives in the national delegation to the Council, which are not allowed to vote on behalf of the Member State.[48] Italy adopts a similar position as to participation. However, the indivisibility of the Italian

---

actors with and without legislative powers. See also Scott, D., 'Constitutional Regions and the European Union', referenced in Loughlin, n.4 above, at n.23.

43 For a detailed discussion of some of these topics, see the work of Panara, n.12 above.

44 Art.16(2) TEU.

45 See in detail Panara, n.12 above, 20–1.

46 Art.23(6) German Basic Law.

47 Panara, n.12 above, 18.

48 Panara, n.12 above, 18–19.

Republic ('the Republic is one and indivisible')[49] limits the de facto role of the regions, which do have legal right of direct participation in decision-making under the Italian Constitution in line with the *agency* model.[50] Similarly, the UK's devolved governments are involved in UK representation but must ensure a common position towards the EU.[51] France is an extreme example of the agency model as its regions are excluded from representation, both as the ministerial representative and as being part of the delegation.[52] Representation thus depends on internal division of competence regarding specific policy areas in combination with division of competence regarding external affairs. As a result, internal competence does not necessarily lead to the competence to represent these interests at the EU level.[53] Since local governments seldom hold (exclusive) legislative competence, they rely heavily on regions to represent their interest, which themselves may be thwarted by the aforementioned process.[54]

Differences in representation are mirrored by differences in responsibility for the implementation and enforcement of EU law. From the EU's perspective, the Member State is exclusively liable for any non-compliance with EU law.[55] However, domestically, this responsibility can be sub-divided between the central and regional government. In Austria,

---

49 Art.5 Italian Constitution.

50 Art.117(5) Italian Constitution.

51 The Brexit referendum has laid bare a stark divide between Northern Ireland and Scotland, and England and Wales, with the former two nations voting 'Remain' and the latter voting 'Leave'. In January 2017, the Supreme Court clarified the legal position of the devolved nations in Brexit, underlining that the Article 50 notification procedure lies within the exclusive competence of Westminster Parliament and that the devolution agreements have not altered its sovereignty in this matter. See *R (on the application of Miller and another) (Respondents) v Secretary of State for Exiting the European Union (Appellant)*, [2017] UKSC 5, specifically paras. 136-151.

52 Panara, n.12 above, 21.

53 See Weatherill, n.4 above, 12.

54 In some Member States, however, they may rely directly on the national government to represent their interest (it is the case of e.g. Italy with the *Conferenza Stato-Città*, in which a European Session takes place at least twice a year. See Art.23 of law no. 234/2012: accessed 31 January at *www.conferenzastatocitta.it/sessioneComunitaria.asp?CONF=CSC*) (I am grateful to an anonymous referee for this suggestion).

55 *Commission v Belgium* Case 72/81 [1982] ECR 183; *Commission v Belgium* (Joined Cases 227–230/85) [1988] ECR 1. See also Weatherill, n.4 above, 5–6 ('[T]he internal reality of local responsibility is simply not recognized at EC level which deals only in State responsibility.')

the federal government has to respect EU obligations *and* domestic divisions of power, which means that the *Länder* have a right, and duty, to implement EU measures that affect their competences.[56] This principle can also be found in the constitutions of the UK, Italy, Germany, Belgium and Spain.[57] When this responsibility is paired with significant discretion in how to implement and enforce, the relevant sub-national actors are indirect subjects of EU law: their participation depends on their domestic positions.

B. Local Objecthood

Local governments can be participatory objects of EU law in two ways: actively, when the EU passes laws that are aimed at affecting the rights and obligations of local governments; and passively, due to EU laws that affect local government action in policy areas under their control, or when they are tasked with the implementation or enforcement of EU laws without discretion.

At first glance, the Member States' exclusive sphere of competence regarding their internal structures appears to foreclose the active objecthood of local governments; the EU is not to adopt laws that affect the relationship between national governments and their subsidiaries. The indirect subjecthood and passive objecthood of local governments shows that rules which are not directly aimed at influencing this relationship may nevertheless be seen to do so by influencing the relative control of these actors over certain policy areas. The European Regional Development Fund is a key example of a policy that, while not aimed at changing the internal division of powers within the Member State, undoubtedly affects it.[58] The European Economic and Social Committee has also issued numerous opinions on the position of cities as drivers for innovation,[59] and the position of metropolitan areas within regional

---

[56] Panara, n.12 above, 24.

[57] Panara, n.12 above, 25.

[58] See Bache, I., and R. Jones, 'Has EU regional policy empowered the regions? A study of Spain and the United Kingdom' (2007) 10(3) *Regional and Federal Studies* 1.

[59] See e.g. Opinion of the European Economic and Social Committee on 'Smart cities as drivers for development of a new European industrial policy' (own-initiative opinion) 17 November 2015.

development more broadly.[60] While theoretically distinct, the dividing line between active and passive objecthood – i.e. rules that affect local governments and rules that affect their relationship with the central government – is often hard to draw in practice. A notable example can be found in Regulation 1302/2013 on European grouping of territorial co-operation (EGTC).[61] The preamble of the Regulation acknowledges the differing status of local and regional actors across the Member States,[62] and urges Member States to allow for the participation of local and regional actors to facilitate specific cross boundary co-operation.[63] Once local actors are part of an EGTC, they will be considered empowered to deliver specific joint services without need for further authorization by national parliament.[64]

As passive objects, local governments are affected by EU laws that relate to areas under their purview. This position can be distinguished from indirect subjecthood based on discretion in implementation and enforcement; as passive objects, local governments do not have meaningful discretion in the application of EU law. The passive objecthood of local governments can be distinguished from the position of individuals under EU law insofar as local governments are subject to certain EU provisions as emanations of the state. An important example of this is public procurement, where EU state aid rules influence local government action.[65] In terms of policy, the 2016 Dutch Council Presidency has made renewed efforts to foster an EU Urban Agenda. While recognizing that 'the EU has no formal authority over urban policy', there are three ways in which the Agenda looks to foster the development of European cities: improved regulation, improved access and workability of the financial

---

[60] Opinion of the European Economic and Social Committee on 'Metropolitan Areas and City Regions in Europe 2020' (own-initiative opinion) 22 December 2011.

[61] EU Regulation 1302/2013, OJ 2013 L 347/303.

[62] N. 61, preamble 7.

[63] N. 61, preamble 11.

[64] For examples, see *ec.europa.eu/regional_policy/en/policy/cooperation/european-territorial/egtc/* (accessed 31 January 2017).

[65] See Caka, F., 'State Aid Given by Local Government Which Distorts Competition' (2012) 14 *European Journal Law Reform* 113. See also *Unión General de Trabajadores de La Rioja (UGT-Rioja)* (Case C-428/06 to C-434/06) [2008] I-06747; *Portuguese Republic v Commission of the European Communities* (Case C-88/03) [2006] ECR I-07115; *Diputacion Foral De Álava v Commission* (Case T-127, 129, 148/99) [2002] ECR II1275; and *Territorio Historico de Álava-Diputacion Foral De Álava v Commission* (Case T-92 and 103/00) [2002] ECR II-1390.

plans supporting EU cities, and the creation of a European platform for urban knowledge.[66] Pilot partnerships under this agenda include projects regarding air quality,[67] housing,[68] inclusion of migrants,[69] and urban poverty.[70] Alongside this agenda, the EU has been involved with urban mobility for some time.[71]

In sum, we find virtually no possibilities for local governments to be included as direct subjects or active objects, and limited formal opportunities for them to act as indirect subjects. As a result, local governments typically find themselves in the position of passive object. Under EU law, local governments thus bear duties, many of which are specific to their state-based roles, without corresponding rights of representation. The most effective methods for influencing EU decision-making tend to depend on informal tools such as lobbying and organizational membership, which is not a route that is equally accessible for all local governments. The status quo thereby emphasizes the role of local governments as service providers over their democratic role.

3. IMPLICATIONS

The picture of local government in the EU is one where local governments' legal positions are firmly based on Member States' constitutional arrangements. This is unlikely to change in the foreseeable future. The 1990s saw the high water mark of EU regionalism with the 'Europe of

---

[66] See *urbanagendaforthe.eu/urban-agenda/* (accessed 31 January 2017). See also Commission Communication, 'The urban dimension of EU policies – Key features of an EU urban agenda', 18 July 2014.

[67] *urbanagendaforthe.eu/partnerships/air-quality/* (accessed 31 January 2017). See relatedly, Declaration of the European Parliament on establishing a green hydrogen economy and a third industrial revolution in Europe through a partnership with committed regions and cities, SMEs and civil society organisations, 22 May 2007.

[68] *urbanagendaforthe.eu/partnerships/housing/* (accessed 31 January 2017).

[69] *urbanagendaforthe.eu/partnerships/inclusion-of-migrants-and-refugees/* (accessed 31 January 2017).

[70] *urbanagendaforthe.eu/partnerships/urban-poverty/* (accessed 31 January 2017).

[71] See e.g. Commission Staff Working Document accompanying Commission Communication – Together towards competitive and resource-efficient urban mobility (17 December 2013) and Opinion of the European Economic and Social Committee on 'Integrating transport and land-use policies for more sustainable city transport' (23 December 2009).

the Regions' movement,[72] which envisaged a federal Europe with regions as the constituent parts, rather than nation states.[73] Strengthened by the Commission's White Paper on Governance, calling for 'stronger interaction with regional and local governments and civil society',[74] the regionalism movement created a window for meaningful formal sub-national inclusion in the EU's multi-level governance system leading up to the Convention on the Future of Europe. This promise has been partially fulfilled: since the Lisbon Treaty reforms the subsidiarity principle includes explicit reference to regional and local government in the subsidiarity principle,[75] and the Committee of the Regions can now question the application of the subsidiarity principle before the Court of Justice (CJEU).[76] However, the most significant change has been the inclusion of national parliaments in the subsidiarity process, rather than regional or local actors – although these may be included in such domestic bodies in some Member States.[77] This change signalled a more general shift in focus towards the balancing of Member State and EU competences,[78] rather than the inclusion of sub-national actors.[79] With

---

[72] Loughlin, n.4 above, 162.

[73] Loughlin (ed.), n.7 above. During this time, there were also a few region-sceptic voices that worried about EU intervention in domestic territorial arrangements of the individual states, even as the regional lobby insisted that it was a sacrosanct constitutional principle: see Loughlin, n.4 above, 165.

[74] COM (2001) 428 final.

[75] This marks a change from the previous iterations of the subsidiarity principle, which did not explicitly reference the regional or local dimension of the Member States. See Art.5 TEC ('In areas which do not fall within its exclusive competence, the Community shall take action, in accordance with the principle of subsidiarity, only if and insofar as the objectives of the proposed action cannot be sufficiently achieved by *the Member States* and can therefore, by reason of the scale or effects of the proposed action, be better achieved by the Community.')

[76] Art.8 of Protocol No 2 on the application of the principles of subsidiarity and proportionality. See e.g. Hönnige, C., and D. Panke, 'The Committee of the Regions and the European Economic and Social Committee: How Influential are Consultative Committees in the European Union?' (2013) 51(3) *Journal of Common Market Studies* 452–471.

[77] For an in-depth discussion of this process and the outcome, see Loughlin, n.4 above.

[78] Loughlin, n.4 above, 157. Academic research into this question continues, see e.g. Panara, n.12 above. For non-legal scholarship see e.g Ballas, D., D. Dorling, and B. Hennig, *The Social Atlas of Europe* (Policy Press, Bristol 2014).

[79] See also Cygan, A., 'Regional Governance, subsidiarity and accountability with the EU's multi-level policy' (2013) 19(1) *European Public Law* 161 at

this in mind, this Section addresses the remaining question as to whether the status quo is problematic, especially with respect to subsidiarity and (representative) democracy.

A. Concerns

The two principal roles of local government are the provision of a forum for political participation and the efficient provision of public services. Measures taken by the EU can affect these roles both positively and negatively. At present, most effects are incidental insofar as the fiction of distinct spheres of influence means that impact assessments of EU legislation do not (adequately) consider local impacts – this is left to the Member States. The empirical question as to the effect of local service provision, for example through the allocation of Regional Development Funds, falls outside the scope of this chapter.[80] It may be noted, however, that while the European position of local governments has stayed relatively stable (and thereby limited) over the past decades, many Member States have been expanding the domestic mandates of local governments through increased decentralization of public service provision.[81] The obligation to assume additional responsibilities is typically not accompanied by corresponding increases in budgetary or legislative powers.[82]

Viewing the EU from the perspective of local government exposes three key democratic concerns. First, it highlights that the current application of the subsidiarity principle – despite the wording of Article 5(3) TEU – is one that excludes sub-national actors to the advantage of national actors. In turn, this can put pressure on hard-won compromises

---

188 ('[T]he [Lisbon] Treaty has failed to sufficiently recognize the political and legislative autonomy of regions').

[80] See e.g. Bache and Jones, n.58 above.

[81] E.g. the delegation of the National Health Service to Manchester in 2014. This example is particularly striking due to the centralized nature of English government. See Memorandum of Understanding on Greater Manchester Health and Social Care Devolution, accessed 1 February at *www.greatermanchester-ca.gov.uk/downloads/file/135/greater_manchester_health_and_social_care_devolution_memorandum_of_understanding*.

[82] See n.81, endnote x ('Where national policies apply, decisions about the implementation of those policies that are made about Greater Manchester will be made with Greater Manchester. As set out in the MoU national government will continue to set overall policy for health services, including setting the Mandate for NHS England.').

between different ethnic, cultural or political constituencies within Member States by skewing the power balance towards the central government.[83] Any grievance that this causes can only be brought before the European Courts if the local government in question shows individual and direct concern, as they do not have privileged access to the Courts.[84]

The second related concern speaks to the democratic pedigree of the EU. The EU's interpretation of the subsidiarity principle can be properly understood only in reference to the principle of conferral and the principle's role in regulating the exercise of the EU's shared competences.[85] Although the subsidiarity principle has always spoken to power-sharing, the underlying presumption in favour of decentralization – founded on a preference for decision-making close to the people – is at least equally important. However, the status quo moves the EU further away from a reality with meaningful links between the Union and its people,[86] despite the fact that the EU espouses the principle of representative democracy and strives for transparent decision-making 'as close as possible to the citizen'.[87] Much has been written about the EU's democratic deficit and the question whether EU decision-making by the Council, Commission and Parliament is sufficiently democratic.[88] In the author's view the exclusion of local governments as democratic actors in the European process shows that in debates on the EU's democratic deficit, the legitimacy of Member States as representatives goes unquestioned. The divergent positions of sub-national actors and the ability of Member States to bypass internal divisions of competence due to their

---

83 Weatherill, n.4 above, 9–10. As also demonstrated by the indirect subjecthood and active objecthood of local governments. As phrased by Weatherill, 'Finding a role for the Regions in checking the EU's competence', in Weatherill and Bernitz (eds), n.4 above, p. 131, '[T]he EU has institutionalized an arena within which national political elites [...] have an opportunity to advance policies that might have been unfeasible had they been pursued solely within a domestic context.'

84 Weatherill, n.4 above, 5–6.

85 Art.5(1) TEU.

86 S. Weatherill, 'Finding a role for the Regions in checking the EU's competence', in Weatherill and Bernitz (eds), n.4 above, at 132 (on the Convention of the Future of Europe's failure to bring the EU closer to the people).

87 Art.10 TEU.

88 For an overview of the rich literature on this topic, see Moravczik, A., 'In Defense of the Democratic Deficit: Reassessing Legitimacy in the European Union' (2002) 40(4) *Journal of Common Market Studies* 603.

exclusive sphere of influence gives reason for pause.[89] The existing presumption of democratic legitimacy of the national government should not go unchallenged. Local governments' long history as centres for democracy,[90] and the relative strength of local affiliations,[91] indicate that sub-national democracy may provide an alternative, or at least a complement, to the national process.

Thirdly, the landscape provided in this chapter shows the formal roles of local government in the EU. It is therefore inevitably incomplete, as it does not include the informal ways in which these actors participate in European governance. The role of interest groups such as REGLEG were mentioned several times but their informal influence deserves more attention than may be provided within the scope of this chapter. The absence of meaningful formal paths of representation enables powerful sub-national actors to influence European law and policy-making without institutional checks on how their interests may relate to those of other sub-national actors.[92] The full range of implications for EU democracy is obscured by the lack of information about these informal processes and the lack of information on individual Member State practices.

B. Solutions

At present, attempts to augment the formal role of sub-national actors – local governments but also regions – in the EU would likely be perceived as infringements into the exclusive competence of the Member States over their institutional arrangements. An increasing number of Member States are uncomfortable by the challenges that the EU poses to the

[89] See importantly Müller, JW, 'Should the EU Protect Democracy and the Rule of Law inside Member States?' (2015) 21(2) *European Law Journal* 141–160.

[90] Frug, n.12 above, at 559.

[91] Su, R., 'Intrastate Federalism' (2016) *University of Pennsylvania Journal of Constitutional Law* (forthcoming, on file with author), at 52. *See generally* Hummon, D.M., 'City mouse, country mouse: The persistence of community identity' (1986) 9 Qual. Sociol. 3.

[92] Weatherill argues that allowing such parties a formal say at EU level would bring differentiated treatment at the national level to the EU level (Weatherill, 'Finding a role for the Regions in checking the EU's competence', n.4 above, at 155). The author submits that this unequal representation is already a reality and that by allowing for it to take place through informal channels, even the most basic procedural checks cannot be applied.

centrality of the nation state,[93] and any changes perceived to move the EU closer to a federalist system. As evidenced by the Brexit referendum, the embattled state of the EU has also led some of its citizens to express a desire to return to state-based sovereignty.[94] Whether or not the popular perception of the locus of democratic governance accurately reflects the geography of power is in many ways irrelevant.[95] In times of crisis, the nation-state is widely perceived to be the 'right' institution to represent national interests. That the 'national' interests may not sufficiently respect the position of minorities – in case of Brexit, this minority constitutes 48 per cent of the British voters – is a compromise inherent to (representative) democracy.[96]

While any changes to the EU that may be seen to infringe on Member State competence are politically improbable, more direct ties between the people and the EU would offer a potentially constructive avenue towards greater EU legitimacy, and longevity. Implicit in this argument is the assumption that local preferences are inadequately captured at the national level, making local governments natural allies of the EU against their Member States.[97] There is no empirical evidence to support this view.[98] Direct participation by local governments could, however, give a better overview of the challenges of implementation and enforcement at the legislative stage.[99] This, in turn, could lead to better regulation, a more complete application of the subsidiarity principle and increased

---

[93] This development relates to the broader globalization movement that has affected the role of nation state over the past decades. See e.g. Stahl, K., 'Local Home Rule in the Time of Globalization' (forthcoming) *BYU Law Review* (on file with author). See also Blank, Y., 'Localism in the New Global Legal Order' (2006) 47(1) *Harvard International Law Journal* 263.

[94] See Swank, D., H.-G. Betz, 'Globalization, the welfare state and right-wing populism in Western Europe' (2003) 1(2) *Socioeconomic Review* 215–245.

[95] See Closa, C. and D. Kochenov (eds), *Reinforcing Rule of Law Oversight in the European Union* (Cambridge University Press, Cambridge 2016).

[96] See e.g. Follesdal, A., 'Democracy, Legitimacy and Majority Rule in the EU' in Nentwich, M., and A. Weale (eds), *Political Theory and the European Union: Legitimacy, Constitutional Choice and Citizenship* (Routledge, London and New York 1998) 34–48.

[97] For a similar observation regarding the United States, see Barron, D., 'A Localist Critique of the New Federalism' (2001) 51 *Duke Law Journal* 377 at 379–80.

[98] For an anecdotal example of EU/local government antagonism, see *www.euractiv.com/section/transport/news/20-cities-challenge-relaxation-of-emissions-standards/* (accessed 1 February 2017).

[99] See e.g. *www.nu.nl/politiek/4248493/grote-steden-willen-honderden-miljoenen-extra-opvang-asielzoekers.html* (accessed 1 February 2017).

input legitimacy for EU governance.[100] Apart from allowing for direct participation, expanding the standing rights of local governments before the European Courts would provide these actors with ways to challenge infringements of their domestic competences due to EU law.[101] Alternatively, the mobilization of local governments in this process could continue through informal means, with the risk of continued and growing inequity in representation.[102] This runs contrary to the normative tenets behind European multi-level governance: the inclusion of non-state actors and support of the peripheries in order to create a higher shared level of social welfare.[103]

In all, in a Union founded on representative democracy ideals, the current exclusion of local governments as participatory subjects and objects requires legitimation beyond the legal fiction of exclusive spheres of EU and Member State competence.

---

[100] See Weiler, J., 'In the Face of Crisis: Input Legitimacy, Output Legitimacy and the Political Messianism of European Integration' (2012) 34(7) *Journal of European Integration* 825 (on the EU's reliance on output legitimacy).

[101] See also Lenaerts, K., 'Federalism and the Rule of Law: Perspectives from the European Court of Justice' 33(5) *Fordham International Law Journal* (2011) 1338 at 1388 ('There are no enclaves of national sovereignty precluding EU law from displaying its pervasive effects. Instead, provided that there is a link with the substantive law of the Union, there is an EU framework that percolates through all areas of national law') and Lenaerts, K. and N. Cambien, 'Regions and the European Court: Giving Shape to the Regional Dimension of the Member States' (2010) 35 *European Law Review* 609 (arguing that the EU treaties recognize the regional dimension of subnational entities).

[102] See Leorke, D., 'Power, mobility, and diaspora in the global city: an interview with Saskia Sassen', accessed 1 February 2017 at *www.saskiasassen.com/PDFs/interviews/Power-Mobility-and-Diaspora-in-the-Global-City.pdf* (arguing that informality is a tool for the powerful as well as the powerless).

[103] See Kukovec, D., 'Law and the Periphery' (2015) 21(3) *European Law Journal* 406–28.

8. Citizenship-for-sale schemes and EU law: can third-country nationals buy their way into becoming subjects of EU law?

Alina Tryfonidou*

1. INTRODUCTION

In 1955, in the famous *Nottebohm* decision, the International Court of Justice pointed out that nationality must reflect a 'genuine connection' between an individual and the State the nationality of which (s)he possesses.[1]

It seems, nonetheless, that nationality in the above sense is a far cry from the status that some EU Member States bestow in recent years, whereby, desiring to enlarge their coffers, they offer, in exchange for large sums of money, their citizenship to rich foreigners who have no – and do not intent to establish any – links with their territory.

The issue came to the forefront in the end of 2013, when the Maltese Government announced a proposed amendment to the Maltese Citizenship Act, which would introduce a scheme that would allow the grant of Maltese citizenship to persons paying a certain sum of money, without any residence (or other integration) requirements having to be satisfied.[2]

* I would like to thank the editors of this book as well as the anonymous reviewers for valuable comments on previous versions of this essay. Needless to say, all errors remain mine.

[1] *Liechtenstein v Guatemala (Nottebohm case) (second phase)*, Judgment of 6 April 1955, [1995] International Court of Justice Reports at 4, 23.

[2] See Carrera, S., 'How much does EU citizenship cost? The Maltese citizenship-for-sale affair: A breakthrough for sincere cooperation in citizenship of the union?' CEPS Paper in Liberty and Security in Europe No. 64/April 2014, accessed 2 February 2017 at *www.ceps.eu/system/files/LSE%20No%2064%20Price%20of%20EU%20Citizenship%20final2.pdf*, pp. 3–6.

One of the questions that emerged was whether such citizenship-for-sale schemes breach EU law. The Maltese issue was resolved at political level, between the Maltese Government and the European Commission, with a compromise which involved an amendment of the proposed scheme by adding a one-year effective residence requirement.[3]

One might ask, however, why is the EU involved in this matter? Is not the bestowal of nationality a matter that falls exclusively within Member State competence? Although this is, indeed, the case, the bestowal of Member State nationality has broader implications for the EU. This is because, when a person acquires the citizenship of a Member State, (s)he automatically also acquires EU citizenship,[4] and thus, by 'selling' their own nationality, Member States effectively also 'sell' EU citizenship. The latter, in fact, remains a completely derivative status, since its gatekeepers continue to be solely the Member States and there is no way for an individual to acquire Union citizenship without first acquiring the nationality of one of the Member States.[5] Accordingly, it is the Member States that define which individuals can be 'subjects' of EU law (through the acquisition of EU citizenship) and thus the question that has emerged – and which this essay aims to consider – is whether it is permissible under EU law for a Member State to offer this possibility (of becoming a subject of EU law) *simply* in exchange for money, without requiring any effective links between the individual and a Member State and/or the EU. In other words, are 'golden passport' programmes (i.e. programmes which provide for the exchange of citizenship for a (high) sum of money) which transform Member State (and EU) citizenship into a tradable commodity, compatible with EU law?

2. SUBJECTS AND OBJECTS OF EU LAW

This collection of essays uses the notions of 'subjects' and 'objects' of law as the research platform for assessing the development and formulation of EU law. The case study presented in this chapter focuses on the question of who can qualify as a 'subject' of EU law and, in particular,

---

[3] See the Joint Press Statement by the European Commission and the Maltese Authorities on Malta's Individual Investor Programme (IIP), accessed 2 February 2017 at *europa.eu/rapid/press-release_MEMO-14-70_en.htm.*

[4] This is clear from the text of Art.20 TFEU.

[5] For a critical account of this see Kochenov, D., '*Ius Tractum* of Many Faces: European Citizenship and the Difficult Relationship between Status and Rights' (2009) 15(2) CJEL 169.

on whether third-country nationals can buy their way into becoming subjects of EU law.

Bederman has noted that a 'subject of international law' is 'an entity that bears international legal rights or duties';[6] accordingly, and transplanting this into the EU context, a subject of EU law is an entity that bears legal rights deriving from EU law and/or is subject to duties imposed by EU law. According to the same author, 'the *objects* of international law are the who, what, and where that are being acted on. The objects of international law are the legitimate topics of international legal regulation'.[7]

When persons were not (yet) recognised as deriving rights directly from EU law but were – merely – affected by EU regulation, they could merely be considered 'objects' of EU law. However, since the 1960s and the Court's judgment in the landmark *Van Gend en Loos* case,[8] it has been made clear that persons who fall within the personal scope of the market freedoms – and, in addition, since 1993, *all* persons who are Union citizens – have been transformed from objects of EU law to subjects of EU law. Conversely, persons who are not Member State nationals (and are thus not EU citizens) and who are not deriving any rights from EU law in some other way, continue to be merely objects of EU law as they may only be 'legitimate topics of [EU] legal regulation'.

Therefore, since all persons who acquire Union citizenship are now considered to be 'subjects' of EU law, the question that this chapter aims to examine is whether the EU can, in certain circumstances (namely, when Member State nationality is 'sold' via golden passport programmes), place some limits on who can be transformed from a mere object of EU law to a subject of EU law by becoming an EU citizen.

3. ORDINARY NATURALISATION PROCEDURES, GOLDEN RESIDENCE PROGRAMMES, GOLDEN VISA PROGRAMMES AND GOLDEN PASSPORT PROGRAMMES

The bestowal of nationality (and, by extension, of Union citizenship) is an area that falls exclusively within Member State competence.

---

[6] Bederman, D.J., *The Spirit of International Law* (University of Georgia Press, Athens GA 2002) 79.

[7] Bederman (2002) n.6 above, 80.

[8] *Van Gend en Loos* (Case 26/62) [1963] ECR 1.

Accordingly, Member States are free to lay down the conditions which must be satisfied in order for a person to acquire their nationality, provided that, when they do so, they comply with EU law.[9] Nationality – in general, not just in the EU context – can be bestowed either by birth or through naturalisation.

As regards the *acquisition of nationality by birth*, two criteria are prevalent around the world, including among the EU Member States: *jus soli* (citizenship by birth) and *jus sanguinis* (citizenship by parentage). Some EU Member States use only the latter as the condition that must be satisfied for acquisition of their nationality, some Member States have adopted a (diluted) form of the *jus soli* criterion, whilst some have employed a combination of the two.

Similarly, when it comes to the acquisition of nationality through naturalisation, each Member State has its own rules regarding the exact criteria that must be satisfied, these (usually) consisting of a requirement of lawful effective residence in its territory for a certain period of time coupled with the successful completion of language and integration tests. The aim of these criteria is to ensure that only persons who have established strong links with the society of a state can acquire its nationality. These criteria are used as part of – what I shall hereinafter call – the ordinary naturalisation procedure.

Virtually all Member States, however, also make provision for acquisition of their nationality through naturalisation, by persons who do not satisfy the above criteria[10] but who have made – or can make – an exceptional contribution to their society as a result of their special achievements. The contribution can be in the fields of research and technology, culture, sports, or the economy.

As regards the latter (i.e. contribution to the economy) two situations must be distinguished.

On the one hand, some Member States have created naturalisation schemes which confer the right to *reside* to persons who make a significant monetary investment in their territory (golden residence programmes) or schemes which provide the right to reside in their territory *together* with the grant of a visa to travel in the Schengen area in exchange for a significant monetary investment (golden visa programmes). It should be highlighted that, in most cases, such schemes do not involve an outright exchange of nationality for an investment but,

---

[9] *Micheletti* (Case C-369/90) [1992] ECR I-4239.

[10] Though, some schemes may require that such persons should build such links following acquisition of their nationality.

rather, the investment merely gives rise to lawful residence for a certain period of time, or lawful residence together with access to the whole Schengen area, which may lead to naturalisation in the future, acquired through the ordinary naturalisation procedure.

On the other hand, in recent years, some Member States have made provision in their laws for procedures that grant their *nationality* to persons who are willing to make a payment of a certain (large) amount of money and/or a significant investment in their territory without requiring that these persons also satisfy any of the criteria imposed under the ordinary naturalisation procedure and, thus, without requiring that such persons have – or work towards building – a link with the society of their new state of nationality. The main example of this in the EU context is Cyprus. Three other Member States (Malta, Bulgaria and Romania), have in recent years introduced what Džankić has characterised as 'hybrid' investment citizenship programmes, because, unlike the programme introduced by Cyprus which does not have *any* effective residence requirement, in order for an investor to acquire citizenship, (s)he does need to satisfy a residence requirement, albeit a short one (one year in Malta and Bulgaria, and four years in Romania).[11]

Realistically speaking, multimillionaires taking advantage of such programmes are not specifically interested in acquiring the citizenship of the particular Member State to which they are applying, but are, rather, after EU citizenship which – as explained earlier – is automatically granted as a result of the bestowal of the citizenship of a Member State. Union citizenship is a particularly attractive 'asset', given that it grants free, unrestricted, access to the whole of the EU, both for economic and non-economic purposes. This is, in fact, the reason why a number of commentators, EU institutions and politicians[12] have questioned the legality of such practices and their compatibility with EU law. Since – the argument goes – Member States are part of the EU and the bestowal of their nationality leads, at the same time, to the grant of Union

---

[11] Džankić, J., 'Investment-based citizenship and residence programmes in the EU', EUI Working Paper RSCAS 2015/08, p. 5, accessed 2 February 2017 at *cadmus.eui.eu/bitstream/handle/1814/34484/RSCAS_2015_08.pdf?sequence=1).*

[12] See, for instance, Carrera, S. (n. 2); V. Reding, 'Citizenship must not be up for sale', Plenary Session debate of the European Parliament on 'EU Citizenship for sale', Strasbourg, 15 January 2014 (full speech available at *europa.eu/rapid/press-release_SPEECH-14-18_en.htm* (accessed 2 February 2017)); European Parliament Resolution of 16 January 2014 on EU Citizenship for sale (2013/2995 [RSP]).

citizenship, their nationality laws should not be entirely free from EU scrutiny but they should, rather, be examined for their compatibility with EU law.

4. OBJECTIONS TO CITIZENSHIP-FOR-SALE PROGRAMMES

There are a number of arguments against the permissibility of citizenship-for-sale-programmes, which provide for the grant of Member State nationality in situations where there are no effective ties between the individual and the society of the state whose nationality (s)he acquires.

The first – which is a general argument, not specific to the EU context – is that it is objectionable to degrade the value of citizenship to a tradable commodity.[13] As Michael Sandel has argued, there are certain things that should in no circumstances be put up for sale because of their inherently 'superior' nature.[14] Citizenship-by-investment schemes are, therefore, 'institutionally corrupt' because '[t]he act of exchanging a higher-value good (citizenship) for a lower value good (money) destroys the value of citizenship and corrodes public trust in that institution in a way that naturalisation on other bases does not'.[15] The EU institutions appear to share this view. In particular, the European Parliament has pointed out that, since 'the rights conferred by EU citizenship are based on human dignity'[16] they should not be 'downgraded' to a tradable commodity.[17]

The second argument relates to the value of the status of EU citizenship and to what it represents. As the European Parliament has noted, 'EU citizenship implies the holding of a stake in the Union and depends on a person's ties with Europe and the Member States or on

[13] Shachar, A., and R. Hirschl, 'On Citizenship, States, and Markets' (2014) 22 *The Journal of Political Philosophy* 231, 250.

[14] Sandel, M., *What Money Can't Buy: The Moral Limits of Markets* (Penguin, London 2013).

[15] Johnston, L.M., 'A Passport at Any Price? Citizenship by Investment through the Prism of Institutional Corruption', Edmond J. Safra Working Papers, No.22, 12 September 2013, accessed 2 February 2017 at *papers.ssrn.com/sol3/papers.cfm?abstract_id=2324101*, pp. 4–5.

[16] European Parliament Resolution (n.12), para.8.

[17] European Parliament Resolution (n.12), especially paras 7 and 8.

personal ties with EU citizens'.[18] However, such links cannot be formed only through the payment of a hefty amount of money, in the absence of other link-building activities. As Ochoa has rightly argued, physical presence in a state is required in order to enable the creation of ties with it.[19]

Thirdly, Member State programmes for the outright sale of citizenship may lead to a regulatory race to the bottom as regards access to EU citizenship.[20] This argument highlights the problems that emerge as a result of the fact that Union citizenship is a purely derivative status: although it is a supranational status imposed 'from above', access to it is determined by the various Member States, which lay down different conditions and is, thus, granted 'from below'. The problems caused in this context are similar to those that emerge in a free trade area with regard to the payment of customs duties: since in a free trade area there is no common external tariff and each Member State can impose different amounts of customs duties on goods coming from outside the area, traders will choose the state with the lowest duties as the state through which to access the area, having in mind that once they enter one of the participating states, they will enjoy free circulation in the whole area. The same is the case with Union citizenship: it does not matter from which Member State a third-country national 'enters' the status of EU citizenship; from the moment that (s)he is a Union citizen, (s)he can move, reside and/or pursue an economic activity in any Member State. Accordingly, Member States that wish to take advantage of this situation and sell their nationality (and by extension, Union citizenship and, through it, access to the whole EU) in order to enhance their coffers, will engage into a competitive game of offering the most attractive package for wealthy third-country nationals that wish to become Union citizens, which is likely to lead to the lowering of the requirements for acquisition of nationality through such programmes.

---

[18] European Parliament Resolution (n.12), para.7.

[19] Ochoa, P., 'What Money Can't Buy: Face-to-Face Cooperation and Local Democratic Life' in Shachar, A., and R. Bauböck (eds), *Should Citizenship be for Sale?*, EUI Working Papers, RSCAS 2014/01, Robert Schuman Centre for Advanced Studies, EUDO Citizenship Observatory, accessed 2 February 2017 at *cadmus.eui.eu/bitstream/handle/1814/29318/RSCAS_2014_01.pdf?sequence=1)*, p. 24.

[20] This concern has been identified by, inter alia, the European Parliament – see European Parliament Resolution (n.12), para.10.

The final – and, for practical purposes, most significant – objection to such programmes is that they lead to discrimination.[21] In particular, they create an unjustifiable distinction between persons who wish to acquire the nationality of a Member State (and through it Union citizenship) who have to satisfy the strict requirements of ordinary naturalisation procedures because they cannot afford to 'buy' citizenship offered for sale in exchange of exorbitant sums of money, and (the slim minority of) persons who can satisfy the requirements of citizenship by investment programmes. As Shachar has noted, '[i]f civic integration is a required precondition to the bestowment of full membership by the state (as restrictive citizenship tests increasingly indicate), how can this demand only apply to some and not to others?'[22]

5. CITIZENSHIP-FOR-SALE PROGRAMMES: ARE THEY IN BREACH OF EU LAW?

The important question for the purposes of this chapter is whether citizenship-for-sale programmes are in breach of EU law and, if yes, whether the EU can stop Member States bestowing their nationality through such programmes. When considering this question, it should be borne in mind that the mere grant of Member State nationality through golden passport programmes is not problematic from the point of view of EU law; this is problematic only because the grant of Member State nationality leads – by extension – to the grant of Union citizenship. Accordingly, the important question is whether the grant of *EU citizenship* through citizenship-for-sale programmes is in breach of EU law.

There are two ways in which the EU can tackle such programmes. Firstly, an Article 258 Treaty on the Functioning of the European Union (TFEU) action can be brought by the Commission against the Member States that have (already) introduced such programmes, on the basis that

[21] For instance, the European Parliament in its Resolution on the matter noted that 'concerns exist as regards possible discrimination because these practices by Member States only allow the richest third-country nationals to obtain EU citizenship, without any other criteria being considered' – European Parliament Resolution (n.12), para.K.

[22] Shachar, A., 'Dangerous Liaisons: Money and Citizenship' in Shachar, A., and R. Bauböck (eds), *Should Citizenship be for Sale?*, EUI Working Papers, RSCAS 2014/01, Robert Schuman Centre for Advanced Studies, EUDO Citizenship Observatory, accessed 2 February 2017 at *cadmus.eui.eu/bitstream/handle/1814/29318/RSCAS_2014_01.pdf?sequence=1),* p. 6.

they are in breach of the principle of sincere co-operation laid down in Article 4(3) Treaty on the European Union (TEU) read in conjunction with a number of Treaty provisions. Secondly, the EU may use the same mode of reasoning as that used by the Court in its judgment in *Airola* (see below), and declare that persons who acquire their Member State nationality through such programmes, will not be recognised as Member State nationals *for the purposes of EU law* and, thus, will not acquire Union citizenship, as otherwise the EU (by bestowing its citizenship in this manner) will be in breach of EU law.

Each of these possible solutions will now be considered in turn.

(i) Enforcement Action

Enforcement actions are brought by the Commission against Member States when they fail to fulfil their obligations under the Treaties. Accordingly, in order for the Commission to be able to bring an enforcement action against Member States that have introduced golden passport programmes, it must be proved that by introducing such programmes the Member States fail to comply with their obligations under the Treaties. The important question, therefore, is which of their obligations under EU law do Member States breach by introducing such programmes?

Carrera has suggested that one way of challenging citizenship-for-sale schemes under EU law is by arguing that they contravene the principle of sincere co-operation.[23] The principle of sincere co-operation applies in all areas, including those in which Member States have exclusive competence,[24] and, hence, the fact that Member States have exclusive competence in the field of nationality does not exclude the application of this principle in this context. The principle – which is now found in Article 4(3) TEU – provides, inter alia, that 'the Member States shall facilitate the achievement of the Union's tasks and *refrain from any measure which could jeopardise the attainment of the Union's objectives*' (emphasis added).

Accordingly, the question that follows is, which of the Union's objectives is breached by the exchange of Union citizenship for money?

Although Carrera has been of the view that golden passport programmes breach the principle of sincere co-operation because they give rise to 'free-riding', in my view the main reason that such programmes

23 Carrera (n.2 above).
24 Carrera (n.2 above), pp. 23–24.

violate this principle is that they breach some of the values of the EU, namely, the prohibition of discrimination on the ground of property and, more broadly, the principle of equality, which form part of the values on which the EU is based. Since one of the EU's objectives is to promote its values, action by Member States which jeopardises the attainment of this objective is liable to amount to a breach of the principle of sincere cooperation.

More specifically, citizenship-for-sale programmes create a difference in treatment between wealthy third-country nationals who can simply 'buy' Member State nationality and, through it, Union citizenship, and third-country nationals who cannot and, as such, have to satisfy a number of burdensome requirements to comply with the ordinary naturalisation procedure. Such programmes, therefore, create a distinction based on the ground of property, since *the only* criterion used to distinguish between persons who can benefit from such programmes (and thus more easily, i.e. without complying with the ordinary naturalisation procedure, acquire Member State nationality and through it Union citizenship) and persons who cannot, is their ability to pay a large sum of money and/or to make a significant investment in the territory of the Member State the nationality of which they wish to acquire. Article 21 of the EU Charter of Fundamental Rights (EUCFR) provides that any discrimination based on the ground of, inter alia, property shall be prohibited; and the reason for introducing such programmes – to raise funds for Member State coffers – is clearly incapable of justifying this difference in treatment under Article 52 of the Charter.

Accordingly, since EU citizenship and the EU more generally have as their basis the fight against discrimination, by instituting and applying citizenship-for-sale programmes Member States are in contravention of the principle of sincere co-operation when this is read in conjunction with the general principles of EU law (fundamental human rights and the principle of equality), Articles 20 and 21 of the EUCFR, Article 2 TEU (which provides that the Union is founded on the values of, inter alia, human dignity, equality, and the respect for human rights) and Article 3 TEU (which states that the Union's aim is to, inter alia, promote its values).

The difficulty with this solution, nonetheless, is that, firstly, it is dependent on the Commission deciding to bring an action against the recalcitrant Member States – something which is clearly politically sensitive – and, secondly, even if a successful action is brought, this does not mean that Member States will comply with the judgment and refrain from applying such programmes, as the net gains from them may be higher than the penalty payment or lump sum that *may* be imposed under

Article 260 TFEU for their failure to comply with the Article 258 judgment which has found them in breach of EU law.

(ii) A Declaration that Member State Nationals who have Acquired their Nationality via Citizenship-for-Sale Programmes are not Member State Nationals *for the Purposes of EU Law*

An alternative solution proposed in this chapter is inspired by the Court's approach in an old staff case – *Airola*.[25]

Mrs Airola was a Commission *fonctionnaire*. When she commenced working for the Commission in Italy in 1964, she held only Belgian nationality. However, in 1965 she married an Italian national and as a result she acquired (also) Italian nationality, in accordance with Italian legislation that provided that the wives of Italian nationals *automatically* obtained Italian nationality *and could not renounce it*, although the same did not apply to men who married Italian women. As a result of her acquisition of Italian nationality, the Commission refused to grant her the expatriation allowance she applied for, on the ground that she was a national of the state to which she had been posted (Italy). When the issue was referred to the ECJ, the latter held that when applying the Staff Regulations, the concept of 'nationals' must be 'interpreted in such a way as to avoid any unwarranted difference of treatment as between male and female officials who are, in fact, placed in comparable situations'.[26] Accordingly, in its judgment in this case, the ECJ indicated that although the grant of nationality is a matter that falls within Member State competence, the EU may need to ignore the bestowal of Member State nationality *for EU law purposes*, if on the facts of the case nationality was granted in a manner contrary to EU law.

Accordingly, it can be argued that the EU institutions may make a declaration that, for the purposes of EU law and, more specifically, the acquisition of Union citizenship, the act of nationality disposition by Member States will not be valid if it is done in exchange for money *and* if the person acquiring Member State nationality has no ties with the said Member State or, more broadly, with the EU. The justification will be that the EU cannot recognise a status which is granted in a manner which breaches its values, by being in breach of the principles of non-discrimination and equality (as noted above).

---

[25] *Airola* (Case 21/74) [1975] ECR 221.
[26] *Airola* (n.25), para.10.

If this suggestion is followed, this will mean that Member State nationals who have acquired their nationality through citizenship-for-sale programmes will not be considered Union citizens and thus will not enjoy any of the rights attached to this status. This – in the vast majority of cases – will defeat the whole purpose of the acquisition of Member State nationality through such programmes (i.e., access to the whole of the EU) and is thus likely to lead to their demise.

The difficulty with this solution, nonetheless, is its enforcement. Member States do not distinguish between their nationals who have acquired a 'golden passport' and all their other nationals. In fact, Member States that operate such golden passport schemes are often very secretive, refusing to publish the names of those who have acquired their nationality in this manner. Accordingly, even if the EU declares that Member State nationals who have acquired their Member State nationality through such programmes shall not be considered Union citizens, it is unlikely that in practice it will be able to identify them and thus exclude them from the EU citizenship status.

6. CONCLUSION

This brief case study sought to consider whether it is permissible under EU law for Member States to transform EU citizenship into a tradable commodity by introducing schemes that provide for the grant of national citizenship (and, by extension, EU citizenship) in exchange of a hefty sum of money; in other words, it was considered whether it is permissible under EU law for third-country nationals to buy their way into becoming subjects of EU law. It was explained that – in the view of this author – citizenship-for-sale schemes give rise to discrimination on the ground of property and amount to a breach of the principle of equality. Accordingly, such schemes go against some of the values on which the EU is founded and which it aims to promote. It was, therefore, considered that there can be two solutions to this issue: a judicial and a political one. The former will consist of an enforcement action brought by the Commission against the Member States that have introduced such schemes, claiming that the latter breach the principle of sincere co-operation under Article 4(3) TEU read in conjunction with a number of Treaty provisions as well as the EU Charter of Fundamental Rights; this, however, as has been explained, can prove difficult to apply in practice. The latter (political) solution will consist of a declaration made by the EU that it does not recognise *for the purposes of EU law* national citizenship granted through such schemes, because the grant of citizenship in this manner gives rise to a breach of some of the EU's values; again, however, as explained, there are likely to be practical difficulties in the application of this solution.

9. The turning of non-state entities from objects to subjects of EU restrictive measures

Sara Poli*

1. INTRODUCTION

The dichotomy 'subjects' and 'objects' of EU law is very specific in the context of the Common Foreign and Security Policy ('CFSP'). Indeed, the target of CFSP measures are in general third countries[1] rather than non-state entities. Therefore, individual rights usually are not directly affected by such measures. The only exceptions are EU 'restrictive measures' or 'sanctions' (these terms are used interchangeably).[2] Enacted

* The research leading to the publication of this piece has been funded with support from the European Commission. The research was carried out during the Jean Monnet Chair (Lifelong Learning Programme) awarded to Professor Sara Poli between 2013 and 2016. This piece reflects the views only of the author, and the Commission cannot be held responsible for any use which may be made of the information contained therein.

[1] EU sanctions against third countries take the form of prohibitions on the import and/or export of arms, goods, and devices which are necessary for internal repression purposes. Bans may also concern investments and the provision of services and technical assistance.

[2] On the EU's sanction policy, see among others, Gestri, M., 'Sanctions imposed by the European Union: legal and institutional aspects', in Ronzitti, N., *Coercitive Diplomacy, Sanctions and International Law* (Brill/Nijhoff, Leiden 2016), p. 70; Bosse-Platière, I., 'Les mesures restrictives adoptées par l'union européenne ou la projection a l'externe d'un acteur singulier', in *Annuaire Français de Relations Internationales*, vol.XVII, 2016, forthcoming; Beaucillon, C., *Les mesures restrictives de l'Union européenne* (Bruylant, Brussels 2014); Cameron, I. (ed.), *EU Sanctions: Law and Policy Issues Concerning Restrictive Measures* (Intersentia, Cambridge/Antwerp/Portland 2013); Gazzini, T., and E. Herlin-Karnell, 'Restrictive measures adopted by the EU from the standpoint of international and EU law' (2011) *European Law Review* 798; Eckes, C., 'EU

through CFSP Decisions,[3] they are widely used to target not only third countries ('bilateral' or 'global' sanctions), but also a broad range of non-state entities such as terrorists and terrorist groups, in addition to third-country citizens, legal or natural persons and other non-state entities for the purposes of the CFSP. These are 'targeted individual sanctions' and, strictly speaking, they are conceptually different from 'targeted sanctions'.[4]

The latter are adopted to 'bring about a change in the policy or in the activity by a target country, part of [a] country, government, entities, or individuals in line with the objectives set out in the CFSP Council decision'.[5] Leaving aside the EU diplomatic sanctions,[6] the EU restrictive measures against non-state actors can take the form of asset freezes and/or travel bans.

The majority of EU sanctions implement those adopted in the context of the United Nations (UN), under the authority of the United Nations Security Council (UNSC). In this respect, the EU does not drift from public international law. However, the EU is also competent to adopt restrictive measures that are autonomous from those of the UN. Since the UN Security Council has been facing increasing difficulty in agreeing on sanctions regimes, the EU has imposed a growing number of autonomous sanctions programmes,[7] particularly after the 'Arab Spring' and the outbreak of the Ukraine-Russia crisis.[8] In addition, the EU has 'mixed

---

restrictive measures against natural and legal persons: from counterterrorist to third country sanctions' (2013) *Common Market Law Review* 888; Portela, C., *European Union Sanctions and Foreign Policy* (Routledge, London 2011); Paladini, L., 'Le misure restrittive adottate nell'ambito della PESC: prassi e giurisprudenza' (2009) *Diritto dell'Unione Europea* 341.

[3] Under the provisions of title V Chapter 2 of the TEU.

[4] Since these sanctions target members of the political or military leadership of third countries. For in-depth analysis on sanctions and non-state entities from the perspective of international law, see White, N.D., 'Sanctions Against Non-State Actors', in Ronzitti (n.2 above), p. 127–60.

[5] Guidelines on implementation and evaluation of restrictive measures in the framework of the Common Foreign and Security Policy, Council document n. 11205/12, 15 June 2012, p. 5.

[6] This expression is used to indicate measures of retorsions adopted by the EU. See *www.consilium.europa.eu/en/policies/sanctions/* (accessed on 2 February 2017).

[7] Doussin, A., 'Navigating the complex word of international sanctions', in (2015) *International Trade Law and Regulation* 58.

[8] Belarus, Bosnia and Herzegovina, Burundi, Côte d'Ivoire, Egypt, Russia, Syria, Ukraine, Egypt, Republic of Guinea (Conakry), Haiti, Iran (for its human right abuses), Myanmar, Yugoslavia (Serbia and Montenegro), Tunisia, United

sanction regimes' that complement UN restrictive measures. For example, in specific cases sanctions are linked to a UNSC resolution but the scope of the targeted sanctions is widened, as a result of an EU's autonomous decision-making power in the field of CFSP.[9]

It should be noted that the normative turn from global[10] to targeted[11] sanctions and sanctions against non-state entities as such[12] first occurred in the context of the UN. Thus, the UN 'constituted' 'non-state entities' before the EU did it.[13]

A variety of designation criteria are selected by restrictive measures that extend to non-state entities in the UN context and the trend is to expand rather than to streamline them.[14] By following a chronological order, we can identify four broad categories of designation criteria identified in the UN practice, which were often further elaborated upon by the EU. Traditionally, UN sanctions list the leaders of armed groups that threaten the peace, security or the stability of their own countries.[15] An example of these sanctions are the EU autonomous restrictive measures targeting a wide range of natural and legal and other entities or bodies that undermine or threaten the territorial integrity, sovereignty and

---

States of America. Sanctions against Moldova are an early case of autonomous sanctions enacted vis-à-vis the Transnistrian leadership (for the first time in 2003).

[9] The EU has expanded the scope *ratione personae* of restrictive measures with respect to those established at UN level; the same has happened with respect to the scope *ratione materiae* of sanctions decided at UN level. Examples of mixed sanction regimes are those of Iran (as far as the regime countering the proliferation of weapons of mass destruction is concerned), Libya, Democratic Popular Republic of Korea (DPRK) and Zimbabwe.

[10] Designating a third country as whole.

[11] Designating the political leadership of a country.

[12] Individuals not exercising a governamental function.

[13] Since the early 1990s the UN has targeted non-state entities. 'The imposition of sanctions against Bosnian Serbs with resolution 820 in April 1993 represented the first time the UN targeted a sub-state entity', UN Security Council, UN sanctions, Special Research Report, 2013, p. 9. Accessed 6 March 2013 at *http://www.securitycouncilreport.org/atf/cf/%7B65BFCF9B-6D27-4E9C-8CD3-CF6E4FF96FF9%7D/special_research_report_sanctions_2013.pdf.*

[14] For the full list of designation criteria see UN Security Council, UN Sanctions (n.13 above), p. 9.

[15] See the example of the Houtis who threaten the territorial integrity of Yemen, groups of individuals affecting the stability of South Sudan, the members of the military command responsible for the coup d'état of 2012 in the Republic of Guinea Bissau, affecting the stability of this country.

independence of Ukraine.[16] These measures were adopted against the Crimean leaders and their supporters as well as against the political leadership of two self-proclaimed Autonomous Republics: Donetsk and Luhansk in 2014.[17]

The UN also designates non-state entities when they give support to their government in violating international humanitarian law and/or commit human rights abuses.[18] The EU autonomously sanctioned serious breaches of human rights when committed by the political leadership and persons associated with the government of the concerned third country in connection with the repression of the political opposition by a military junta (Myanmar in 1996[19]), in the aftermath of elections (i.e. the targeted sanctions against Zimbabwe in 2002[20] and Belarus in 2006[21]), or, more recently, the crackdown on political opposition (the Republic of Guinea in 2010[22]). Serious human right abuses also attracted sanctions (as in the

---

[16] Council Decision 2014/145/CFSP of 17 March 2014 concerning restrictive measures in respect of actions undermining or threatening the territorial integrity, sovereignty and independence of Ukraine, OJ [2014] L 078/16 and Council Regulation (EU) No 269/2014 of 17 March 2014 concerning restrictive measures in respect of actions undermining or threatening the territorial integrity, sovereignty and independence of Ukraine, OJ [2014] L 078/6.

[17] Further categories of non-state entities targeted by Decision 2014/145 as subsequently amended are: a) certain natural or legal persons, entities or bodies actively supporting, materially or financially, or benefiting from, Russian decision-makers responsible for the annexation of Crimea or the destabilisation of Eastern Ukraine and b) certain natural or legal persons, entities or bodies conducting transactions with the separatist groups in the Donbass region of Ukraine. Accessed 7 February 2017 at *eeas.europa.eu/archives/docs/cfsp/sanctions/docs/measures_en.pdf.*

[18] See for examples the UN Security Council, UN Sanctions (n.13 above), p. 9.

[19] 96/635/CFSP: Common Position of 28 October 1996 defined by the Council on the basis of Article J.2 of the Treaty on European Union, on Burma/Myanmar, OJ [1996] L 287/2.

[20] Council Common of 18 February 2002 concerning restrictive measures against Zimbabwe, OJ [2002] L 50/1.

[21] Council Regulation (EC) No 765/2006 of 18 May 2006 concerning restrictive measures against President Lukashenko and certain officials of Belarus, OJ [2006] L 34/1.

[22] Council Decision 2010/638/CFSP of 25 October 2010 concerning restrictive measures against the Republic of Guinea, OJ [2010] L 280/10.

cases of Iran (in 2011)[23] and Burundi (in 2015)[24]); finally, the violent repression of the civilian population and the use of violence against protesters were at the basis of sanctions respectively in Syria (in 2013)[25] and Ukraine (in 2014).[26]

A further designation criterion is the perpetration of terrorist acts or the engagement in activities that, broadly speaking, facilitate these acts. On this basis members of groups, such as Al Quaida and the ISIL (Da'esh) and other individuals or undertaking associated to these entities[27], are designated by the competent sanction committee.[28] The UN has increased its use of sanctions for the purpose of counter-terrorism since the attack on the World Trade Center in 2001[29] and has extended them in 2015 to

---

[23] Council Decision 2011/235/CFSP of 12 April 2011 concerning restrictive measures directed against certain persons and entities in view of the situation in Iran, OJ [2011] L 100/11.

[24] Council Decision (CFSP) 2015/1763 of 1 October 2015 concerning restrictive measures in view of the situation in Burundi, OJ [2015] L 257/37.

[25] Council Decision 2013/255/CFSP of 31 May 2013 concerning restrictive measures against Syria, OJ [2013] L 147/14. See Arts 27 and 28.

[26] This is the case of restrictive measures imposed on members of the government using violence against the Maidan Square protesters in early 2014. See Council Decision 2014/119/CFSP of 5 March 2014 concerning restrictive measures directed against certain persons, entities and bodies in view of the situation in Ukraine, OJ [2014] L 66/30.

[27] Council Decision (CFSP) 2016/368 of 14 March 2016 amending Common Position 2002/402/CFSP concerning restrictive measures against members of the Al-Qaida organisation and other individuals, groups, undertakings and entities associated with them, OJ [2016] L 68/17.

[28] On EU and UN counter terrorism initiatives see inter alia Murphy, C., *EU Counter-Terrorism Law: Pre-Emption and the Rule of Law* (Hart Publishing, Oxford 2012); Eckes, C., *EU Counter-Terrorist Policies and Fundamental Rights-The Case of Individual Sanctions* (Oxford University Press, Oxford 2009).

[29] However, the first time that groups of individuals were sanctioned was with the UNSC Resolution 1267 (1999). The latter imposed on UN members the freezing of funds and other financial resources, including funds derived or generated from property owned or controlled directly or indirectly by the Taliban, or by any undertaking owned or controlled by the Taliban.

the ISIL. The EU has implemented the UNSC Resolutions in this area[30] and has also set up its own anti-terrorist regime.[31]

In addition, the UN has imposed a freeze on the funds and other resources of persons and entities involved in the nuclear and ballistic missiles programmes of Iran (2006)[32] and the Democratic Republic of Korea (2006),[33] and the EU has expanded these regimes.[34]

As of 2011, the EU has autonomously listed persons responsible for the misappropriation of state funds in its restrictive measures concerning neighbouring countries. More precisely, the former political leadership of the EU neighbour countries affected by geopolitical events (for example, the 'Arab Spring' or the Ukraine/Russia crisis) are targeted when they have been identified as responsible for misappropriation of state funds within their domestic jurisdictions.[35] The aim of the EU's action is to assist countries that are in transition towards democracy through judicial co-operation or, in the case of Ukraine, to strengthen the rule of law.

The overview over the breadth of the designation criteria 'imported' by the UN or chosen by the EU shows that the EU's chances to expand the number of non-state entities targeted by sanctions have multiplied over the years.

Having concisely framed the EU's sanction policy, it is now time to articulate the object of the research. The chapter examines the emergence of non-state entities as 'subjects' of EU restrictive measures. It argues

---

[30] Council Regulation (EC) No. 881/2002 of 27 May 2002 imposing certain specific restrictive measures directed against certain persons and entities associated with the Al-Qaida network, OJ [2002] L 139/9, amended 247 times. Accessed 2 February 2017 at *eeas.europa.eu/archives/docs/cfsp/sanctions/docs/measures_en.pdf*.

[31] Council Common Position of 27 December 2001 on the application of specific measures to combat terrorism, OJ [2001] L 344/93. As of September 2016, the EU is also authorised by the UN to adopt autonomous restrictive measures against members of ISIL/Da'esh and Al-Qaida.

[32] UNSC Resolution 1737 (2006) of 27 December 2006.

[33] UNSC Resolution 1718 (2006) of 14 October 2006.

[34] See below, Section 2 for the Iranian regime. Regarding the Korean sanction regime, the EU has expanded the scope of prohibitions defined by relevant UNSC Resolutions with Council 2013/88/CFSP of 18 February 2013 amending Decision 2010/800/CFSP concerning restrictive measures against the Democratic People's Republic of Korea, OJ [2013] L 46/28.

[35] The number of persons held responsible for misappropriating state funds, who are targeted by the EU, is modest. In the case of Ukraine asset freezes and travel bans were imposed on 18 persons who breached human rights and were identified as responsible for the misappropriation of Ukrainian state funds. Similar restrictions were imposed on 48 individuals in Tunisia and 19 in Egypt.

that these addressees of sanctions have been 'objects' of EU law and have turned into 'subjects' of EU law as a result of Treaty changes that were inspired by the case law of the European Union ('CJEU'). It is also contended that the position of non-state entities, seeking judicial review of restrictive measures, could be further strengthened by the Court. The chapter is structured as follows. Section 1 deals briefly with EU competence to adopt restrictive measures in order to show how the legal position of non-state entities has changed from 'objects' to 'subjects' of EU restrictive measures. Indeed, the EU started to target non-state entities at a time when there were no legal bases in the Treaties to do so. For these reasons non-state entities could be qualified as 'objects' of EU law rather than 'subjects' as in the case of third countries. In this section, it is also stressed that the CJEU has ruled on annulment actions introduced by non-state entities against Regulations, instituting economic sanctions, at a time when the Court did not have an explicit competence to review the legality of restrictive measures targeting non-state entities. The first section concludes with a short description of the legal bases that in the Lisbon Treaty has made non-state entities 'subjects' of EU law. The transformation from 'objects' to 'subjects' of EU law is considered as a positive development which is consistent with the principle that the EU is based on the rule of law: if natural and legal persons can be selected by restrictive measures these subjects should also be able to challenge these measures before the Court.

Section 3 explains the reasons why the EU addresses its sanctions to non-state actors and dwells on the typology of entities who are targeted in the Council's practice; it then examines whether the CJEU has limited the Council's discretion in selecting the kind of non-state entities that should be targeted in order to achieve the objective of the restrictive measure. Sections 4 and 5 focus on CJEU case law. First it is shown how the Court has given substance to the right of non-state entities to challenge restrictive measures; the section then provides examples of situations in which the inclusion in the list of addresses of restrictive measures was annulled as well as the reasons why they were vitiated. The attention then turns to the Court's contribution in defending the rights of non-state entities as 'subjects' of EU restrictive measures. It is shown how the Court has improved in respect of due process rights of individual addresses of restrictive measures and has forced the Council to increase the evidentiary burden to insert a non-state entity in the EU lists of persons subject to asset freezes and/or travel bans. The last section draws some concluding remarks and suggests how the position of non-state entities as litigants could be further improved by the Court.

2. TURNING NON-STATE ENTITIES FROM OBJECTS TO SUBJECTS OF EU LAW WITH THE LISBON TREATY

Although the EU adopted sanctions against third countries as early as 1982,[36] it was not until the Maastricht Treaty that primary law explicitly gave the EU the competence to do so. Post-1993, a number of non-state entities with links to a third country's political leadership were also targeted by the EU. By contrast, non-state entities as such[37] were included in the list of EU restrictive measures only after 2001 with the EU counter-terrorism legislation,[38] adopted to implement the UNSC resolution 1373 (2001), following the 9/11 terrorist attacks. The legal bases for the exercise of this competence were so weak that reliance on former Article 308 TCE was necessary to support the EU legislation.[39] Thus, non-state entities were mere 'takers' of EU law. The Treaty of Lisbon has filled the competence gap by introducing an ad hoc legal basis to impose restrictive measures on non-state entities (Article 215, para.2 of the Treaty on the Functioning of the European Union (TFEU)).[40] This provision specifically enables the EU to designate 'natural or legal persons and groups or non-State entities' as addressees of sanctions.[41] Therefore, it is only in 2009 that these entities are first

---

[36] Cremona, C., 'EC competence, smart sanctions and the Kadi case', in Cremona, C., F. Francioni, and S. Poli, 'Challenging counter terrorism measures through the Courts', *EUI working papers*, Academy of European law, n. 2009/10, p. 72.

[37] Without any form of connection with a third country or with the ruling class of a third country.

[38] This is Council Regulation 2580/2001 of 27 December 2001 on specific restrictive measures directed against certain persons and entities with a view to combating terrorism, OJ [2001] L 344/70.

[39] After the Maastricht Treaty the legal bases used to adopt restrictive measures were Arts 60 and 301 of the Treaty of the European Community (TEC). Only third countries could be targeted on the basis of these Treaty provisions. The secondary legislation designed to counter terrorism was based on those provisions couple with Art.308 TCE. See, for example, Council Regulation 2580/2001 (n.38 above).

[40] 'Where a decision adopted in accordance with Chapter 2 of Title V of the Treaty on European Union so provides, the Council may adopt restrictive measures under the procedure referred to in paragraph 1 against natural or legal persons and groups or non-State entities.'

[41] It should be noted that the Lisbon Treaty provides for a specific legal basis, Art.75 TFEU, allowing for the adoption of measures necessary to achieve

formally 'constituted' as 'subjects' of the EU primary law, within the meaning of the famous statement of the Court in *Van Gend en Loos*.[42]

When the EU started to address economic sanctions to non-state entities deprived of a link with a third country it did so through Regulations. This enabled the CJEU to review restrictive measures challenged by non-state entities to the extent these entities were 'individually and directly concerned' by these acts, within the meaning of Article 263(4) TFEU. However, at the time the notorious Mr Kadi sought the annulment of the EU's asset freezes inflicted on him by Regulation 881/2002,[43] the Court did not have the power to review sanctions addressing non-state entities. This is logical, since the latter could not in principle be targeted by EU restrictive measures. The difficulties of the Courts in upholding the legal basis of restrictive measures targeting non-state entities in *Kadi I* has been widely remarked on.[44] This situation made it clear that it was necessary to amend the Treaty so as to recognise an explicit competence to adopt sanctions against non-state entities.

In the Lisbon Treaty the adoption of restrictive measures is subject to a double-track procedure. First of all, a CFSC Decision is adopted on the basis of Article 29 of the Treaty on the European Union (TEU). The names of the persons that the EU wants to target are included in 'black lists' in the annexes of this measure. When the latter foresees the adoption of an asset freeze, a non-CFSP act is needed to give effect to the CFSP measure instituting the sanctions, since the EU needs to ensure the uniform application of this economic sanction in all Member States.

---

the objectives of the Area of Freedom, Security and Justice (AFSJ) as regards preventing and combating terrorism and related activities. However, this provision has not been used to enact counter-terrorism measures against non-state entities. The Court of Justice has legalised Art.215(2) as the legal basis for all restrictive measures including those countering terrorism. See *Parliament v Council* (C-130/10). For a comment on this case see Herlin-Karnell, E., and C. Matera, 'External dimension of the EU counter-terrorism policy', *CLEER Working Paper*, 2014/12, p. 17.

[42] '[...] the Community constitutes a new legal order of international law [...] and the subjects of which comprise not only Member States but also their *nationals*' (emphasis added). *Van Gend en Loos* (Case 26/62) ECLI:EU:C:1963:1. The quotation is taken from p. 12. See Weiler, J., 'Van Gend en Loos: the individual as subject and object and the dilemma of European legitimacy' (2014) 12 (1) *International Journal of Constitutional Law* 94–103.

[43] Council Regulation (EC) No. 881/2002 of 27 May 2002 (n.30 above).

[44] Pantaleo, L., 'Case C-376/10 *P Pye Pyho Tay Za v Council*, Judgment of the European Court of Justice (Grand Chambre) of 13 March 2012' (2012) *Common Market Law Review* 1780.

The mentioned act is enacted on the basis of Article 215 TFEU. While the first paragraph of the latter provision concerns restrictive measures against third countries, the second one refers to measures 'against legal and natural persons and other non-state entities'. Sanctions targeting persons and entities connected to third-country regimes fall under Article 215(2).[45] By contrast, where the CFSP Decision provides for travel bans, these sanctions are implemented directly by the Member States.

While the Lisbon Treaty has made non-state entities subjects of EU law, it has also complemented the change of status with a right to challenge these measures before the Court. The latter's competence vis-à-vis CFSP Decisions has been recognised by Article 275(2) TFEU as an exception to the general lack of competence to review acts adopted on the basis of the provisions of the Treaties related to the CFSP.[46] Article 275(2) TFEU entitles natural and legal persons and other non-state entities to seek the annulment of the CFSP measure instituting the sanction on the conditions laid down by Article 263(4) TFEU.[47]

To sum up, as a result of Treaty changes, non-state entities have become not only official addresses of EU measures but also potential applicants in the context of annulment actions brought against sanctions, in accordance with the principle that the Union is based on the rule of law. The outcome of this change is certainly positive; however, as we shall see in Section 5, further improvements could be made in strengthening the position of the non-state entity as litigant.

---

45 Eckes, C., 'EU restrictive measures against natural and legal persons: from counterterrorist to third country sanctions' (n.2 above) at 882.

46 See Art.24(1) TEU, para.2, stating that the CJEU 'shall not have jurisdiction with respect to [Title V chapter 2] provisions' and Art.275 TFEU, para.1, which excludes the CJEU's jurisdiction with respect to the provisions relating to the CFSP and 'acts adopted on the basis of those provisions'. See Hillion, C., 'A Powerless Court? The European Court of Justice and the Common Foreign and Security Policy', in Cremona, M., and A. Thies (eds), *The ECJ and External Relations: Constitutional Challenges* (Oxford: Hart Publishing, 2014), p. 47; Brkan, M., 'The Role of the European Court of Justice in the Field of Common Foreign and Security Policy After the Treaty of Lisbon: New Challenges for the Future', in Cardwell, P. (ed.), *EU External Relations Law and Policy in the Post-Lisbon Era* (Springer, Berlin and Heidelberg 2012), p. 97.

47 'Any natural or legal person may, under the conditions laid down in the first and second paragraphs, institute proceedings against an act addressed to that person or which is of direct and individual concern to them, and against a regulatory act which is of direct concern to them and does not entail implementing measures.'

3. NON-STATE ENTITIES TARGETED BY THE EU

The CFSP Decisions instituting restrictive measures, enacted on the basis of Article 29 TEU, are intended to influence the behaviour of the targeted state and non-state actors who act in contradiction of the EU CFSP objectives. Thus, the EU may seek to cut the financing to the activities of non-state entities such as terrorist groups[48] (and individuals or other entities associated with these groups or owned or controlled by these entities) or to isolate the leaders of anti-government militias, and the political and military leaders of self-proclaimed states (as in the case of the sanctions against the leaders of self-proclaimed Republics in Ukraine and the Transnistrian leadership in Moldova).[49]

In addition, EU sanctions are aimed at putting pressure on third countries through traditional arms/trade embargos, but also through targeted sanctions. Such sanctions are aimed at individuals who represent a third country (for example, the leaders of third-country regimes) and who are responsible for violations of international law, which may also amount to *erga omnes* violations, and of EU values.[50] A common feature of restrictive measures against many neighbour countries such as Egypt, Belarus, Libya, Syria, Tunisia and Ukraine is that they stretch to cover non-state entities such as family members of the ruling class of the third country concerned. Sanctions against Belarus, Syria and Libya extend to

---

[48] The EU has an autonomous sanction regime, including among others, terrorist groups such as the PKK, Al Aqsa, Hamas and the Liberation Tigers of Tamil Ealan and a UN-dependent sanction regime, including members of the Al Quaida network and the ISIL (Da'esh).

[49] Council Common Position 2003/139/CFSP of 27 February 2003 concerning restrictive measures against the leadership of the Transnistrian region of the Moldovan Republic [2003] OJ L 53/60.

[50] See, for example, the sanctions against selected EU neighbour countries. Sanctions against Tunisia and Egypt (2011) target people responsible for the misappropriation of funds who undermined the development of democracy and deprived the Egyptian and Tunisian people of the benefits of the sustainable development of their economy and society. Sanctions against Ukraine (2014) inflict sanctions on persons identified as responsible for the misappropriation of Ukrainian State funds and persons responsible for human rights violations, with a view to consolidating and supporting the rule of law and respect for human rights in Ukraine (2014). For a more detailed account see Poli, S., 'Promoting EU Values in the Neighborhood Through EU Financial Instruments and Restrictive Measures', in Poli, S. (ed.), *The European Neighbourhood Policy: Values and Principles* (Routledge, London 2016), p. 51.

persons/entities supporting the repressive policies of the leadership[51] and persons benefiting from the regime such as businessmen.

Usually, there is a certain degree of progressivity in the infliction of sanctions. When the first wave of restrictive measures does not work – these measures target the political/military leadership of the country – subsequent rounds of sanctions extend their scope *ratione personae* to include persons who render the sanction regime more effective. For example, the EU extends its sanctions to entities (i.e. banks or companies) controlled or owned by the concerned third-country regime. In addition, a number of legal and natural persons and other non-state entities that are 'associated' with members of the government of the third country concerned, or 'support' it or 'benefit' from its support, are inserted in blacklists.[52] In this case non-state entities are used as instruments to weaken the ruling class of a third-country regime. The Iranian sanction regime (linked to the non-proliferation of weapons of mass destruction) is an illustration of the progressive extension of the sanction regime to non-state actors. The set of sanctions enacted in 2007 against Iran[53] were expanded in 2010 and in 2012 as a reaction to the lack of engagement by Iran with the International Atomic Energy Agency (IAEA). As a result of the changes in 2012, the EU has imposed restrictions on admission and the freezing of funds and economic resources to 'persons and entities providing support to the Government of Iran allowing it to pursue proliferation sensitive nuclear activities or the development of nuclear weapon delivery systems, in particular persons and entities providing financial, logistical or material support to the Government of Iran.'[54]

Depending on the specific situation of the concerned third country, the EU may decide to extend the sanctions to numerous non-state entities, for example companies operating in broad economic sectors of the concerned third country, such as those of transport and energy. The Iranian

---

[51] The support may be direct, as in the case of militia involved in the repression of the civilian population in Syria or indirect. There are many examples of 'indirect support'. This is provided by persons providing logistical and economic support to a third-country regime but also political support, as in the case of journalists.

[52] Legal persons and other entities owned or controlled by the mentioned persons are also listed.

[53] Common Position 2007/140/CFSP of 27 February 2007 concerning restrictive measures against Iran, OJ [2007] L 61/49.

[54] Council Decision 2012/35/CFSP of 23 January 2012 amending Decision 2010/413/CFSP concerning restrictive measures against Iran, OJ [2012] L 19/22, recital 13.

sanction regime lists the highest number of non-state entities (about 500) that facilitate the development of the nuclear and missile programmes by the government. In addition to persons designated by the UNSC or the concerned sanction Committee, the EU imposes restriction on admission and freezes the funds of persons that are 'engaged in, directly associated with, or providing support for Iran's proliferation of sensitive nuclear activities or for the development of nuclear weapon delivery systems, including through the involvement in procurement of the prohibited items, goods, equipment, materials and technology, or persons acting on their behalf or at their direction, or persons that have assisted designated persons or entities in evading or violating the provisions of UNSCR 1737 (2006), UNSCR 1747 (2007), UNSCR 1803 (2008) and UNSCR 1929 (2010)'[55] or the EU Decision instituting restrictive measures. 'Other persons that provide support to the Government of Iran, and persons associated with them'[56] are also included. As of April 2015, visa bans apply to 94 persons; 43 of these had been designated by the UN, the others were designated autonomously by the EU.[57]

We may question whether the Court has somehow limited the Council's discretion in selecting the kind of non-state entities that should be targeted in order to achieve the objective of the restrictive measure. The answer is negative. On the contrary, the Court has widely interpreted the notion of 'associates' of members of the government of a third country. This is witnessed by the rulings in *Tomana*[58] and *Sarafraz*,[59] in which the

---

[55] Art.20(1)b of Council Decision 2010/413/CFSP of 26 July 2010 concerning restrictive measures against Iran and repealing Common Position 2007/140/CFSP, OJ [2010] L 195/39.

[56] Art.20(1)c.

[57] Information note, *The EU and the Iran*, document 140124/02, April 2015, p. 7.

[58] In *Tomana and others* (Case T-190/12) the Court held that people who were members of the government of Zimbabwe or could be considered as associates to that government at a time when human right abuses were committed in that country could still be considered as associate to that government after they left their posts. The sanctions were justified by the engagement in criminal conduct, leading to human rights abuses against the Zimbabwean people in 2002. The GC rejects the action introduced by a number of addresses of those measures and its ruling was upheld on appeal (see *Tomana and others* (Case C-330/15 P)).

[59] *Sarafraz* (Case T-273/13). This action was brought by Mr Sarafraz, the Director of a TV channel who had broadcast the interview of a journalist and the content of the interview was in fact a forced confession of a detainee. The EU had listed the applicant on the ground that he had worked with the Iranian

Zimbabwean and Iranian sanction regimes are respectively challenged. In addition, the Court has accepted the Council's presumption that, given the context, certain legal/natural persons, on account of their position of successful businessmen in the concerned country, support the ruling regime. However, this does not mean that the Court has been deferent to the Council in reviewing restrictive measures. Indeed, it has annulled a CFSP Decision when the Council has not provided sufficient evidence to substantiate its allegations that a certain person provided financial support to a third-country regime.[60] The Court has also required the Council to identify a set of indicia 'sufficiently specific, precise and consistent'[61] in order for a person to be considered as supporting the government's repressive policies.[62]

4. THE COURT OF JUSTICE AS A FORUM FOR ACCESS TO JUSTICE FOR THE 'SUBJECTS' OF RESTRICTIVE MEASURES

As possible subjects of EU restrictive measures, non state-entities have been able to question the legality of their inclusion in the list of persons whose assets and economic resources have been frozen by the EU.[63] In the EU legal order the position of non-state entities is privileged with respect to third countries addressed by EU sanctions, since the Treaty explicitly confers on them the right to impugn the CFSP Decisions before the Courts.

The CJEU has given substance in a number of ways to the right of natural and legal persons and other non-state entities to challenge their

---

security services to broadcast forced confessions of detainees in breach of the right to due process and fair trial.

60 By way of example, see *Hassan* (Case T-572/11).

61 *Anbouba* (Case C-630/13 P), para.53. In *Anbouba* the Court found that that there was a sufficient link between the person subject to a measure freezing his funds and the regime being combated in Syria. By contrast, the Council had not discharged its burden of proof in *Tri-Ocean Trading*. The latter was a company operating in the oil shipping field whose funds were frozen for organising covert shipment of oil to the Syrian regime: *Tri-Ocean Trading* (Case T-709/14), para.54.

62 *Anbouba* (n.61 above), para.52.

63 In principle, non-state entities could also challenge CFSP Decisions insofar as they impose travel bans. This is not prohibited under Art.275(2) TFEU. However, non-state entities are more interested in seeking the annulment of administrative sanctions freezing their financial resources.

inclusion in the blacklists of the EU. It is possible to identify several strands in the case law that reinforce the right of non-state entities to challenge restrictive measures. First of all, when applicants challenge the CFSP Decision to the extent that this measure inserts their names in the blacklist, they easily pass the admissibility test, under Article 263 para.4 of the TFEU.[64] Second, the terms 'legal and natural persons', enshrined in Article 275(2) TFEU, were widely interpreted to include entities that are 'emanations of non-member countries', as in the case of banks[65] or companies controlled by Iran. The Council and the Commission have contested that these entities fulfilled the conditions to challenge Decisions setting up restrictive measures; indeed, in the ECHR system[66] (but also in other systems) these applicants would not have legal standing to bring proceedings, the *ratio legis* being that a state cannot enjoy fundamental rights. However, the Court has not found similar limitations either in the Charter of Fundamental Rights of the European Union or in the Treaties. On the contrary, the provisions of the Charter, in particular Articles 17, 41 and 47, guarantee the rights of '[e]veryone' or '[e]very person, a formulation which includes legal persons such as legal persons controlled by a third country.

Third, turning to the scope of judicial review, this is in principle limited.[67] The Council enjoys a wide margin of discretion in adopting its CFSP Decisions, including restrictive measures; yet, the EU has to comply with due process and fundamental human rights, even when it

---

[64] By contrast, when private applicants have challenged measures of general application of a CFSP decision and not their individual listing, the CJEU has declared the action inadmissible on the basis of the Court of Justice's lack of competence, under Art.275(2) TFEU. *Hemmati* (Case T-68/12), paras 32–33.

[65] *Council v Bank Saderat* (Case C-200/13 P); *Council v Bank Mellat* (Case C-176/13 P).

[66] See Art.34 of the European Convention of Human Rights.

[67] As the GC put it: 'As the European Union Courts may not, in particular, substitute their assessment of the evidence, facts and circumstances justifying the adoption of such measures for that of the Council, the review carried out by the Court of the lawfulness of decisions to freeze funds and economic resources must be restricted to checking that the rules governing procedure and the statement of reasons have been complied with, that the facts are materially accurate, and that there has been no manifest error of assessment of the facts or misuse of power.' *Al Tabbaa* (Cases T-329/12 and T-74/13). The first case in which the Court had the chance of examining the standard of judicial review with respect to restrictive measures, targeting individuals for their support to the government conduct, is *Bank Melli Iran* (Case T-390/08), para.37.

acts under the CFSP.[68] Fourth, the Court has not limited its review in consideration of the impact that this would have on the effectiveness of the sanctions.[69]

Fifth, a further interesting aspect of the case law concerns the situation in which the Council cannot provide the Court with confidential information giving evidence that a non-state entity fulfils the designation criteria. In this case the Court has upheld annulment actions brought by the addresses of restrictive measures on the ground that they were not supported by evidence even where the Council could not disclose to the Court the information at the basis of the listing due to its confidential nature.[70] This is in line with the Court's position in *Kadi II*.[71]

Next, the Court has afforded individuals the right to protect their reputation, by laying down the principle that the interest of the applicant in bringing proceedings may continue to exist despite the removal of his name from the list at issue. This case law applies both in relation to restrictive measures designed to counter terrorism[72] as well as in relation to third-country regimes.[73] Finally, when the listing decision has caused

---

[68] The CJEU recognises that in principle, it is competent to fully review these measures, in the light of the fundamental rights forming an integral part of the European Union legal order. See *Council v Fulmen and Mahmoudian* (Case C-280/12 P), para.58.

[69] *Al-Tabbaa* (n.67 above), para.77. However, in other cases the GC has interpreted the designation criteria of restrictive measures so as to safeguard the *effet utile* of Decision instituting these measure. See *Ben Ali* (Case T-200/14), para.133.

[70] See *Jaber* (Case T-653/11), paras 79–86; for further references see Poli, S., 'L'Unione europea e le misure restrittive individuali a carattere economico: tendenze evolutive del quadro normativo e giurisprudenziale' *Studi sull'integrazione europea*, forthcoming. See the important changes to the Rules of procedure of the GC and to those of the CJEU with respect to the treatment of information affecting the EU or the Member States' international relations made available to the GC and the CJEU by a party in annulment proceedings. This kind of information will often be used in the adoption of restrictive measures by the Council; the courts will now be able to use this information to rule on annulment actions brought by the addressees of these measures without disclosing this information to the applicant. See, in particular, Art.105 of the Rules of Procedure of the General Court, as published in OJ [2016] L 217/69, and Art.190 *bis* of the Rules of Procedure of the CJEU, OJ [2016] L 217/69.

[71] *Commission and Others v Kadi* (Cases C-584/10 P, C-593/10 P and C-595/10 P), para 123.

[72] *Abdulrahim* (Case C-239/12 P), paras 71 and 82.

[73] See, amongst others, *Ali Sedghi* (Case T-66/12) and *Portnov* (Case T-290/14).

actual damage to the applicant, the EU may incur non-contractual liability. In *Safa Nicu*[74] the Iranian applicant has successfully claimed damages from the EU on the grounds that the Council has committed a sufficiently serious breach of a rule of law intended to confer rights on this firm and the latter has incurred actual damage as a result of the Council's mistake.[75]

5. THE CASE LAW AND THE SUCCESSES OF THE APPLICANTS BETWEEN 2013 AND 2016

The legality of restrictive measures is the object of numerous cases introduced before the GC.[76] Thus, the trust of the addresses of restrictive measures in the EU judiciary is high. Looking at the outcome of the case law on restrictive measures,[77] it is striking that the number of restrictive measures annulled by the GC is not negligible. In 2013, 29 annulment actions were considered admissible; about half of them were upheld.[78] In

[74] *Safa Nicu Sepahan* (Case T-384/11). For a comment see Micheva, K., and D. Duic, 'The EU Restrictive Measures – What if the Court of Justice of European Union finds them not Being Legal: Cases in Croatia and Republic of Macedonia' (2015) *Balkan Social Science Review* 30.

[75] In particular, the Council listed the applicant for providing equipment to the Fordow (Qom) facility built without being declared to the IAEA, without having evidence of this.

[76] The number of challenges to restrictive measures examined by the GC comes second only to cases concerning competition law. Bertrand, V.B., 'La particularité du contrôle juridictionnel des mesures restrictives: les considérations impérieuses touchant à la sûreté ou à la conduite des relations internationales de l'Union et de ses Etats membres' (2015) *Révue Trimestrielle de Droit Européen* 555.

[77] The time lag covered by the analysis of the case law post-Lisbon is three and a half years (2013–2016); this period is considered sufficiently long to appreciate how the case law has evolved.

[78] Cases *Islamic Republic of Iran Shipping Lines and others* (IRISL)(T-489/10); *Persia International Bank plc* (T-493/10) (partially upheld); *Bank Saderat* (T-494/10) (partially upheld); *Bank Saderat* (T-495/10) (partially upheld); *Bank Mellat* (T-496/10); *Bank Melli Iran* (Joined Cases T-35/10 and T-7/11); *Export Development Bank of Iran* (Joined Cases T-4/11 and T-5/11) (partially upheld); *Iran Insurance Company* (T-12/11) (partially admissible); *Post Bank Iran* (T-13/11) (partially admissible); *Bank Refah Kargaran* (T-24/11) (partially upheld); *Europäisch-Iranische Handelsbank AG* (T-434/11) (partially annulled); *Trabelsi* (T-187/11) (partially upheld); *Chiboub* (T-188/11); *Al-Matri* (T-200/11); *Iran Transfo* (T-392/11); *Turbo compressor manufacturer* (T-404/11); *Naser Bateni*

2014 the GC examined on the merit roughly the same number of applications for annulment. However, the legality of the impugned measures was confirmed only in eight cases.[79] The bulk of the successful actions concern restrictive measures against Iranian applicants; however, the listings of Belarusian, Zimbabwean and Syrian applicants were also annulled.[80] Legal action was also introduced by terrorist groups.[81] Turning to the year 2015, the trend of successful actions continued: about 40 actions were considered admissible; in about half the cases, restrictive measures enacted in view of the situation in Iran, Belarus, Ukraine, Ivory Coast, Egypt or against persons financing terrorism were annulled (or partially annulled).[82] In 2016[83] the GC examined 11 admissible actions

---

(joined cases T-42/12 and T-181/12); *Good Luck Shipping* (T-57/12); *Nabipour* (T-58/12) (partially upheld); *Iranian Offshore Engineering & Construction Co* (T-110/12); *HTTS* (T-128/12 and T-182/12); *North Drilling* (T-552/12).

[79] Cases *Ipatau* (T-646/11); *Ezz and others* (T-256/11); *Syrian Lebanese Commercial Bank SAL* (Joined Cases T-174/12 and T-80/13); *Bouchra Al Assad* (T-202/12); *Manufacturing Support & Procurement Kala Naft* (T-263/12); *Aguy Clement Georgias* (T-168/12); *Adib Mayaleh* (Joined Cases T-307/12 and T-408/13).

[80] Cases *Aliaksei Mikhalchanka* (Joined Cases T-196/11 and T-542/12); *Ali Sedghi, Ahmad Azizi* (T-66/12); *Sina Bank* (T-67/12) (partially annulled); *Hemmati* (n.64 above) (partially annulled); *Sharif University of Technology v Council* (T-181/13); *Moallem Insurance Co* (T-182/13); *Safa Nicu Sepahan Co.* (T-384/110); *Ahmed Mohammed Kadhaf Al Dam* (T-348/13); *Syria International Islamic Bank PJSC* (T-293/12); *Mohamad Nedal Alchaar* (T-203/12); *Al-Tabbaa* (n.67 above); *Hani El Sayyed Elsebai Yusef* (T-306/10); *National Iranian Tanker Company* (T-565/12); *Zanjani* (T-155/13); *Ben Ali* (T-133/12); *Sorinet Commercial Trust Bankers Ltd* (T-157/13); *Central Bank of Iran* (T-262/12); *BelTechExport ZAO* (T-438/11); *Jaber* (n.70 above) (partially admissible and partially annulled); *Samir Hassan* (T-572/11) (partially admissible and partially annulled); *Sport-pari ZAO* (T-439/11); *BT Telecommunications PUE* (T-440/11).

[81] *Liberation Tigers of Tamil Eelam (LTTE)* (Joined Cases T-208/11 and T-508/11); *Hamas* (Case T-400/10).

[82] *Klyuyev* (T-244/15); *Kurchenko* (T-248/15); *Yanukovych* (T-173/15); *Portnov* (T-290/14); *HTTP* (T-95/14); *Petropars Iran* (T-433/13) (partially upheld); *Gossio* (T-406/13) (partially upheld); *Iralco* (T-158/13) (partially upheld); *Oil Pension fund* (T-121/13) (partially upheld); *Iran liquefied gas* (T-5/13) (partially upheld); *Chyzh* (T-276/12) (partially upheld); *Dynamo-Minsk* (T-275/12) (partially upheld); *Bank Tejarat* (T-176/12) (partially upheld); *Ternavsky* (T-163/12); *Sabbagh* (T-652/11) (partially upheld); *Akhras* (T-579/11) (partially upheld); *Ocean capital administration* (T-420/11 and T-56/12) (partially upheld); RENV *Ayadi v Commission* (Case T-527/09), RENV *Abdulbasit Abdulrahim v Commission* (Case T-127/09).

[83] The data examined cover the period 1 January 2016 to 30 September 2016.

and in six of them private applicants[84] prevailed.[85] However, in the same year, in most of the cases the addresses of restrictive measures lost on appeals presented to the CJEU against the GC's unfavourable rulings. Out of seven appeals, private applicants did not succeed in five cases; by contrast the Council's appeals were rejected in only two cases.[86] As a general trend, when the CJEU has examined appeals introduced by the addresses of sanctions against the GC's court rulings, the appellants did not succeed.[87] In a couple of instances only the judgments at first instance, holding the challenged restrictive measures illegal, were set aside and referred back to the GC.[88]

Looking at the grounds leading to the annulment of restrictive measures, in most of the cases these were: the lack of motivation[89] or, more often, the Council's error of assessment in listing a certain non-state actor. In this context, it is particularly instructive to focus on the case law which led to the annulment of a restrictive measure due to the commission of a mistake by the Council.

It is possible to identify several situations in which the Council's Decision was annulled insofar as it listed a certain non-state entity. In a first group of cases the inclusion in the list of an applicant was quashed when there was insufficient evidence to show that the person concerned fulfilled the designation criteria. The leading successful action is *Fulmen and Mahmoudian*,[90] decided in 2012, concerning sanctions adopted in view of Iran's nuclear programme. Here, the Court examined the listing of a company and of his major shareholder accused of installing electrical equipment on a clandestine Iranian site before its existence was

---

[84] Former members of a government of a third country are also counted amongst private applicants.

[85] Cases *Farahat* (T-830/14); *Tri-Ocean Energy* (T-719/14); *Tri-Ocean Trading* (T-709/14); *Stavytskyi* (T-486/14); *Arbuzov* (T-434/14); *Oleksii Mykolayovch Azarov* (T-332/14).

[86] *Council v Bank Saderat* (Case C-200/13 P) and *Council v Bank Mellat* (Case C-176/13 P).

[87] See, by way of example, Cases *Ezz* (C-220/14 P) *Anbouba* (C-605/13 P); *Ipatau* (C-535/14 P); *Council v Fulmen & Fereydoun Mahmoudian* (n.68 above); *Europäisch-Iranische Handelsbank* (C-585/13 P); *Council v Manufacturing Support & Procurement Kala Naft* (C-348/12 P).

[88] These concern the anti-terrorism regime and in both cases the challenged Decision listing the applicants was annulled. RENV *Ayadi v Commission* (Case T-527/09), RENV *Abdulbasit Abdulrahim v Commission* (Case T-127/09).

[89] The duty to motivate sanctions is codified by *Council v Bamba* (C-417/11 P), para.49 and the case law cited.

[90] Cases *Fulmen* (T-439/10) and *Mahmoudian* (T-440/10).

officially discovered. However, since the Council had not produced information or evidence in support of the reasons relied on in the contested measures,[91] the latter were annulled. In this case the link between the non-state entity and the government in power was too remote to consider it as a supporter of such a government. In this situation, the EU through its Courts provides the addresses of sanctions with access to justice. But there are numerous other cases in which the GC annulled the Council Decision, targeting a legal[92] or natural[93] person, for its support of a third-country regime or for its assistance in evading the sanctions,[94] for lack of sufficient evidence.

In a third group of cases there was a mismatch between the reasons for the listing decision and the designation criteria chosen by the Council Decision instituting restrictive measures. This led to the annulment of the listing acts.[95] In a fourth group of successful actions applicants were

---

[91] Para.102.

[92] Just to quote a few examples: in the case *University of Sharif of Technology* (Case T-181/13) the applicant was accused of having assisted designated entities to violate the provisions of the EU legislation concerning restrictive measures against the Islamic Republic of Iran, or provided direct support to Iranian nuclear activities. In *North Drilling* (Case T-539/14) the applicant was a company in the energy sector that was listed since it was controlled by the Iranian government and had bought prohibited goods. In *Iran Liquefied Natural Gas* (Case T-5/13) the applicant was an Iranian company in the energy sector that was included in the list since it was a subsidiary of National Iranian Oil Company. See also a similar case *Oil Pension Fund Investment Company* (Case T-121/13).

[93] In *Mikhalchanka* (Cases T-196/11 and T-542/12), the applicant was listed since, as the political commentator of a TV programme covering the Belarusian election of 2010, he had commented on the elections of 2010, which were held in violation of international electoral standards. He was targeted since he was a 'Journaliste haut placé et influent à la télévision publique, ONT'. The GC found that the Council had not disclosed any evidence capable of demonstrating the influence, actual impact or responsibility that Mr Mikhalchanka or, as the case may be, the television programme he presented, could have had for the violations of international electoral standards and the repression of civil society and the democratic opposition. The CJEU confirmed this ruling in the appeal (Case C-693/13 P). See also Case *Al-Tabbaa* (n.67 above) (paras 95–96) concerning restrictive measures in view of the situation of Syria; the applicant was a businessman and member of Assad's family. Finally, see *Sabbagh* (T-652/11), in which the applicant was a lawyer listed for providing financial support to Assad and for his links with other designated persons.

[94] *Iranian Aluminium Co (Iralco)* (Case T-158/13); *Bank Tejerat* (Case T-176/12).

[95] This happened in challenges to Council Decisions, listing people responsible for the misappropriation of state funds. Applicants in these actions were

included in the blacklist at a stage when they did not yet fall within the designation criteria.[96]

In a fifth group of actions the decision to maintain the applicant on the blacklist was annulled, since the circumstances leading to his inclusion in the list were changed.[97] The decision to keep an applicant on the list was annulled even where the applicant was a former member of the political leadership of a third country.[98]

---

wrongly included in the list since they were considered responsible for money laundering and not for misappropriation of state funds. *Ben Ali* (n.80 above), *Al Matri* (n.78 above), *Chiboub* (n.78 above), *Ezz* (n.79 above). However, to the extent that these persons were subsequently considered responsible for misappropriation of funds, the re-listing of these persons on that ground, if challenged, is doomed to fail. A recent judgment of the GC may be considered a confirmation of this trend. See *Ben Ali* (n.69 above).

[96] This is the case of Council Decisions designating people responsible for the misappropriation of Ukrainian state funds; in this group of cases the objective of the restrictive measure was to consolidate the rule of law in Ukraine. Members of Janukovich's government were listed since investigations were opened against them at national level. However, a number of people were included in the list at a time when the investigations were not yet authorised by a judicial authority. This led to the annulment of the impugned act in *Portnov* (Case T-290/14).

[97] This is the case of Gaddafi's cousin. Since 1995, he was believed to have had command of an elite army battalion in charge of Gaddafi's personal security. He had been involved in planning operations against Libyan dissidents abroad and was directly involved in terrorist activities. The impugned measure was annulled because the Council had not revised the designation criteria in view of the changes of the political situation in Libya. The grounds relied on by the Council in 2011 – which have remained unchanged since then – do not explain why Mr Qadhaf Al Dam's name was retained on the list in 2013, that is to say, nearly a year and a half after the fall of the regime responsible for the repression which led to the Council adopting those measures. See *Ahmed Mohammed Qadhaf Al Dam v Council* (Case T-348/13).

[98] This is the case of the former Minister of economy of Assad's regime, Mr Alchaar. He was maintained on the blacklist after he resigned from the government. The Council erred in law since its decision to keep Alchaar on the list was based on the presumption that the applicant was still associated with the regime and was jointly responsible with the government for the repression of the civilian population. Thus, the Council had reversed the burden of proof and had failed to carry out an impartial examination. This case is interesting since the Council has decided not to re-list the applicant. See *Mohamad Nedal Alchaar* (Case T-203/12), in particular paras 170–171.

It should be emphasised that sometimes the Council re-lists applicants who successfully challenged their listing Decisions.[99] This may happen when the Council re-articulates the motivation at the basis of the listing or provides new evidence to justify the inscription in the list. However, there are also cases in which the Council de-lists an applicant as a result of the GC's ruling[100] and there are cases in which at first instance the Court annuls the re-listing of applicants.[101]

6. CONCLUSIONS

Before the Lisbon Treaty entered into force, non-state entities were 'objects' of EU restrictive measures; they were upgraded to 'subjects' of EU law after 2009 and were also provided the right to challenge these measures, by contrast with third countries. As a result, in the Council's practice legal and natural persons and other entities, not presenting any link with a third state, have been listed by CFSP Decisions, when they directly or indirectly supported third-country regimes or qualified as terrorist groups or as persons supporting terrorism.

The CJEU has made non-state entities subjects of EU law before primary law recognised them as possible addresses of restrictive measures. The Treaty followed suit by extending the Court's power of judicial

---

[99] By way of example see the re-listing of Hassan in 2014 after his listing decision was annulled in *Hassan* (Case T-572/11), the re-listing of National Iranian Tanker Company in 2015 after its listing was annulled in *National Iranian Tanker Company* (Case T-565/14) for lack of evidence, the re-listing of Iran Insurance Company and Post Bank Iran in 2013 after their listing decision was annulled in *Iran Insurance* (Cases T-12/11 and T-13/11), the re-listing of Oil Industry Pension Fund Investment Co in 2015 after its listing decision was annulled in Case T-121/13, the re-listing of Jaber, Kaddour, Mohammed Hamcho in 2015, after their listing decision was annulled in Cases T-653/11, T-654/11 and T-43/12, the re-listing of Oleksander Yanukovich and Adriy Klyuyev in 2016 after their listing was annulled in *Klyuyev* (Case T-340/14) and *Yanukovich* (Case T-348/14). The validity of the re-listing decisions was confirmed in the subsequent cases.

[100] This has happened to Mr Mahmoudian, Alchaar, Tabbaa, Sabbah, the company Fulmen and the bank Syria International Islamic bank. For more details see Poli, S., 'L'Unione europea e le misure restrittive individuali a carattere economico: tendenze evolutive del quadro normativo e giurisprudenziale' (see n.70 above).

[101] For example in *Good Luck Shipping* (Joined Cases T-423/13 and T-64/14) the GC annulled the applicants' relisting decision of 2013 after its listing was annulled in case *Good Luck Shipping* (n.78 above).

review to restrictive measures instituted against natural and legal persons (under Article 275(2) TFEU), thus providing for access to justice for non-state entities designated by the EU.

The judiciary has contributed to strengthening the position of non-state entities as subjects of EU law by widely interpreting the notion of 'private parties' in the mentioned provision, by imposing on the Council to improve the procedural standards applicable when these measures are enacted vis-à-vis non-state entities, and by requiring the Council to provide evidence in order to list or to continue to list a person. The non-insignificant number of successful actions proves that the Court has set itself as the gatekeeper of the legality of CFSP measures and its role has been fundamental in securing respect for the legal guarantees of the addresses of restrictive measures, as provided for by Article 275(3) TFEU. Thus, the Court has not been deferent towards the Council: it is possible for a non-state entity to be deleted from the list. However, this does not mean that the judiciary has acted ultra vires or has excessively curtailed the Council's discretion. Indeed, as an EU institution, the Court is subject to the duty to 'practice mutual sincere cooperation'[102] with the Council, even when it acts in the context of the CFSP. As a result of this duty, the Court has widely interpreted the notion of 'associate' of the government targeted by sanctions, has acknowledged that the Council enjoys discretion in selecting the designation criteria[103] and in some cases it has interpreted the Decisions instituting restrictive measures in such a way as to preserve their '*effet utile*'.[104]

One last point is worth making. Is there scope for improvements in the position of non-state entities as litigants before the Court? It is submitted that the Court could be more open than it currently is to challenges brought by this category of applicants. First of all, the possibility of questioning the validity of a CFSP Decision, instituting restrictive measures vis-à-vis natural or legal persons and other entities, should be recognised not only in annulment actions but also in the context of a

---

[102] See Art.11(2) TEU, imposing such a duty on all EU institutions.

[103] C-348/12 P (n.87 above), para.120, C-605/13 P (n.87 above), para.41. However, the Decisions targeting natural and legal persons must be based on clear and distinct criteria. This is specified in Declaration n.25 attached to the Lisbon Treaty on Arts 75 and 215 of the TFEU.

[104] See Case T-200/14 (n.69 above).

preliminary ruling procedure. This would expand the existing phenomenon of the 'legalisation of the CFSP'.[105] This issue will be settled in the *Rosneft* case which is pending before the Court.[106] Secondly, the Court could change its case law on the legal standing of non-state entities and make it possible for private parties to challenge the provisions of a CFSP Decision instituting a restrictive measure even if the applicant is not listed but falls within the general and abstract categories of non-state entities that are addressed by such a measure. So far this has not been possible, since the GC interprets Article 275(2) as excluding its competence in this situation.[107] Finally, the Court, in reviewing restrictive measures that list non-state entities supporting a third-country regime, should clarify whether or not the standard of review is the same for sanctions of UN-origin and EU autonomous restrictive measures. This point has not been discussed by the Court, yet; the *Qaddafi*[108] case will offer the first opportunity to settle this issue and it is to be hoped that the above-mentioned question will receive a positive answer.

---

[105] See Cardwell, P., 'The legalisation of the European Union Foreign Policy and the use of sanctions' (2015) *Cambridge Yearbook of European Legal Studies* at 292, 297–298, 309.

[106] *OJSC Rosneft Oil Company* (Case C-72/15), pending (OJ [2015] C 155/12). So far Art.275(2) TFEU has been interpreted to enable private parties to directly challenge Decisions instituting restrictive measures against natural or legal persons or other non-state entities. The letter of the provision does not say anything on the possibility of questioning the validity of such a Decision in the context of a preliminary ruling procedure. On the contrary, it could be argued that since Art.275/2 TFEU refers to the conditions set out by Art.263(4) TFEU, the Court has jurisdiction to rule on the legality of a restrictive measure in the context of an annulment action (Art.263 TFEU) but not in that of a preliminary ruling (Art.267 TFEU). In his Opinion, released on 31 May 2016, A.G. Whatelet argued in favour of extending the Court's competence to rule on these acts in the framework of a preliminary ruling procedure.

[107] *Sina Bank* (n.80 above), paras 37–43.

[108] *El-Qaddafi* (T-681/14), pending (OJ [2014] C 431/31).

PART III

The external-internal nexus of EU law and its subjects and objects

10. The EU as an international person between functionalism and constitutionalism

Andrés Delgado Casteleiro*

1. INTRODUCTION

As with any dichotomous relations; the distinction between objects and subjects of law can be seen as a purely reductionist exercise. Any legal system enshrines much more nuance in the way it approaches its objects and subjects than a dual epistemological way of thinking.[1] When it comes to reflecting on the European Union (EU) as an international subject, the nuances and perspectives become even more relevant. Depending from which perspective the EU is observed, the characterization of what the EU is could differ substantially. The different debates on the sui generis and/or the constitutional nature of the EU are a testimony to the different perspectives from which the EU can be approached.

Yet at the root of all our thinking about the EU there is a certain sense of manifest destiny.[2] The EU is a creation designed to achieve certain objectives and has been vested of certain functions and competences to accomplish them. The *telos* of the EU not only justifies its existence[3] but determines how it functions.[4] Unlike states that just exist, the being of the

* The author would like to thank Dr Elaine Fahey and Dr Samo Bardutzky for their useful comments and suggestions. The usual disclaimer applies.

[1] See chapter 1 in this edited collection.

[2] Weiler, JHH, 'The political and legal culture of European integration: An exploratory essay' (2011) 9 *International Journal of Constitutional Law* 683.

[3] Article 1 of the Treaty of the European Union (TEU) provides that the Member States establish among themselves the EU on which they confer competences to attain objectives they have in common.

[4] The fundamental role that the aims and objectives of the EU play in the CJEU's case law on a legal basis could be seen as an example that the EU can

EU, as with any other International Organizations (IO), depends on the pursuit of its objectives conferred by the states that created it.[5] In this regard, it is often mentioned that the EU has an incomplete legal personality inasmuch as, first, it is conferred by the Member States, and second, it is limited by those powers conferred upon it by them.[6]

Against this background of borrowed existence, the discussion of the EU as subject takes a very interesting focus; this contribution examines how the limited or functional nature of the EU continues to play a fundamental role in its conceptualization as a subject. After briefly dealing with how international law deals with its subjects by assigning them human-like features (Section 2), this chapter moves to provide an overview of how functionalist theories continue to play a fundamental role in our understanding of the EU as subject (Section 3). The chapter identifies a general tension between the functional nature of the EU and its Member States' quest for control over the EU which tends to disregard other aspects of the EU's actions as subject. Furthermore, most of the attempts to overcome the EU's functionalist theories have not been as successful as could have been expected both internally (Section 4) and externally (Section 5).

2. PERSONIFICATION IN INTERNATIONAL LAW

It is clear that in international law the discussion has moved away from the dichotomy between objects and subjects to the existence of different

---

operate only when it needs to achieve a certain objective. See generally, Opinion 2/00 Re: *Cartagena Protocol* [2001] ECR I-09713; Cullen, H, and A Charlesworth, 'Diplomacy by other means: The use of legal basis litigation as a political strategy by the European Parliament and Member States' (1999) 36 *Common Market Law Review* 1243–1270; De Baere, G, 'From "Don't Mention the Titanium Dioxide Judgment" to "I Mentioned it Once, But I Think I Got Away with it All Right": Reflections on the Choice of Legal Basis in EU External Relations after the Legal Basis for *Restrcitive Measures* Judgment', in Barnard, C, et al. (eds), *Cambridge Yearbook of European Legal Studies* (Hart, Oxford 2012–2013) 537–562; Koutrakos, P, 'Legal Basis and Delimitation of Competence in the EU' in Cremona, H, and B de Witte (eds), *EU Foreign Relations Law* (Hart, Oxford 2008) 171–198.

[5] Klabbers, J, *Advanced Introduction to the Law of International Organizations* (Edward Elgar Publishing, Cheltenham and Northampton MA 2015) 15.

[6] Stein, E, 'External Relations of the European Community: Structure and Process' (1991) 1 *Collected Courses of the Academy of European Law*; Schermers, HG and NM Blokker, *International Institutional Law*, 5th rev'd edn (Martinus Nijhoff, Leiden 2011) 993.

subjects within international law. The International Court of Justice laid down the crux of the issue in the *Reparations Opinion* when it acknowledged that "the subjects of law in any legal system are not necessarily identical".[7]

As a starting point, any discussion on the subjects of international law entails a certain level of abstraction or even imagination.[8] Would anybody think of the EU when they are told to say what first comes to mind when they imagine a subject, a person or a participant? The consideration the EU as a subject entails, first, a certain level of personification. Likewise, parallels can be drawn with imagining a state as a subject. Imagining the state as a subject or a person entails giving it human-like features, thinking of international law through analogies with human societies and domestic legal orders. For Hobbes, the essence of the state is the creation of an artificial person.[9] Similarly for Vattel and Kant, the state was a moral person.[10]

While, nowadays, it has been argued that this personification of the state is a relic of the past,[11] the reality on how lawyers continue to speak about states shows how these analogies are well entrenched in the way we think about international law.[12] O'Donoghue highlights how the personification of the state "goes beyond metaphor in more than aiding

---

[7] Reparations for Injuries Suffered in the Service of the United Nations (Advisory Opinion), ICJ 1949 Rep. 174.

[8] This level of abstraction is also present in other approaches to the issue of subjectivity under international law. For instance, Higgins, though favouring the term 'participant' instead of subject as a way of trying to break the link between sovereignty and personhood under international law, continues to regard states as single unitary actors within the international decision-making processes. Higgins, R, 'Conceptual Thinking about the Individual in International Law', in Higgins (ed.), *Themes and Theories. Selected Essays, Speeches, and Writings in International Law* (Oxford University Press, Oxford 2009), 77.

[9] Nijman, JE, *The Concept of International Legal Personality: An Inquiry into the History and Theory of International Law* (TMC Asser Press, The Hague 2004), 51.

[10] Jouannet, E, *Emmer Vattel et l'émergence doctrinale du Droit international classique* (Pedone, Paris 1998), 323.

[11] D'Aspremont, J, 'The Doctrine of Fundamental Rights of States an the Anthropomorphic Thinking in International Law' (2015) 4 *Cambridge Journal of International and Comparative Law* 511.

[12] For an analysis of how the classical doctrines of international law continue to play a role in current international law see generally: Koskenniemi, M, *The Gentle Civilizer of Nations: The Rise and Fall of International Law 1870–1960* (Cambridge University Press, Cambridge 2001).

the reader to understand a process or aspect but to also assign characteristics intended to elicit a particular perspective on what is being considered".[13] For instance, Charlesworth and Chinkin have shown how the language of personification continues to influence international law. In particular, they demonstrate how that language is gendered when it comes to the theory of subjects:[14] by default, states are assigned male-like features.[15] Similarly, O'Donoghue argues that:

> 'in personifying the state as male or female there is thus an attempt to not only represent something we are familiar with, such as the 19th Century state as a person but to then give specific attributes to those states holding particularised characteristics.'

Therefore, if the state is a man, what is the EU? For Chinkin and Charlesworth, any other kind of subject besides the states is regarded as some sort of deviant in international law[16] and interestingly, IOs are commonly described using monster-like features. For instance, Guzman speaks of the 'Frankenstein problem' when dealing with the issue of the control of IOs by its Member States.[17] Similarly, Klabbers opens his textbook on International Institutional Law with a quote from Mary Shelley's *Frankenstein*[18] and Weiler compares the EU to the Golem.[19] Take this last comparison for instance: the traditional Jewish legend of the Golem, by which the rabbi of Prague created a monster to protect the Jewish community from pogroms, evokes the idea of the EU as a means of protecting its Member States from the horror and the violence of the past. In the best-known account of the legend, when the Golem tried to be something more than a defence mechanism, fell in love and was rejected, it turned into a violent monster.[20] Similarly, Frankenstein's monster tells the story of a man-made creation that revolts against its

---

[13] O'Donoghue, A, '19th Century Personifications of the State in International Law' (on file with the author), 5.

[14] Charlesworth, H and CM Chinkin, *The Boundaries of International Law* (Manchester University Press, Manchester 2000), 137.

[15] Charlesworth and Chinkin, n.14, 125.

[16] Charlesworth and Chinkin, n.14.

[17] Guzman, A, 'International Organizations and the Frankenstein Problem' (2013) 24 *European Journal of International Law* 999–1025.

[18] Klabbers, J, *An Introduction to International Institutional Law* (Cambridge University Press , Cambridge 2009) 1.

[19] Weiler, n.2, 693.

[20] It is worth mentioning that the Golem was created without a mouth so it would not be able to speak and thus express any ideas of its own.

master in the pursuit of being something more than a monster. While these stories highlight the dangers of trying to behave like God, they also teach an important lesson about the fate of monsters and man-made creatures: they may be beings, but they will never be human beings.

Given that these fictional stories have been used to describe the EU, what kind of story do they tell about the EU as a subject?[21] At first sight, they could be seen as notes of caution about the dangers entailed in the creating an organization such as the EU. Likewise, Guzman spoke of the Frankenstein problem as a way to explain the risk that IOs, and the EU among them, might act against the interest of its Member States.[22] These stories, however, could also be seen in another light. They show how these monsters had more aspirations than those for which they were created. The Golem fell in love, and the Frankenstein monster in Shelley's version yearns for a partner. They could no longer be defined just by the functions and aims that their masters conferred on them. These metaphors show how the EU is not regarded as a complete person or subject but as something instrumental, that somehow cannot be completely controlled.

Moreover, these metaphors illustrate how engrained the functional conceptual of the EU within our thinking about the EU is, as well as other IOs.[23] The EU, like the Golem, was created to achieve certain objectives through the exercise of certain competences and abide by the will of the Masters of the Treaties (the Member States). It is their objectives and functions that define the EU and allow it to exist as a subject.

---

[21] On law's aesthetic dimension and the ideological purposes that those images harness, see Rackley, E, 'Representations of the (woman) judge: Hercules, the little mermaid, and the vain and naked Emperor' 22 *Legal Studies* 602–624.

[22] Guzman, n.17, 1000.

[23] Klabbers, J, 'The Transformation of International Organizations Law' (2015) 26 *European Journal of International Law* 26. See generally: Alvarez, JE, *International Organizations as Law-makers* (Oxford University Press, Oxford and New York NY 2005) 25. Only disagregagionist accounts of international law would to a certain extent depart from functionalist perspectives. See Slaughter, A-M, *A New World Order* (Princeton University Press, Princeton NJ 2004); Kennedy, D, *A World of Struggle. How Power, Law and Expertise Shape Global Political Economy* (Princeton University Press, Princeton NJ 2016). Yet for all the explanatory force that these theories might have they nevertheless see IOs through the prism of the functions they should achieve.

3. THE EU AS A FUNCTIONAL SUBJECT

Metaphors can be seen as evidence of the underlying rationale of a legal system,[24] and the conceptualization of the EU as a monster identifies a tension within its subjectivity. The EU could be seen as a functional subject, vested with certain competences and geared towards the pursuit of the objectives defined by its Member States. The EU is a creation of its Member States, they are its masters and the EU should abide by them. Nevertheless the internal dynamics of the transfer of powers constitute a challenge to the conception of the EU as a functional subject. In other words, within the EU's subjectivity there is a struggle between its 'borrowed' existence and the articulation of its functions.

3.1 The Function of the EU and How it Relates to its Powers: A Brief Account

Any examination on the nature of an IO like the EU and how it relates to its Member States usually begins with the work of Virally. His work was one of the first to provide a theoretical account of the legal personality of IO.[25] Moreover, Virally's work is often regarded as a functionalist manifest of sorts.[26] Functionalism or the functionalist theory of IOs flows from Virally's enquiries into the nature of IOs. For Virally, the acknowledgement that IOs are the result of the state's needs to co-operate within an institutional framework[27] shows the instrumental nature of the IO in contrast to the complete nature of the state.[28] This difference in nature shows also that the finality of states and of IOs is different. States have what Virally calls *finalité integrée.* This *finalité* gives states their raison d'être and is so embedded within the DNA of the state that it no longer needs to justify its action or decisions.[29] On the contrary, insofar as their existence is inextricably related to their functions and objectives (*finalité fonctionelle*) IOs need to justify their existence by

---

[24] Rackley, n.21, 603.

[25] Schermers and Blokker, n.6, 8.

[26] Klabbers, n.23, 22.

[27] Virally, M, 'La notion de fonction dans la théorie de l'Organisation Internationale' in Virally, M (ed.), *Le droit international en devenir—Essais écrits au fils des ans* (Presses Universitaires de France, Paris 1990) 273.

[28] Klein, P, 'Les Compétences et pouvoirs de l'Organisation internationale' in Lagrange, E, and J-M Sorel (eds), *Droit des Organisations internationales* (LGDJ, Paris 2013) 716.

[29] Virally, n.27, 275.

constantly referring to their functions and objectives.[30] IOs' actions refer back to the scope of their mandate and how it relates to their objectives. For instance, even the doctrine of implied powers refers back to the objectives that the IO pursues.[31]

To put it briefly, the functional finality of IOs would embody three different normative elements. First, the functional finality enshrines a structural element by which the functions authorize IOs to have a structure, competences and instruments of substantive law, all geared towards the achievement of the objectives for which the IO was created. Second, it acts as a limit inasmuch as the objectives determine what the IO might and might not do. Third, the functional finality would encapsulate an obligation: the organs of the organization are obliged to perform the functions entrusted to it.[32]

These normative elements revolve mainly around how the relation between the IO and its Member States is articulated. Moreover, they formulate the relation from a principal-agent mindset by which the Member States are the principals entrusting the agent of certain functions to achieve certain objectives. Yet, as with most principal-agent dilemmas, the principal does not completely trust the agent to create mechanisms which can safeguard their collective interests.[33] All in all, functionalist accounts of IOs boil down to a single issue: control.[34] The transfer of powers to the EU needs to be somehow supervised so as to be sure that it does not depart from its mandated objective and functions.

The three normative elements of functionalism serve that purpose of controlling the EU. The structural element establishes a first layer of control by giving the EU only a limited toolbox. For instance, the pre-eminent role that the Council of Ministers plays within the EU's decision-making process shows how the institutional design embeds that notion of control. Moreover, the agenda-setting powers of the European Council would further reflect how the institutional design responds to a functional view of the EU. The limiting element would concern the division of competences and the extent to which those competences must only serve the purpose of achieving the objectives for which the EU was created.[35] The fact that the EU has competence over trade policy, but that

---

30 Virally, n.27, 275.

31 Klein, n.28, 727. E.g. Case Opinion 2/94 Re: *Accession to the ECHR* [1996] ECR I-1759, para.26.

32 Schermers and Blokker, n.6, 18. Cf Virally, n.27, 281.

33 Klabbers, n.23, 10.

34 Klabbers, n.5, 19.

35 Virally, n.27, 285.

when conducting that policy it must achieve certain objectives as laid down in the Treaties, would be an example of how this limiting element in practice aims to control how the EU behaves when exercising its functions. Finally, the third normative element of obligation means that the EU is not merely entitled to act in certain ways but is also under an obligation to do so.[36] The EU should actively pursue its objectives. In other words, the EU as a subject is defined by its actions. The idea that the EU's personhood is inextricably linked to an obligation to act could explain how concepts like output legitimacy have figured prominently in the analysis of the EU.[37] In other words, the EU's (internal) output legitimacy is an expression of this third normative element: the EU needs to be continuously acting to show that it has legitimacy to ultimately exist as a person.

Furthermore, as Klabbers shows, functionalism focuses upon only one of the three legal relationships that inform the EU's functioning.[38] In general, functionalism is primarily concerned with the relations between the IO and its Member States. Still, the relations between organs within the IO, and especially the relations between the IO and the outside world, cannot be fully explained through the prism of functionalism.[39] Functionalism as a theory struggles when explaining how the different organs of an IO interrelate and, more importantly, how the IO relates to other subjects besides its Member States.

Virally and international law's functionalist accounts of the subjectivity of entities like the EU boil down to the articulation of control mechanisms. Functionalism shows how the subjectivity of the EU is dependent on that of its Member States which aim to control it so as to ensure that the EU objectives are achieved. The EU's personhood is not only limited by these objectives but more importantly is shaped and defined as a subject inasmuch as it pursues those objectives.

3.2 The Internal (Integrationist) Dynamics of the Transfer of Powers

Yet, for all the checks and balances that the Member States might have set up to control the EU, the dynamics of the transfer of powers by

---

36 Klabbers, n.23, 23.

37 See generally: Scharpf, F, *Governing in Europe. Effective and Democratic?* (Oxford University Press, Oxford and New York NY 1999); Lindseth, PL, *Power and Legitmacy: Reconciling Europe and the Nation-State* (Oxford University Press, Oxford and New York NY 2010).

38 Klabbers, n.5, 12.

39 Klabbers, n.23, 23.

themselves constitute a threat to traditional functionalist thinking. According to Schmitter when States transfer powers to the EU, they set the initial terms of that transfer, but they do not exclusively determine the direction and extent of subsequent change:

> 'Rather, regional bureaucrats in league with a shifting set of self-organized interests and passions seek to exploit the inevitable "spill-overs" and "unintended consequences" that occur when states agree to assign some degree of supra-national responsibility for accomplishing a limited task and then discover that satisfying that function has external effects upon other of their interdependent activities.'[40]

Schmitter's theory, often referred as neo-functionalism,[41] challenges the traditional functional accounts presented by Virally[42] and others to the extent that it shows how the normative elements underpinning functionalism do not effectively constrain the IO in the pursuit of its objectives. However, it should be noted that, as Klabbers argues, functionalism and neo-functionalism ask different questions:

> '[Neo-functionalism] is predominantly interested in questions relating to the optimal conditions for inter-state cooperation and whether and how cooperation could beget further cooperation. By contrast, the functionalism of international organizations law concentrates on how organizations are legally structured, particularly in relation to their member states'[43]

Though Klabbers is right in acknowledging that functionalism and neo-functionalism ask different questions; the latter's explanation of the internal integrationist dynamics that the EU's legal structure triggers highlights the main flaws of the classical functionalist thinking. When it comes to the principal-agent dilemma (which underpins both theories), Schmitter identifies two relevant factors that show how the dynamics of EU integration transcend a narrow reading of the EU's functions. First,

---

[40] Schmitter, PC, 'Neo-neo-functionalism', in Wiener, A, and T Diez (eds), *European Integration Theory* (Oxford University Press, Oxford and New York NY 2003) 3.

[41] Neo-functionalism was first coined by Haas, EB, *Beyond the Nation-state: Functionalism and International Organization* (Stanford University Press, Redwood City CA 1964), with Schmitter being its most ardent proponent. Rosamond, B, 'The Uniting of Europe and the Foundation of EU Studies: Revisiting the Neofunctionalism of Ernst B. Haas', (2005) 12 (2) *Journal of European Public Policy* 237–54.

[42] See above, n.27.

[43] Klabbers, n.23, 20–21.

the EU, but especially actors like the Commission, profits from the collective nature of the principal (28 Member States) and the diverging interests that they might have.[44] Second, the functions conferred on the EU institutions are sufficiently interdependent in their effects that 'they cannot be performed alone without incurring increasing costs or diminishing returns'.[45] Consequently, regardless of the initial intentions of the Member States, 'there will be a tendency to "spillover" within each function, as well as across them, and, hence, an (uneven) trend toward task expansion in both scope and level of authority'.[46]

In other words, classical functionalism cannot satisfactorily explain why the EU might develop more powers and competences than those that it had been initially allocated by the Member States. Functionalism defines the EU by contraposition to the Member States that created it. It is a subject not because it interacts with other subjects, but because the Member States have decided for the EU to be considered a subject.

4. TAMING THE MONSTER (INTERNALLY): THE CONSTITUTIONALIZATION OF THE EU AND THE RETURN OF FUNCTIONALISM

4.1 The Problem with the Constitutional Narratives and the EU's Functional Being

As seen above, functionalism cannot really explain how the EU relates to subjects other than its Member States. Moreover, the internal dynamics that are set in motion by the transfer of powers have the consequence of diluting accountability mechanisms, both vis-à-vis the Member States (as seen in the previous section) but also, and more importantly, towards other EU citizens.[47]

Constitutional narratives of the EU have been deployed to overcome this democratic deficit.[48] Without democracy, the rule of law, and legitimacy anchored in popular ownership, the EU 'rapidly becomes

---

44 Schmitter, n.40, 9.

45 Schmitter, n.40.

46 Schmitter, n.40.

47 On the issue of how the transfer of powers exacerbates the democratic deficit at all levels (both national and supranational) see Mair, P, *Ruling the Void: The Hollowing Out of Western Democracy* (Verso, London 2014).

48 It would be almost impossible to provide a comprehensive review of the literature on the constitutionalization of the EU. For a recent overview see:

alienating and, like the Golem, turns on its creators'.[49] Regardless of the type of constitutionalism that might be used to approach the EU, be it normative, descriptive, formal or material,[50] the constitutional discourse has tried to overcome the paradoxes and the tensions inherent to functionalism. Notwithstanding, constitutionalism retains a certain sense of a functional ethos embedded within it.[51] Broadly speaking, constitutionalism would be concerned with two aspects of the organization of a polity. By contrast to functionalism, constitutionalism aims to overcome the limited subjectivity of the EU by not only focusing on issues having to do with the division of powers but also extending its scope to focus on the application of liberal principles such as rule of law and fundamental rights in the EU.[52]

Still, in constitutionalist terms, the EU is regarded as something more than an expression of the concerted wills of its Member States.[53] The most radical exponent of constitutionalist theory applied to other subjects besides states would be Petersmann.[54] For Petersmann, constitutionalism

---

Schütze, R, 'Constitutionalism and the European Union' in Barnard, C, and S Peers (eds), *European Union Law* (Oxford University Press, Oxford 2014).

[49] Weiler, n.2, 693.

[50] Schütze, n.50, 72.

[51] See Dashwood, A, *Reviewing Maastricht* (Kluwer, The Hague 1996), Dashwood used the term 'a constitutional order of states' as a means to capture both the emerging constitutional thinking about the EU whilst still reaffirming the limited subjectivity of the EU.

[52] Von Bogdandy, A, and J Bast, *Principles of European Constitutional Law* (Hart, Oxford 2011) 2; Schütze, n.50, 92; Pernice, I, 'Does Europe Need a Constitution? Achievements and Challenges After Lisbon' in Arnull, A, et al. (eds), *A Constitutional Order of States? Essays in EU Law in Honour of Alan Dashwood* (Hart, Oxford 2011) 79.

[53] Klabbers, J, 'Contending approaches to international organizations: between functionalism and constitutionalism' in Klabbers, J, and A Wallendahl (eds), *Research Handbook on the Law of International Organizations* (Edward Elgar Publishing, Cheltenham and Northampton MA 2011) 15.

[54] These are just a few examples: Petersmann, E-U, 'National Constitutions, Foreign Trade Policy and European Community Law' (1992) 2 *European Journal of International Law* 1–35. Petersmann, 'Time for a United Nations "Global Compact" for Integrating Human Rights into the Law of Worldwide Organizations: Lessons from European Integration' (2002) 13 *European Journal of International Law* 621–50; Petersmann, 'Human Rights, International Economic Law and Constitutional Justice' (2008) 19 *European Journal of International Law* 769–98. For a critique of Petersmann's approach see: Howse, R, 'Human Rights in the WTO: Whose Rights, What Humanity? Comment on Petersmann' (2002) 13 *European Journal of International Law* 651–9; Alston, P, 'Resisting

would serve a double purpose within the constitutional discourse. On one hand, it acts as a set of normative values that would act as controlling mechanism. The EU, the Member States and its citizens are kept in check by the constitution, and especially by the fundamental rights recognized by the EU Treaties.[55] On the other hand, it puts the citizen at the heart of the system through the elevation of human rights. Therefore, constitutionalism would aim to limit and control the actions of the EU.[56]

Yet, for all the explanatory and transformative power that constitutionalism carries on, as with functionalism, there is a tension between the internal dynamics that the transfer of powers triggers and constitutionalism. The internal integrationist dynamics identified by Haas would be somehow tamed by a constitutional understanding of the separation of powers and also would establish certain limits by virtue of the rule of law and fundamental rights. However, as Howse and Nicolaidis show, the proposed adoption of a 'constitutional' mode of thinking has important practical or policy implications.[57] First, individuals become subjects of EU law.[58] Second, they argue that:

> 'constitutional law is generally regarded as higher law, with a presumption against the change of basic structures. Constitutionalizing discourse tends to serve a "door closing" function against claims that [the EU] has gone too far and may need to be scaled back to give greater scope for democracy at the national level.'[59]

Constitutionalism has the consequence of shutting down any internal contestation to the development of powers by the EU. Constitutionalism, thus, would further enhance the internal dynamic of ever closer integration inasmuch as the EU Constitution recognizes those internal dynamics. Yet, there seems to be an inherent contradiction between the constitutionalist narrative and the ever-closer integration dynamics identified by the

---

the Merger and Acquisition of Human Rights by Trade Law: A Reply to Petersmann' (2002) 13 *European Journal of International Law* 815–44.

55 Petersmann, n.54, 19.

56 Klabbers, n.53, 15.

57 Howse, R, and K Nicolaidis, 'Enhancing WTO Legitimacy: Constitutionalization or Global Subsidiarity?' (2003) 2003 *Humanity* 73, 75. Even though they use the example of the WTO, the logic and the implications of the constitutional discourse to the EU are also quite clear.

58 See *Van Gend en Loos* Case 26/62 [1963] ECR 0001. See also Chapter 1 of this edited volume.

59 Howse and Nicolaidis, n.57, 75.

neo-functionalists. The constitutionalization of the EU has the consequence of reifying it. It becomes a single structure one is either for or against,[60] since the venues for contestation are closed.

Thus, ironically, the constitutionalization of the EU would lead to a legitimacy crisis.[61] This crisis would be articulated not in terms of whether certain parts of the EU should be scaled down, but instead it would be an interrogation of the legitimacy of the EU as a subject. Inevitably, a legitimacy crisis of the EU would be framed in terms of the overall project which would favour narratives highlighting the functionalist accounts of the EU instead of the constitutional ones. What was the EU originally created for? Has the EU gone too far? Should we rethink what the EU is for?

The failure of the Constitution for Europe in 2005 could be seen as the trigger of the current legitimacy crisis that the EU is going through. From a functional perspective, the legitimacy crisis is an existential crisis for a subject like the EU. To the extent that the EU is still regarded as a functional – and consequently incomplete – subject, questioning its legitimacy amounts to questioning why it should exist at all.[62] Constitutionalist narratives tried to solve that issue by bringing forward liberal constitutional values which aimed to show that the EU was something more than an IO created with a limited set of objectives. In other words, constitutionalism attempted to complement the output legitimacy inherent to the EU's nature with an input legitimacy that could shield the EU from such existential/legitimacy crises. However, constitutionalism has had the unintended consequence of exacerbating the legitimacy claims against the EU which at their root question the function and consequently the existence of the EU as subject.

4.2 The Influence of Functionalism in the Conceptualization of the EU as an International Person

The incomplete nature of the EU as a subject has logically figured prominently in the analysis of its external relations. Given that functionalism struggles to explain how the EU relates to the outside world, it is somewhat paradoxical that most of the legal literature on EU external relations is clearly marked by a functionalist approach. The leading books on that subject either begin delving directly into the articulation of

---

60 Howse and Nicolaidis, n.57.

61 Howse and Nicolaidis, n.57.

62 See above, n.37.

the division of powers between the EU and its Member States,[63] or focus on the incomplete legal personality of the EU when compared with a state.[64] Furthermore, the analysis of the constitutional principles that inform EU external relations law can be easily explained through the prism of functionalism. The structural principles guiding the EU's external action, principle of conferral, the loyalty principle or the principle of the autonomy of the EU legal order[65] articulate the relation between the EU and its Member States when acting externally. The focus on the relationship between the EU and its Member States in the EU's external action is exemplified by the prominent role that mixed agreements play within the EU external relations legal literature.[66] Mixed agreements are those agreements concluded jointly by the EU and its Member States on one hand and a third party in the other. While there are many reasons behind the adoption of mixity as the formula for concluding an international agreement,[67] all of them in one way or another concern the tensions created by the transfer of powers to the EU.

---

63 Eeckhout, P, *EU External Relations Law* 2nd edn (Oxford University Press, Oxford 2011); Koutrakos, P, *EU International Relations Law* (Hart, Oxford 2006).

64 Macleod, I, et al., *The External Relations of the European Communities: A Manual of Law and Practice* (Clarendon Press, Oxford 1996); Van Vooren, B, and RA Wessel, *EU External Relations Law. Text, Cases and Materials* (Cambridge University Press, Cambridge 2014); Kuijper, PJ, et al., *The Law of EU External Relations. Case, Materials and Commentary on the EU as an International Legal Actor* (Oxford University Press, Oxford 2013). It is interesting to note that to a certain extent these textbooks follow the traditional template of the classical functionalist International Institutional Law textbooks such as Schermers and Blokker.

65 Koutrakos, n.63, 5.

66 O'Keeffe, D, and HG Schermers, *Mixed Agreements* (Kluwer Law and Taxation, Deventer and Boston MA 1983); Neuwahl, NA, *Mixed Agreements: Analysis of the Phenomenon and their Legal Significance* (European University Institute, Florence 1988); Heliskoski, J, *Mixed Agreements as a Technique for Organizing the International Relations of the European Community and its Member States* (Kluwer Law International, The Hague 2001); Neframi, ET, *Les accords mixtes de la Communauté européenne:aspects communautaires et internationaux* (Bruylant, Brussels 2007).

67 Rosas, A, 'The European Union and Mixed Agreements' in Dashwood, A, and C Hillion (eds), *The General Law of E.C. External Relations* (Sweet & Maxwell, London 2000) 200–220; Hoffmeister, F, 'Curse or Blessing? Mixed Agreements in the recent practice of the European Community and its Member States', in Hillion, C, and P Koutrakos (eds), *Mixed Agreements in EU Law Revisited: The EU and its Member States in the World* (Hart, Oxford 2010) 249–68.

EU external relations law scholarship shows how functionalism plays a prominent role in the way the EU is regarded as an international subject. It is significant that the other relational legal dynamics (between the EU organs and with third parties) do not figure prominently in the way EU external relations lawyers conceptualize the EU as an international actor. The overall role that each of the institutions plays in the configuration of the EU's external action has not been as prominent in the scholarship as the interactions between the EU and its Member States. Issues closely linked to the constitutional nature of the EU, such as rule of law, fundamental rights, or democracy, have not been the centre of many constitutional analyses of the EU's external action. Few authors focus on these issues when analysing the constitutional principles of EU external relations law.[68]

Likewise, the relations with third parties tend to be disregarded as well. It is significant that the issues having to do with the responsibility vis-à-vis other parties to international agreements have been analysed primarily from the perspective of how the division of competences plays a role in establishing the breach.[69] Consequently, questions closely related to functionalist visions of the EU arise when conducting this

---

[68] De Baere, G, *Constitutional Principles of EU External Relations* (Oxford University Press, Oxford and New York NY 2008) 159–200.

[69] Gaja, G, 'Some reflections on the European Community's International Responsibility' in Schermers, HG, et al. (eds), *Non-contractual Liability of the European Communities* (Martinus Nijhoff, Leiden 1988) 169–76; Pigrau Solé, A, 'La Responsabilidad Internacional de la Comunidad Europea' in Menéndez, FM Mariño (ed.), *Acción exterior de la Unión Europea y comunidad internacional* (Universidad Carlos III : Boletín Oficial del Estado, 1998) 171–217; Björklund, M, 'Responsibility in the EC for Mixed Agreements' (2001) *Nordic Journal of International Law* 373–402; Tomuschat, C, 'The International Responsibility of the European Union' in Cannizazaro, E (ed.), *The European Union as an Actor in International Relations* (Kluwer Law International, The Hague 2002) 177–91; Neframi, E, 'International Responsibility of the European Community and of Member States under Mixed Agreements' in Cannizzaro, E (ed.), *The European Union as an Actor in International Relations* (Kluwer Law International, The Hague 2002) 193–205; Gaja, G, 'How does the European Community's International Responsibility relate to its exclusive competence?' in *Studi di Diritto Internazionale in Onore di Gaetano Arangio-Ruiz* (Editoriale Scientifica, Naples 2004) 747–55; Talmon, S, 'Responsibility of International Organizations: Does the European Community require special treatment?' in Ragazzi, M (ed.), *International Responsibility Today. Essays in Memory of Oscar Schachter* (Martinus Nijhoff, Leiden 2005) 405–21; Eeckhout, P, 'The EU and its Member States in the WTO – Issues of Responsibility' in Bartels, L, and F Ortino (eds), *Regional Trade Agreements and the WTO Legal System* (Oxford University Press,

analysis. For instance, the issue of the lack of responsibility of the EU under international law is normally approached from a functionalist perspective.[70] The discussion would revolve around the division of powers and who should be responsible while to a certain extent neglecting the third party which suffered because of the actions of the EU and/or its Member States.[71]

The approach taken in the literature reflects the importance that functionalism has in the conceptualization of the EU as an international person. The analysis of the EU as an international subject relies on the how to characterize the EU in relation to its Member States and the role that the latter play in shaping, influencing or even curtailing the EU's international subjectivity.

Oxford and New York NY 2006) 449–64; Kuijper, PJ, 'International Responsibility for EU Mixed Agreements' in Hillion, C, and P Koutrakos (eds), *Mixed Agreements Revisited. The EU and Its Member States in the World* (Hart, Oxford 2010) 208–27; Casteleiro, A Delgado, and J Larik, 'The "Odd Couple": The Responsibility of the EU at the WTO' in Koutrakos, P, and MD Evans (eds), *The International Responsbility of the European Union: European and International Perspectives* (Hart, Oxford 2013) 233–55; Martín, JM Cortés, 'European Exceptionalism in International Law? The European Union and the System of International Responsibility' in Ragazzi, M (ed.), *Responsibility of International Organizations: Essays in Memory of Sir Ian Brownlie* (Martinus Nijhoff, Leiden 2013) 189–200.

[70] Casteleiro, A Delgado, *The International Responsibility of the EU: From Competence to Normative Control* (Cambridge University Press, Cambridge and New York NY 2016) 90. Cf Paasivirta, E, 'Responsibility of a Member State of an International Organization: Where Will It End? Comments on Article 60 of the ILC Draft on the Responsibility of International Organizations' (2010) 7 *International Organizations Law Review* 49–61; Hernández, GI, 'Beyond the Control Paradigm? International Responsibility and the European Union' (2012–2013) 15 *Cambridge Yearbook of European Legal Studies* 643–68; Quirico, O, 'The International Responsibility of the European Union: A basic interpretative pattern' (2013) *Hungarian Yearbook of International and European Law* 63–74; Sarvarian, A, 'EU Accession to the ECHR and the Law of International Responsibility' in Kosta, V, et al. (eds), *The EU Accession to the ECHR* (Hart, Oxford 2013) 87–104.

[71] Naert, F, 'The International Responsibility of the Union in the context of its CSDP Operations' in Evans, MD, and P Koutrakos (eds), *The International Responsibility of the European Union: European and International Perspectives* (Hart, Oxford 2013) 313–38.

5. OUTSIDE BUT NOT LOOKING IN: INTERNATIONAL LAW, THE EU AND THE SUBJECTS OF INTERNATIONAL LAW

As has been argued, EU law scholarship has struggled to overcome functionalist rationales when thinking about the EU as a subject. Yet, the efforts in the EU legal scholarship to detach the EU from its functions through constitutionalism signal a willingness to regard the EU as a complete autonomous subject distinct from its Member States.[72] In public international law, the discussions have moved in two directions when speaking about the subjectivity of actors like the EU.

First, as with the EU, constitutionalizing accounts of IOs have played a prominent role in dealing with the shortcomings of the inherent functionalist vision of IOs as subjects. Yet these projects suffer from the same shortcomings identified by Howse and Nicolaidis, discussed previously.[73]

Second, in recent years a more orthodox functionalist approach has been brought forward by the International Law Commission. The most recent projects concerning IOs, including the EU within the international legal order, reaffirm the limited nature of the EU as a person from an international perspective.

5.1 International Responsibility of the EU and the ILC's Articles on Responsibility of International Organizations (ARIO)

In 2011 the UN approved, on second reading, the ILC's ARIO.[74] This project aimed to propose a legal framework to approach issues having to do with the responsibility of IOs towards third parties (i.e. non-members). Yet the most prominent issue during the discussions leading to the ARIO was not how better to structure the reparations towards third parties, but instead how the functional nature of the IO should be reflected in the final outcome.[75] In principle, responsibility concerns the third legal dynamic identified by Klabbers (IOs' relation with the outer

---

[72] For an original application of constitutionalism to EU External Relations see Larik, J, *Foreign Policy Objectives in European Constitutional Law* (Oxford University Press, Oxford 2016).

[73] Howse and Nicolaidis, n.57.

[74] International Law Commission, 'Articles on the responsibility of international organizations' (2011) *Yearbook of the International Law Commission*, vol. II, Part Two.

[75] Nollkaemper, A, 'Constitutionalization and the Unity of the Law of International Responsibility' (2009) 16 *Indiana Journal of Global Studies* 536.

world),[76] yet the ILC focused mainly on the relationship between an IO and its Member States.

Article 61 ARIO, entitled 'Circumvention of international obligations of a State member of an international organization', would constitute a perfect example of how the ILC adopted a pure functionalist approach. The provision reads as follows:

> 1. A State member of an international organization incurs international responsibility if, by taking advantage of the fact that the organization has competence in relation to the subject-matter of one of the State's international obligations, it circumvents that obligation by causing the organization to commit an act that, if committed by the State, would have constituted a breach of the obligation.
>
> 2. Paragraph 1 applies whether or not the act in question is internationally wrongful for the international organization.

This provision calls for three comments. First, the provision provides a straightforward functionalist solution to the issue of responsibility of a state for a breach committed by an IO. Insofar as the IO is no more than the institutionalization of the concerted will of its Member States, the latter should be held responsible for the actions of the IO.[77] Second, inasmuch as IOs are created to achieve a certain common good and their functions are tailored to achieve that common good objective, any wrongdoing on the part of the IO can only be explained by a special dolus (see the notion of circumvention) by the states that created the IO. Article 61 ARIO shows that Member States will engage in responsibility when they knowingly and willingly used the IO to breach international law.[78] Third, leaving aside how this article subverts the classical view on

---

[76] Klabbers, n.5, 15.

[77] Brownlie, I, 'The Responsibility of State for the Acts of International Organizations' in Ragazzi, M (ed.), *International Responsbility Today. Essays in Memory of Oscar Schachter* (Martinus Nijhoff, Leiden 2005) 355–62.

[78] Blokker, N, 'Abuse of the Members: Questions concerning Draft Article 16 of the Draft Articles on Responsibility of International Organizations' (2010) 7 *International Organizations Law Review* 35–48; Blokker, N, 'Preparing articles on responsibility of international organizations: Does the International Law Commission take international organizations seriously?' in Klabbers, J, and A Wallendahl (eds), *Research Handbook on the Law of International Organizations* (Edward Elgar Publishing, Cheltenham and Northampton MA 2011) 313–41; Reinisch, A, 'Aid or Assistance and Direction and Control between States and International Organizations in the Commission of Internationally Wrongful Acts' (2010) 7 *International Organizations Law Review* 63–77; Kuijper, PJ, and E Paasivirta, 'Further Exploring International Responsibility: The

how international responsibility rests on objective factors and not subjective elements,[79] the attribution of a sort of subjective element to the commission of the wrongful act reaffirms how the functionalist views go hand in hand with the personification of the state. The state in this article is a single unitary person with the clear idea that it wants to breach international law and consequently decides to co-operate with other states to create another person to be able to breach the law without suffering the consequences. The states in this scenario would be profiting from the fact that IOs are not in principle bound by the same rules that bind the state that created them.[80]

Applied to the EU, this provision would completely diminish the EU's personality inasmuch as any action conducted by the EU would entail holding EU Member States responsible for the actions of the EU. For instance, none of the relevant human rights treaties is open to signature by subjects other than the state, thus, were the EU to breach one of the provisions enshrined in one of those treaties, the EU Member States would bear the legal responsibility. Yet one cannot but wonder about this functional approach; why not instead challenge the structural bias of the international legal system towards the State, and open those Treaties to IOs?

5.2 The Development of Customary International Law and the Functional Nature of the EU

While it could be argued that the discussions on the responsibility of the EU draw a picture where functionalism is only the consequence of the inherent asymmetries of any consent-based legal system, the discussions on the development of Customary International Law (CIL) currently being held within the ILC highlight how functionalism not only reduces the EU to its functions, but also limits its international normative scope.

In his second report ILC Mr Wood mentioned that

> 'States remain the primary subjects of international law and, as explained in the second report, it is primarily their practice that contributes to the

---

European Community and the ILC's Project on Responsibility of International Organizations' (2004) 1 *International Organizations Law Review* 111–38; Paasivirta, n.70.

[79] D'Aspremont, J, 'The Articles on the Responsibility of International Organizations: Magnifying the Fissures in the Law of International Responsibility' (2012) 9 *International Organizations Law Review* 18.

[80] Paasivirta, n.70.

> formation, and expression, of rules of customary international law. It is also States that (for the most part) create and control IOs, and empower them to perform, as separate international legal persons, a variety of functions on the international plane in pursuit of certain goals common to their members.'[81]

As a general rule IOs cannot develop CIL by themselves. Notwithstanding this fact, the SR acknowledges that the EU might be a special case. Yet, the logic behind the speciality of the EU has nothing to do with the fact that its legal personality might very well be the most rounded and defined of all IOs. Instead, for the ILC, if one were not to equate the practice of the EU with that of states, this would mean not only that the EU's practice would not be taken into account, but also that its Member States would themselves be deprived of or reduced in their ability to contribute to state practice.[82]

The EU's ability to contribute to the development of international law rests on the fact that international law could benefit from different voices and perspectives for it to develop. Instead, the EU practice is considered relevant only inasmuch as it is seen as an expression of the practice of its Member States.

Functionalism as a theory not only limits the EU personhood by inextricably linking it to its Member States, but also its contribution to the development of international law. While Article 3(5) TEU establishes that the EU shall contribute to the development of international law, international law does not allow the EU to fully contribute to that development. Only insofar as the EU's actions can be regarded as the actions of its Member States will its practice be taken into account to develop new customary rules. Functionalism as a theory reduces the role of the EU to a mere instrument of its Member States. Furthermore, this vision of the EU as an instrument of its Member States also restricts the impact that its actions can have in the outer world: the subsidiary responsibility of its Member States and the minimal role that it can have in developing international law are testaments to it.

---

81 Wood, M, Third report on identification of customary international law, UN Document N A/CN.4/682, para.70. Accessed 5 February 2017 at *legal.un.org/docs/?symbol=A/CN.4/682*.

82 Wood, n.81 above, 77.

6. CONCLUSIONS: MORE HUMAN THAN HUMAN?

Ridley Scott's *Blade Runner* could be seen as providing one of the most poignant explanations of the problems created by functionalism and the limited nature of the EU. In the movie, the Tyrrell Company (with 'More Human than Human' as its motto) design human-like subjects (replicants). These replicants are entrusted with certain functions and objectives and are defined solely by them. It is only when these replicants begin to be something more than a vessel to serve the humans that created them that they become a problem, inasmuch as they cannot be fully controlled. The functional nature of the replicant clashes with its (or better, his/hers) personhood.

Likewise, functionalism as a theory not only shows how the classical dichotomy between subjects and objects of the law cannot fully grasp the current articulation of the EU as an international subject, but more importantly, struggles to explain the EU's internal dynamics. Furthermore, the instrumental view on one hand has an alienating power, inasmuch as the subject might not feel that it has to fully engage with the system.[83] On the other hand, it pushes aside any meaningful discussion of the substance of the EU as an actor, moving the debate towards false choices of being in favour of or against the EU.

Moreover, this chapter has shown how functionalism continues to play a role in the EU law scholarship. While the constitutionalist turn might have hidden some of the functionalist tendencies within the EU, we are currently witnessing a resurgence of functionalism in the EU both at a political level (for example Brexit) and within the scholarship. Yet, the question remains, how to approach the EU as a subject without contraposing it to the Member States. Only by advancing new ways of understanding the EU as a person would it be possible to gain better insight into its functioning and better scrutinize its actions. A better understanding of the EU as a subject will make it a completely different object to study and analyse.

---

83 *Yassin Abdullah Kadi, Al Barakaat International Foundation v Council of the European Union and Commission of the European Communities* (C-402/05 P and C-415/05 P) [2008] ECR I-06351.

11. Evolution of the role of third countries in EU law – towards full legal subjectivity?

Emilia Korkea-aho*

1. INTRODUCTION

This chapter concerns the evolution of the role of third countries in EU law, asking in particular whether third countries are, or could one day be, full legal subjects of the EU legal order.

The EU is a member-only organization, and each membership application will, upon approval, require and bring about profound legal, political and institutional reforms in the candidate country. One of the many changes is the transformed relationship of the aspiring candidate not only in relation to existing Member States (who become fellow Member States) but also in relation to countries outside the EU. For the new EU member, these non-member nations become, irrespective of the potential existence of special long-term relations, legally 'third countries', countries that are not formally part of the Union. This group is heterogeneous, comprising countries in the European Economic Area (EEA), EU Partnership countries, as well as the EU's main political and industrial allies, and, in the future, former members, when, as is likely, the UK leaves the EU.[1] Despite the large factual differences between

* This chapter has benefited from generous discussion with, and comments from, colleagues.

[1] Note that Norway, Iceland, Liechtenstein and Switzerland closely participate in a number of EU activities through provisions in the EEA Agreement or on the basis of bilateral agreements with the EU. These agreements are not discussed here. See Eriksen, Erik, and John Fossum (eds), *The European Union's Non-Members. Independence under Hegemony?* (Routledge, Abingdon 2015). Note also that the terms 'third country' and 'third-country actor' are used in a generic sense, covering both governmental as well as non-governmental actors (NGOs and economic operators) in third countries. Finally, 'a third-country

third countries, they constitute a single category in EU legislation. Therefore, what is meant by 'third country' in this chapter refers to this legislative category.

The concepts of 'subject' and 'object' are, as is clear from the introduction to this volume, open to much debate. I argue, however, that despite certain incompleteness, the subject-object framework provides an alternative (or complement) to a traditional internal-external distinction to study third countries. This distinction is central to much of EU law, from internal market law to security policies, and especially external relations law: as explained above, the meaning of the phrase 'third country' in the EU treaties expressly refers to an outsider country that is not a party to the treaty agreed upon by insider countries.[2] Shifting the perspective to the subject-object framework may reveal new insights that would be inaccessible to the research that operates with the internal-external framework. One such insight is the main thesis put forward in this contribution: third countries are in the process of becoming subjects of the EU legal order. Unlike the internal-external distinction, the subject-object framework allows us to observe the gradual movement in identifying and conceptualizing 'new subjects' of the EU legal order.

Traditionally, many authors have claimed that the subjects of the law are those entitled to have rights, powers and duties under law. One such right would seem to be a right to participate in the process in which the content of those rights, powers and duties is determined.[3] A legal subject is not only capable of shaping the law by which she is governed, but is also subject to a duty of compliance with that law. If this is how we determine the meaning of a legal subject, can we give a separate meaning to the position of a legal object? Is a legal object simply someone who is an addressee of the law? But can one be the addressee of the law without simultaneously being a legal subject?

Within nation state or regional borders such as the EU, this does not seem possible, as we are attuned to thinking that people participate in making the laws under which they live, whether directly or through representatives elected by them. Everyone is both author and the

---

national' is used in the context of migration and refers to an individual who is neither from the EU country in which she currently is, nor from other Member States. Specific EU rules concerning the rights of third-country nationals are not part of the present analysis.

[2] See *www.eurofound.europa.eu/observatories/eurwork/industrial-relations-dictionary/third-country-nationals* (accessed 5 February 2017).

[3] Fahey and Bardutzky, chapter 1 in this volume.

addressee of the law.[4] Yet we are, admittedly, on shakier ground when we bring third countries into the picture. First of all, are third countries subject to norms the EU adopts? Does the EU address its rules to the wider world beyond its territorial borders? More controversially, can third countries become full legal subjects of EU law? The question is controversial, particularly as we claimed above that legal subjectivity traditionally denotes the capability to change the law by which one is governed. This is, indeed, a democratic understanding of a legal subject. Consequently, third countries can be legal subjects only if they are the authors of legal obligations placed on them by the EU. Are third countries the authors of EU law – and could they be?

It is certainly polemical to speak of fully-fledged subjectivity of a third country in the EU, and I do not purport to claim that third countries are already full legal subjects or even that they should have legal subjectivity. Rather, this contribution will serve as an exploration of the impact and effects of Article 11 of the Treaty on the European Union (TEU) on the development of third-country legal subjectivity in the EU. The scope of the chapter is limited to the extent that it is engaged only in finding out whether the incorporation of third-country interests in EU level participatory processes has, since the Lisbon Treaty, been required by the law. Justificatory questions such as whether the EU should consult third countries irrespective of legally binding obligations, and why the EU should consult third countries without international reciprocity on the issue, are not asked.[5]

Article 11 TEU is a key element in discussing the subjectivity of third countries.[6] At first sight, the provision concerns the internal aspects of

---

[4] For an early judicial formulation, see *NV Algemene Transport- en Expeditie Onderneming van Gend & Loos v Netherlands Inland Revenue Administration* (Case 26/62) EU:C:1963:1. This principle is now enshrined in Art.10 TEU on representative democracy.

[5] Benvenisti argues for reinterpretation of sovereigns as trustees of humanity and, even absent any specific treaty obligations, for minimal obligations to take into account the interests of foreigners in formulating and implementing domestic policies. See Benvenisti, Eyal, 'Sovereigns as Trustees of Humanity: On the Accountability of States to Foreign Stakeholders' (2013) 107 *American Journal of International Law* 295.

[6] Note though that this is not the only possibility for third countries to contribute to the EU law-making process. One example is the influence that third countries may exercise on EU law through international or global regimes. In this chapter I will focus exclusively on Art.11 TEU and the opportunities provided by it. More generally on the possibilities of third countries to influence EU's decision-making, see Korkea-aho, Emilia, '"Mr Smith Goes To Brussels": Third

decision-making – the need to consult civil society, EU citizens and non-governmental organizations (NGOs) in decisions taken at EU level – rather than third-country actors as such. Since the Lisbon Treaty, Articles 10 and 11 TEU have served to lay down the foundations of democratic participation in the Union. Whilst the former is written to provide the *citizens* of the EU with participation through the European Parliament and Council, the latter is arguably more inclusive in its approach, and the opportunities of participation it provides are not restricted to EU citizens or representative associations.

I begin by inquiring in Section 2 whether the consequences of EU regulatory action abroad render third countries as the objects of EU law. Section 3 focuses on third countries as potential subjects of the EU legal order and assesses the territorial dimension of Article 11 TEU and the EU's new Better Regulation (BR) guidelines that operationalize Article 11 through impact assessments and public consultations. One essential dimension of legal subjectivity is, as noted above, the capacity to enforce one's rights.[7] Section 4 thus asks whether third-country actors can take any redress in situations where they believe that their rights under Article 11 TEU have not been upheld. The final section provides conclusions and explores the future. If third countries are becoming subjects of the EU legal order, what are the theoretical and practical implications of this process?

2. THIRD COUNTRIES AS OBJECTS OF EU LAW?

As set out above, the main difficulty with the notion of a legal object is that it is difficult to distinguish from legal subject, and the idea of an object as an addressee of the law has hardly any independent content, especially if we adopt a standard meaning of 'legal subject' as someone having rights, powers and duties under the law. However, given the rapid

---

Country Lobbying and the Making of EU Law and Policy', CYELS, accessed 5 February 2017 at *doi.org/10.1017/cel.2016.1.1*. For the special situation of EEA countries, see Gullberg, Anne Therese, 'Lobbying in Oslo or in Brussels? The case of a European Economic Area country' (2015) 22 *Journal of European Public Policy* 1531.

[7] In international law a legal subject is defined as an entity capable of having rights and duties and the capacity to enforce its rights by bringing claims in court. See Cassese, Antonio, *International Law*, 2nd edn (Oxford University Press, Oxford and New York 2005), or Klabbers, Jan, *An Introduction to International Institutional Law*, 2nd edn (Cambridge University Press, Cambridge 2009).

globalization of markets, and the emergence of transnational regulatory environments, the concept of object understood as an 'addressee of the law' has relevance as a tool to probe the territorial limits of political and social action of the EU.

Although conventional wisdom provides that laws are addressed to the citizenry, other audiences can be seen both in what legal texts say and how they say it. In the EU too, third countries are recognized in their own right in the Treaties, although the primary audience is the citizens of the EU. Important in this respect is Article 21 TEU that sets general parameters intended to guide the Union's action on the international scene. Third countries are specifically mentioned in paragraph 2: 'The Union shall seek to develop relations and build partnerships with third countries, and international, regional or global organisations which share the principles referred to in the first subparagraph.' With its emphasis on multi-state relations and promotion of democracy and rule of law in the wider world, Article 21 nevertheless offers a vastly incomplete picture of relations and partnerships between the EU and third countries, even at the treaty level. Primary EU law makes a total of 50 specific references to 'third countries': five are located in the TEU and the remaining 45 in the Treaty on the Functioning of the European Union (TFEU).[8] As a comparison, 'Member States' receive 499 (99+400) references, whilst 'citizens' receive 19 references (14+5). If one takes the figures from all decisions of the Court of Justice of the European Union (CJEU), the numbers tell a similar story: Member States (9834), third countries (2702) and citizens (1077).

A similar exercise cannot easily be repeated for EU secondary law or for relevant literature. However, third countries seem to be the subject of increased attention by scholars working in different fields of EU law. The theme is especially prominent in the literature on the global reach of EU law that has expanded on the picture painted by the treaties. Within this literature, scholars have elaborated the normative and factual implications of the EU legal order for those operating in third countries in policy fields as diverse as merger control, aviation emissions, chemical safety, data protection and animal welfare.[9] The concrete ways in which EU law

---

[8] Fahey and Bardutzky, chapter 1 of this volume. All references to third countries in the TEU are references to states as an entity, whereas in the TFEU references are occasionally made to 'third country nationals'. Neither contains references to third-country economic operators.

[9] Fiebig, Andre, 'The Extraterritorial Application of the European Merger Control Regulation' (Fall 1998/Winter 1999) 5 Colum. J. Eur. L. 79; Scott, Joanne, 'Extraterritoriality and Territorial Extension in EU Law' (2014) 62

affects third-country conditions vary according to the context, as does the nature of this reach that can range from extraterritorial effects of EU legislation to power that the EU exerts through its internal market.[10] The effects of EU law on third countries may also be a result of judicial intervention, as demonstrated by a recent ruling. The European Court of Justice ruled that animal tests performed outside the EU should not be used for product safety assessment inside the EU, effectively extending the reach of a ban on animal testing in cosmetics outside the EU.[11]

The effects in the internal market fields are especially straightforward, as disregard for EU rules may result in denied access for third-country origin goods.[12] Does this mean we can now assume that these EU rules that are de facto binding on third-country operators thereby turn them into objects of EU law? There are at least two objections to this approach. First, the argument can be made that third-country actors are not objects of EU law, as they can decide whether or not to obey the law, using again the internal market example, by simply avoiding the EU market. Freedom to not obey does not, however, convince, as it does not differentiate third-country actors from EU actors who can also choose to exit. In addition, the choice is often purely hypothetical if operators have no real possibilities to bear financial and otherwise consequences of the exit decision.

Second, although EU law regulates the conduct of third-country actors, the primary direct addressees and those who could face liability prescribed by the law are EU actors. This is a valid consideration, and in

---

American Journal of Comparative Law 87; Scott, J, 'The New EU "Extraterritoriality"' (2014) 51 *Common Market Law Review* 1343; Scott, J, 'The Geographical Scope of the EU's Climate Responsibilities' (2015) 18 CYELS; Kuner, Christopher, 'Extraterritoriality and Regulation of International Data Transfers in EU Data Protection Law' (2015) 5 *International Data Privacy Law* 235; Fahey, Elaine, *Global Reach of EU Law* (Routledge, Abingdon 2016).

[10] For the ways in which the EU can influence third countries even without imposing 'binding' rules on them, see Bradford, Anu, 'The Brussels Effect' (2012) 107 *Northwestern University Law Review* 1 and Damro, Chad, 'Market Power Europe: Exploring a Dynamic Conceptual Framework' (2015) 22 *Journal of European Public Policy* 1336.

[11] *European Federation for Cosmetic Ingredients v Secretary of State for Business, Innovation and Skills and Others* (Case C-592/14) EU:C:2016:703.

[12] In EU chemicals legislation this rule is called 'no data no market'. See Regulation (EC) No 1907/2006 of the European Parliament and Council of 18 December 2006 concerning the the Registration, Evaluation, Authorisation and Restriction of Chemicals (REACH), establishing a European Chemicals Agency [2007] OJ L396, Art.5.

order to uphold this idea in the era of the globalized internal market, the EU has developed new legal constructs. In EU chemicals law, for instance, chemicals manufacturers are obliged to register their substances and this requirement extends to substances manufactured outside the EU if they are intended for the internal market.[13] Third-country operators per se do not incur duties, and the obliged entity is instead an EU-based representative ('only representative') appointed by a third-country operator to take care of the duties under EU law.[14]

However, third-country actors can also be directly affected on the basis of application of EU law on several occasions. For instance, in the context of an EU-wide system for monitoring and enforcing aviation safety, non-EU airlines may be banned from operating in European airspace if they are found to be unsafe and/or they are not sufficiently overseen by their own authorities.[15] If a third-country airline is in this manner subject to a duty of compliance and may rely on enforcement mechanisms, then it might be difficult to qualify the airline merely as an object/addressee of EU law.

Although not settling the issue of third countries as objects of EU law conclusively, the ideas discussed above helped to establish that EU law addresses, indirectly at least, third countries, limiting their autonomous agency. The analysis also demonstrated that in an increasing number of situations the concept of object understood as an 'addressee of the law' is insufficient to capture the significance of EU law for third countries, necessitating an analysis of third countries as subjects of EU law.

3. THIRD COUNTRIES AS SUBJECTS OF EU LAW? THE EXTRATERRITORIALITY OF ARTICLE 11 TEU

3.1 Article 11 TEU as an Obligation

Since it was introduced by the Treaty of Lisbon, much has been written about the legal nature of Article 11 TEU.[16] Although the Lisbon Treaty

---

13 REACH, Art.1.

14 REACH, Art.8.

15 Regulation (EC) No 2111/2005 of the European Parliament and the Council of 14 December 2005 on the establishment of a Community list of air carriers subject to an operating ban within the Community and on informing air transport passengers of the identity of the operating air carrier.

16 Mendes, Joana, *Participation in EU Rule-Making. A Rights-Based Approach* (Oxford University Press, Oxford 2011) ('Mendes 2011(a)'); Mendes,

did not retain the title of 'participatory democracy' originally envisaged by the Constitutional Treaty, it is clear that Article 11 sets out the democratic principle of participation. Participatory democracy, at least how it is understood by the treaties, can take many forms, from open consultations and civil society dialogues to citizens' legislative initiative. Although Article 11 is a novelty, its incorporation by the Lisbon Treaty, with the exception of citizens' legislative initiative, amounts more to 'a symbolic recognition of a long-established custom than an innovation in the democratic foundations of the European Union'.[17]

It would, however, be a mistake to think that nothing changed. The treaty enshrinement constitutionalized the custom and contributed to cementing participation as an essential element of the Union's political and institutional framework.[18] Whilst Article 11 is undeniably premised on instrumental reasoning – participation enhances transparency and predictability, promotes trust and acceptability and so on – it is clear that, for the first time, a Treaty article links participation to democracy, elevating participation to one of the foundations of democracy in the EU. Has the constitutionalization of the principle of participation given rise to rights that can be directly enforced by individuals before the courts? Commenting on a general level, Mendes argues that 'the fact that it is now a Treaty norm is not without consequences. At least, what is in essence a discretionary choice of the institutions is a now *a norm of conduct by which the institutions need to abide*, irrespective of the means chosen to give it effect'.[19]

The normative bite of Article 11 is, however, considerably weakened due to difficulties in establishing the precise meaning of Article 11. The terminological uncertainties that prevail are the effect of inconsistent use

---

J, 'Participation and the role of law after Lisbon: A legal view on Article 11 TEU' (2011) 48 *Common Market Law Review* 1849 ('Mendes 2011(b)'); Marxsen, Christian, 'Participatory Democracy in Europe – Article 11 TEU and the Legitimacy of the European Union' in Fabbrini, Federico, et al. (eds), *What Form of Government for the European Union and the Eurozone?* (Hart Publishing, Oxford 2015) 151–69; Mendes, J, 'The Democratic Foundations of the Union: Representative Democracy, Complementarity and the Legal Challenge of Article 11 TEU' in Lazowski, Adam, and Steven Blockmans (eds), *Research Handbook on EU Institutional Law* (Edward Elgar Publishing, Cheltenham and Northampton 2016).

[17] Mendes 2011(a), 140.

[18] Von Bogdandy, Armin, 'Founding Principles' in Von Bogdandy, Armin, and Jürgen Bast (eds), *Principles of European Constitutional Law* (Hart, Oxford 2010) 21–3.

[19] Mendes 2011(a), 140 (emphasis added), also Mendes 2016, 180.

of concepts such as 'civil society' and 'representative associations' in different parts of the Article. Much depends on how EU institutions, especially the Commission, interpret the nature and scope of the obligations it lays down. Legal rules are required to give effect to Article 11 and, as yet, the procedures and conditions required for the implementation of Treaty rights have been determined only for the citizens' initiative.[20] Some guidance can be found in the EU's Better Regulation (BR) guidelines which I will analyze below. Prior to this, I will determine whether Article 11 TEU has a scope of application outside the EU.

3.2 Territorial Scope of Article 11 TEU

Article 11 TEU is divided into four specific provisions. The first requires the institutions to give citizens and representative associations the opportunity to make known and publicly exchange their views in all areas of Union action. There is profound recognition that political ownership needs to go beyond the institutions themselves, with a critical role to be played by 'citizens' and 'representative associations'.

Neither concept is explicitly associated with any particular region or geographical background, suggesting that to the extent that the exchange of views concerns matters falling in the scope of Union action, entitled actors do not need to claim to be EU citizens or associations operating in the EU. However, what can potentially emerge as a territorially limiting factor to the expansive reading of Article 11(1) is that the concepts are commonly considered as part of the vocabulary of representative democracy. The rights under Article 10 TEU, which lays down the maxim that the EU is founded on representative democracy, benefit only the citizens of the Union. Should the more (territorially) restrictive approach taken in Article 10 apply to Article 11 as well? The interpretation of the geographical scope of the rights granted by Article 11(1) should be determined in conjunction with other Article rights. The second subparagraph is also addressed to the institutions, obliging them to maintain an open, transparent and regular dialogue with representative associations and civil society. It builds on Article 11(1) but complicates the determination of the scope of application by introducing a new concept: 'civil society'. No further guidance is provided as to what constitutes civil society: Is it a concept used narrowly to cover only EU citizens and their associations or can it serve as a framework for forging a global civil society out of those affected by EU activities?

---

[20] Mendes 2016, 176.

The third specific provision enshrined in Article 11 concerns the Commission's responsibility to organize public consultations with a view to regulating in a coherent and transparent manner.[21] This particular provision is unlike the other two in several respects. First, the institution bound by Article 11(3) is the Commission. Second, those entitled on the basis of Article 11(3) potentially constitute a large group, as the provision has a distinctly broader scope than the previous provisions, covering 'parties concerned'. The definition is neither used in the same article nor anywhere else in the treaties, but the plain English meaning refers to those having an interest or involvement in something. Third, whilst the other two provisions seem to indicate that the functioning of civil society is a (democratic) value in itself, the consultation process under Article 11(3) is tied up with the instrumental view of participation, ensuring the coherence and transparency of Union action.

The final provision leaves no leeway for interpretative argument as far as its territorial scope is concerned. Article 11(4) contains provisions on a European citizens' initiative: No fewer than one million citizens who are *nationals of a significant number of Member States* may take the initiative of inviting the Commission, within the framework of its powers, to submit any appropriate proposal on matters where citizens consider that a legal act of the Union is required for the purpose of implementing the Treaties.[22] Article 11(4) undeniably excludes third-country actors from its scope, which suggests that EU legislature clearly indicated that its purpose was not to extend this form of participation beyond the boundaries of the EU.

If one looks closely at this Article of the Treaty, the provisions it lays down can be categorized, according to their content, into three groups of rules. First, the breadth of Article 11(3) is clear in the definition of 'parties concerned' which includes a wide range of actors. It seems

---

[21] See also Protocol No. 2 on the application of the principles of subsidiarity and proportionality annexed to the Treaty that stipulates that, before proposing legislative acts, the Commission shall consult widely. Apart from this general requirement in Article 11 TEU to consult widely, are there any specific provisions obliging the EU to consult third countries? These are rare, but recently adopted EU financial market legislation includes provisions that require the EU to take into account international developments and include the views of foreign entities as it adopts delegated or implementing acts or amends Annexes. See, for example, Recital 71 of Regulation 1060/2009 Credit Rating Agencies (CRAs) [2009] OJ L146.

[22] Regulation (EU) No 211/2011 of 16 February 2011 on the citizens' initiative [2011] OJ L65. See Dougan, Michael, 'What are we to make of the citizens' initiative?' (2011) 48 *Common Market Law Review* 1807.

plausible not to differentiate between actors on the basis of where they are located geographically, as EU and non-member actors are both capable of proving an interest in EU action as a prerequisite for eligibility for participation. Besides citizens, civil society and representative associations already referred to, the parties concerned may also comprise third-country governments, corporations or other entities physically based or legally established outside the EU. Second, there is Article 11(4), which contains a clearly worded exclusion of nationals of other than Member States. Between these two poles are Articles 11(1) and (2) which together constitute the third relevant category.

Whilst admitting that there is some ambiguity in defining their scope of application, the view defended here is that Articles 11(1), (2), and (3) TEU should not be interpreted narrowly to cover only EU citizens and representative associations.[23] In my view, limiting the scope of application of Treaty provisions must be based on an unequivocal limitation in the treaties themselves, as in Article 11(4) or Article 15(3) TEU, which restricts right of access to documents to 'any citizen of the Union, and any natural or legal person residing or having its registered office in a Member State'.[24]

Would the broad scope of application result in a surge in a multiplicity of administrative procedures that the EU organizes in the legislative process, thereby increasing concerns about the EU's capability of coping with unlimited participation rights? The worry is not entirely unfounded, as the Commission struggled to process a total of 149,399 online contributions on its public consultation on investor protection and ISDS in the proposed Transatlantic Trade and Investment Partnership (TTIP) negotiation outcome.[25] Although non-EU companies and NGOs were among the respondents, their overall contribution was marginal, and it is

---

[23] No case law exists on the issue. It is not unlikely that the Court would interpret these provisions in a teleological manner. One could argue that the idea of Article 11 is to pay tribute to the EU demos, which is limited to people residing in Member States. However, it is equally plausible to argue that its purpose is to extend participation to those affected by EU law.

[24] Another matter that cannot be discussed here is that the territorially limited scope of Article 15(3) TEU hinders the effective exercise of rights provided by Article 11 TEU.

[25] The final report on the consultation was published on 13 January 2015, accessed 5 February 2017 at *trade.ec.europa.eu/doclib/press/index.cfm?id=1234*.

unlikely that the numbers of non-EU participation would ever threaten the proper functioning of the EU legislative process.[26]

In May 2015, six years after the entry into force of the Lisbon Treaty, the Commission adopted the updated Better Regulation Package with two distinct sets of rules. The main guidelines set out the mandatory requirements and obligations for each step in the policy cycle, while the "toolbox" rules provide additional guidance and advice which is not binding unless expressly stated so.[27] Below I analyze rules on impact assessments and public consultations as a means of concretizing Article 11, in particular from the perspective of how inclusive they are of third-country actors.

3.3 Operationalization of Article 11 TEU through Impact Assessments

Coordinated by the Commission, impact assessment (IA) is an administrative exercise intended to analyze diffent policy options on the basis of their economic, social and environmental impacts. Since 2005, the EU's IA guidelines have contained a section on international impacts.[28] Every IA had to establish whether a proposed policy option has an impact on relations with third countries, with specific reference to three issues: the competitiveness of European business, trade relations with third countries, and impacts on developing countries.[29] New BR guidelines strategize differently. They make no attempt at a systematic treatment of the subject 'third countries', nor devise a particular policy recommendation for third countries; instead, references to third countries are found everywhere in the guidelines and the accompanying toolbox rules. The

---

[26] Public consultations are published on the Commission 'Your Voice in Europe' website. Approximately 100 public consultations are organized annually. For modest numbers of non-EU participation, see Rasmussen, Anne, and Petya Alexandrova, 'Foreign interests lobbying Brussels: participation of non-EU members in Commission consultations' (2012) 50 *Journal of Common Market Studies* 614.

[27] European Commission, *Better Regulation Guidelines*, COM(2015) 215 final 4.

[28] For a comparison of EU and US IA and public consultation practices, see Berman, Ayelet, 'Taking Foreign Interests into Account: Rulemaking in the US and EU' (1 May 2016) Int' J. Const. Law, forthcoming. Accessed 5 February 2017 at SSRN: *ssrn.com/abstract=2722635*.

[29] European Commission, *Impact Assessment Guidelines*, COM(2009) 42.

main message is, nevertheless, the same as before: impacts outside the EU are part of the analysis.[30]

What types of impact outside the EU are detected through an IA? The recognition and elaboration of external effects of EU action in the BR guidelines is a trade-focused exercise geared towards detecting market barriers as it has been in the past. Neither societal impacts nor impacts on developing countries receive much attention.[31] In the BR guidelines there is only one explicit reference to employment, social protection or poverty impacts in non-Member States,[32] and one concerning environmental impacts in third countries.[33] Much like its predecessor, the new BR guidelines require that possible inconsistencies with obligations undertaken at the World Trade Organization (WTO) or in international agreements have to be explained and removed if possible.[34] However,

---

[30] European Commission, *Better Regulation "Toolbox"* (2015) 47.

[31] The same could be said of the old EU rules. They also included predominantly EU-centric impacts, as in, how does the proposal impact the EU's relationship with these actors, not how does it impact the third country.

[32] Better Regulation "Toolbox", 107.

[33] Better Regulation "Toolbox", 107. The EU has an obligation to ensure that its trade agreements do not harm human rights abroad. See Council of the European Union, *Strategic Framework and Action Plan on Human Rights and Democracy*, Luxembourg 25 June 2012 11855/12. See also European Commission, Directorate-General for Trade, *Guidelines on the analysis of human rights impacts in impact assessments for trade-related policy initiatives*, accessed 5 February 2017 at *trade.ec.europa.eu/doclib/docs/2015/july/tradoc_153591.pdf*. According to Commission guidelines, human rights impact assessment consultation 'is as broad as possible, both inside and outside the EU'. See *Guidelines on the analysis of human rights impacts in impact assessments for trade-related policy initiatives* (above) 11.

[34] Better Regulation Guidelines, 23, also 83. The EU is bound by the commitments it has made under public international law and in particular by the requirements of WTO law to give consideration to third-country interests. For instance, the Agreement on Agriculture determines that 'Where any Member institutes any new export prohibition or restriction on foodstuffs … it shall give due consideration to the effects of such prohibition or restriction on importing Members' food security … before any Member institutes an export prohibition or restriction, it shall give notice in writing, as far in advance as practicable.' See Agreement on Agriculture, 15 April 1994 Marrakesh Agreement Establishing the World Trade Organization, Annex 1A, Art.12. Similarly, the Agreement on Technical Barriers to Trade (TBT) lays down that 'Members shall ensure that technical regulations are not prepared, adopted or applied with a view to or with the effect of creating unnecessary obstacles to international trade.' See Agreement on Technical Barriers to Trade, 15 April 1994, Marrakesh Agreement Establishing the World Trade Organization, Annex 1A, 1868 U.N.T.S. 120,

mere 'technical' compliance with international agreements will no longer be sufficient, with the BR guidelines having shifted the focus from compliance to actively pursuing convergence with third countries. The IA must verify whether or not the proposal will contribute to greater regulatory convergence with the EU's main trade partners (such as US, Japan, China).[35] In addition, when developing a new regulation or standard, the analysis should contain an evaluation of the main regulations affecting the products/services covered by the proposal in major third countries' markets and a comparison between these regulations. Therefore, it is stressed that the final IA Report 'will need to recall the reasons for any divergence from international standards as well as from regulation with similar ambition in major jurisdictions whenever regulatory divergence may have a significant negative impact on trade and investment flows'.[36]

Consulting interested parties is an obligation for every IA and it must follow the minimum standards and guidelines described in the BR guidelines. An open and internet-based consultation is required for all impact assessments 'as it ensures transparency and accountability and gives *any* interested party the possibility to contribute'.[37] Relevant constituencies will depend on the nature of the problem, and the identification of affected groups is always a highly contextualized assessment.[38] The Commission instructs its officials to 'think beyond the

---

Art.2(2). Pursuant to this agreement, the EU notifies other WTO members of the proposed technical regulations. For the notification process, see Sørensen, Karsten Engsig, 'Technical Regulations and Their Notification' in Gaines, Sanford E, Birgitte Egelund Olsen and KE Sørensen (eds), *Liberalising Trade in the EU and the WTO: A Legal Comparison* (Cambridge University Press, Cambridge 2012). Note that under WTO law only those technical regulations with a significant effect on trade of other Members need be notified. See ibid. 275.

[35] Better Regulation "Toolbox", 157.

[36] Note 35, 102.

[37] Note 35, 57 (emphasis added). The EU 2009 IA Guidelines specifically instructed that the Commission must 'always include all target groups and sectors which will be significantly affected by or involved in policy implementation, *including those outside the EU*'. See COM(2009) 42, 14 (emphasis added).

[38] For the non-exhaustive definition of the 'affected parties, groups or regions', see Better Regulation Guidelines at p. 26: 'businesses of different sizes (SMEs or not), citizens, workers, learners, consumers, public administrations, third country actors, developing countries, different territories and regions (less developed or prosperous regions, cities, rural areas, border regions, overseas territories etc.)'. See also Better Regulation "Toolbox", 48 and 97.

narrow boundaries of the specific policy sector': specific instructions exist to distinguish within categories (i.e. micro, small, medium-sized and large enterprises), to look at non-EU actors (i.e. developing countries, non-EU producers etc.) and to differentiate across Member States and/or EU regions.[39]

The especial status of trade impacts is also visible from the concern that the Commission raises with regard to public consultations in IAs: it is important 'when consulting stakeholders in the IA context to provide *equal* opportunities for third country operators and EU importers to express their views'.[40]

3.4 Operationalization of Article 11 TEU through Public Consultations

Consultation is a formal Commission-driven process by which, early in the policy-making process, the EU collects input and views from stakeholders about its policies to precede their implementation. In 2002, the Commission published a Communication laying down general principles and minimum standards for consultation: the objective of consultations, how and when the consultations should occur, who should be consulted, and how stakeholder comments should be considered.[41] The Communication is still applicable, and the new BR guidelines should only complement and clarify the existing principles and practices.[42]

A general principle underlying the 2002 Communication is the idea that consultation should target everyone 'affected by the policy', a formulation that appears to cover parties irrespective of where they are in the world. Wide consultation is generally held to be useful in developing effective policies, and the usefulness of the consultation is maximized if the proposals are endorsed by the widest possible constituency of interests.[43] Third countries are also explicitly mentioned: '[d]epending on the issues at stake, consultation is intended to provide opportunities for input from representatives of regional and local authorities, civil society organisations, undertakings and associations of undertakings, the

---

[39] Better Regulation "Toolbox", 66.

[40] Better Regulation "Toolbox", 155 (emphasis added).

[41] See European Commission, *Towards a reinforced culture of consultation and dialogue – General principles and minimum standards for consultation of interested parties by the Commission*, COM(2002) 704 final (emphasis added).

[42] Better Regulation Guidelines, 55.

[43] Better Regulation Guidelines, 8.

individual citizens concerned, academics and technical experts, *and interested parties in third countries*'.[44]

The BR guidelines further explicate that the purpose of consultations is to seek a balanced and comprehensive coverage of interests, covering 'social, economic and environmental bodies; large and small organisations or companies; wider constituencies (e.g. religious communities) and specific target groups (e.g. women, the elderly, the unemployed, ethnic minorities), *organisations in the EU and those in non-member countries* (e.g. candidate, associated or developing countries or major trading partners of the EU)'.[45] Concern for third-country economic actors is evident in the BR guidelines' repeated emphasis that businesses can be affected differently by the concrete initiative, depending on, among other things, whether they are located in the internal market or in third countries, and therefore careful differentiation within specific stakeholder categories is necessary.[46]

While the new BR guidelines provide much greater detail than the 2002 Communication, describing extensive methodologies for 'stakeholder mapping' and setting out consultation methods for 'relevant' stakeholders based on pre-established criteria, they still ultimately rely on individual Commission staff to identify the relevant target groups and avoid excluding those potentially affected. For the US this seems to be a cause for concern: 'Given the breadth of these potentially interested parties in many cases, it would appear to be quite challenging for a single Directorate-General to be confident that it has identified all "relevant parties" in the European Union, *not to mention "stakeholders and citizens outside the European institutions and bodies"*'.[47] Another difference between the earlier policy and the new BR guidelines is that the former required consideration of external voices in situations in which the proposal is thought to have international relevance. For instance, the Commission in the 2001 White Paper on European Governance committed itself to 'improve the dialogue with governmental and non-governmental actors of non-member countries *when developing policy*

[44] Note 41, 4.

[45] Better Regulation Guidelines, 75.

[46] Better Regulation Guidelines, 74.

[47] Comments of the United States on the European Commission's Public Consultation Document setting out Draft Stakeholder Consultation Guidelines, published on 30 June 2014, 13, accessed 6 February 2017 at *photos.state.gov/libraries/useu/231771/PDFs/USresponseConsultGuidelinesfinal.pdf*.

proposals with an international dimension'.[48] That the BR guidelines have dropped references to the international dimension as a prerequisite for an international dialogue contains a powerful message that the participation of actors of third countries is now a norm rather than a cosmetic exception.

The conclusion from the preceding sections is twofold. First, what clearly arises from the above is the care that the EU takes in including third-country actors, in particular economic operators, in impact assessments and consultations. There is no trade-off between nationality and access to the legislative process for third-country actors. Instead, what can best be described as 'access deficit' emerges between economic and non-economic actors, not between EU actors and those in third countries.[49] Second, the analysis would seem to suggest that the question we should be asking is not whether third countries 'are' legal subjects or not. It is more about whether they are de facto treated as subjects regardless of their formal status, and whether the regularity of such factual treatment is capable of creating legitimate expectations of third-country subjectivity.

4. CAN THIRD COUNTRIES ENFORCE THEIR RIGHT TO BE CONSULTED?

An important part of legal subjectivity is the capability to enforce rights in courts, hence contributing to the implementation and enforcement of the law.

There are, however, several problems in even raising the question of enforcement in relation to Article 11. Whilst participation is one of the fundamental principles that now underlie the EU as a legal and political system, Article 11 does not necessarily translate into legally enforceable provisions. It has been argued that it is only Article 11(1) that would support the recognition of rights,[50] and the essence of duties under

---

[48] See European Commission, *European Governance – A White Paper* COM(2001) 428 final, 22 (emphasis added).

[49] An argument which cannot be discussed here is that the BR guidelines on public consultation and impact assessment are drafted to advance economic virtues, not, for instance, to contribute to inclusiveness and equality of representation, thus disregarding the origin of these processes in normative requirements flowing from Art.11.

[50] Mendes 2011(b), 14. The same provision would possibly also support the finding of direct applicability.

Article 11(2) and (3) is found in the norm of conduct guiding the institutions' choices as they give them effect. It is not at all unlikely that any annulment actions introduced to contest the lack of consultation would fail on the merits.

Moreover, the Commission itself has long been opposed to what it sees as the juridification of participation, arguing that it has wide discretion as to how to discharge its obligations to consult and communicate effectively with civil society.[51] Painstaking efforts have been made by the Commission to ensure that no rights can be derived from the content of the new BR guidelines. Article 11 duties are treated as a means to an end, as a means to ensure that the institutions have enough information to make decisions, not as giving normative shape to the position of citizens as holders of legally protected interests.[52] The right to be consulted is better understood as a right of the Commission to receive information. This general philosophy is also well encapsulated by the opening statement of the BR guidelines: 'the aim of the guidelines is not to respect procedural requirements per se but to ensure that the Commission is equipped with relevant information on which to base its decision in a timely manner.'[53]

To be sure, legal challenges would be difficult to envisage even in the hypothetical situation where the Commission is required by express provisions of the law to consult the main trading partners in impact assessment. The conditions which private applicants must satisfy to establish standing to bring annulment proceeding under Article 263 TFEU are strict, and non-privileged applicants are almost certainly destined to fail. This is true for all private applicants, both EU and non-EU. Other EU institutions, as privileged applicants, have never challenged the way in which the Commission has undertaken impact assessments. The European Parliament (EP) could perhaps use its preferential status under Article 263 TFEU and start annulment proceedings against the Commission. However, it is likely that the EP would use this rather strong weapon sparingly, since legal proceedings inevitably upset good working relations between the two institutions. The EU Ombudsman could intervene in the non-application of hypothetical rules on impact assessment, but in the absence of legal norms it is unlikely that

---

[51] See COM(2001) 428 final.

[52] Mendes 2011(a), 141. The latter, what Mendes calls 'a thicker meaning of participation', is restricted to procedures that lead up to the adoption of formal individual decisions.

[53] Better Regulation Guidelines, 4.

the EU Ombudsman would find that the lack of consultation constitutes maladministration.

No effective accountability mechanisms are in place to provide redress in situations where actors feel that their views have not been taken into account. However, the point to be proven lies elsewhere. Except for the EU Ombudsman, all other avenues discussed above are accessible to third-country actors.[54] Third-country actors do not need to overcome any additional procedural hurdles in order to challenge EU measures: as provided by Article 19(3) TEU, actions can be 'brought by a Member State, an institution or a natural or legal person'. EU actions are open to challenge, irrespective of the geographical location of the complainant.

5. CONCLUSIONS: ON THE ROAD TOWARDS FULL LEGAL SUBJECTIVITY?

Contributing to a larger body of evolving literature on the EU as a global actor, this book chapter deployed the subject-object theoretical framework to interrogate the extent to which the EU conceptualizes and identifies third countries as addressees of its rules and whether, as a consequence of such developments, third countries are becoming full legal subjects in the EU legal order.

The description 'third country' entails a starting point of the analysis, for the meaning of the phrase relies on the fact that third countries do not belong to the legal order created by the constitutive treaty of EU Member States. Third countries are, nevertheless, recognized in their own right in the Treaties, and the EU courts' case law and secondary legislation affect and constrain the conduct of third-country actors both in market and non-market contexts. Consequently, viewing third countries through a prism of an object/addressee of the EU legal order is an increasingly insufficient account of a multiplicity of rights, duties and responsibilities contained in, and attached to, the role of third country.

The question whether third countries have then gained the subject status was answered by exploring the impact and effects of Article 11 TEU on participation of third countries in the legislative process in the EU. The argument put forward is that, notwithstanding the citizens' initiative which is unequivocally limited to EU actors, the Treaty provision should not be interpreted narrowly to cover only EU citizens

---

[54] The EU Ombudsman's mandate is territorially limited to citizens or residents of a Member State as well as to businesses, associations or other bodies with a registered office in the Union, see Art.228(1) TFEU.

and representative associations, and the EU is legally required to extend practices of participation to all those affected by EU law, also including third countries. Analysis of the EU's BR rules on public consultation and impact assessments from the perspective of how inclusive they are of external interests shows that third-country consultation is more a norm than an exception in practice.

Those concerned with the existence of the EU as a political union might now be tempted to argue that there should be formal limits to the participation of third-country actors, as communities must be finite and cannot be held accountable for including every possible interest outside their territories.[55] This may well be the case, but such an argument can be good only up to the point that the EU accepts that some limits are needed to circumscribe its own global role, as well.[56] Allowing third-country actors to participate in the making of EU law goes some way towards counterbalancing the important role that EU rules have in the wider world.

Perhaps more critical and urgent than the imposition of limits on the participation of third countries is to ask why the EU consults third countries. There is very little said of rationales for extending participation beyond the EU. For the Commission, third-country participation is a high-level political mechanism to ensure global regulatory convergence and compliance with the EU's international obligations. The special role afforded to concerns of economic operators underlines the instrumental view. The issues that are then raised in relation to the equality of representation and whether third-country economic actors may be advantaged over EU non-economic actors need to be further explored.

Where does this lead us in identifying and conceptualizing third-country subjectivity? Is third-country subjectivity possible – and could it be? Perhaps the evolution of the role of third countries in EU law could be best described as a gradual movement towards full legal subjectivity. They started off as little more than the objects of EU legislation, but as time has passed they have taken on rights and obligations in much the

---

55 In the EU context, see especially Maduro, Miguel, 'The Importance of Being Called a Constitution: Constitutional Authority and the Authority of Constitutionalism' (2005) 3 Int'l J. Const. Law; Regan, Donald H, 'An Outsider's View of Dassonville and Cassis de Dijon: On Interpretation and Policy' in Maduro, Miguel, and Loïc Azoulai (eds), *The Past and Future of EU Law: The Classics of EU Law Revisited on the 50th Anniversary of the Rome Treaty* (Hart, Oxford 2010). See also Joseph Corkin, Chapter 5 of this volume.

56 For the thin constitutional limits of the EU's global role, see Fahey 2016, note 9 above.

same way as Member States and citizens.[57] Whilst their position is still incomplete, third countries are factually treated as subjects in Article 11 processes, consequently giving rise to third countries' normatively grounded expectations of legal subjectivity. Then again, taking into account the unique way in which EU law functions, incompleteness and complexity of factual and normative considerations may very well be traits that characterize all its subjects, not just those outside the EU.

[57] Cities appear to be undergoing a similar process, see Josephine van Zeben, Chapter 7 in this volume.

12. From objects to subjects: paving the way for third countries and their natural and legal persons

Ilaria Vianello*

INTRODUCTION

The Treaty of Lisbon makes clear that the Union, when acting on the international scene, shall not only promote the rule of law, but shall also respect it in the development and implementation of its external action.[1] Even if it is easy to belittle such idealistic ambition, this obligation implies the need to address the principles that should govern the EU's conduct towards its international partners and their citizens in a relational sense. It requires redefining the 'actorness' of the European Union (EU) in its relations with third countries as well as the 'actorness' of the third countries themselves. Respect for the rule of law demands that the framework of external action (not the substance of its policies!) should abide by certain procedural standards.[2] The development of procedural standards that would regulate the relations between the Union and third states (including their natural and legal persons) is hindered by – among

* Helpful comments were provided by the editors of this book Samo Bardutzky and Elaine Fahey, as well as by Edoardo Chiti and the anonymous reviewers. This chapter has also benefited from the discussions with Marise Cremona and Joana Mendes. All remaining mistakes and inconsistencies are, of course, of my own making.

[1] Articles 3(5), 21(1) and 21(3) of the Treaty on European Union [2010] OJ C83/01, (hereafter TEU).

[2] Vianello, I., 'Taking a look outside: the rule of law structuring the relations between the EU and its external partners', in Cremona, M. (ed.), *Structural Principles in External Relations Law* (Hart, Oxford, forthcoming).

others – the CJEU's narrow understanding of subjects in EU law.[3] By defining as subjects only those entities which are recognised under a body of principles and rules, the Court constrains itself from the possibility of moving from the grammar to the pragmatics of the law. In other words, by limiting the definition of subjects of EU law to 'rights holders', the Court misses the opportunity to discuss and evaluate the numerous developments in European law which do have an impact on third countries and their natural and legal persons beyond legally recognised rights.[4]

The aim of this chapter is to discuss how a more encompassing definition of subjects of EU law could support the articulation of the rule of law in the external domain, and could consequently challenge the classical approach of treating third states and their natural and legal persons as objects of EU law and policies. While such a discussion could be the topic of an entire monograph, this chapter will focus only on the Union's policies towards the Western Balkans (Stabilisation and Association Process)[5] and towards its Eastern and Southern neighbours (European Neighbourhood Policy).[6] The EU recreates with these countries a

---

[3] The original framing of subjects of EU law was developed and formulated by the Court in its famous *Van Gend en Loos* case: *NV Algemene Transporten Expeditie Onderneming Van Gend en Loos v Nederlandse Administratis der Belastingen* (Case 26/62) ECLI:EU:C:1963:1. See Fahey, E., and S. Bardutzky, chapter 1 of this book for an in-depth analysis of the case.

[4] For example, see: *Yedaş Tarim ve Otomotiv Sanayi ve Ticaret AŞ v Council of the European Union and Commission of the European Communities* (Case T-367/03) ECLI:EU:T:2006:96; *Krikorian v European Parliament, Council and Commission*, Case T-346/03 ECLI:EU:T:2003:348; *Cemender Korkmaz, Corner House Research, and The Kurdish Human Rights project v Commission* (Case T-2/04) ECLI:EU:T:2006:97; *P Mugraby v Council and Commission* (Case C-581/11) ECLI:EU:C:2012:466.

[5] The Stabilisation and Association Process (SAP) is the Union's regional approach initiated by the Commission in 1999 in order to assist the Western Balkan countries in meeting the relevant EU accession criteria and ultimately be accepted as Member States. For a comprehensive analysis of the policy see: Blockmans, S., *Tough Love: The European Union's Relations with the Western Balkans* (T.M.C. Asser Press, The Hague 2007).

[6] The European Neighbourhood Policy (ENP) is chiefly a bilateral policy between the EU and each neighbouring country (e.g. Ukraine, Moldova, Georgia, Egypt, Tunisia, Morocco, etc.) and it does not envisage accession. The EU offers its neighbours a privileged relationship including political association, deeper economic integration, increased mobility, and a very concrete set of opportunities through its sector policies. For a comprehensive analysis on the policy see: Cremona, M., 'The European Neighbourhood Policy More than a Partnership?',

mode of foreign governance that sees a proliferation of administrative activities that have a significant impact on the third states to which they are addressed and on the life of their citizens.[7] The Stabilisation and Association Process (SAP) and the European Neighbourhood Policy (ENP) are particularly interesting for the purpose of this chapter because the relations between the Union and the states taking part in these two policies are – despite their impact – not always framed within clear legal procedures, especially if compared to the relations between the Union and the EFTA countries.[8] Thus, they best exemplify the importance of embracing a more comprehensive definition of subjects of EU law. Finally, the analysis will not cover third-country nationals relaying on the direct effect of international treaties provisions concluded by the Union with a third state. This chapter is not so much interested in the obligations stemming from the international agreements concluded by the Union with third states, but rather with those that develop outside a clear legal framework.

The chapter will proceed as follows. First, it will highlight how the Union's neighbours have so far been considered by the Union legal order as passive receivers of Union policies. Second, it will explain how the obligation to respect the rule of law in the way the EU develops and implements its external policies demands rethinking the role of third states (including their citizens) within the Union policy cycle. Finally, the paper will discuss how a broader definition of subjects of EU law could support moving the Union's neighbours from being passive objects to being active subjects in the SAP and the ENP framework.

---

in Cremona, M. (ed.), *Development in EU External Relations Law* (Oxford University Press, Oxford 2008), 245–300.

[7] Tulmets, E., 'Experimentalist Governance in EU External Relations: Enlargement and the European Neighbourhood Policy', in Sabel, C.F., and J. Zeitlin (eds), *Experimentalist Governance in the European Union Towards a New Architecture* (Oxford University Press, Oxford 2010), 297, 312; de Búrca, G., 'EU External Relations: The Governance Mode of Foreign Policy', in Van Vooren, B., S. Blockmans and J. Wouters (eds), *The EU's Role in Global Governance: The Legal Dimension* (Oxford University Press, Oxford 2013), 39, 42.

[8] Fenger, N., M. Sanchez Rydelski and T. Van Stiphout, *European Free Trade Association (EFTA) and the European Economic Area (EEA)* (Wolters Kluwer Law & Business, Alphen aan den Rijn 2012), Part II, 53–165.

1. OBJECTS: PASSIVE RECEIVERS OF UNION EXTERNAL ACTION

The external relations of the European Union besides agreements – the most traditional form of conducting international relations – are characterised by an increasing use of alternative instruments (for example, progress reports, action plans, memoranda of understanding) which do not find a clear categorisation under the current legal literature.[9] These instruments are administrative in nature since they are essentially geared towards meeting the objectives of these two policies.[10] If we picture the decision-making machinery of the SAP and the ENP as a cycle, on the left side of the cycle we have the instruments defining the Union's primary political choice; while on the right side of the cycle we have the administrative instruments aimed at their implementation. This cycle can also be replicated for the study of other EU external policies: the European Council sets out the strategic interest and objectives of the Union in external relations, the Council defines those policies, and it is the European Commission (the Commission) which executes them and gives them effect.[11]

The ensemble of administrative activities aimed at achieving the goals set forward by the SAP and ENP are not neutral. At first glance, the impact exercised by the administrative activities seems to be legally irrelevant. However, it is neither incidental nor unforeseeable; it is often the outcome of processes crystallised over time. The administrative activities are capable of influencing the policy choices of third countries and they incur the risk of raising expectations about the Union's future conduct. The instruments implementing the SAP and the ENP, even if addressed, for example, to the Council, have as main addressee the third country which should follow the suggestion made in the document, adopt

---

[9] Some authors have categorised them as soft law. However, this definition has so far taken an inward-looking approach, by focusing on the role that these instruments have internally. See for example Van Vooren, B., 'A case-study of soft law in EU external relations: the European Neighbourhood Policy' 2009 *European Law Review* 34(5); Van Vooren, B., *EU External Relations Law and the Neighbourhood Policy: A Paradigm for Coherence* (Routledge, Abingdon 2011).

[10] Hofmann, H.C.H., G.C. Rowe and A.H. Türk, *Administrative Law and Policy of the European Union* (Oxford University Press, Oxford 2013), 11.

[11] See in this respect Opinion of Advocate General Sharpston delivered on 26 November 2015 on *Council v Commission* (Case C-660/13) ECLI:EU:C:2015:787, para.106.

the standards indicated in the latter, and address the lacks identified unless they want to trigger negative sanctions or renounce benefits.[12] The impact exercised by the Union's administrative activities on the neighbouring states rests on the empirical insight that many acts can in the end effectively curtail third countries' freedom in the same way as legally binding acts.[13] The latest EU practice of providing macro-financial assistance to the ENP states represents a good example. The Union's ability to deny funds or to suspend disbursement of a loan or credit implies that a failure by Tunisia or Ukraine to comply with the Union's policy prescriptions, as set out in the Memoranda of Understanding (MoU) agreed with the borrowing states, can be enforced.[14] Despite the impact that these administrative activities have and the presence of enforcement mechanisms in case of non-compliance, third countries are still treated by the Union legal system as objects as opposed to subjects (to be understood in the *Van Gend en Loos* definition of the term).[15] For example, third states could be denied macro-financial assistance due to their inability to fulfil the conditions set out in the MoUs concluded with the Union, without having the guarantee of being heard.[16]

The impact of the administrative activities on the position of individuals can be clearly sensed by the cases that reached the Court of Justice of the European Union (CJEU) and the European Ombudsman (the Ombudsman) in which individuals from third countries challenged

---

[12] For example, if lack of progress is registered in the way in which a third country implements its e.g. association agenda or its visa liberalisation action plan, the entry into force of the association agreement or the implementation of the visa liberalisation free regime might be postponed.

[13] von Bogdandy, A., 'Common principles for a plurality of orders: A study on public authority in European legal area' (2014) 12 *International Journal of Constitutional Law*, 988; Vianello, I., 'EU External Action and the Administrative Rule of Law: A Long-Overdue Encounter' (EUI PhD Thesis document on file).

[14] Decision (EU) 2015/601 of the European Parliament and of the Council of 15 April 2015 providing macro-financial assistance to Ukraine [2015] OJ L100/1, Art.3(1); Decision (EU) 534/2014 of the European Parliament and of the Council of 15 May 2014 providing macro-financial assistance to the Republic of Tunisia [2015] OJ L151/9, Art.3(1).

[15] Note 3, and on this point see also Korkea-aho, E., chapter 11 in this book.

[16] For example, EU-Ukraine MoU on macro financial assistance at point 3: 'The Commission will also continuously verify the financing needs of Ukraine and may reduce, suspend or cancel the assistance in case they have decreased fundamentally during the period of disbursement compared to the initial projections.' Commission Implementing Decision of 18 May 2015 approving the Memorandum of Understanding between the European Union and Ukraine related to macro-financial assistance to Ukraine, C(2015)3444/F1.

the action *or* inaction of the European Commission in developing and implementing the Union's external action.[17] The Union's positive and active involvement in the neighbouring states too often clashes with its passive behaviour in front of, for example, human rights violations. The adoption of administrative instruments increases the predictability of how a certain policy will be implemented; thus, the expectations of individuals increase as to the determination of the Union to enforce its policies.[18] For example, the Union has made it clear in a number of Commission communications that it will activate sanctions in the event that a third country fails to respect human rights.[19] The adoption of this type of communication, as well as of progress reports indicating the failure on the side of the third country to respect human rights, increases the expectations of individuals, whose human rights are violated, that measures – such as suspension of aid – will be taken by the Union at the moment when their own country violates their human rights.[20] Third countries' citizens are no longer content to be passive objects. They have begun to understand that they have a role to play in the EU external administrative processes, and that public administration involves striking

---

[17] Note 4 for CJEU case law and the following European Ombudsman decisions: Decision on 26 October 2000 of the European Ombudsman on complaint 530/98/JMA against the European Commission, breach of Art.4 ECGAB; Decision on 28 June 2005 of the European Ombudsman on complaint 933/2004/JMA against the European Commission, breach of Art.4 ECGAB; Decision on 26 February 2016 of the European Ombudsman on complaint 1409/2014/JN against the European Commission, Art.4 ECGAB and duty of care, Decision on 2 September 2016 of the European Ombudsman on complaint OI/7/2015/ANA against the European Commission, breach of Art.23 ECGAB.

[18] Hofmann, H.C.H., G.C. Rowe and A.H. Türk (n.10), 536.

[19] Among others: Commission Communication of 23 May 1995, 'The inclusion of respect for democratic principles and human rights in agreements between the Community and third countries', COM(95) 216 final; Commission Communication of 8 May 2001, 'The European Union's role in promoting human rights and democratisation in third countries', COM(2001) 252 final.

[20] The agreements concluded by the Union with each SAP and ENP state foresee suspension mechanisms in case of violations of human rights. For example, Art.133 of the agreement concluded by the Union (and its Member States) with Montenegro stresses that: 'Either Party may (1) suspend this Agreement, (2) with immediate effect, (3) in the event of non-compliance by the other Party of one of the essential elements of this Agreement.' The essential elements of the agreement include, among others, human rights. Stabilisation and Association Agreement between the European Communities and their Member States, of the one part, and the Republic of Montenegro, of the other part, [2010] OJ L108/3.

a balance among conflicting interests and competing principles. Nevertheless, in these cases the Court ignored – or maybe thwarted? – the opportunity of going beyond a purely formalistic approach in favour of one that would take into account the social reality, the implication of the Union's activities outside its borders, and the context in which the administrative activities operate. On the other hand, the Ombudsman's decisions are slowly paving a trail in recognising the role of third countries' citizens as receivers of Union policies.[21]

2. ARTICULATING THE RULE OF LAW EXTERNALLY: FROM OBJECTS TO SUBJECTS

As mentioned at the beginning of the chapter, the Treaty of Lisbon makes clear that, when developing and implementing its external action, the Union shall respect the principles that inspired its own creation – among which is the rule of law.[22] The CJEU in its recent case law did not hesitate to use both Article 3(5) TEU and Article 21 TEU to enforce the obligation on the side of the Union to respect the rule of law when acting externally.[23] The Court underlined how respect for the rule of law applies to all external action of the EU, including the Common Foreign Security Policy (CFSP).[24] In these cases, despite the Treaties' limitations, the

---

[21] AG Wathelet, in his Opinion on the *Front Polisario* case, cites a decision of the European Ombudsman in order to stress the importance that the Commission and the Council carry out human rights impact assessments before the Union concludes an agreement with a third state. The decision cited by the AG is 1409/2014/JN on the Commission's failure to carry out a prior human rights impact assessment of the free trade agreement between the EU and the Socialist Republic of Vietnam. Opinion of Advocate General Wathelet delivered on 13 September 2016 on *Council v Front Polisario* (Case C-104/16 P) ECLI:EU:C:2016:677, para.263. More generally on the role of the Ombudsman as catalyst in promoting the respect of the rule of law in way the Union interacts with third states see: Vianello, I., (n.13).

[22] Articles 3(5), 21(1), and 21(3) TEU.

[23] *European Parliament v Council of the European Union* (Case C-263/14) ECLI:EU:C:2016:435; *H v Council, Commission and EUPM* (Case C-455/14) ECLI:EU:C:2016:569.

[24] 'As regards, in particular, provisions of the EU-Tanzania Agreement concerning compliance with the principles of the rule of law and human rights, as well as respect for human dignity, it must be stated that such compliance is required of all actions of the European Union, including those in the area of the CFSP, as is clear from the provisions, read together, set out in the first subparagraph of Article 21(1), Article 21(2)(b) and (3) TEU, and Article 23

Court used Article 21 TEU in order to extend its jurisdiction to disputes having a CFSP dimension.[25] While these cases are relevant in order to underline the obligation on the side of the Union to respect the rule of law when acting externally, they do not inform the articulation of the rule of law in the way the Union interacts with its external partners. The cases, even if dealing with Union external action, have an internal dimension. One deals with the choice of correct legal basis for the conclusion of an international agreement between the EU and Tanzania;[26] while the other is a staff case concerning an EU citizen working for the European Union Police Mission (EUPM) in Bosnia and Herzegovina.[27] The cases were not about the EU's conduct towards third states and their citizens.

If the Court had (and still has) a crucial role in developing the principles giving effect to the administrative rule of law internally,[28] this does not seem to be the most evident path in cases dealing with the administrative phase of the Union external action. The final decision as to whether to open accession negotiations for EU membership or to suspend economic relations with a third country due to human rights violations is political. Third countries cannot acquire a right as to how the Union should act towards them (for example, they cannot challenge a decision

---

TEU.' *European Parliament v Council of the European Union* (Case C-263/14) ECLI:EU:C:2016:435, para.47; 'it must be noted that, as is apparent from both Article 2 TEU, which is included in the common provisions of the EU Treaty, and Article 21 TEU, concerning the European Union's external action, to which Article 23 TEU, relating to the CFSP, refers, the European Union is founded, in particular, on the values of equality and the rule of law […]. The very existence of effective judicial review designed to ensure compliance with provisions of EU law is inherent in the existence of the rule of law.' *H v Council, Commission and EUPM* (Case C-455/14) ECLI:EU:C:2016:569, para.41.

[25] 'The Court of Justice of the European Union shall not have jurisdiction with respect to the provisions relating to the common foreign and security policy nor with respect to acts adopted on the basis of those provisions.' Article 275(1) Treaty on the functioning of the European Union, [2010] OJ C83/01 (hereafter TFEU).

[26] *European Parliament v Council of the European Union* (Case C-263/14) ECLI:EU:C:2016:435.

[27] *H v Council, Commission and EUPM* (Case C-455/14) ECLI:EU:C:2016:569.

[28] Administrative law scholars share the recognition that both the Court of Justice of the European Union (CJEU) and the EU legislature have gradually established an administrative rule of law applicable to the various components of the EU administrative system. Chiti, E., 'Is EU Administrative Law Failing in Some of Its Crucial Tasks?' (2016) *European Law Journal* 22(5).

not granting them candidate status), and citizens of third countries cannot acquire a right to determine how the Union should behave towards their own states. However, the administrative processes leading to political decisions of this type are not deprived of relevance. As discussed in the previous section of this chapter, the mode of foreign governance established by the SAP and the ENP is an example. The articulation of the respect for the rule law externally, in policies such as the SAP and the ENP, might be aided by a more comprehensive definition as to the subjects of EU law.

A more comprehensive definition as to the subjects of EU law might help explain the necessity of protecting third countries and their citizens from EU action despite the lack of enforceable rights on their side. The definition of subjects ought to be more encompassing than the one provided by the Court in *Van Gend en Loos*. As stated by the editors of this book in their introductory chapter, 'a different understanding of the term subject, one that does not rely on being a bearer of rights, is liberating'.[29] This is particularly important in the external dimension of EU action, where third states and their citizens (even if heavily influenced by Union action) are not recognised under a body of principles and rules which acknowledges their claims. The attempt to go beyond the definition of subject of EU law – as so far provided by the CJEU – does not necessarily render the term devoid of meaning. Rather, it demands rethinking the criteria that make an entity a subject. The application of the rule of law in the way the Union interacts with its external partners may benefit from a definition of 'subjects' which openly acknowledges the role granted to third states (including their citizens) within the system of foreign governance developed and implemented by the EU.

3. SUBJECTS: ACTIVE RESPONDENTS TO UNION EXTERNAL ACTION

The lack of a powerful court determined to give effect to the administrative rule of law externally does not imply a complete vacuum of norms. The most active and instrumental actors in supporting the operationalisation of the administrative rule of law externally are: the EU administration itself and the Ombudsman. This section will discuss how a more comprehensive approach to the definition of subjects – one that does not focus on rights but rather on the relation established by the

[29] Fahey and Bardutzky, (n.3).

Union with third states – could aid the full operationalisation of administrative rule of law externally. Participatory mechanisms (the duty to hear the other side and the duty to consult) have been chosen as examples of duties which derive and give effect to the administrative rule of law.[30] The duty to hear the third state and the duty to consult natural and legal persons will be analysed in turn. This distinction should possibly help in understanding the differences between third states and individuals as separate groups of subjects.

The Duty to Hear the Third Country

The Commission and European External Action Service (EEAS) internal guidelines as to how to compile progress reports foresee the participation of third countries in the process.[31] For example, third countries are invited to provide written inputs, and meetings are encouraged between the EU Delegation and third countries in order to clarify the written contributions.[32] However, the guidance notices stress the importance of consulting the neighbouring countries in order to gather information from the widest array of sources, rather than specifically acknowledging the self-defence aspect of it. In order to fully operationalise the duty to hear the other side in the Union external context, the duty needs to be analysed against the background of the relation established by the administration of the Union and third states, rather than on third countries' rights. The relation between third countries and the administration is based on two incorrect assumptions. First, the belief that the activities implementing the SAP and the ENP do not have as de facto addressees the third states; second, that the relation between the Union

---

[30] Waldron, J.,'The rule of law and the importance of procedure', in Fleming, J.E. (ed.), *Getting to the Rule of Law* (New York University Press, New York and London 2011), 16 and 22.

[31] The SAP progress reports are Commission working documents. The European Council invites the Commission to present the assessment of what each SAP country has achieved over the last year on preparing for EU membership. The ENP progress reports are Joint Staff working documents between the Commission and the External Action Service (EEAS); before 2011 they were only Commission Staff working documents. The aim of these documents is to assess the progress made in the implementation, by each ENP country, on the priorities listed in their respective Action Plans.

[32] European Commission, Directorate General for Enlargement, *Guidance Note Enlargement package 2015*, Access to Documents request GESTDEM reference 2016/450; EEAS, *Guidance Note ENP Package 2014*, Access to Documents request GESTDEM reference 2013/5084.

and the third state is one between two equal partners. By taking these two assumptions into account more appropriately, it will become clear why the third state ought to be heard in the process of adoption of the administrative activities implementing the Union's wider neighbourhood policies.

Most of the administrative activities characterising the EU wider neighbourhood are not directly addressed to the SAP and ENP states; however, the fact that the instruments do not have the third countries as a clear addressee should not be misleading. As discussed in Section 1, the instruments – even if addressed to, for example, the Council – have as main addressee the neighbouring states, which should follow the suggestions made in the document; adopt the standards indicated in the latter; address the lacks identified; or adapt its political agenda to the strategy papers unless they want to trigger negative sanctions or renounce benefits.[33] The possibility of suspending funding flowing from the Union to the SAP and ENP states due to non-compliance with EU conditions makes the requirements contained in the administrative activities implementing the two policies legally binding and hence theoretically enforceable.[34] Administrative activities, whether binding or non-binding, acquire legal authority from the moment in which non-compliance or compliance has legal consequences.[35] Therefore, the belief that the relation between the Union and its neighbouring states is one between two sovereign entities with equal powers is illusionary. It is the Union which decides when positive incentives are to be granted or negative sanctions are to be imposed. The third state, depending on its willingness to integrate in the Union, will always find itself in a subaltern position. Visa liberalisation

[33] Examples are: suspension of financial aid, postponement of the signature of an agreement, etc. The 2014 Bosnia and Herzegovina progress reports states that: 'Bosnia and Herzegovina also still refuses to adapt this Agreement [i.e. SAA Interim Agreement] to take into account its traditional trade with Croatia before it joined the EU. The Commission has undertaken steps to suspend Bosnia and Herzegovina from certain trade benefits if the adaptation process is not finalised by the end of 2015.' Commission Staff Working Document Progress Report on Bosnia and Herzegovina accompanying the EU Enlargement Strategy of 8 October 2014 SWD(2014) 305 final.

[34] Lannon, E., K.M. Inglis and T. Haenebalcke, 'The Many Faces of EU Conditionality in Pan-Euro-Mediterranean Relations', in Maresceau, M., and E. Lannon (eds), *The EU's Enlargement and Mediterranean Strategies, A Comparative Analysis* (Palgrave, Basingstoke and New York 2001), 111.

[35] Mendes, J., 'Rule of law and participation: A normative analysis of internationalized rulemaking as composite procedures' (2014) 12 *International Journal of Constitutional Law* 377.

regimes are granted once the neighbour state respects the criteria identified by the Union in the visa liberalisation action plans. It is only once the Union decides that SAP countries are ready that accession negotiations will be opened. Finally, it should not be forgotten that some states, such as Ukraine and Tunisia, are also dependent on the EU for macro-financial loans.[36]

The point here is not to question whether it is correct morally or legally to impose certain standards on third states. Rather, the point here is to recognise the type of relation that the Union has developed with the third state so as to grant to the third state some procedural protections. The duty to hear the third country ought to be included as an essential element in the pre-legal relationship between the Union and the neighbouring states. The pre-legal relationship is the phase leading to an eventual sanction or denial of benefits. Here the idea is that the entity whose situation is under scrutiny has a special status in defending itself before sanctions would be imposed, despite the lack of legally recognised rights.[37] The third state ought not only to defend itself from the potential action of the Union, which has the power to limit through conditionality its wellbeing by cutting down their relations, but also ought to be heard in light of the impact that the administrative activities have on the state itself. In other words, the establishment of participatory rules at the administrative level affords anticipated procedural protection to actors that might be affected by the intervention or non-intervention of the Union. This should particularly be the case in light of the difficulties faced by third states in challenging the final decision.[38]

The Duty to Consult Natural and Legal Persons

The latest Commission internal guidelines on how to draft SAP progress reports require EU Delegations to organise broader consultations with

[36] Commission Implementing Decision of 18 May 2015 approving the Memorandum of Understanding between the European Union and Ukraine related to macro-financial assistance to Ukraine, C(2015) 3444 final; Commission Implementing Decision of 16 July 2014 approving the Memorandum of Understanding between the European Union and Tunisia related to macro-financial assistance to Tunisia, C(2014) 5176 final.

[37] Galligan, D.J., *Due Process and Fair Procedures: A Study of Administrative Procedures* (Clarendon Press, Oxford 1997), 143.

[38] Third countries might not be able to challenge a final decision (e.g. suspension of aid) either due to its non-legally binding nature or for the Court's restrictive standing rules.

local organisations and civil society.[39] These meetings are, according to the Commission, 'crucial to ensure proper consultation of local partners'[40] and their function is to guarantee that reports draw on the widest possible array of sources.[41] Likewise, the EEAS internal documents on how to draft ENP progress reports requires EU Delegations to contact and collect information from the civil society organisations in partner countries.[42] According to the EEAS, the rationale for embracing such an inclusive approach is twofold: ensuring transparency and objectivity of the reports; and to 'demonstrate the interest of the European institutions to make use of all sources available and help identify areas where further information needs to be collected'.[43] Also, the EEAS internal guidelines on how to adopt ENP action plans[44] state that EU Delegations must hold consultations with civil society prior to the start of negotiations.[45] Individuals – like their states – are consulted in order to gather information, rather than with the aim of recognising them as subjects within the process.

In order to operationalise the duty to consult in external relations as a tool to protect individuals affected by the exercise of external administrative power, beyond the obvious obstacles (for example, the absence of rights), it is fundamental to frame its impact within the context of the Union external action. For example, the expectations of the individuals, who went all the way to Court to challenge the Commission action (or inaction),[46] might not be defined as 'legitimate' under EU law and, thus, lack legal protection. However, other obligations imposed on the administration might come as a safety net in order to protect individuals from wrongfully relying on the administrative activities implementing the

---

39 European Commission, Directorate General for Enlargement, *Guidance Note Enlargement package 2015*, Access to Documents request GESTDEM reference 2016/450.

40 Note 39.

41 Note 39.

42 EEAS, *Guidance Note ENP Package 2014*, Access to Documents request GESTDEM reference 2013/5084.

43 Note 42.

44 Action Plans lay down the strategic objectives of the cooperation between each ENP country and the EU. Their implementation helps fulfil the provisions of the agreements concluded by the EU with each ENP country and build ties in new areas of cooperation. The elaboration of the Action Plans is in the hands of the Commission and – only recently – also of the EEAS.

45 EEAS, *Non-Paper: Guidelines for Future ENP Action Plan* 05.01.2012, Access to Documents request SG1 – Corporate Board Secretariat.

46 Note 4.

Union external action. The duty to consult is one among others. It offers the individuals with the opportunity to present their cases of, for example, human rights violations before the administration, and to better understand the administrative phase of the Union's external action (i.e. that Commission progress reports denouncing human rights violations do not necessarily lead to sanctions). Recognising the importance and the functions that consultations procedures play and ought to play is not without consequences. In this respect, further reflections are essential. For example, as to who is to be invited for consultations, and as to the need of openness in order to guarantee sincere participation.

In a recent case the Ombudsman was asked to determine whether the Commission was guilty of maladministration by failing to disclose its comments on the draft of the Serbian Free Legal Aid Act in the context of pre-accession negotiations between the EU and Serbia. The Ombudsman, in her brief assessments, agrees with the Commission's decision not to disclose the document; but at the same time offers some suggestions for increasing openness. First, she encourages the administration to make the document available at a later date – for example, after the entrance into force of the Serbian Legal Aid Act or the provisional closure of Chapter 23 of the accession negotiations. Even if this choice is not ideal for the Serbian civil society, the states lagging behind in the enlargement process could benefit from greater openness and the inclusion of natural and legal persons in the process. For example, Bosnia and Herzegovina's civil society could have access to the Commission's recommendations on the Serbian Legal Aid Act when such act will be discussed in their own country. Second, the Ombudsman in her assessment indicates that some of the information contained in the requested document will be incorporated in the Serbia progress report, 'which should adequately inform the public of the general recommendations directed at the Serbia authorities'.[47] The Ombudsman in this decision – by taking into account the pre-accession context – recognises the importance of keeping the local population informed. The rationale is to allow them to better participate in the process.

[47] Decision on 2 September 2016 of the European Ombudsman on complaint OI/7/2015/ANA against the European Commission, external relations, breach of Article 23 ECGAB, point 26.

CONCLUSION

The respect for the rule of law in the relations between the Union and third states faces numerous challenges. The dogmatic attention given by the EU legal literature and the jurisprudence of the Court to the subjects of EU law as rights-bearers is one among many. Such an obsession limits the possibility of understanding the importance that procedural duties (such as participatory mechanisms) might have in protecting third countries and their citizens from the Union's exercise of power. Third countries and the natural and legal persons of third countries belong to two separate groups of subjects. The first are the direct addressees of the Union's measures; while the second are indirectly addressed. Nevertheless, the proposal of this chapter to look beyond the understanding of a legal subject as a bearer of rights and duties applies to both categories. The logic of embracing a more encompassing definition of subjects may support academics, as well as the EU institutions and the European Ombudsman, in operationalising the respect for the rule of law externally beyond the obvious obstacles. A more encompassing definition ought to focus on the type of relation that the Union develops with third states and their individuals.

In particular, third countries and natural and legal persons of third countries ought to be recognised as subjects in the administrative phase of the Union's policy cycle. If it is true that final decisions in external relations (for example, the suspension of funds, the opening of accession negotiations, etc.) are of a pure political nature; the administrative activities regulating the relations between the Union and third states are not deprived of consequences. It is specifically in this administrative phase – as exemplified by the case of the SAP and ENP – that third countries and their citizens ought to be framed as subjects rather than objects of EU action. Here the rule of law ought to be seen not just as a system of control imposed from above and external to the relationships developed between the Union and third states; but as a system of regulation occurring within the relation. The subjects of this relation are entities whose role ought to be recognised in light of a system of established procedures imposed on them over time.

Finally, if the framing of subjects of EU law in *Van Gend en Loos* was 'a prelude to a drift in EU law from the logic of public international law';[48] the framing of third countries and their citizens as subjects of EU

---

48 Fahey and Bardutzky (n.3).

law in the administrative phase of the Union's external action might have consequences in the development of Global Administrative Law. This is an important question for further research.

13. Beyond rhetoric? Social conditionality in the EU's external trade relations

Samantha Velluti

1. INTRODUCTION

1.1 Context and Background

That a flourishing economy leads to a flourishing life is little disputed. And yet, this rather intuitive idea of the world conceals a much more complex scenario. Debates about what is meant by a flourishing economy and a flourishing life (*eudaimonia*), how to frame their relationship and, within it, who is or should be the subject or object of contemporary law and governance, remain as divisive and contentious as ever. Is it enough to foster trade to ensure people's well-being? Do questions about trade necessarily incorporate concerns about sustainability, fairness and human rights? There is no agreement as to whether trade measures should consider a future for humanity predicated on the fulfilment of all persons to achieve dignifying living standards. There is equally no agreement as to whether decision-makers should adopt trade policies that enable people to live the kinds of lives that they value and have reason to value. Nevertheless, the way we address these questions has important normative implications and impacts directly on the place that social issues should occupy vis-à-vis trade policies and, significantly, the role of the EU as a global promoter of values and human rights.

EU law must constantly put forward claims about itself centred around the idea of self-betterment which underpins the justification for any EU legal norm.[1] European *eudaimonia* 'requires EU law to grant individuals the structures, entitlements, responsibilities and protection to make better

[1] Chalmers, Damian, 'Gauging the cumbersomeness of EU law' (2009) 62 *Current Legal Problems* 405.

and more successful lives for themselves'.[2] This idea of self-betterment has significant normative and deontological implications for EU intervention; particularly for the authority of EU law beyond its borders given that it claims to offer something that cannot be offered by national law.

Against this backdrop, the chapter looks at the legal subjects and objects of the EU's law and practice of promoting social rights and labour standards in its external trade relations. Since the mid-1990s – and pursuant to the Treaty of Maastricht's reshaping of the EU as an international organization with a human face – the EU has been using its strong global commercial leverage to progressively promote and strengthen the social dimension of globalization through the combined use of hard and soft trade measures, focusing chiefly on the promotion of labour standards internationally through increased cooperation with the International Labour Organization (ILO) and its external trade policies. To varying degrees and with mixed success, many of the EU's trade agreements (both bilateral and regional) include an element of social conditionality, namely social incentive clauses that condition trade concessions and market access on the respect and implementation of internationally recognized human rights, social and environmental standards.[3]

The increased commitment of the EU to the social dimension of its external trade policy, that is the object of regulation, and the methods by which it is regulated, raise an apparently very simple question: who are the real beneficiaries of such change? Or, to put it differently, who are the real legal subjects of the purported self-betterment that social conditionality in the EU external trade relations is meant to ensure? As the analysis will go on to show, answering these questions is far from straightforward as it requires a clear definition of subjects and objects of EU law and then specifically an understanding of who the subjects and objects of EU social conditionality are.

---

2 Chalmers, n.1, 406.

3 ILO, Assessment of labour provisions in trade and investment arrangements, Geneva, Switzerland, July 2016, accessed 6 February 2017 at *www.ilo.org/global/about-the-ilo/newsroom/news/WCMS_499348/lang–en/index.htm*; Velluti, Samantha, 'The EU's social dimension in its external trade relations' in Beke, Laura, Axel Marx, Jan Wouters and Glenn Rayp (eds), *Global Governance of Labor Rights* (Edward Elgar Publishing, Cheltenham and Northampton MA 2015).

1.2 Rationale and Focus of Analysis

This chapter embraces the notion of 'legal subject' as being an entity – either a natural or a juristic person – recognized or accepted as being capable of holding rights, duties and capacities, and 'legal object' as something or someone in respect of which a legal subject may hold rights, duties and capacities.[4] Everyday life comprises a network of legal relationships among legal subjects concerning their rights or duties and covering claims that a legal subject has or may have on a legal object. In this context it is possible to identify two types of relationship: a 'subject-subject relationship' between the bearer of the right and other legal subjects, and a 'subject-object relationship' between the right-bearer and the legal object of his or her right.[5] Strictly linked to the notion of subjects and objects of law is that of 'rights', here conceived as basic guarantees, with both a moral and political component, that people in all countries are endowed with, can enjoy and exercise and invoke against others.[6] Rights act as standards of justification and parameters for criticism. In this context, compliance with them is mandatory. Rights, however, do not act solely as 'trumps'[7] held by individuals to be used when a collective goal is not a sufficient justification for denying them what they wish, as individuals, to have or to do, or not a sufficient justification for imposing some loss or injury upon them. Contemporary human rights practice has also come to encompass the aspirational component of policy objectives. This is the case of participatory rights, which from the perspective of democratic legitimacy are particularly important in the context of the EU's social conditionality in its external trade relations and is of direct relevance to framing its subjects and objects. In this specific context participation refers to ensuring ownership to all relevant subjects chiefly at the local level in developing the appropriate infrastructure to promote social rights and labour standards. As pointed out by Bardutzky and Fahey, the

---

4 Kruger, Hannaretha, and Ann Skelton (eds), *The Law of Persons in South Africa* (Oxford University Press, Oxford 2010), 11–13.

5 N.4; there is some resonance here with Hohfeld's concept of rights; this notion is used insofar as it helps us to understand the meaning and purpose of rights and how they relate to certain aspects of legal reasoning and legal interpretation. See Hohfeld, Wesley Newcomb, 'Fundamental Legal Conceptions as Applied in Judicial Reasoning' (1913) 23 *Yale Law Journal* 710.

6 Nickel, James, *Making Sense of Human Rights*, 2nd edn (Blackwell, Malden MA and Carlton, Australia 2007).

7 Dworkin, Ronald, *Taking Rights Seriously* (Harvard University Press, Cambridge MA 1978), xi.

primary concern here is the social legitimacy of EU law in light of the evolving objects of EU law and a mutating subjects-objects relationship.[8] The aim is to rethink the existing philosophy of EU law so that it does not rest 'upon a theory of interpretation at the expense of a theory of justice',[9] thereby avoiding the risk of conceiving questions of justice in a way that wrongly excludes certain subjects from consideration, which in turn would lead to a situation of 'meta-injustice' in the form of 'meta-political misrepresentation'.

At this juncture a caveat is in order. The formal distinction between subject and object of law is required by decision-making itself, which is intrinsically associated with choice. In turn, choice forces us to embrace a dichotomic vision in respect of all aspects of life including the notions of legal subjects and objects. This notwithstanding, such distinction may be too rigid and not bode well with the EU's multi-layered and multi-faceted system of governance.[10] This is because the subjects and objects of EU law change depending on the layer of governance we consider and whether we are looking at the internal or external dimension of EU action. Increasingly, subjects of EU law become its objects, thus illustrating the fuzziness of the subject-object divide.[11] This also requires a rethinking and new ways of conceptualizing the actorness of the EU.[12] The interchangeability or blurred divide between subjects and objects of EU law is visible in the EU international trade agreements, which contain social conditionality provisions. Its legal subjects are the EU and/or the Member States[13] and third parties and its objects will include EU citizens, third-country citizens and/or third-country services, goods and capital, but also environment and human rights protection[14] in respect of which the EU and the Member States on the one hand and third parties

[8] Bardutzky, Samo, and Elaine Fahey, Chapter 1 of this volume.

[9] Williams, Andrew, 'Taking values seriously: towards a philosophy of EU law' (2009) 29 *Oxford Journal of Legal Studies* 552.

[10] Bardutzky and Fahey (n.8).

[11] eg Member States (traditionally subjects of EU law), Union citizens, third countries, third-country nationals, parties to an agreement, third or contracting parties.

[12] Bardutzky and Fahey (n.8); Korkea-aho, Emilia, Chapter 11 of this volume and Vianello, Ilaria, Chapter 12 of this volume.

[13] This will depend on whether or not we are considering mixed agreements requiring the ratification of both the EU and the Member States. See Hillion, Christophe, and Panos Koutrakos (eds), *Mixed Agreements Revisited. The EU and its Member States in the World* (Hart, Oxford 2010).

[14] This is not an exhaustive list as EU international agreements cover a fairly wide range of areas.

on the other, as legal subjects of a given international agreement, will hold rights, duties and capacities. This is at one layer of decision-making, namely at the international level. At the domestic level, thus another layer of decision-making, the objects of the EU international agreements acquire the role of legal subjects. Hence, in addition to the state and the public authorities, we will have natural and/or legal persons with right-claims that can be exercised and invoked against other natural and legal persons. The analysis is situated within this conceptual framework of subjects and objects of EU external trade relations law. The chapter looks at the EU's increased practice of promoting social rights and labour standards in its external trade relations, focusing largely on its bilateral agreements, which encompass reciprocal or non-reciprocal preferential trade links with third countries. The aim of the chapter, therefore, is to critically examine the EU's new social clauses and provisions on labour standards in the context of the broader debate about the purpose and effectiveness of EU social trade and to see what this tells us about the subject-object divide.

The chapter starts by looking at the role of the EU as a global social actor following the entry into force of the 2009 Treaty of Lisbon. It then proceeds to evaluate the EU's social conditionality in its bilateral and regional trade agreements. After having identified its strengths and limitations, it considers how to bolster the impact of its trade agreements to promote and uphold social rights externally. The chapter posits that one such way could be through revised social impact assessments (SIAs)[15] together with the strengthening of the involvement of civil society organizations and social partners under the Trade and Sustainable Development Chapter of the EU's new trade agreements.

---

[15] The 2011 Joint Communication of the European Commission and High Representative of the European Union for Foreign Affairs and Security Policy on *Human Rights and Democracy at the Heart of EU External Action – Towards a More Effective Approach*, COM(2011)886 final.2011 explicitly refers to the importance of impact assessments; see also the 2012 EU Strategic Framework and Action Plan on Human Rights and Democracy, of 25 June 2012, Luxembourg, Luxembourg 11855/12 which expressly calls for the insertion of human rights in Impact Assessment, as and when it is carried out for trade agreements that have significant economic, social and environmental impacts. The new generation of trade SIAs reflect this goal.

2. THE EU'S PROMOTION OF SOCIAL RIGHTS AND LABOUR STANDARDS IN ITS EXTERNAL TRADE RELATIONS

2.1 The Role of the EU as a Global Social Actor Post-Lisbon

Since the entry into force of the 2009 Treaty of Lisbon, and chiefly through Articles 3(5) and 21 Treaty on European Union (TEU), the EU has constitutionalized its commitment to human rights obligations to the extent that non-commercial objectives are now clearly within the remit of EU internal and external action.

The EU constitutes a formidable platform for developing an integrated system to further diverse goals through the coordinated action of various institutions. As a regional entity with a 'global vocation'[16] to promote global human rights, the EU now has a regulatory framework enabling it to mobilize various instruments of governance in a social perspective.[17] In this context, the EU stands as a model of a highly competitive social market economy[18] 'reflecting the ambition of furthering diverse economic and social aims simultaneously, however much that model is both incomplete and under threat'.[19] The Treaty of Lisbon has refocused attention on a holistic approach to European integration and the goals of full employment, social progress and cohesion have been relaunched in the context of a new 'highly competitive social market economy'.[20]

The reconceptualization of EU trade policies as exemplified by the *Trade, Growth and World Affairs* and *Trade for All* strategies[21] are evidence of a growing support in the EU's internal and external policies

---

[16] Cremona, Marise, 'Rhetoric and Reticence: EU External Commercial Policy in a Multilateral Context' (2001) 38 *Common Market Law Review* 359.

[17] Perulli, Adalberto, 'Fundamental Social Rights, Market Regulation and EU External Action', 30 (2014) *International Journal of Comparative Labour Law and Industrial Relations* 37.

[18] Article 3(3) TEU.

[19] Reddy, Sanjay, 'Foreword. International Trade as a Means to Diverse Ends: Development, Workers, the Environment, and Global Public Goods' in De Schutter, Olivier, *Trade in Service of Sustainable Development* (Hart, Oxford 2015), xv; for further analysis, see Damjanovic, Dragana, 'The EU Market Rules as Social Market Rules: Why the EU can be a Social Market Economy' 50 (2013) *Common Market Law Review* 1685.

[20] Perulli (n.17), 34.

[21] European Commission, *Trade for All – Towards a More Responsible Trade and Investment Policy*, accessed 6 February 2017 at *trade.ec.europa.eu/doclib/docs/2015/october/tradoc_153846.pdf*.

and actions for International Labour Organization (ILO) labour standards and reflect the increasing importance in the EU of decent job creation, social dialogue and social protection for ensuring inclusive growth and sustainable development in the broader context of the global economic crisis. The promotion of ILO labour standards is mostly visible in the EU's trade arrangements, at the unilateral, regional and bilateral levels.

The EU's social ambition has grown exponentially in the past decade as exemplified by the increasing number of trade agreements containing social conditionality clauses.[22] Many EU trade agreements include social incentive clauses and condition trade concessions and market access on the respect and implementation of internationally recognized human rights and social and environmental standards.[23]

The strong normative connotation that the trade-labour linkage has come to acquire within the EU can be explained by various interrelated factors. First, with the Treaty of Lisbon. the European Parliament – a strong advocate of the inclusion of labour in trade arrangements – has gained increased competences in external trade policy.[24] All the main political groups in the European Parliament, while having different motivations, agree on the need for trade arrangements to include labour provisions.[25] The inclusion of labour provisions makes it easier to find public support, given that they act as a counterweight to the market liberalizing provisions of the EU's trade agreements. In addition, the framing of labour (and environmental) provisions as part of 'sustainable development' reduces their objection.[26]

---

[22] Velluti, Samantha, 'The Promotion of Social Rights and Labour Standards in the EU's External Trade Relations' 5 (2016) *Centre for the Law of EU External Relations* (CLEER) Papers 83.

[23] ILO, Assessment of labour provisions in trade and investment arrangements, Geneva, Switzerland, July 2016, accessed 6 February 2017 at *www.ilo.org/global/about-the-ilo/newsroom/news/WCMS_499348/lang–en/index.htm*.

[24] Raube, Kolja, and Jan Wouters, 'The Many Facets of Parliamentary Involvement and Interaction in EU External Relations', Leuven Centre for Global Governance Studies, Working Paper No. 174 – April 2016.

[25] Van den Putte, Lore, 'Divided We Stand – The European Parliament's Position on Social Trade in the Post-Lisbon Era', in Marx, Alex, et al. (eds), *Global Governance of Labour Rights: Assessing the Effectiveness of Transnational Public and Private Policy Initiatives* (Edward Elgar Publishing, Cheltenham and Northampton MA 2015), 63.

[26] Van den Putte, Lore, and Jan Orbie, 'EU Bilateral Agreements and the Surprising Rise of Labour Provisions' (2015) 31 *International Journal of Comparative Labour Law and Industrial Relations* 263.

Nevertheless, the effectiveness and credibility of the EU's approach has been called into question because of the uneven application of social conditionality, often leaving labour rights violations unpunished.

The next sections map out and assess the relevant labour provisions provided under selected EU trade agreements as well as the key monitoring and enforcement mechanisms put in place to ensure their compliance in order to see what this tells us about the subjects and objects of EU social conditionality more generally.

2.2 EU Bilateral and Regional Trade Agreements

2.2.1 The rise of the EU's social dimension in its external trade relations

The shift in focus of the EU towards bilateral and regional trade agreements for promoting the trade-labour linkage can be explained as a response to the lack of progress at multilateral level and, in particular, as an alternative solution to the failure to include a trade-labour linkage in the World Trade Organization (WTO) context. The EU has been including social clauses in its bilateral agreements since the 1990s with a widening and deepening of the trade-labour linkage in EU trade agreements since the mid-2000s. The content of social clauses has become more detailed and their scope has been expanded. In particular, in addition to technical cooperation in social policy, trade agreements include a commitment to the respect for the ILO's core labour standards (CLS) as fundamental labour rights.[27] Since the mid-1990s, sustainable development has become increasingly important in the EU's trade policy and the Treaty of Lisbon has elevated it to one of the key principles underlying EU external action.[28] This overarching legal commitment has been given further effect with the adoption of the so-called 'new

[27] The four CLS are embodied in eight ILO Conventions: (i) freedom of association and the right to collective bargaining (Conventions 87 and 98); (ii) the elimination of all forms of forced or compulsory labour (Conventions 29 and 105); (iii) the effective abolition of child labour (Conventions 138 and 182); and (iv) the elimination of discrimination in respect of employment and occupation (Conventions 100 and 111).

[28] Article 21(2)d and (3) TEU; Bartels, Lorand, 'Human Rights and Sustainable Development Obligations in EU Free Trade Agreements' (2013) 40 *Legal Issues of Economic Integration* 297; on its notion and operationalization, Zaccai, Edwin, 'Over Two Decades in Pursuit of Sustainable Development: Influence, Transformation, Limits' (2012) 1 *Environmental Development* 79 and De Schutter, Olivier, *Trade in the Service of Sustainable Development. Linking Trade to Labour Rights and Environmental Standards* (Hart, Oxford 2015).

generation' of free trade agreements (FTAs) containing a 'Trade and Sustainable development' chapter, which includes provisions for the respect of labour and environmental standards. The agreements contain provisions on cooperation and obligations to respect and 'strive' to improve multilateral and domestic labour and environmental standards.[29] In particular, a first set of obligations contain minimum obligations to implement certain multilateral obligations and other obligations which require the parties to the agreement not to reduce their levels of protection and encouraging them to raise their levels of protection, subject to a proviso that this is not done for protectionist purposes.

Examples of such agreements are the 2010 EU-Korea FTA,[30] the 2012 EU-Central America Agreement[31] and the 2012 EU-Colombia/Peru Agreement.[32] The 2013 EU-Singapore FTA[33] and the 2016 EU-Vietnam FTA[34] (both awaiting ratification) also contain such a chapter. The 2008 EU-CARIFORUM agreement is also important in this context as it is the first economic partnership agreement (EPA) concluded with a regional

---

[29] For further analysis, Bartels, Lorand, 'Social issues: Labour, environment and human rights' in Lester, Simon, and Bryan Mercurio (eds), *Bilateral and Regional Trade Agreements* (Cambridge University Press, Cambridge and New York NY 2009), 342.

[30] Free Trade Agreement between the European Union and its Member States of the one part, and the Republic of Korea of the other part (EU-Korea FTA) [2011] OJ L127/6, 14 May 2011, p. 6. It entered into force in July 2011 and it is the EU's first trade agreement with an Asian country. It is also the first completed agreement in a new generation of FTAs launched by the EU in 2007 as part of its strategy to create 'deep and comprehensive' free trade agreements (DCFTA) with selective partners following the Doha round standstill at the WTO.

[31] Agreement establishing an Association between the European Union and its Member States, on the one hand, and Central America on the other (EU-CAAA) [2012] OJ L346/3.

[32] Trade Agreement between the European Union and its Member States, of the one part, and Colombia and Peru, of the other part [2012] OJ L354/3.

[33] It is the first bilateral agreement concluded by the EU with an ASEAN (Association of Southeast Asian Nations) country and it will probably provide the blueprint for future bilateral agreements with other ASEAN countries; Free Trade Agreement between the European Union and Singapore, 17 October 2014, Authentic text as of May 2015, accessed 6 February 2017 at *trade.ec.europa.eu/doclib/press/index.cfm?id=961*.

[34] Free Trade Agreement between the European Union and the Socialist Republic of Vietnam, Agreed Text as of January 2016, accessed 6 February 2017 at *trade.ec.europa.eu/doclib/press/index.cfm?id=1437*.

group.[35] In general terms, while there is some variation between the provisions contained in the different agreements, there seems to be some level of commonality as to the substantive standards and the institutional set-up envisaged.

2.2.2 Governance and implementation of the social clauses

A particularly salient aspect of these trade agreements from the perspective of the subjects and objects of EU social conditionality and their interaction is the governance and implementation of the social clauses which has also been expanded so as to include a wide range of actors, including high-level labour officials, civil society and business actors of the partner countries to a given trade agreement who are involved in monitoring and promoting social clauses.[36] The new generation of EU trade agreements are enabling third countries – as legal subjects qua partner countries – to acquire a renewed role: from one of mere public power recipients to one of co-shapers.[37] In particular, they provide for the setting up of a Sub-Committee/Board on Trade and Sustainable Development in the context of which senior government officials regularly meet to oversee the implementation of the labour (and environmental) commitments of the agreement.[38] In addition, civil society actors officially have

---

[35] The regional group comprises 15 Caribbean countries: Antigua and Barbuda, Bahamas, Barbados, Belize, Dominica, Dominican Republic, Grenada, Guyana, Haiti, Jamaica, St Lucia, St Vincent and the Grenadines, St Kitts and Nevis, Suriname and Trinidad and Tobago; Economic Partnership Agreement between the CARIFORUM States, of the one part, and the European Community and its Member States, of the other part [2008] OJ L289/3.

[36] For further analysis, Orbie, Jan, Deborah Martens and Lore Van den Putte, 'Civil Society Meetings in European Union Trade Agreements: Features, Purposes and Evaluation' 3 (2016) *Centre for the Law of EU External Relations* (CLEER) Papers 1.

[37] For further analysis on this point, particularly from the perspective of the application of the rule of law principles in EU external action and participation as a procedural rule giving effect to the rule of law and as determining a new subject of EU law, namely third countries and citizens of third countries, see Vianello (n.12).

[38] Douma, Wybe, 'The Promotion of Sustainable Development through EU Trade Instruments' in Pantaleo, Luca, and Mads Andenas (eds), *The European Union as a Global Model for Trade and Investment*, University of Oslo Faculty of Law Legal Studies Research paper Series No 2016-02, 86; de Andrade Correa, Fabiano, 'The Integration of Sustainable Development in Trade Agreements of the European Union' in Kleimann, David, 'EU Preferential Trade Agreements: Commerce, Foreign Policy and Development Aspects', International Trade Observatory and Relex Working Group, European University Institute, Robert

a role in monitoring the implementation of sustainable development provisions,[39] although their role and the key features of civil society meetings vary significantly from agreement to agreement.[40] Government officials of the partner country/ies and the EU meet annually with labour and environmental experts in the Sub-Committee on Trade and Sustainable Development, which has been established to oversee the implementation of the Trade and Sustainable Development chapter. As regards civil society and social partners, the 2011 EU-Korea agreement is illustrative. It provides for Domestic Advisory Groups for each party made up of civil society, business, social partners and other experts from relevant stakeholder groups, which meet at an annual Civil Society Forum.[41] Similarly, the 2012 EU-Colombia/Peru[42] and EU-CAAA[43] agreements mandate each party and the subcommittee/board to meet with existing national advisory groups (or to create new ones) and civil society on a regular basis.

The above illustrates that the EU's approach to social conditionality is to a large extent promotional in nature and based on cooperation. The promotional approach combines binding and non-binding commitments to labour standards, domestic or international, with provisions on cooperation, knowledge sharing, technical assistance, dialogue and monitoring, thus allowing third countries to strengthen their capacity-building to address labour concerns.[44]

By its very nature, and to some extent due to a lack of transparency of what happens in practice, any evaluation concerning the results that the promotional approach of the EU's social conditionality has achieved so far cannot be definitive. It is difficult to establish a causal link between the implementation of measures and the results yielded, also due to the significant degree of variation between the de jure and the de facto configurations of the plurality of actors, and thus subjects, that can be involved. Second, it is not possible to make generalized conclusions as to

---

Schuman Centre for Advanced Studies, accessed 6 February 2017 at *cadmus.eui.eu/handle/1814/27661*, 141.

39 Bartels, Lorand, 'The Role of Civil Society in Monitoring Free Trade Agreements', Report for the EU European Economic and Social Committee, EESC/COMM/16/2012.

40 Orbie, Martens and Van den Putte (n.36), 12–25.

41 2011 EU-Korea FTA, Art.13.12(3)–(5) and Art.13.13.

42 2012 EU-Colombia/Peru, Art.282.

43 2012 EU-CAAA, Part III.

44 ILO, Report on *Social Dimensions of Free Trade Agreements*, International Institute for Labour Studies, Geneva, Switzerland, 2013, Chapter 3.

the effects of promotional labour provisions due to the differences between the new trade agreements and the way they are operationalized in practice. Third, there are significant cultural, political and socio-economic differences between the partner countries with which the EU signs these agreements. More specifically, the fact that new subjects such as civil society organizations and social partners are envisaged in promoting social trade may be insufficient in terms of results because much will depend on the domestic context. For example, empirical studies of the 2012 EU-Colombia agreement show that, despite the country putting in place a fairly robust legal and institutional framework to protect labour rights, to date it has not yielded much impact. This is due to shortcomings in the way the Trade and Sustainability chapter of this agreement has been designed in the first place and then applied.[45] This unsatisfactory state of affairs is explained by the fact that there are still deeply rooted political and social inequalities in the country and institutionalized anti-union practices continue in spite of the new labour laws that have been put in place in the country.

A textual analysis of these new trade agreements also shows that social clauses are not given the same importance as its counterpart, the trade provisions of these trade agreements. Hence, we can see a difference in the weight that each of the main objects of these agreements has with the trade provisions carrying more weight than the social clauses. Furthermore, the latter do not strive for increased compliance but rather aim at preserving what is already in place, requiring the parties to the trade agreement to uphold and not lower their already existing labour commitments; they are conceived as aspirations together with the environmental provisions. Labour provisions are conceived as an element of sustainable development to be pursued through the trade agreement itself. They are not considered as having conditioning force on which to base trade relations.[46] This is well illustrated in the 2011 EU-Korea FTA agreement, which requires the parties to uphold their international commitments, namely the four CLS, which they should already adhere to automatically via their ILO membership.[47] It is thus a formal reaffirmation by the parties to uphold these labour standards within their own territory, in law

---

[45] Marx, Axel, Brecht Lein and Nicolás Brando, 'The Protection of Labour Rights in Trade Agreements. The Case of the EU-Colombia Agreement' 50 (2016) *Journal of World Trade* 587.

[46] Van den Putte, Lore, *The European Union's trade-labour linkage: Beyond the soft approach?* (July 2016) (unpublished doctoral thesis, on file with author).

[47] eg Art.13.4 subpara.3 and Art.13.7 subpara.2 of the 2011 EU-Korea FTA.

and in practice.[48] It also contains a commitment by the signatory parties that they will not lower their domestic labour standards to attract trade and foreign direct investment (FDI).[49] This provision seems to weaken rather than strengthen the parties' commitment to the respect for labour rights as it still enables them to lower the standards of labour protection in their countries if no causal link with increased trade or investment can be found. In addition, the commitment is loose: none of the agreements sets out specific steps that should be undertaken by the signatory parties to increase respect for social clauses. In the case of a labour dispute, EU trade agreements foresee a cooperative approach, which relies on dialogue and cooperation between the parties and between government officials and civil society. If the issue cannot be resolved in this way, a panel of experts can be established.[50] However, the recommendations of this panel lack enforceability.

While these promotional features of the 'new generation' of trade agreements contribute to injecting a social dimension into the EU's trade policy through cooperation and social dialogue, it remains to be seen whether they entail an effective improvement of the implementation-capacity of developing countries to respect and protect labour standards.

2.2.3 The subjects and objects of EU social conditionality in EU bilateral trade agreements

What is particularly interesting for the purposes of our study is the engagement and more generally the role of civil society organizations and social partners in the governance of the Trade and Sustainable Development chapter, namely the legal subjects of social conditionality in charge of its application. Their role has been attributed to them via the provisions of the trade agreements negotiated by the parties to the agreement. While the inclusion of these actors is meant to ensure better input democratic legitimacy, the lack of clarity as to their role means that it is difficult to evaluate their effective contribution to the objectives of the Trade and Sustainable Development chapter.[51] Some argue that their involvement is purely instrumental to the 'real' economic purpose of the agreement: they are used to forge broad support by 'helping the parties to

---

[48] Marx, Lein and Brando (n.45), 5.

[49] eg Art.13.7 subpara.2 of the 2011 EU-Korea FTA.

[50] eg Art.13.15 of the 2011 EU-Korea FTA.

[51] For further analysis of alternative forms to representative democracy, their legal force and the credibility of the EU's meaningful use in decision-making and implementation processes, particularly in relation to Art.11 TEU, see Korkea-aho (n.12).

"sell" the agreement to their constituencies and can thus be reduced to a public relations stunt to improve the reputation of the trading partners'.[52] Taking this further, it is argued that, through direct involvement in the governance of the social clauses, civil society organizations and social partners are 'being co-opted and their opposition is being neutralized'[53] despite being assigned the role of legal subjects in the operationalization of the agreement. Hence there is a risk of 'meta-injustice' in the form of 'meta-political misrepresentation' adverted to earlier in the chapter. By becoming institutionalized as such it becomes more difficult to oppose the instrumental nature of the Trade and Sustainable Development chapter. On a more positive note, and in spite of the limited enforceability of labour provisions in the short term, their inclusion may nevertheless have important policy learning effects in the longer term, such as providing the ground for transnational advocacy building or facilitating the functioning of existing transnational networks.[54] This form of experimentalist governance which is emerging in the context of these new trade agreements[55] may provide a better understanding of the challenges faced by a given third country, thus reducing negative externalities on affected stakeholders and communities.[56]

3. STRENGTHENING EU SOCIAL CONDITIONALITY THROUGH IMPACT ASSESSMENTS

3.1 The Use of Impact Assessments by the EU

Impact assessments of EU trade agreements have been carried out for some time.[57] Three types of evaluation can be conducted during the life

[52] Orbie, Martens and Van den Putte (n.36), 28.

[53] Orbie, Martens and Van den Putte (n.36).

[54] Keck, Margaret, and Kathryn Sikkink, 'Transnational Advocacy Networks in International and Regional Politics' 51 (2002) *International Social Science Journal* 89.

[55] In this sense, see Orbie, Martens and Van den Putte (n.36), 47–48; for an analysis of experimentalist governance in the context of EU external action, see Zeitlin, Jonathan (ed.), *Extending Experimentalist Governance? The European Union and Transnational Regulation* (Oxford University Press, Oxford 2015).

[56] Velluti (n.22), 110.

[57] The 2011 Joint Communication of the European Commission and High Representative of the European Union for Foreign Affairs and Security Policy on *Human Rights and Democracy at the Heart of EU External Action – Towards a More Effective Approach*, COM(2011)886 final explicitly refers to the

of a trade initiative:[58] an Impact Assessment (IA) at the initial design stage, a SIA during the trade negotiations,[59] and an evaluation after implementation.

The EU has been systematically conducting ex ante 'trade sustainability impact assessments' ('trade SIAs') prior to the conclusion of each trade agreement, as part of the EU's sustainable development policy (focusing in particular on economic development, social development and environmental protection) to establish what the impact of a given international agreement could be, particularly the likely changes and trade-offs caused by trade liberalization, and to identify certain measures which may reduce its negative effects.[60] Once the Council gives a mandate to conduct trade negotiations, the Commission initiates the

---

importance of impact assessments; see also the 2012 EU Strategic Framework and Action Plan on Human Rights and Democracy, of 25 June 2012. Luxembourg, Luxembourg. 11855/12 which expressly calls for the insertion of human rights in Impact Assessment, as and when it is carried out for trade agreements that have significant economic, social and environmental impacts. The new generation of trade SIAs reflect this goal.

[58] Further information is available at *ec.europa.eu/trade/policy/policy-making/analysis/index_en.htm#_bilateral-regional*, accessed 6 February 2017.

[59] There are also economic assessments of the negotiated outcome (EANOs). Once the negotiations are concluded, and before the trade agreement is signed, an economic analysis of the proposed agreement for the EU is prepared by the services of the Directorate-General (DG) Trade of the Commission for the European Parliament and the Council. The analysis assesses the impact of the actual outcome of the negotiations with regard to the reduction of trade barriers. This economic assessment is distinct from SIAs in which estimation of the likely impact of a proposed trade agreement is based on assumptions about the level of such reductions that will be achieved. It should also be noted that the economic assessment of the negotiated outcome is a trade-specific instrument and relates only to negotiations conducted by DG Trade: Nilsson, Lars, 'EU Trade Policy: Recent Progress and Analytical Advances' (GIFTA Workshop on 'Social and Labour Impacts of Free Trade Agreements', German Marshall Fund, Brussels, July 2016).

[60] European Commission, *Handbook for Trade Sustainability Impact Assessment 2016* (2nd edn), accessed 6 February 2017 at *trade.ec.europa.eu/doclib/docs/2016/april/tradoc_154464.PDF*; for a list of completed and ongoing assessments, *ec.europa.eu/trade/policy/policy-making/analysis/sustainability-impact-assessments/assessments/*, accessed 6 February 2017; for further analysis, Cote, Kyle, 'European Union Trade Sustainability Impact Assessments: Developing Coherence between Trade Agreements and Labour Standards' in Wouters, Jan, et al. (eds), Special Issue on 'Protecting Labour Rights in a Multi-polar Supply Chain and Mobile Global Economy' (2014) 89 *Bulletin of Comparative Labour Relations* Chapter 6.

process of a trade SIA. The EU trade SIAs are outsourced to competitive agencies and experts selected by the Commission who will employ a specific methodology, deliver economic analysis, carry out a preliminary assessment, provide detailed sector studies and a final synthesis report. Potentially these agencies and experts have a role as legal subjects in carrying out these SIAs. Economic, social and environmental impacts outside the EU are explicitly part of the analysis.[61] The scope of the impact is broad so as to cover a variety of objects, namely third countries and within countries, regions, businesses, firms, different categories and status of citizens, services, goods, the environment and the overall ecological system.[62] The relevant type of object will depend on the specific sector and/or nature of the issue addressed, as SIAs are generally highly contextualized.

These trade SIAs have been increasingly subject to criticism by many non-governmental organizations (NGOs) as they have failed to provide a proper assessment of how a given trade agreement will impact on human rights.[63] In particular, it is argued that they do not adequately consider the real problems that developing countries (particularly Least Developed Countries (LDCs)) have. This is mainly because not all sectors are assessed as illustrated by the SIAs carried out in relation to the EU–African, Caribbean and Pacific States (ACP) Economic Partnership Agreements (EPAs), which have not fully taken into account the impact that market integration has on small-scale farmers. A 2007 study on EPAs for the UN Human Rights Council concluded that the treaties would 'result, at least in the short run, in huge losses in revenue and restricted access to the EU market, making it highly likely that the social and

[61] European Commission, Better Regulation Guidelines, COM(2015) 215 final; European Commission, Better Regulation Toolbox, accessed 6 February 2017 at *ec.europa.eu/smart-regulation/guidelines/docs/br_toolbox_en.pdf*, Toolbox 16, Identification/Screening of Impacts.

[62] See n.61.

[63] Jones, Emily, 'Partnership or Power Play? How Europe Should Bring Development into Its Trade Deals with African, Caribbean, and Pacific Countries' (2008) Oxfam Briefing Paper, accessed 6 February 2017 at *www.oxfam.org/sites/www.oxfam.org/files/bp110_europe_EPAs_trade_deals_with_acp_countries_0804.pdf*; Office of the United Nations High Commissioner for Human Rights (OHCHR), Human Rights Impact Assessments for Trade and Investment Agreements, Report of the Expert Seminar, 23–24 June 2010, Geneva, Switzerland, accessed 6 February 2017 at *www2.ohchr.org/english/issues/food/docs/report_hria-seminar_2010.pdf*.

economic human rights of millions will be adversely affected'.[64] The European Commission's own SIAs of EPAs warned that, without adequate safeguards, ACP countries could be negatively exposed to lost tariff revenue and increased competition from EU exports, resulting in a damage to the local production that could disproportionately threaten the livelihoods and food security of rural populations.[65]

It has to be added that trade SIAs involve highly complex studies concerning a wide spectrum of sectors, stakeholders and economic, social and political variables that, as some IAs recognize, are very difficult to disaggregate and measure. To some extent, therefore, trade SIAs have inherent limitations, which explains why they can only provide a limited perspective on a given trade agreement and its potential impact.

3.2 Preliminary Remarks

The analysis carried throughout the chapter has shown that there are separate channels to feed into and thus ways to improve the nature and implementation of the Trade and Sustainable Development chapter. The first is through the involvement and monitoring function of civil society organizations and social partners under the Trade and Sustainable Development chapter. The second is through revised SIAs and, in particular, through the combined use of ex ante trade SIAs and ex post evaluations which could significantly contribute to strengthening the EU's practice of social conditionality in trade agreements. For this to be possible the

---

[64] Human Rights Council, 'Application of the criteria for periodic evaluation of global development partnerships – as defined in Millennium Development Goal 8 – from the right to development perspective: the Cotonou Partnership Agreement between the European Union and ACP Countries (Report by Professor James Thuo Gathii), UN doc. A/HRC/8/WG.2/TF/CRP.6 (21 December 2007), 2.

[65] PricewaterhouseCoopers, 'Sustainability Impact Assessment of the EU-ACP Economic Partnership Agreements', May 2007, accessed 6 February 2017 at *www.eesc.europa.eu/resources/docs/jochen-krimphoff-sia4-en.pdf*; see also Bilal, Sanoussi, et al., 'Global Financial and Economic Crisis: Analysis of and Implications for ACP-EU Economic Partnership Agreements (EPAs), ECDPM Discussion Paper No. 92, July 2009, accessed 6 February 2017 at *ecdpm.org/publications/analysis-of-and-implications-for-acp-eu-economic-partnership-agreements-epas/*; CEPII-CIREM, 'An Impact Study of the EU-ACP Economic Partnership Agreements (EPAs) in the six ACP Regions', Final Report – January 2008, accessed 6 February at *trade.ec.europa.eu/doclib/docs/2008/march/tradoc_138081.pdf*.

methodologies employed in the ex ante trade SIAs and ex post evaluations would need to take into full consideration the social rights impact of EU trade agreements. Most importantly, the EU would need to act upon their findings in a way which is not limited to maximizing the benefits of trade agreements and minimizing their potential negative impact, but also in a way that ensures a strengthening of social rights and labour standards in the EU and the third country concerned. These different channels correspond to different layers of decision-making within which we have different subjects of EU law. What is required for EU social conditionality to have more impact without resorting to negative conditionality is a strengthening of this subject-subject relationship. Specifically this requires that, as suggested above, the improved SIAs are combined together with a strengthened socialization process within the trade agreements.

4. CONCLUSION

The chapter examined the legal subjects and objects of EU social conditionality in its bilateral and regional trade agreements with a particular focus on the new generation of FTAs. This is a particularly interesting typology of agreements to study as it illustrates the way the EU – the main legal subject of these new agreements – is exercising its authority and economic leverage to promote social objectives outside its borders. Indeed, this type of trade agreement, and the promotional social conditionality therein, while serving a multifarious purpose, is a vivid manifestation of the current 'global reach of EU law'[66] with important effects in relation to the other legal subjects on the one hand and the legal objects that are covered by the trade agreement on the other. First, with regard to the institutional set-up we see a combination of traditional legal subjects, namely the EU, EU Member States and third countries, with less conventional legal subjects such as civil society organizations and social partners involved in the implementation and monitoring of the social clauses of these trade agreements. In this context, the aim of the EU is to strengthen the legitimacy input as well as the governance aspects of its social conditionality. The so-called 'global governance dilemma' illustrates this: 'the more global regulation is needed and implemented, the more demands are necessarily going to rise from the

[66] Fahey, Elaine, *The Global Reach of EU Law* (Routledge, Abingdon and New York 2016).

bottom up for democratic legitimacy and accountability of decision-makers'.[67] This development is thus to be welcomed because it gives voice to important legal subjects at the domestic and local levels where the required change in relation to social rights and labour standards needs to be injected. On another level, it also fosters the creation of transnational advocacy groups or strengthens existing transnational networks, thus promoting new types of subject-subject relationships. Nevertheless, the analysis suggests that this aspiration on the part of the EU has yet to materialize, in part because of a particular type of democratic ideology and mind-set which seems to stifle any attempt to give concrete meaning to participatory forms of democracy within the EU external trade relations context.[68] Second, with the promotion of social rights and labour standards through this new typology of trade agreements – their legal objects – we see the EU attempting to 'transcend the separation between economic growth and social institutions, in which the utopia of a market "civilization" coexists with the "dogma of universal competition"'.[69] To some degree the EU has acknowledged that trade and international economic law can have a significant impact on much more than economic activity and that they can raise profound questions of social concern. This is demonstrated by the increased social ambition of the EU in most of its international trade arrangements and not just in its new generation of FTAs.

However, what follows from this recognition with respect to the identification of adequate and effective institutional and legal arrangements remains uncertain and to some extent unsatisfactory. In addition, the insertion of social clauses in trade agreements is also debatable if not contestable, as the promotional nature of the EU's social conditionality may run the risk of watering down the human rights dimension of these social clauses, thus weakening their enforceability.

Overall, this seems to indicate that social conditionality in the EU's trade agreements remains premised on a standard mode of decision-making based largely on representative democracy. The voice and space of those legal subjects who are largely non-state actors and involved in the application and monitoring of EU social conditionality remain insufficiently meaningful. In turn, this results in a meagre impact in

---

[67] Telò, Mario, 'Introduction: The EU as a model, a global actor and an unprecedented power' in Mario Telò (ed.), *The European Union and Global Governance* (Routledge, London and New York 2009), 19.

[68] See in this sense, Korkea-aho (n.12).

[69] Perulli (n.17), 29, citing Supiot, Alain, *L'esprit de Philadelphie. La justice sociale face au marché total* (Seuil, Paris 2010).

respect of social rights and labour standards protection in the partner countries concerned, the legal object of the agreements, with unsatisfactory change in terms of results. Further empirical studies need to be carried out to assess whether this state of affairs is in the process of changing.

PART IV

Subjects and objects in Europe's crises

14. European integration in a crisis scenario: easy steps to revitalise the EU as a subject and to avoid disintegration?

Matthias Ruffert

1. THOSE WERE THE TIMES … ?

Few will disagree that the EU is in the deepest crisis since the inception of the integration process in the early 1950s. If the European institutions only had the support they were always granted in the past! Truly? In fact, there never was such full support. The history of European integration knows many setbacks. It all started with one of them when the French Assemblée nationale, pushed by the leader of the then radical socialist party, rejected the treaty on the European defence community.[1] It was not long before another French leader tried to block the whole process in the 1960s, preventing the UK from accessing (!) the Communities and blackmailing the Council until the Luxembourg compromise brought some relief.[2] The 1970s were considered a quiet time altogether, but also one of Eurosclerosis, culminating in a leaderette claiming her money back and handbagging her male co-leaders to the point of harassment. To continue: Whoever was in Brussels around 1992–93 when the Single Market was completed must have felt the dark mood among the eurocrats around the Danish and French referenda on the Maastricht treaty and the

[1] On the early history of the EU see Schulz-Forberg, Hagen, and Bo Stråth, *The Political History of European Integration: The Hypocrisy of Democracy-through-market* (Routledge, London 2010).

[2] Cf. Streinz, Rudolf, *Die Luxemburger Vereinbarung* (VVF, Munich 1984).

German *Bundesverfassungsgericht* (Federal Constitutional Court) established its ultra vires-control.[3] The following years were by no means easy. It took from 1992 to 2009 to collect the Maastricht leftovers, with two smaller treaty reforms (Amsterdam and – ridiculous in terms of reform – Nice), the blow against the constitution project by the referenda in France and the Netherlands, countless referenda in Ireland, and the masterpiece of saving what was agreed in the constitution project in the Treaty of Lisbon – albeit against the resistance of more leaders who, seven years later, are almost forgotten.

Looking at the past allows us to see the present difficulties in proportion. But if we consider Brexit, the problems with the refugee crisis, the ongoing state-debt crisis and the emerging coalition of wrongdoers against basic European values, we should take preceding developments into account to assess these topical issues. Unfortunately, we cannot do this. There is a quantum leap between the problems of the past and those of the present. We reasonably fear that all those efforts of integration could be lost by a general turn in disintegration. The EU would deteriorate from a subject designing the future of Europe into an object of forces operating against it.

2. WHAT IS AT STAKE IN THE CURRENT MULTI-CRISIS?

There is a vast range of criticism against the EU institutions: their lack of transparency, their poor accountability and their remoteness to the citizen-voters meant that the EU would not be admissible as a Member State if it were a state because it did not fulfil the minimum requirements of democratic government. The deficit in democracy of the Union is discussed broadly, the validity of the critical arguments to be set aside here.[4] Using an illustrative, albeit simplified wording, this criticism – whatever its validity – is about the input-legitimacy of the Union.

It is submitted that for the first time the current crisis calls into question the output-legitimacy of the EU. Again, there are historical

[3] The French population voted in favour of the treaty (51 per cent), the Danish population only in a second referendum. Cf. also 89 *Entscheidungen des Bundesverfassungsgerichts* 155.

[4] Cf. Ruffert, Matthias, in Calliess, Christian, and Matthias Ruffert, *EUV/AEUV – Das Verfassungsrecht der Europäischen Union mit Europäischer Grundrechtecharta*, 5th edn (C.H. Beck, Munich 2016), Art.9 EUV, paras 4 *et seq*., with references to relevant literature.

instances of criticism related to the output of the European institutions. There were butter mountains and milk lakes until the 1980s – but the Common Agricultural Policy was successful in feeding European bellies and the agricultural industry's pockets. The EU was totally taken by surprise by what happened in Yugoslavia in the 1990s, and it was unable to react adequately – but a common foreign policy was not at the core of the integration project, at least not at that time. There are the tractor seats design, the amount of curvature of cucumbers, the lightbulbs, SEPA-codes and plastic bags – but such factual or alleged underperformances are nothing more than mere molestations of everyday life. What we are experiencing today is far worse: the EU is blamed for failing to provide its citizens with basic public functions in the fields of security and economic welfare. Some prefer to convert the EU into an object of their criticism or even aversion instead of recongnising its active role in solving the problems mentioned and enabling it to do so.

The functioning of the blaming mechanism is obvious. If there is an external, even stronger actor outside national politics, it is not so difficult to make voters believe that the real problem lies elsewhere than in failures at home or in the problem itself. Thus, the frightening youth unemployment rate in the Mediterranean, including France, is highly deplorable and must be reacted upon with all available means, but it can be contested whether it is really caused by the EU's politics and not by the closure of domestic labour markets for young newcomers or deficits in vocational training. Similar questions may be asked with respect to the situation in Greece. Of course, the suffering of ordinary citizens due to the abysmal economic situation of the country is not acceptable. However, there are strong indications that this has little to do with the EU intervening in 2010. Suppose the first package for Greece in May 2010 had not been tied. The EU could not have been blamed for 'austerity' in the following six years, but Greece would have gone bankrupt as financial markets would have demanded repayment of their loans. The inquiry into whether there was no more money in the purse in late 2009 hints more towards domestic mismanagement and corruption than towards anything else.[5]

[5] This is further explained in Ruffert, 'The EMU in the ECJ – a new dimension of dispute resolution in the process of European integration', in Daniele, Luigi (ed.), *The Democratic Principle and the Economic and Monetary Union*, forthcoming, at III. 4. Cf. also the contributions in Dimitropoulos, Giorgios, Athanasios Gromitsaris and Martin Schulte (eds.), *State Reform for a Better Europe* (Duncker & Humblot, Berlin 2016), a Greek-German project the author participated in.

The political background to the refugee crisis is different, but by no means easier. The potential mistakes made in late summer 2015, under pressure of thousands of people on the roads, in railway stations or trains, were made at national level. However, politics cannot modify a problem to give it its ideal shape instead of solving it. We know from United Nations reports that there is a huge number of people in large parts of Africa and Asia who are heading towards Europe, if they are not already crossing the Sahara desert or the Mediterranean.[6] This challenge exists – whether the EU is politically active in the field or not. Can governments, such as the Hungarian, really claim that the enormous wave of refugees was brought to the country following a decision of the EU? It is ridiculous to say that the existence or the politics of the EU caused the refugees to leave their countries, but of course it is a viable strategy to do so in domestic politics.

It does not come as a surprise, therefore, that the EU, in its post-Brexit activity, addresses its political output first. The 'Bratislava roadmap' of 16 September 2016[7] lists certain measures to protect the EU's borders as well as 'work to be continued to broaden EU consensus in terms of long term migration policy, including on how to apply the principles of responsibility and solidarity in the future'. It foresees measures to provide for the security of the citizens in the EU, and undertakes to fight youth unemployment. These are all output-oriented measures – no shift of powers, no institutional reform being necessary to implement them.

3. THE DUAL CHARACTER OF SOVEREIGNTY REVISITED

The factual or alleged failures in delivering the output which is so necessary for the legitimacy of the EU are calling into question one of the most important narratives of the whole integration process. The EU is – among other functions – a co-operative endeavour of the Europeans to enhance the problem-solving capacity of public power. The supranational EU shall be better able to tackle the pertinent problems if or when the capacities of the Member States are not sufficient.

Once that belief fades, the idea of sovereignty regains ground. In democratic elections and votes people chose to close up their country

[6] The figures at *www.unhcr.org/figures-at-a-glance.html* alone should suffice for illustration (accessed 7 February 2017).

[7] Accessed 7 February 2017 at *www.consilium.europa.eu/en/press/press-releases/2016/09/16-bratislava-declaration-and-roadmap/*.

behind a fence, ban EU flags from public presentations – or leave the EU straight away. Other nations claim that their national sovereignty is in peril because of financial colonialism exerted by EU-led institutions, formerly called the 'Troika'. But we can also discern a more input-related approach towards sovereignty: the German *Bundesverfassungsgericht* establishes a link between sovereignty, democracy and individual personality. Within the democratic process, the individual takes part in sovereign governance and thus realises her or his inherent human dignity which would be at stake in the case of dominance from outside. In this rationale, the nation state becomes the 'primary space' for democratic rule, the EU at some sort of a secondary level.[8]

4. THE FADING OF THE SUPRANATIONAL INSTITUTIONAL DESIGN

i. The Challenge

This re-concentration on the nation state in Europe has repercussions on the performance of the EU's institutional design. If some important reforms are not undertaken, there is a serious risk that this unique design will fade and lose its supranational character. The shift is from subject to object: from an actor in European politics to a mere platform of interstate negotiations.

ii. The European Parliament

The European Parliament has seen a significant rise in its powers since the Lisbon Treaty. Co-decision became the ordinary legislative procedure, and the election in 2014 was parliamentarised by means of the creation of the *Spitzenkandidaten*.[9] However, as explained, institutional weaknesses remain that prevent the Parliament from being a strong actor in the current crisis.

The core deficit lies in the rules for electing the European Parliament, which still largely rely on domestic voting systems. MEPs continue to be elected in national contingents and at national level. This causes at least

---

[8] 123 *Entscheidungen des Bundesverfassungsgerichts* 267, summed up in the OMT-decision: Bundesverfassungsgericht, 43 *Europäische Grundrechte-Zeitschrift* (2016) 440.

[9] Cf. Goldoni, Marco, 'Politicising EU Lawmaking? The *Spitzenkandidaten* Experiment as a Cautionary Tale' (2016) 22 ELJ 279.

three negative effects on the supranational institutional design of the EU. First, it affects all progress in building European political parties. As long as voters elect national parties, which then form transnational groups in the European Parliament, there is an obstacle to the creation of supranational democratic rule in Europe.[10] Second, it leads to disproportion in representation. It is not by coincidence that the equality of voters is not mentioned in the core provision Article 14(3) TEU. As long as national borders are cogent limits to MEPs' constituencies, there is no way out of this problem.[11] Third, there are different limitations on how many votes are needed for a party or political group to enter the European Parliament. Most Member States apply limits (5 per cent or 3 per cent), but others explicitly reject this idea.[12]

In the light of these facts, the core problem of the European Parliament does not lie in its lack of powers or its position between a mere assembly and a parliament of a state, but in the electoral law of the EU. Its reform is indispensable. According to Article 223(1) TFEU, the initiative lies with the Parliament itself. The latest resolution of the European Parliament has not so far ripened into a formal proposal, and it is more reluctant than former reports (viz., the Duff-Report[13]), but at least it proposes a joint constituency for the *Spitzenkandidaten*, an overall threshold (albeit variable from three to five per cent) and a better identification of the European parties for the voters in the Member States.[14] If we consider the many proposals for reform discussed in the current crisis, the reform of the electoral law of the European Parliament appears to be a lot easier. Although it would require ratification by all Member States (Article 223(2) TFEU), there is no need for Treaty

[10] This is made clear by Grimm, Dieter, *Europa ja – aber welches? Zur Verfassung der europäischen Demokratie* (C.H. Beck, Munich 2016), 24 *et seq.*

[11] Cf. only Peuker, Enrico, 'Das Wahlrecht zum Europäischen Parlament als Achillesferse der europäischen Demokratie', (2008) *Zeitschrift für Europarechtliche Studien* 453, and of course 123 *Entscheidungen des Bundesverfassungsgerichts* 267 at 373 *et seq.*

[12] Cf. the debate around 129 *Entscheidungen des Bundesverfassungsgerichts* 300, and 135 *Entscheidungen des Bundesverfassungsgerichts* 259, with dissenting opinions at 352 and 306 respectively.

[13] Second Report on a proposal for a modification of the Act concerning the election of the members of the European Parliament by direct universal suffrage of 20 September 1976, 2 February 2012 (2009/2134(INI)), Doc. A7-0027/2012.

[14] European Parliament resolution of 11 November 2015 on the reform of the electoral law of the European Union (2015/2035(INL)), Doc. P8_TA-PROV(2015)0395.

amendment. This reform must be faced if the Parliament is not to be downgraded to a mere platform for negotiation.

The same holds true for the current parliamentary practice of deciding a vast majority of legislative proposals in a Trilogue procedure. True, Article 295 TFEU, first sentence foresees consultations between Parliament, Council and Commission. However, it should be recognised that the European Parliament – probably like all parliaments of the world – is not an ideal partner for interinstitutional negotiations.[15] The interest and political input of the European Parliament is represented in these negotiations by a delegation led by the rapporteur of the relevant committee. Negotiations are confidential, which means that the inherent advantages of any parliamentary procedure – debate, persuasion, compromise – get lost to the benefit of a self-organised bargaining system. The underlying pre-Lisbon interinstitutional agreement was concluded nearly ten years ago. To modify it in such a way as to bring forward the aforementioned 'parliamentary virtues' is not difficult; there is no need for ratification or any other lengthy procedure. As a result, however, the EU could benefit substantially from such modification. Its position as a strong subject of European politics and not a mere negotiation platform could be significantly strengthened.

iii. The Executive in Europe

(a) From Community method to Union method

The creation of parliamentary rule was not the beginning of the integration process, to say the least. In terms of institutions, it all started with a strong executive, the High Authority which was later transformed into the European Commission. For decades, the presence of the EU as a subject was guaranteed by this particular executive.[16] Recent years brought significant changes.

The Treaty of Lisbon secured a prominent position for the European Council, reforming the presidency of the Council by introducing the European Council's president as an institutional invention. In the eurozone's state debt crisis, the European Council and its 'sub-group', the eurozone summit, took the lead in reshaping the economic constitution of the EU. Though not endowed with legislative functions (explicitly

---

[15] Cf. the critique in the seminal article by von Achenbach, Jelena, 'Verfassungswandel durch Selbstorganisation: Triloge im europäischen Gesetzgebungsverfahren' 55 *Der Staat* (2016), 1.

[16] Cf. in general Ruffert, 'Personality under EU Law: A Conceptual Answer towards the Pluralisation of the EU' (2014) 20 ELJ, 346.

Article 15(1) TEU, second sentence), it transformed political programming into detailed input for legislation. The European Stability Mechanism was created as an International Organisation outside the EU, and – for different reasons that may be obsolete after Brexit – the control mechanism of the European Fiscal Compact was equally positioned outside the Treaties.[17]

In the beginning, the euphemism 'Union method' as opposed to the Community method was used to justify the ongoing rise of intergovernmental elements in the institutional framework of the EU.[18] After about six years of muddling through, following that alleged Union method with an emphasis on intergovernmental bargaining instead of supranational decision-making, we know the disadvantages. Bargaining conflicts oppose Member States – the North versus the South, the Visegrád East versus the established West, the Nordic versus the Mediterranean, Germany versus all the rest. The political advantage of the heads of state or government preserving their power in interstate negotiations is outweighed by the disadvantages of visible conflicts. To quit this impasse, some propose the supranationalisation of the European Council.[19] However, the complexity of such a Treaty is bound to block its realisation. We can also observe that the Court of Justice makes some (successful) efforts to integrate all the intergovernmental elements into the EU framework, be it in terms of institutions (*Pringle*)[20] or substantive law/human rights (*Ledra Advertising*).[21] The crisis certainly did not take a course to advance optimism excessively, but here it might be useful to see whether the advantages of supranational rule would not have a chance of returning. It is also not too far-reaching to require that the limits of Article 15(1) TEU be taken seriously. The EU as a subject could only benefit.

---

[17] Cf. only Ohler, Christoph, *Bankenaufsicht und Geldpolitik in der Währungsunion* (C.H. Beck, Munich 2015), para.3/79.

[18] The term was coined by Chancellor Angela Merkel: Rede von Bundeskanzlerin Merkel anlässlich der Eröffnung des 61. akademischen Jahres des Europakollegs Brügge, 2 November 2010, accessed 7 February 2910 at *www.bundeskanzlerin.de/ContentArchiv/DE/Archiv17/Reden/2010/11/2010-11-02-merkel-bruegge.html.*

[19] Fabbrini, Federico, *Economic Governance in Europe* (Oxford University Press, Oxford 2016) at 236 *et seq.*

[20] ECJ, Case C-370/12, ECLI:EU:C:2012:756, paras 153 *et seq.* (Pringle).

[21] ECJ, Cases C-8/15 P to C-10/15 P, ECLI:EU:C:2016:701 (Ledra Advertising).

(b) From high authority to polycentric administration

At first sight, the pluralisation of the EU's administration – illustrated as 'agencification' – has little to do with the issue of disintegration. The proliferation of agencies in the last ten years or so (the current number of decentralised agencies alone now being 34 – divergences in the counting method notwithstanding) has often been described and analysed.[22] The issues treated are the legal basis for the creation of an agency, the democratic legitimacy of agencies as well as judicial review of agency action and damages following agency negligence. A closer look at the structure of the agencies, however, reveals a deeper problem for the institutional design of the Union. Usually, the board of management of an agency (whatever its precise name) is composed of Member States' representatives. On the one hand, it is perfectly correct to consider such a co-operative framework as part of the EU's composite administration.[23] On the other hand, the agencies shape a network of 'mini-EUs' subdivided according to the subject matter of their competence, which might degenerate into a plethora of negotiation platforms.

It has been proposed elsewhere that a more coherent integration of the agencies in the pluralist institutional setting of the EU should be developed.[24] One element to effect this could be the establishment of a supervision of the legality of the agencies' actions, taking up a pan-European concept of administrative organisation from the tradition of public legal persons in Member States' law. According to Article 17(1) TEU, second, third and fifth sentences, the ideal institution for the exercise of such supervision is the European Commission. Following these provisions, the Commission shall be the guardian of EU law ('… shall ensure the application of the Treaties, and of measures adopted by the institutions pursuant to them'). The Commission 'shall oversee the application of Union law under the control of the Court of Justice of the

---

[22] Literature on this point is vast. Cf. Busuioc, Madalina, *European Agencies* (Oxford University Press, Oxford 2013); Craig, Paul, in Patrick Birkinshaw/Mike Varney (Hrsg.), *The European Legal Order After Lisbon* (Kluwer, The Hague 2010), 93; Curtin, Deirdre, *Executive Power of the European Union* (Oxford University Press, Oxford 2009); Groß, Thomas, *Die Legitimation der polyzentralen EU-Verwaltung* (Mohr Siebeck, Tübingen 2015); Hofmann, Herwig, and Alessandro Morini, 'Constitutional Aspects of the Pluralisation of the EU Executive Through "Agencification"' (2012) 37 EL Rev., 37; Weißgärber, Kirsten, *Die Legitimation unabhängiger europäischer und nationaler Agenturen* (Nomos, Baden Baden 2016).

[23] Augsberg, Steffen, in Terhechte Jörg Philipp (ed.), *Verwaltungsrecht der Europäischen Union* (Nomos, Baden-Baden 2011), paras 6/31 *et seq.*

[24] Ruffert (n.16 above) at 361 *et seq.*

European Union' and exercise executive and management functions. As it stands at the top of the European administration, which is first mentioned in Article 298(1) TFEU, it is the supervisory body par excellence. Its responsibility towards the European Parliament under Article 17(8) could provide the link between democratic legitimacy and administrative legality. For the executive agencies, the supervisory function of the Commission is already recognised by the relevant regulation.

Generally, the supervisory activity of the Commission has to be integrated into its action as provided for by the relevant statute of the agency, for example in co-operative proceedings for the creation of delegated legislation or in complaints procedures. It has further to be limited to the control of legality to avoid substantial intervention in the policies of the agencies which might lead to an incursion into their recognised administrative autonomy.

5. THE TASK OF LEGAL SCHOLARSHIP

Advancing the reforms of the electoral law of the European Parliament, reducing trilogues and making them more transparent, limiting intergovernmental decision-making by means of political practice and structuring the polycentric administration of the EU – these are, it cannot be denied, very modest proposals. What is worse is that there is certainly no guarantee of success. If European politics does not generate a better outcome, institutional reforms are futile.

For a (legal) scholar, it might be tempting to present blueprints for the solution of one problem or another. Some authors cannot resist it. The risk, however, is to leave the scope of methodologically sound analysis. After all, the law is not everything; there is a framework shaped by other disciplines such as economy or political science, and there is political choice by the persons and institutions in charge of political decision-making. What we can offer as European legal scholars is a set of principles, rules and institutions, functioning and content of which has been scrutinised over the years and can be foreseen in its effects. The explanation of the said set may serve the political process, if only in demonstrating that the existing institutional arrangement of the EU is groundwork to be further built on. It is impossible to convince the fierce representatives of populism, currently more right-wing but also, in some countries, sometimes left-wing. The general public, however, deserves valid information about what has already been achieved in creating a powerful subject of European politics.

15. *Homo objectus*, *homo subjectus* and Brexit

Dora Kostakopoulou and Anastasia Tataryn

1. INTRODUCTION

When the result of the British referendum on EU membership was confirmed, on the morning of 24 June 2016, the people in the United Kingdom woke to an altered nation. Citizens of the European Union who had for decades lived as equals with citizens of the UK felt the ground shift beneath their feet: from equal legal citizen-subjects, they were *becoming* different and foreign. The objectification of the 'other', as an outsider without equal entitlement or claim to the laws of the nation-state, had even before the Brexit vote been a reality for persons living in the UK without citizenship, permanent status or access to citizenship, namely those who were without documentation and legal immigration status. Their 'irregular' position in the nation-state falls between the gaps of legal categories that look to citizenship as recognition of status and subjectivity under the law. The EU citizen in a post-referendum Britain likewise risks being left in such an 'irregular' space.

Previously recognised as subjects of the law, these individuals have the threat of non-recognition within a national law that sees them as outsiders, as objects objectified by their condition. In other words, *homo subjectus* is transformed into *homo objectus*. Yet the anticipated transition of *homo subjectus* into a rightless *homo objectus* can only take place in an unambiguous way if all the movers and actors of its initial (subject) and terminal (object) situations are the same. This is even more the case if the activity of the social life that constitutes status – including work and economic, social reproduction – is recognised only through formal legal distinctions and if these are allowed to be the sole demonstration of democratic participation. If, however, all those affected by the outcome of the Brexit vote who, in this particular example, had been precluded from taking part in it, could embrace a status of *homo activus* and take part in shaping the subsequent unfolding of the event, then we could end up with multiple events or multiple endings.

To this end, we argue that the relationship between *homo subjectus* and *homo objectus* is neither predetermined nor inevitable. It is, rather, interrupted by *homo activus*. The *homo activus* opens up processes that are unknown but which offer the possibility of democratic participation reflective of the individuals who are living and working in a given territory, in the United Kingdom, away from predetermined subjectivities and restrictive categories of identification.

2. *HOMO OBJECTUS, HOMO SUBJECTUS* AND CONDITIONING EVENTS

In 1920 Alfred North Whitehead published a companion book to his previous work, *An Enquiry concerning the Principles of Natural Knowledge*. It was entitled *Concept of Nature* and included a chapter on 'Objects'.[1] In this chapter, Whitehead mapped the relation between objects and events and in so doing he used the term 'ingression'. He wrote, 'I am using the term ingression to denote the general relation of objects to events. The ingression of an object into an event is the way the character of the event shapes itself by virtue of the being of the object. Namely, the event is what it is because the object is what it is; and when I am thinking of this modification of the event by the object, I call the relation between the two "the ingression of the object into the event".'[2]

The ingression of objects into events is more visible in political life than in nature. This is because political life becomes crystallised in institutions, practices and policies following events that modify relations and turn objects into subjects.[3] Events could also undo meaningful relations and transform subjects into objects. In both cases, institutions, law and policies are undergoing fundamental change. For instance, the entry into force of the European Communities Act in 1972 made UK and EU nationals the subjects of rights derived from European Community law. Free movement, one of the four fundamental freedoms,[4] became the cornerstone of the building of an internal market and an EU-wide

1 *Concept of Nature* (Cambridge University Press, Cambridge 1920).

2 N.1, p. 144.

3 See chapter 1 of this volume by S. Bardutzky and E. Fahey.

4 The other three freedoms are free movement of goods, capital and services.

citizenship[5] anchored on mobility and with this the desirability of crossing borders with a view to creating new opportunities for individuals and more prosperity and openness for communities.

The application of the new legal order to the United Kingdom made individuals holders of rights that authorities in the UK and other Member States had to recognise and to respect. Human mobility was no longer viewed as a nuisance or a problem. Instead, it was seen as a positive and enriching socio-political and juridical reality. It had to be actively encouraged and promoted as a source of great strength for the economy, society and the individual. It is true that mobility has always been differential; in the main it is 'privileged' EU citizens who have taken advantage of their free movement rights. But its regulation and promotion by a supranational body, such as the European Union, supersedes national autonomy over the grant of entry and residence rights to EU citizens and their family members and, recently, the residence rights of third-country national parents of children who are EU citizens.[6]

The UK's 1975 referendum on the continuation of its EC membership did not alter this legal reality. The decision in favour of continued membership led the then Prime Minister, Harold Wilson, to state in the House of Commons that 'the historic decision has been made … We look forward to continuing to work with [our partners] in promoting the Community's wider interests and in fostering a greater sense of purpose among the Member States'.[7] That event thus did not change the *homo juridicus* status of EU nationals. In contrast, the Brexit outcome of the referendum on 23 June 2016 gave rise to the prospect of EU citizens becoming former subjects of EU law rights and thus objects when the withdrawal agreement between the UK and the European Union enters into force.

Of course, critics might argue here that the transformation of *homo subjectus* into *homo objectus* owing to active conditioning events is neither a new nor an unexpected development. States have not hesitated to denationalise even their own citizens under the shadow of oppressive

---

[5] The Maastricht Treaty (1 November 1993) institutionalised European Union citizenship and declared that 'every person holding the nationality of a Member State shall be a citizen of the Union'; formerly Art.8(1) EC, then Art.17(1) EC on renumbering, and now Art.20 TFEU.

[6] *Baumbast and R v Secretary of State for the Home Department* (Case C-413/99) [2002] ECR I-7091; *Zhu and Chen* (Case C-200/02) [2004] ECR I-9925; *Zambrano* (Case C-34/09), Judgment of the Court of 8 March 2011.

[7] Cited in Dinan, D., *Ever Closer Union: An Introduction to European Integration* (Palgrave, Basingstoke 1999), 74.

ideology and/or fear about their continued security. For example, a century ago, France withdrew the French nationality of 'citizens of enemy origin' (in 1915).[8] Belgium proceeded to denaturalise non-patriotic citizens in 1922, while Italy denaturalised dissidents on the ground that they were 'undeserving of Italian citizenship' in 1926.[9] Austria and Germany enacted similar laws in 1933 and 1935, respectively. Following such events, the *homo juridicus* status of citizens was erased; they were relegated outside the scope of the law and were given a non-recognised *status objectus*. As Chief Justice Warren noted with respect to processes of denationalisation in the US in the late 1950s, such events result in 'the total destruction of the individual's status in an organised society'.[10]

Although events may not always be effective and the forces of change are not always eruptive and thus clearly visible, one must not lose sight of how easy it is for political life to change direction and to transform equals into unequals[11] and 'unwanted objects'.[12] In such cases, new practices are invented, new policies are devised and new documents are produced. Not long ago, developments in Eastern Europe showed the 'ingression' of subjects into events and their transformation into objects. Former citizens, who were Russian-speaking, became non-citizens in the newly independent countries of Estonia and Latvia in 2004 and, in 1992, 18,000 permanent residents originating from other republics of the former Yugoslavia, mostly of non-Slovene or mixed ethnicity, were 'erased' in Slovenia, that is, they were removed from the register of permanent residents, thereby becoming quasi foreigners.[13] This meant

---

[8] Bill to Revoke Naturalisation in France, *The Law Times*, Vol. 188-21, 2 January 1915.

[9] For more detail on denaturalisations, see *www.newworldencyclopedia.org/entry/Naturalization*, accessed 7 February 2017.

[10] *Trop v Dulles*, 356 US 86, 101 (1958).

[11] I have borrowed this from Kostakopoulou, D., 'Ideas, Norms and European Citizenship' *Modern Law Review* Vol. 65(2) (2005), 233–67.

[12] Birmingham, P., *Hannah Arendt and Human Rights. The Predicament of Common Responsibility* (Indiana University Press, Bloomington IN 2006); Honig, B., *Democracy and the Foreigner* (Princeton University Press, Princeton NJ 2001); Kostakopoulou, D., *Citizenship, Immigration and Identity in the European Union: Between Past and Future* (Manchester University Press, Manchester 2001).

[13] In 1999, the Slovenian Constitutional Court declared the erasure unlawful and unconstitutional; Case No. U-I-284/94, accessed 7 February 2017 at *odlocitve.us-rs.si/en/odlocitev/AN01683*.

that the status of EU citizenship was not available to them.[14] In addition, Hungary's contemplation of granting external or extraterritorial citizenship to persons of Hungarian origin living in non-EU states, such as in Serbia, Montenegro and Ukraine, thereby altering unilaterally the personal scope of EU citizenship, gave rise to concern.[15]

Human vulnerability increases when political events lead to authoritative decisions and policies that undo, or threaten to undo, legal rights and that unsettle human lives. In such cases, the temporal happening is not simply a process, but is also a variation in so far as it alters legal realities. The latter manifests itself in the removal of rights protection.[16] This is noticeable in the UK following the announcement of the outcome of the EU membership referendum on 23 June 2016. As both the status of *homo subjectus* and the practices associated with that status are to be negotiated following the activation of Article 50 TEU, EU citizens living permanently in the UK, as well as UK nationals living in other EU Member States, are struggling to come to terms with the unexpected transition from recognised subjects to objects of governmental negotiations and actions. As a consequence, there has been a surge in naturalisation applications in the UK and certain Member States.

Making EU citizenship conditional on domicile for a period of five years in the territory of the EU would make the social fact of community membership a true determinant of belonging and provide an answer to the insecurity of UK nationals living in host Member States. Although this may be deemed to be a radical proposal unlikely to meet with national executives, it has been proposed and defended since the 1990s

---

[14] Instead, imperfect solutions were sought in the lesser status of quasi-civic citizenship entailed by Directive 2003/109/EC of 25 November 2003 Concerning the Status of Third Country Nationals who are Long-Term Residents in the EU (OJ L 16/44 of 23 January 2004) and the EU anti-discrimination directives (Directive 2004/43/ EC of 29 June 2000 implementing the principle of equal treatment between persons irrespective of racial and ethnic origin [2000] OJ L 180/22 and Directive 2000/78/EC of 27 November 2000 establishing a general framework for equal treatment in employment and occupation [2000] OJ L 303/16). Yet, the panoply of rights afforded by these Directives is imperfect and partial.

[15] Article 16 of the Hungarian Constitution establishes the state's responsibility to support Hungarians living abroad, but the 2001 legislation granted them limited access to the Hungarian labour market, thereby falling short of awarding state nationality.

[16] Compare Arendt, H., *The Origins of Totalitarianism* (Houghton Mifflin Harcourt, New York NY 1976).

and has featured on policy agendas at the European level.[17] However, this proposal would not assist EU citizens living in the UK who would have to opt either for naturalisation or for permanent leave to remain in the United Kingdom.

While naturalisation might furnish a secure and fully recognised status for certain EU citizens, one cannot sidestep the fact that their transition from subjects to objects of governmental negotiations and actions has happened without their consent and involvement since they were excluded from taking part in the referendum on 23 June 2016. The new reality will thus be constructed in their name but without them. Their gradual disassociation and their ensuing non-recognition are acts 'done to them'.[18] They have no power to contest this development and to object to their de-citizenisation and reclassification as either third-country nationals or EU nationals living in a third country. A decision taken by a transient majority in late June 2016, therefore, effectively shatters individuals' lives, the life horizons they have built following decades of residence, socio-economic and (partial) political membership in the host Member States and the future of their families.

In addition to the gradual process of 'othering' that happens without their consent in the place of their residence, they also experience a temporal violence. They become distanced in time; they are aware that official discourses redefine them as 'unwanted' due to their 'foreign' nationality, but, at the same time, their inability to uproot themselves, to live anywhere else and to establish new life horizons creates a 'uchrony', that is, a world of no time. While in the past they could easily oscillate between the past and the future, their memories and their expectations and dreams, the flow of this process has now been seriously disrupted. The disruption is caused not only by the absence of a political commitment guaranteeing them security of residence and thus by the ambiguity of the future; it is also caused by the fact that in the temporal process of

---

[17] It was suggested by the European Union's Migrants Forum in its proposals for the revision of the TEU at the 1996 IGC. For early normative justifications of this policy option, see Kostakopoulou, D., 'Towards a Theory of Constructive Citizenship in Europe' *Journal of Political Philosophy* Vol. 4(4) (1996), 337–58 and Rubio-Marin, R., and J. Monar's contributions in La Torre, M. (ed.), *European Citizenship: An Institutional Challenge* (Kluwer, The Hague 1998).

[18] Bauman observed that the other 'becomes an irrelevant presence, a non-recognised being, a non-admitted existence'; 'Effacing the Face: On the Social Management of Moral Proximity', *Theory, Culture and Society*, Vol. 7 (1990), 5–38 at 25. See also Levinas, E., 'La Trace De L'Autre', trans. A. Lingis, *Tijdschrift voor Philosophie* (September 1963), 605–23.

going backwards and forwards they can no longer contemplate a smooth transition from the past to the present and to the future. There has been a disruptive and path-altering 'interval', that is, a new reality brought about by an accidental happening, namely, the Brexit referendum decision. Because the succession of 'tomorrows' cannot slide smoothly into the past, EU nationals living in the UK and UK citizens living in the EU experience disorientation and distress.

Nevertheless, a national identity is just one of the 'multiple constituents' of selfhood.[19] To ignore this reality would be tantamount to disregarding the concreteness of human beings and thus the concern and respect they deserve.[20] While it is so true that for centuries peoples' lives have been monopolised, and to a large extent disregarded by all sorts of elites, monarchical, ecclesiastical and state elites as well as political parties, one cannot expect that in the twenty-first century people will merely observe their lives drifting away according to collective currents. Nor should they be expected to be willing to exchange their real lives as EU citizens for the imaginary ones which their own states of origin or residence may harbour for them. For in these lives, forged over years and often decades, 'there is too much of them and too little of their country of origin'.[21]

3. RECREATING DEMOCRACY: *HOMO ACTIVUS*

There exists a visible democratic deficit in the forthcoming transformation of *homo subjectus* into *homo objectus* caused by the Brexit referendum decision. All those profoundly affected by it in the UK were not allowed to take part in the referendum, while more than a few British expatriates in other Member States encountered problems in registering their votes. From a pragmatic point of view, one might be inclined to advise the acceptance of the new situation and counsel flexibility in coping with its implications.

---

19 Dewey, J., *Human Nature and Conduct* (Dover Publications, Mineola, 2002 [1922]), at 138. Here I have drawn on Kostakopoulou, D., 'When EU Citizens Become Foreigners', *European Law Journal*, Vol. 20(4) (2014), 447–463.

20 Kant, I., *Groundwork of the Metaphysics of Morals* (trans. H.J. Paton) (Harper, New York NY and London 1964 [1948]); Dworkin, R., *Taking Rights Seriously* (Harvard University Press, Cambridge MA 1977); *A Matter of Principle* (Harvard University Press, Cambridge MA 1985).

21 The phrase is borrowed from Sanatayana, G., *Middle Span: The Background of My Life* (Constable, London 1947), 7.

Yet, self-governing societies do not merely accommodate events; they display determination and inventiveness in enhancing democratic practices and refusing to dismantle democratic legal orderings which regulate the lives of millions of human beings. In this respect, although one is more often than not tempted to conclude that an event, be it political or otherwise, has one determinate ending, political inventiveness and an activist approach to law and politics may require us to contemplate the possibility of multiple endings.[22]

We recall, here, an observation made by Rikker: '… if all the movers and actors of the initial situation are not in the terminal situation, then the event ends more than once, so that there are really as many events as endings. This means that it is impossible to generalise about events with multiple endings because the scientist does not know which of these events to include in the generalisation. Similarly, if movers and actors other than those in the initial situation are in the terminal situation, then the event must begin more than once, with similar consequences for generalisation.'[23]

In other words, the anticipated transition of *homo subjectus* into a rightless *homo objectus* can take place in an unambiguous way only if all the movers and actors of its initial and terminal situations are the same. If, on the other hand, all those affected by the outcome, who had been precluded from taking part in it, could embrace the status of *homo activus* and take part in shaping the subsequent unfolding of the event, then we may end up with multiple events or multiple endings. Similarly, a different evaluation of the implications of an event and its relation to a different set of circumstances or situations would give us a different ending. What is suggested here is not a process of manipulation of the passage of time. We suggest an interruption in order to prevent injustice and to preserve the freedom of relating to, and co-operating with, human beings without discrimination on the ground of nationality.

Beyond the statuses of 'subject' and 'object' lies the possible ingression of *homo activus* into events with a view to shaping them in ways that enhance the democratic way of life. For, as Dewey has observed, 'everything which bars freedom and the fullness of communication sets up barriers that divide human beings into sets and cliques, into antagonistic sects and factions, and thereby undermines the democratic way of

---

22 It is possible that an event may never have an end if the end in view becomes absorbed by its multiple and diffuse implications.

23 Rikker, W., 'Events and Situations', *The Journal of Philosophy*, Vol. 54(3) (1957) 57–70 at 61–2.

life'.[24] *Homo activus* thus takes part in producing the 'coming time'. This is not the same as the process of becoming a subject or an object. Instead, it is a creative process; a movement that forces us away from an oppositional subject versus object binary, towards another way of being. *Homo activus* makes things happen, creating thereby the conditions of possibility for becoming and unbecoming. By engaging with the world, interrupting, contesting, questioning, rethinking and effectuating change, as well as failing to do so, *homo activus* challenges the subject or object positions devised by those in power, changes the direction of events, the surrounding environment and his/her personal experiences. He/she is an agent of socio-political change.[25]

4. *HOMO ACTIVUS* AND IRREGULARITY

Homo activus is not a status that needs to be sought out or created. Nor are EU citizens the only non-UK citizens living and working as *homo activus* in Britain. Persons considered to be migrants without 'regular' status, whether due to pending asylum applications, suspended work permits or awaiting residency permits, are considered to be objects of immigration law. Yet, these so-called 'irregular' migrants are persons who are, and have often been for years, active in their communities and workplaces. Recognition of their participation and activity is denied within a legal architecture that relies on holding citizenship for a person to be a subject of the law.[26] To be recognised as a legal subject, with an active claim and access to the law, a person is often reliant on recognition through citizenship. When that person can affirm that he/she is a citizen of the nation state, or deservingly/legitimately on the path to securing citizenship, then from this status follows a claim to the law of the nation state and access to the nation's justice system. With reference to the Aristotelian construction of 'subject', Costas Douzinas looks at the legal

---

[24] Dewey's address in New York City on 20 October 1939, entitled 'Creative Democracy: The Task Before Us', p. 4.

[25] See Kukovec, D., Chapter 3 of this volume.

[26] Legal architecture refers to the regime of nation state-centred law … not only the English legal system, but the processes whereby an individual can have access to justice, such as access to legal representation, access to legal advice and education, and the power to affirm legal entitlements that are afforded to persons in a given nation state.

subject as split between subjectum and subjectus.[27] The citizen is meant to have both: subjectum is the subject of the law and subjectus is the subject to the law. However, this binary split is not enough to characterise the recognition that is withheld from 'irregular' migrants for they are neither subjectus nor subjectum. In other words they are the rejects, the others, the foreigners-without-a-name. Thus, so long as legal status, namely citizenship status, is the arbiter of identity and belonging, the legal recognition of persons without determined legal immigration status is suspended. This renders these individuals 'irregular', where recognition of their participation as subjects of the law is denied, as is their access to the rights and status afforded to legal subjects. Instead, they are objects – bodies broadly labelled as 'migrant' and practically excluded from the community of the nation state. Their existence as *homo objectus* is enacted through the practice of a legal system that looks for citizenship as identification, and their prospects of achieving status as *homo subjectus* are slim, particularly as borders are reinforced.

4.1 The Nation State, Citizenship and Legal Recognition

Citizenship under the law tends to universalise belonging.[28] As an indicator of belonging and membership, citizenship poses as if it were an attainable legal status for all persons within a territory, one that 'irregular' migrants have in one way or another failed to achieve. The possibility of losing rights as citizens, a reality for many EU citizens living in the UK as Brexit is implemented, reinforces the ostensible value and importance of citizenship as an arbiter of subjectivity. Nevertheless, like 'migrants' before them, persons losing their status and subjectivity continue to live and work and thus continue to be active beings. Their activity as *homo activus* is unhindered by subject or object distinctions since activity and participation is the defining feature of status as opposed to legal, formal, subjectivity. Democracy, recreated through

---

[27] Douzinas, C., *The End of Human Rights: Critical Legal Thought at the Turn of the Century* (Hart, Oxford and Portland OR 2000), 183. Douzinas further notes, 'We think of the subject as the exclusive vehicle of freedom, perhaps because the split is no longer fully apparent as it was in pre-revolutionary Europe; the subjectum/subjectus dyad has been fully internalised and the law, self-given and externally imposed, already inhabits and conceals itself in the recesses of the self.', 226.

[28] Fudge, J., 'Precarious Migrant Status and Precarious Employment' *Comparative Labor Law and Policy Journal* Vol. 34(1) (Fall 2012), 110, in reference to Cohen, J., 'Changing Paradigms of Citizenship and the Exclusiveness of the Demos' *International Sociology* (1999), 245–268.

homo activus, does not exist if the action and activity of all individuals in a given space and territory is taken into account, recognised, and reckoned with. Such a democracy would entail a law that is in process of becoming and unbecoming, rather than aimed at securing subjectivity, however precariously. A law that is in process of becoming and unbecoming is one that explicitly takes into account all persons who constitute the community governed by it, because communities emerge as a result of the interactions and relationships that are happening on a daily basis in all spheres, from economic markets to neighbourhoods, from workplaces to homes.[29]

The possibility of thousands of citizens formally losing their status as a consequence of the Brexit vote may force the informalisation of status and employment of EU citizens in the UK. In other words, the practices and activities of these individuals may be pushed into less regulated and more insecure forms of work and residency. For instance, informalisation into more precarious, short-term or seasonal forms of work in agricultural, hospitality, fashion/clothing and food sectors as well as consultancy, including high-waged consultancies, where individuals are working as 'migrants' rather than as citizens.[30] The informalisation of work and status renders former subjects irregular – they are suspended, precarious, ostensibly distinct from the fixed, settled, subjectivity of UK citizens. Yet this irregularity is not a complete dismissal of their presence or activity, it is a suspension where quasi-legal or semi-legal regulatory practices are exercised with little accountability. Moreover, there is no explicit determination of 'irregularity', rather a quiet conformity or non-conformity with what is considered to be 'good' behaviour of citizen-subjects.[31] Like citizenship's tendency to universalise belonging, there is a pervasive belief within modern legal thought that if only the law is applied 'correctly' and 'effectively', then justice, order and the rule of law will prevail. However, if that effective and correct application is practically impossible because of citizenship demands, then is the *homo*

---

[29] For more on such a rethinking of law and sociality, see Tataryn, A., 'Labour and Migration in the "Suspended Step"', in Mulqueen, T., and D. Matthews, *Being Social: Ontology, Law, Politics* (Counterpress, Oxford 2015), 90–100.

[30] Welter, F., D. Smallbone and A. Pobol, 'Entrepreneurial activity in the informal economy', *Entrepreneurship & Regional Development* Vol. 27 (5–6) (2015), 292–306; Slavnic, Z., 'Political Economy of Informalisation' *European Societies* Vol. 12(1) (2010).

[31] Anderson, B., *Us & Them: The Dangerous Politics of Immigration Control* (Oxford University Press, Oxford 2013).

activus outside the law? In other words, is there an order that exceeds status under the law? Individual lives can be, and are, subjugated, but rather than see the loss of a particular subjectivity as a transition from 'subject' to 'object', attention to the active process of being may allow recognition of actors and activity that transgress and transform predetermined legal categories, such as those envisaged in the Brexit discussions. Saul Newman refers to this as an 'anarchic dimension to life that exceeds and resists control'.[32] It is anarchic because it is a parallel life to law[33] – one that happens *in spite of* law.

This life exceeds the legal categories of 'subject' or 'object' of the law. As various acts of citizenship demonstrate,[34] recognition does exist beyond these frames if only our analysis steps beyond the limiting frame of formal citizenship and/or subjectivity to recognise such activity. For this reason, we suggest the *homo activus* as giving place to the existence that *is* in spite of formal legal categories and subjectivities, in spite of recognition through citizenship status. A post-Brexit United Kingdom will have to address this excess of formal legal categories, if previously recognised EU citizens risk becoming 'irregular', in that they will remain vital in their communities and economies but will be formally excluded from citizenship under UK law. The ingression of *homo activus* is, moreover, disruptive because the *homo activus* demands access to justice and access to rights in resistance to being silenced and marginalised.

The ingression of *homo activus* brings to light how access to rights and justice is enacted. As Bridget Anderson's work demonstrates, political and socio-economic factors facilitate recognised citizenship in what she calls a 'community of value' versus ostensibly holding citizenship.[35] In other words, the possible loss of formal recognition for EU citizens in the UK is less of a concern than having access to work, access to livelihood and access to justice, which is withheld for some citizens and non-citizens ('irregular' migrants) alike. Persons with a precarious immigration status, as well as persons in precarious work arrangements or who are marginalised due to factors such as disability, education, language or experience in the prison system, often lack access to basic needs and

---

32 Newman, S., *Post-Anarchism* (Polity Press, Cambridge 2010), 18.

33 Loizidou, E. (ed.), *Disobedience: Concept and Practice* (Routledge, London 2013), 120–121, with reference to Emma Goldman.

34 See for instance Butler, J., and G.C. Spivak, *Who Sings the Nation-State?* (Seagull Books, London, New York NY, Calcutta 2010), 58–63; Isin, E., and G. Nielsen (eds.), *Acts of Citizenship* (Palgrave Macmillan, London 2008).

35 Anderson, n.31 above.

justice.[36] They are 'irregular' in that they slip through the cracks of the legal and political system. In spite of existing rights under European laws, in practice these are not individuals who are pursuing claims under courts of law, rather they are striving to maintain an income, a home and a livelihood. In the present climate in the UK, individuals considered 'irregular' could include non-British EU citizens as well as those not considered to be *fully*-citizen (whether by virtue of their gender, age, disability, spent or unspent criminal convictions), together with non-national, migrant workers. These are all persons who can be excluded from accessing rights, protections and status, while still being included as necessary actors in communities and, more broadly, the economic market. The process of subject-turning-object by virtue of the changing legal status and citizenship of EU citizens in the UK thus requires an alternative analysis, such as recognition of *homo activus*, which would encompass not only the changing status of EU citizens in the UK but existing marginalised and 'irregular' individuals, already active and yet denied recognition.

5. CONCLUSION

As is the case with almost all terms, *homo subjectus* and *homo objectus* are constructs. They are abstractions which make sense within particular settings and guide our thinking about these settings. These thought constructs become animated by the activities and experiences of ordinary actors, who, irrespective of how the state and the law will view them, will continue to live, act, cooperate, think, love and suffer in their daily lives. It is this common-sense reality that ultimately leads individuals to defy the assumptions and classifications of governmental elites and to act as *homo activus* in a world of significance to them.

---

[36] Anderson, n.31 above, 4; Anderson, B., 'What does "The Migrant" tell us about the (Good) Citizen?' *Centre on Migration, Policy and Society Working Paper*, University of Oxford, 94 (2012), 1, 4.

16. Who do we think we are? Citizenship post-Brexit

Michelle Everson

1. COSMOPOLITANS EXCLUDED

Post Brexit, the (European) world, or at least our perception of it, is very different. Contrary to the comfortable intellectual certainties of the post-Cold War era, a significant segment of the population demonstrably does not perceive itself to have benefited from economic liberalisation or global free trade. Equally, to the degree that a similarly decisive section of UK popular opinion proved itself malleable during campaigning, or highly receptive to press-driven concerns that immigration posed a threat to the social cohesion of the nation, the ascendancy of notions of human-rights-based global community has also been checked. At the same time, however, Brexit would appear to have been a chronicle foretold, at least within the setting of the European Union. As long ago as 2008, the economic sociologist, Neil Fligstein, found a clear signal within Eurobarometer data warning of the increasing alienation of a number of Europeans, broadly defined as a working class, from an integrationist project, which they saw as further diminishing their already precarious social standing. More worryingly still, data similarly confirmed that a far larger and more comfortable middle class, though happy, especially when on holiday, to engage with and benefit from cultural and economic Europeanisation processes, retained a contingent outlook towards the Union, content to support it in good times, but ambivalent with regard to the bad.[1]

Brexit explained: although Fligstein's work went largely unremarked within the Europeanist canon,[2] the emphatic vote of proud labour

---

[1] Fligstein, Neil, *Euro-clash: The EU, European Identity and the Future of Europe* (Oxford University Press, Oxford 2008).

[2] Reflecting, perhaps, a general lack of attention to sociological approaches to the integration of Europe.

heartlands for Brexit, together with middle England's mistrustful rejection of a European Union which they also perceived to be in the grip of economic and border crises, underlines the fragility of our still predominantly functionalist model of European integration. This is a model that, for many, is still founded upon the vehicle of the European *homo economicus*, the active yet culturally unattached citizen-forger of the internal market, who is nonetheless without the necessary degree of political allegiance to the EU that might sustain it in more difficult times.[3] Extrapolating from this analysis, Brexit may be argued to also have been a result of the depoliticised approach to the creation of European community through establishment of a European economy, which, and despite the intensified constitutionalisation of the Union through the Lisbon Treaty, has demonstrably failed to create a European 'community of fate', or a sense of solidarity between European citizens.[4]

So far so European: nevertheless, in the terms of this analysis Brexit must be seen as far more than Brexit, or as far more than an isolated case of a shocking UK secession from the European Union. Distilling the underlying issue down to the question of legal objects and legal subjects, as well as their reconciliation within paradigms of citizenship, the various posited rationales for the Brexit vote may thus also be argued to be a reflection of a deeper and global malaise. The vote is a mirror to an inability or unwillingness on the part of many worldwide to accept the unravelling of an exclusionary core of national citizenship through the two new universalisms of (nationality-law-busting) human rights, and an economic science that promotes and secures the right of passage of the *homo economicus*. To the degree that the Brexit vote may also be taken as an, admittedly vague, first response of a global public to global cosmopolitanism, albeit mediated through a UK and Europeanisation lens, a degree of light is also shed on the always vexed issue of individualism, belonging and community, or the public perception of it, in a global age.

Exclusion still matters: the primary core and primary contradiction of the inclusionary citizenship paradigm is again revealed to be its exclusive character, its self-limitation of its integrative benefits and protection to the few. Citizenship is still treasured and fiercely defended by some,

---

[3] Everson, Michelle, 'The Legacy of the Market Citizen', in Shaw, Jo, and Gillian More (eds), *New Legal Dynamics of European Union* (Clarendon, Oxford 1995).

[4] The community of fate is the core of redistributive regimes, and denotes the preparedness of a community to share our suffering as well as gain.

precisely because, in all of its transformation of the post-feudal individual from an object of law into a dual subject and empowered citizen, it creates its protected and empowered sphere for individuals within a closed community of belonging that excludes just as it includes. Where we consider globalisation processes from the viewpoint of the individual, the vehicle of citizenship has accordingly become one of the fronts upon which the battle for the exact character of post-national order is being fought out; the point at which our more modern universalisms, personified by migrants bearing human or economic rights, meet resistant and sometimes resentful national citizens.

As the months since the Brexit vote within the UK also demonstrate, a sad corollary of resistance through rejection of cosmopolitanism can also be a parochialism that verges on or descends into racism, a retrograde nationalistic recalibration, which similarly denigrates the cosmopolitan rights-bearer who has seized, either by virtue of want or by reason of outlook, on the opportunities presented by our modern universalisms. The worries of the final years of Weimar hang heavy over the juxtaposition of cosmopolitanism and community; over the now very tangible and seemingly intractable paradox of cosmopolitan opportunity versus national community.[5] We have now entered a worrying period of challenge to post-national orders. Yet, in this context, we should not forget that the history of citizenship is itself no more than a history of paradox. Beyond inclusion and exclusion, the citizenship story is similarly one of intractable juxtaposition; one of conflicts, not just between communitarianism and contractualism, but between right and obligation, between individualism and community, between social classes, or between contingent opportunity and secured welfare.[6] The exact value of citizenship is accordingly also to be measured in its ability to contain paradox, to defuse and stabilise conflict, or to strike the social balance that acts as lodestone for constant constitutional settlement.

This contribution accordingly investigates our new citizenship paradox, or the tense relationship established between citizenships of cosmopolitan

---

[5] See only the worrying speech made by Theresa May to the Conservative Party Conference in 2016, and her assertion (paraphrasing) that citizens of the world have no home. Press commentators have already noted the worrying similarities to the rhetoric of 1930s Germany. See *www.theguardian.com/politics/2016/oct/09/theresa-may-rejection-of-enlightenment-values* (accessed 7 February 2017).

[6] Everson, Michelle, and Ulrich K. Preuβ, 'Konzeptionen von Bürgerschaft in Europa' (1996) 26 *Prokla* 4, 543.

opportunity and citizenships of (nationalised) security within the post-national order. Seeking first to distinguish the particular issue of exclusion, and to highlight the always conflictual nature of citizenship (Section 2), it then investigates the two new universalisms of our post-national order, which have played their part in the creation of a new-old tension between individual opportunity and individual security (Section 3). How has the humanism of human rights offered us a perspective to engage with individuals as citizens beyond our own community? How has economic science and a newly virulent character of the *homo economicus* presented new opportunities, but simultaneously challenged traditional securities? The contribution concludes with a closer look at how paradigms of citizenship have historically stabilised the conflicts and contradictions of citizenship, asking whether the post-national order might ever find its own stabilising mechanism. The outlook is nevertheless highly uncertain, above all with regard to the subjects or objects of law (Sections 4 and 5).

2. SPATIALITY, OR THE TIES THAT BIND

Writing in the *European Law Review* in 2004, Hans Lindahl sought to remind European lawyers of the continuing currency of boundaries and barriers to movement in notions of exclusionary belonging, or of the on-going relevance of Hannah Arendt's concept of 'spatiality'. Investigating the consequences of an emergent European 'securitisation' discourse, Lindahl noted that spatiality is:

> '[N]ot merely a geographical term. It relates not so much, and not primarily, to a piece of land as to the space between individuals in a group whose members are bound to, and at the same time separated and protected from each other by all kinds of relationships, based on a common language, religion, a common history, customs, and laws.'[7]

Lindahl's aide memoire has only proved more relevant with time, as EU borders have become an ever more potent focus for a resurgently extreme right throughout the continent, and the Union has been taken far beyond its comfort zone to engage with the politics of cultural conflict. Arendt's underlying themes, however, similarly retain their poignant and regretful power: '[F]reedom', or the freedom of the politically enabled and

---

[7] Lindahl, Hans, 'Finding a Place for Freedom, Security and Justice: The European Union's Claim to Territorial Unity' (2004) 29 *European Law Review* 461 at 466.

protected citizen, 'where it existed as tangible reality, has always been spatially limited.'[8] Also encompassed within Arendt's notion of the 'right to have rights', is the Janus-like character of citizenship, or the inevitability of exclusion as the binding together of individuals within a framework of citizenship empowerment appears to have been achievable historically only within a space of cultural obligation.

Spatiality, however, is a very deep concept indeed. It is far, far more than the relatively simple matter of the delineation of the nation upon communitarian or, alternatively, contractual terms. The two great alternative sources for award of nationality, birth or heritage may be founded in grand historical themes: on the one hand, the notion of a pre-political belonging of common blood, language or culture; and, on the other, the revolutionary contrast, which posits community by virtue of philosophical concordance within Rousseau's nation. Yet, cultural nationalism or French revolutionary zeal are only one element within an all-encompassing citizenship paradigm, which tackles the perennial and all-pervasive problem of how we might not only live peaceably together, but also prosper in community.

As such, the core of citizenship is formed by conflict, but no longer simply by a conflict of the symbolic city, which, as Karl Marx noted, created the core fault-line of antiquity between those who possessed citizenship and those who did not; between citizens and the slaves who were present within, but were never a part of the community, or spatiality, of the city. By virtue of its totalisation of the individual within the community, a first classical citizenship that subsumed the citizen within the *polis* such that an individual had no autonomy or personality absent the *polis*, could, as a simple matter of its own restricted philosophical outlook, assume a dearth of conflict amongst its citizenry. The 'second citizenship' of modernity,[9] however, was informed, first, by natural rights and Judaeo-Christian visions of the individual before God, but also, secondly, by the imperative of maintenance of the *res publica*, or a community of individual citizens. As such, it could not but address the need to create not just rights, but also obligations between individual citizens; the primary one of which was allegiance, or the sense that

---

[8] Arendt, Hannah, *On Revolution* (first published Viking Press, New York *c*.1963) (Penguin, London and New York 1994), p. 262.

[9] Heater, Derek, *Citizenship: The Civic Ideal in World History, Politics and Education* (Manchester University Press, Manchester 1990).

citizens were 'bound to one another by the personal bond of fellow-membership of one body'.[10] In other words: community may be built upon the individual, but individuals are, by very their nature, a fractious group, and must be induced or constrained to respect one another's individuality within their commonality.

Further, given that individuals are fractious across the whole of their lived experiences, the political-philosophical creation of the nation of citizens through communitarian recollection, or alternatively, by repeated proclamation of universally-oriented rallying calls, such as secularism (*laicité*), each of which is designed to diffuse conflict in a public sphere, is only one side of a citizenship story. Instead, citizenship reaches far into the private. T.H. Marshall's seminal description of the emergence of citizenship within the United Kingdom,[11] thus also underlines the complexity of an allegiance that is owed, not simply to the state, but also to the citizenry, in all of its joint and individual parts, and in all of its civic or economic being.

Seen from the sociological perspective, Marshall's analysis illuminates as it tackles the most problematic facet of common life, or tackles intractable conflict between the opportunities and the securities of human existence. Marshall's story, beginning at the troublesome death of feudalism, finds a first expression of citizenship in civic rights, but not in those of conscience, and rather in those of economic opportunity, and primarily in the right to contract. From status to contract: the post-feudal subject, no longer a legal object beholden to the whim of overlords, is simultaneously the first iteration of the *homo economicus*, forging a new marketplace of opportunity, or of economic self-determination though the abstract medium of legal right. For the first time, and following the Black Death, freedom could be a material as well as spiritual experience, also to be forged in relative autonomy from oppressive social mores. Nevertheless, opportunity for one can also be measured in disadvantage for the other, especially within the context of markets, which are anything but egalitarian in their operation. From contract to status: four centuries later, and within the context of an industrialising world, 'free' markets were now only to be experienced by some as a new and brutally depersonalised form of feudalism, within which the possession or not of property, rather than force of arms, played its role in determining degrees of personal autonomy.

---

[10] Salmond, J.W., 'Citizenship and Allegiance' (Part II), [1902] 17 *Law Quarterly Review* 49 at 50.

[11] Marshall, T.H., *Citizenship and Social Class* (first published 1953) (Pluto Press, London 1992).

Today, centuries away from the death of feudalism and the emergence of industrialisation, it has become an understandable and easy commonplace to conceive of the tryptic of civic, political and social citizenship rights solely in their abstract constitutional form, at least within legal science. Nevertheless, a simple enumeration of what are now typically viewed as civic rights of conscience, political rights of self-expression and social rights of pecuniary rectification, only obscures the Marshallian picture of conflictual paradox within the citizenship paradigm. With political emancipation acting as the great facilitating fulcrum for the expression of the dispossessed, the threefold scheme of rights represents, for Marshall, far more than a constitutional device, and is instead a reflection of a continuing clash of class interests, of a demand for the opportunities of economic self-determination and a matching claim for security, or protection from market forces. Certainly, the market might unleash the autonomous genius of the nation; at the same time, however, to the degree that the market creates a spectrum of class, it must be reconfigured, bought back into redistributive social equilibrium; a balance fought for in politics and given expression in the social rights of the individual citizen. Citizenship is not a comfortable concept. At core, the ties that bind the citizenry are every bit as conflictual and divisive as the concepts that expel the globe from the nation. Individualism and community, rights and obligations, and opportunity and security are always uncomfortable bedfellows, but are especially so in a globalising world where universalism has become a measure both of our consciences and of our economic self-determination.

3. A TALE OF TWO UNIVERSALISMS

> '[I]t would be neither satisfactory nor true to the development of the case law to reduce freedom of movement to a mere standard of promotion of trade between member states. It is important that the freedoms of movement fit into the broader framework of the objectives of the internal market and European citizenship. At present, freedoms of movement must be understood to be one of the essential elements of the 'fundamental status of nationals of the member states.' They represent the cross-border dimension of the economic and social status conferred on European citizens.'[12]

In a world of economic and constitutional European law, it has long been an unthinking commonplace that the legal freedoms of the Single Market

---

[12] Opinion of AG Poiares Maduro in *Alfa Vita Vassilopoulos AE v Greece* (Cases C-158 and 159/04) 2006 ECR I-8135, para.192.

coalesce seamlessly with and reinforce the character of the individual living across the space of Europe, as a European citizen; a citizen who is made so by virtue of his/her movement within, or as an ancillary to the European market. This blind collapse of the civic and social into the economic is nevertheless far more incendiary than the dry formulations of the Advocate General of the Court of Justice of the European Union (CJEU) might anticipate. Above all, however, both in its linkage of European citizenship with the pursuit of the integrated European market, and in its doctrinal reduction of that citizenship to a bundle of interwoven economic and social rights, the statement not only unveils the economic functionalism that often underpins European and globally cosmopolitan outlooks on citizenship. It also understates the more fundamental challenges posed to the civilising or integrative aspects of the citizenship paradigm by our two new universalisms: on the one hand, the universalism of human rights; on the other hand, the universalism of economic science and the transformative power of an unleashed *homo economicus*.

3.1 A Humanising Universalism

Perhaps inevitably, however, in a New World Order of civilising possibility, the core problem is one of good intent. Hannah Arendt is far from being alone in her ambivalence towards her own concept of spatiality, or her regret that freedom can only be found in commonality. Instead, in its by now legendary citizenship jurisprudence, stretching from the case of *Maria Martinez Sala* to *Zhu & Chen*, to *Baumbast* and to *Luis Zambrano*,[13] the CJEU has developed its own spatiality-busting weapon in the application of human rights, and more particularly the right to a family life, in order to uncouple enjoyment of the benefits of European Union citizenship both from the concept of the European *homo economicus*, and from the nationality and social security law of its Member States.

In simple terms of legal doctrine, the CJEU's jurisprudence is undoubtedly revolutionary: first, detaching the right of free movement of European citizens (Article 20(2a) TFEU) from the more restrictive status of 'European as worker' under Article 45 TFEU (*Maria Martinez Sala*); secondly, cutting the Gordian knot between citizenship and nationality, extending 'associative' rights of EU citizenship to third country nationals (TCNs); thirdly, questioning constructed solidarity and opening up closed

---

[13] *Maria Martinez Sala* v *Freistaat Bayern* (Case C-85/96) [1998] ECR I-2691; *Zhu and Chen* (Case C-200/02) [2004] ECR I-9925; *Baumbast* (Case C-413/99) [2002] ECR I-7901; *Ruiz Zambrano* v *Office National de l'Emploi* (Case C-34/09) [2011] ECR I-1177.

national benefits systems to EU nationals and their associates; and finally, albeit in a very restricted formulation, even seeming to suggest that rights of EU citizenship have 'substance' of their own and will accrue even where there is no question of movement across national borders. Nevertheless, the true revolution is perhaps in the Court's thinking, or its refusal to restrict itself within conceptual straitjackets and to respond instead to the emotional and material wants of the individual.

Thus, breaking the exclusionary 'blind-side' of traditional citizenship constructs to treat persons in movement within the European space, not as philosophical constructs, but rather as individuals captured by their own material circumstances, the CJEU simply discards the citizenship-nationality law linkage, responding emotionally to a simple human happening, or to the birth of a child within the EU, allowing her mother and 'primary carer', a Chinese national, to travel freely with her across Member State frontiers (*Zhu and Chen*). The nation is hostile to both child and mother. The CJEU and its EU citizenship are not. Similarly, the *ius Europeaum* also furnishes a 'good' outcome, or engages with a tangible other far beyond imagined solidarity communities, thereby extending the EU citizenship regime to matters of access to welfare. In *Baumbast*, where a German national had not satisfied UK requirements that he maintain sufficient sickness insurance for himself and his family, the Court declared that national legislation must nevertheless be proportionate in its application. Contractual citizenship and solidarity is blind to Mr Baumbast's, or the geographical stranger's, need for immediate medical care for his family. This need not be so, the CJEU intones: the measure of solidarity within Europe is not to be negated by spatially-bounded belonging. Instead, a miracle of European recognition is generated as the Court's sympathetic act of observing and responding to the needs of individual citizens transforms proportionality from a technical yardstick of procedural legal review into a far more indistinct instrument of material adjudication, open to an emotionally-founded response to individual circumstance within which a miracle of European solidarity might be born.

This burgeoning, judicially-driven citizenship, founded in emotional judicial response to material circumstance, is necessarily also sometimes inconsistent, especially with regard to social welfare cases, and has perhaps now met its most potent limits in pushback response to the case of *Zambrano*, which, although generally regarded has having furnished the 'correct result' in simple terms of reactive justice, also causes concern within formalist legal thinking, seemingly overturning the CJEU's established line of jurisprudence limiting enjoyment of EU citizenship rights to instances of cross-border movement.[14] As a consequence, the Court has subsequently clarified and limited its revolutionary jurisprudence, whereby Mrs and Mrs Zambrano, failed Colombian asylum seekers, resident in Belgium and who had never moved across European frontiers, were still afforded the protection of the *ius Europeaum* as primary carers of their children who had become Belgian by virtue of their birth in that country.[15] Nevertheless, to the degree that the European Court is also mirroring global legal evolution by engaging in a new form of universalist legal reasoning, it also represents the very best of a legal movement that is dogged in its struggle finally to fulfil the promise of the European Enlightenment. Where the universalising aim continues to be one of achieving Emmanuel Kant's nation of nations, the CJEU has done much to reconcile the universality of the individual before God with a spatial protection that lies far beyond the limiting conceptual formulations of the age of nationalism.

3.2 *Homo Economicus* Unleashed

The judges of the European Court are highly unlikely to have had them in mind, but the philosophical antecedents underlying their judicial activism stretch long. From Emmanuel Kant to Jürgen Habermas: in their material recognition of the third-country national (TCN), the Court echoes the procedural speech act, which similarly imputes to the moment of emotional concord a preparedness to treat, or to contract, thus renewing the post-feudal moment, and exhibiting a readiness to view the individual in his/her material autonomy rather than their abstract personification. From status to contract: the TCN is no longer a simple legal object, but achieves personality, or legal subjectivity and citizenship, in a moment that is constitutionalised by the coeval legal norm that springs into existence in the act of recognition.[16]

---

[14] Nic Shuibhne, Niamh, 'Editorial, Seven Questions for Seven Paragraphs' (2011) 36 *European Law Review* 161.

[15] Most notably, in the case of *Dereci* (*Murat Dereci and Others v Bundesministerium für Inneres* (Case C-256/11) (Grand Chamber) [2011] ECR I-0000), where the Court reiterated that, in *Zambrano*, the operative point was that the children of the Zambrano family remained dependent upon their parents, such that, as Union citizens, they would still have been required to leave the European continent. The five TCNs of Dereci, wishing to join their families in Austria, were non-dependants and therefore not so fortunate.

[16] For simple explanation of a very complex theory, see Eriksen, Erik O., and Jon Weigard Eriksen, *Understanding Habermas: Communicative Action and Deliberative Democracy* (Continuum Press, London and New York NY 2003).

Deep waters indeed: yet, philosophical theory also finds its more pragmatic political theory counterpart in post-Cold War demands for development of forms of universalism that reflect the economic and social realities of globalisation. For citizenship, the authoritative voice in this regard is that of Ralf Dahrendorf, who argued that traditional notions of citizenship should be opened up in response to globalisation and social fragmentation, or should now be informed by a material universalism that might allow us to escape the double binds of conceptualised history that exclude just as they integrate.[17] Citizenship should also reflect and integrate the new non-spatial freedoms and new behaviours that have evolved in the liberalised post-Cold War era, or in European in particular, our freedom to:

> '[d]o new things across national borders; go shopping for cheaper petrol or wine; buy cottages in charming rustic villages; look for work in a foreign cosmopolitan city; take holidays in new destinations, move to retire in the sun, buy cheaper airline tickets; plan international rail travel; join cross-national associations between twinned towns; use a common currency without having 5% stolen by the bank—and a thousand other actions facilitated by the free movement accords.'[18]

From the sublime to the ridiculous, or from philosophical universalisms to shopping: Adrian Favell's sociological research, founded within a behavioural approach to the study of the European citizen, has, on the one hand, famously revealed the cultural barriers that still impede full emotional integration of cosmopolitans within local communities.[19] On the other hand, however, in highlighting the new transaction and exchange opportunities afforded to the mobile 'stars' of European integration, Favell's research nonetheless gives form to Dahrendorf's appeal to take seriously the positive impacts of the 'contingent opportunities' given form in new transnational complexes of economic rights, and especially so within the European Union, that have played a dual function in challenging spatiality. Both a *cultural* function in at least opening up the perspectives of the citizen beyond her own national

---

[17] Dahrendorf, Ralf, 'Citizenship and Social Class', in Dahrendorf, *The Modern Social Conflict: The Politics of Liberty* (Transaction, New Brunswick NJ 2008).

[18] Favell, Adrian, 'European citizenship in three Eurocities: a sociological approach to the European Union' (2010) 30 *Politique Européenne* 187, 194.

[19] A finding founded within a literary approach to qualitative interviews, see above, n.18.

border, and an *economic* function in generating a new wealth to underwrite further what were, for Dahrendorf, the always integrative bundles of social rights of citizenship, typically still guaranteed at nation state level.

With a keen eye, not simply to Dahrendorf's dictum that social rights must be paid for, but also to the centrality of market creation within the emancipation of human autonomy, the emergence of a European *homo economicus* within the character of an economic citizen, constituted by their economic rights, must be viewed as a part of the good intent inherent in all efforts to ameliorate the negative externalities of spatiality. Considering the centrality of the European market within the integration project, it is no surprise that CJEU jurisprudence has endowed and continues to endow the individual European with an economic character. At the same time, where judicial extrapolation of the European treaties has perforce entailed a scientifically-informed reallocation of economic opportunities within an emerging European market, individual economic and cultural potential is no longer constrained by national borders. The corollary to the dismantling of the barriers to trade that distinctive national regulatory regimes have constituted has been the emergence within the four freedoms of a 'frontier-busting' pioneer of European market formation; a pioneer who has not only often contributed to the freeing of the individual European from the 'infantilising' excesses of post-war regulation;[20] but has also, and more generally, reinforced the spatially-blind parameters of a sphere of economic opportunity that is no longer fragmented and constrained by distinct (national) traditions and mythologies. In the jurisprudence of the CJEU responding to individual assertion of European economic rights, the universalisms of science, and in particular of economic science, are instead determinative:[21] a ban on wholemeal pasta could not, after all, be demonstrated to be proportionate – it could not be shown to protect the health of Italian diners.[22]

Vitally, at global level, this new universalism is also a feature of free trade regimes, similarly facilitating (at least to a degree) the rise of post-colonial economies: market forces are famously ahistorical and non-philosophical, blind to the antecedents, characters, desires and intentions of producers, service-providers, employees or consumers. And, to

---

[20] Dani, Marco, 'Assembling the Fractured European Consumer' (2011) 36 *European Law Review* 362, 371.

[21] Everson, Michelle, and Christian Joerges, 'Reconfiguring the Politics–Law Relationship in the Integration Project through Conflicts–Law Constitutionalism' (2015) 18 *European Law Journal* 5.

[22] Dani, see above, n.20.

this extent, a global ideal of *homo economicus* as corrective to the spatialities both of the age of nationalism and the age of empire, contains its own undeniable promise. In short, in a quest for materialisation beyond philosophical conceptualisation or emotionalism, scientific universalisms, even and perhaps especially of the economic variety that attach to the *homo economicus*, are powerful tools, not only establishing a legitimating universality, as legal norm is informed by material methods of fact recognition, but also sweeping away the lazy complexes of opportunity-denying prejudice that history inevitably weaves into its own spatialities.

3.3 Misplacing the Ties that Bind

Yet, as Brexit may be argued to demonstrate, resistance to our global universalism is growing, and may similarly be argued to derive from the growing misfit between calls for a post-national recalibration of the character of the citizen and the exact nature of our reborn *homo economicus*. At core, Dahrendorf remains wedded to the story of citizenship told by T.H. Marshall: the fruits of economic progress, unlocked by heightened private autonomy, must be redistributed within the national collective, must still reattach to spatiality and to the community of fate that wins the allegiance of all citizens. Equally, Adrian Favell calls for a behavioural approach to the study of citizenship in order to reflect the post-national realities of our age. But, as he does so, he still registers the importance of community in the life of the individual.[23] By stark contrast, however, today's *homo economicus* is an atomistic being, maximising joint welfare, but doing so, not as part of spatial collective, but as a social agent within a new ideology, generally given the shorthand sobriquet of neo-liberalism, and within an economic science whose primary postulate is that the risks or negative impacts of markets can be held in check, such that their economic benefits will always be felt generally, as well as individually.

The distinction is vital: the primary significance for the traditional concept of citizenship of the global dominance of ideological and scientific economic universalisms is one of a postulation that the core Marshallian paradox of intractable conflict within the citizenship paradigm, expressed in the inequalities of the market, can be overcome, or can be fully dissolved within a welfare maximisiation, which will secure the status of all. Concomitantly, this universalism negates the need for the

---

[23] See above, n.18.

spatiality expressed in the constraining and 'embedding' of national economies within social rights.[24] The rhetoric of economic universalism is one of 'trickle-down', of joint gain from global free trade; its structural mechanism is the disembedding of national economies from complexes of labour and market regulation; and its willing servitor is supranational and international technocracy and law, drawn like a magpie to its glittering sheen of decisional (adjudicational) neutrality.

Yet, at least since the 2008 financial crisis, the complacency, or pragmatic limits, of our post-Cold War model have been brutally exposed, at least to the extent that private credit can no longer be relied upon to substitute for public welfare. Equally, however, to the degree that the modern welfare-maximising *homo economicus* has also become a denatured creature, the marketised society within which it operates has only proved itself to be equally vulnerable to a political demagoguery, which is similarly content to play on the (relatively) dispossessed, in order to roll back all of our universalism.

3.3.1 Economic uncertainty denied

Pinpointed ex ante as the villain of financial crisis, the issue of systemic risk, or of transmission of poor financial risks throughout the global financial system, often repackaged as financial opportunity, is now the subject of intense regulatory and supervisory activity worldwide, not least within the European System for Financial Supervision.[25] It nevertheless remains the nemesis of economic universalisms founded in 'privatised Keynesianism', or wholesale substitution of public funding and welfare through supposedly never-ending lines of private credit, wherein all citizens assume their own welfare function in myriad acts of financial borrowing.[26] The intensity of state intervention in this area is an immediate signal that the term 'neo-liberalism', if conceived of as denoting a sphere of freedom for aggressive market forces, is not only

---

[24] For the concept of 'embedded economies', see Polanyi, Karl, *The Great Transformation* (first published Farrar & Rinehart 1944) (Beacon Press, Boston MA 2002).

[25] Establishing at European Union level a series of agencies charged with overseeing European financial markets, and including a European Systemic Risk Board, with the participation of the European Central Bank. For details, see Black, Julia, 'Restructuring Global and EU Financial Regulation: Capacities, Coordination and Learning' *LSE Law, Society and Economy Working Papers* 18/2010 (LSE 2010).

[26] Crouch, Colin, *The Strange Non-Death of Neo-Liberalism* (Polity Press, Cambridge 2011).

now a simple misnomer; but always has been, as governments of the left and of the right, within Europe and far beyond, have felt secure within an abdication of state welfare function, or complacent in their certain knowledge that application of intrusive frameworks of risk regulation to the financial sector might underpin an exponentially-infinite process of global capital generation.

> '[M]odels of risk and of information only change perceptions about uncertainty. It can never go away ... [a]nd in economic debates, uncertainty is "ideologically" neutral. A wide diversity of economists insists on uncertainty, therefore a conspiracy of silence is implausible. Perception cannot change the distinction ... that risk is assessable and insurable but the uncertain future can never be identified or therefore calculated.'[27]

All a fallacy of misplaced scientific outlook: from the birth of modern economics in the writings of the Chicago economist, Frank Knight, through the aggressively liberalising economic studies of Hayek, and the socially integrative policies of Keynesianism, the core humanism of markets is only underlined in the inherent uncertainties of their cumulative transactional operations. For Knight, making the distinction between risk and uncertainty, the former was calculable and controllable; but it was the latter, or the readiness to engage with uncertainty, or knowingly face ruin, that lay at the core of individual entrepreneurial activity. For Hayek, uncertainty, or the unknowable, formed the normative basis for a social theory of the legitimate market society; a society that, in stark contrast to socialist and national socialist models, never purported to be able to furnish individual or collective certainty, and thus negated the personal autonomy of individual citizens. And finally, for Keynes, uncertainty was a simple fact of economic life, to be adjusted to if and where possible; but always only with reference to the political authority of the spatially bounded community of fate.

Political abdication, and the collapse of uncertainty into risk was unmasked by financial collapse, but has not ended. If anything, the belief that free markets can maximise welfare for all has emerged in an intensified form within European regimes designed to correct sovereign debt crisis. It has achieved unparalleled dominance within the economic conditionality of technocratically-led governance regimes, such as those envisaged within the new European Treaty for Stability, Growth and Coordination, and the further assaults made upon the labour and welfare

---

[27] Pixley, Jocelyn, 'Uncertainty: the Curate's egg in financial economics' (2014) 65 *The British Journal of Sociology* 2, 200 at 203.

regulation of debtor nations within the eurozone by European Memoranda of Understanding.[28] Within Europe, at least, the vital connection to political authority, underpinned by a community of fate, giving social authority to redistributive restructuring of market forces, has yet to emerge.

3.3.2 Subjectivity negated

In his writing's, Ernst-Joachim Mestmäcker, the last living link with the creators of German ordo-liberalism, or a theory of the economic constitution developed in the 1930s as a defence against the autonomy-extinguishing economic machinations of the Nazi state, rails powerfully against the totalising counterfactuality of modern economic theories which impute to all social relationships the transactional characteristics of the market and thus mould their regulatory prescriptions according to the founding precept that all individual action is rationally calculated.

> 'Ideology in the service of unlimited government and socialism [sic]; the refutation of a concept of justice ignoring viable negative tests of justice that identify unjust norms.'[29]

For Mestmäcker, the methodological falsehood is readily apparent. Application of a Hayekian rational choice analysis primarily serves a moment of normative limitation, a restriction of political power within the realm of autonomous markets. Where such analysis instead takes on the character of a scientific force to be applied far beyond limited spheres of rational individual interaction in an 'arbitrary mimicking' of competition, it becomes a counterfactually totalising force all of its own. Mestmäcker's ire, however, could equally be directed against the pseudo-scientism of modern political abdication within the collapse of uncertainty and risk, or an absolutism that is as counterfactual as it is all-pervasive. And it is perhaps within the synthesis of the two phenomena that a realm of denied falsehood arises within which political demagoguery can only thrive.

---

[28] Fabbrini, Stefano, 'The Euro Crisis and its Constitutional Implications' in Champeau, Serge, Carlos Closa, Daniel Innerarity and Miguel Poiares Maduro (eds), *The Future of Europe: Democracy, Legitimacy and Justice after the Euro Crisis* (Rowman and Littlefield, Lanham MD 2015).

[29] Mestmäcker, Ernst Joachim, 'A Legal Theory Without Law – Posner v. Hayek on Economic Analysis of Law', *Beiträge zur Ordnungstheorie und Ordnungspolitik* (Mohr-Siebeck, Tübingen 2007), p. 55.

As Michèl Foucault noted in his final lectures at the Collège de France, seeking to trace the genealogy of our modern economic liberalism, the core problem in this regard is the growing dominance of a form of economic thinking that construes itself as a science, locating its claim not only to a universal applicability, but also to a universal justice, within the posited facts of market operations themselves, rather than within the place that the market is afforded within society as whole.[30] In Foucault's descriptive terminology of 'anarcho-liberalism', the market achieves a totality within human organisation as the sole point of reference for action and reaction, such that the modern *homo economicus* is denatured, or stripped of all non-economic subjectivities, including the power of political voice within the now withered state. Diverging radically from Ralf Dahrendorf's hopeful ascription to the pioneering post-national citizen of a wealth-generating role that might, in its turn, reinforce the state's ability to supply social welfare, the anarcho-liberal *homo economicus* simply dissolves all need for a community of fate within an 'idolatory of the factual',[31] where justice now becomes a simple given within the optimal outcomes of the market.

Paradigmatically, a powerful echo of the anarcho-liberal approach may be found in the jurisprudence of the CJEU, and above all in AG Maduro's assertion, in the by-now infamous case of *Viking*, that a justice standard of 'allocative efficiency' might play its role in the determination of the proportionality of strikes, called legally under national law to prevent social dumping,[32] that nevertheless, in their effects, limit the reach of European economic rights of establishment and services. For many commentators, the particular problem in *Viking* and the liberalising jurisprudence that has followed in its wake is not simply a pragmatic one of the overall depression of wage rates and working conditions as free labour markets within the EU have seen, in particular, but not only, Eastern European workers being required to compete themselves to integrative parity. Instead, as Alain Supiot has cogently noted, the core issue is one of the CJEU's failure to maintain the European legal tradition that labour and economic constitutions are distinct orders which may not

---

[30] Foucault, Michèl, *Birth of Biopolitics: Lectures at the College de France* (Routledge, London and New York NY 2008).

[31] Mestmäcker, see above, n.29.

[32] *International Transport Workers' Federation, Finnish Seamen's Union v Viking Line ABP, OÜ Viking Line Eesti* (Case C-438/05) 2007 ECR I-1079; See also *Laval un Partneri Ltd v Svenska Byggnadsarbetareförbundet, Svenska Byggnadsarbetareförbundets avdelning 1, Byggettan and Svenska Elektrikerförbundet* (Case C-341/05) 2007 ECR I-11767.

be weighed against one another within the adjudicative balance, or that labour and its regulation is distinct from the rational market order, being informed instead by non-marketisable ethical and social values.[33]

Famously, no new Marshall Plan followed the fall of the Berlin Wall, such that the reintegration of Eastern Europe with the western Member States of the EU has been a matter of economics rather than a communitarian project, and, in this, the EU is simply following a global trend, within which all development concerns have been subsumed within (anarcho-)economics, or within a totalising certainty that the universalism of the global market with furnish just results that maximise the welfare of all.

4. GLOBAL WEIMAR

> 'For many, complaints about foreign workers coming here and taking their jobs are disturbingly reminiscent of the atmosphere whipped up in Britain's cities during the 1960s and 1970s, when the backlash against Commonwealth immigration was reflected both in the ballot box – in support for extreme right-wing parties – and, in many cases, in street violence.[34]

How quickly the world changes: a decade ago, the UK media responded to a blockade of the Lindsey Oil Refinery in protest at the hiring of European labour ('British jobs for British workers') within a trope of cultural clash, of racism and xenophobia. For a broadsheet media, the existence of European legal norms facilitating cross-border agency work and the circumvention of local collective bargaining agreements were secondary questions if considered at all, marginalised as a curiosity within an unthinking correlation of liberal-cultural advance with global economic progress. Today, however, and following the ugly aspect of a slow-burning tabloid coup d'état that has mobilised the problem of the social and economic impacts of a cross-border competitive labour advantage against all movement of peoples, the workers of Lindsey will no doubt be being celebrated by some as Brexit heroes; the vanguard of the workers' movement which, their political marginalisation as voiceless xenophobes notwithstanding, managed subsequently to overthrow the arrogant economic dirigisme of European and UK governing elites.

---

33 Supiot, Alain, 'A legal perspective on the economic crisis of 2008' (2010) 2 *International Labour Review* 149.

34 *The Times*, 'Editorial Comment' (30 January 2009), relating to protest by UK workers of importation of (skilled) labour from Portugal and Italy and typical of public comment on the dispute both on the right *and on the left*.

Clearly, the Lindsey workers never were, and are not now heroes, or even villains. They are merely people who are trying their best to establish a measure of social justice for themselves within the only framework available to them: a spatially delineated paradigm of (nationalised) citizenship, which is exclusionary in its impact and the upholding of which can be, and is being, seized upon by forces of political demagoguery, with racism both in their rhetoric and in their hearts. Hannah Arendt's ambivalence towards her own paradigm of spatiality, her hostility to her own recognition that an effective citizenship of (economic and social) security is founded within a bounded right to have rights still pertains; and has just found its most potently upsetting expression in the vote of old Labour heartlands for Brexit, as well as in the chasm in understanding that has opened up between economically dispossessed England and cosmopolitan London. Neil Fligstein's work is once again illuminating, especially where he also recalls the guiding cynicism of emergent citizenships in his paraphrasing of Karl Deutsch's dictum that:

> '[T]he historical trick to the rise of a nation state will be to find a horizontal solidarity for the existing [class] stratification and a rationale that using a state apparatus to protect the nation makes sense.'[35]

Where in Europe a propertied class enjoys the greater part of the benefits of European Union, and labour competition, rather than solidaristic rapport, is made the norm between European workers, between those who move and those who do not, class stratifications can never make sense, let alone act as focal a point for the building of European identity rationales. Europe has misplaced its own historical trick, cannot persuade its own populations that its legal, if not state, apparatus makes sense.

The disjunction, however, is even more fundamental than a mismatch of posited welfare maximisation and a lived experience of relative dispossession. Rather, the opportunities presented by economic universalisms must likewise be seen in the light of the release of new identities, also at national and global level. Adrian Favell's emphasis upon shopping may appear facetious, but his underlying frustration with that aspect of the Marshallian triptych of industrial citizenship,[36] which, in its deification of the historic emergence of class-based rights, can also be seen as entrenching outmoded and oppressive constructs of social organisation, is

---

[35] See, above n.1, p. 130.

[36] Favell, Adrian, 'The Changing Face of "Integration" in a Mobile Europe' *Council for European Studies Newsletter* (June 2013).

in deadly earnest. The ossification of historically conditioned stratifications within bounded societies, governed by their own rousing, class-based narratives of citizenship evolution, have similarly obscured a myriad of social cleavages founded, for example, in gender, sexual orientation or ethnicity, and have played their own part in retarding material claims for justice that are not expressed within traditional national narratives of belonging and cohesion. The core underlying problem is thus not simply one, or at all one, that cosmopolitan London or even Brussels has been wholly deaf to social justice demands asserted against dominantly abusive economic forces: the notion of 'Social Europe', after all, is firmly entrenched in European discourse. Rather, within our current citizenship discourse, a disjunction has opened up, and an old-new antagonism has been recreated between a social justice of economic security that is still bounded within communitised spatiality, and a reinvigorated, often economically so, citizenship of opportunity, which possesses its own potential for an evolutionary justice more sensitive to old-new identities, be they located at national, global or supranational level.

5. WHO DO WE THINK WE ARE?

Brexit is perhaps only the first explosive expression of the unbearable cultural, social and political tensions that have intensified during the aggressive wave of capital-driven economic liberalisation that established itself following the fall of the Berlin Wall. Global Weimar: in less than 30 years, globalisation (together with technology) has transformed the world, opening up unparalleled opportunities for the formulation of new cultural identities, for the redefinition of novel demands for justice (in opportunity), and for the assertion of never-before-heard voices outside the conventional political realm. Yet, just as in Weimar, pluralism, self-expression and opportunity lack the cynicism of the 'historical trick'; are inimical to the dirigisme of traditional citizenship paradigms, which sought to persuade their constituents that stratification made sense.

In this global setting, we are confronted with the task of managing pluralism, of overcoming a new-old cleavage within the citizenship status of individuals throughout the globe; a potentially explosive cleavage of opportunity versus security. Nevertheless, as we struggle finally to address and to overcome the paradoxes inherent to outlook of spatiality, we surely can and must buy ourselves time to perfect, for cogent example, our understanding of the means in which class and identity intersect; or buy time through a comprehensive modification within a global economic system that threatens constantly to amplify the contradictions within our social organisation to their breaking points, or to open up an irresistible space for political demagoguery. With its efficiency lodestone, its emphasis on the asocial calculations of the rational actor, and its unbridled pursuit of growth, modern economics has established a totalitarianism of purpose that is deaf to all social mores that cannot be expressed within its parameters: There Is No Alternative. But, alternatives do exist, and do so not merely in the very different outlooks of a global south, or in the basket-weaving dreams of alternative economic thinkers. The Habermasian universalism that can be argued to inform CJEU citizenship jurisprudence may also have its flaws, and especially so beyond an occidental zone of comfort with the moral imperative, but it similarly confronts us with an ethical outlook lying far beyond the factual idolatry of the welfare-maximising *homo economicus*. We can recognise our eternal companion of economic uncertainty, and fill its space with non-economic moralities. Equally, however, capitalism and markets existed prior to the birth of modern economics and functioned adequately without the guiding star of efficiency. They provided opportunity in the absence of perfect competition, and can surely do so again, even if we surrender some economic growth in the meantime.

Who do we think we are? The truth of this matter is one that we are uncertain of, and perhaps more profoundly so than ever before. The genie of opportunity cannot, however, be forced back into the bottle any more than it could 600 years ago, even and especially where it has outlived both nationality and class. The task of finding new forms of citizenship that hold our modern antagonism of opportunity and security in check within the ever broader spatialities of a globalising world is perhaps not one for the law. It is one for cultural enquiry and for politics. Nevertheless, law at national, supranational and global level are in a front line, challenged to act by economic rights-holders (subjects of law) and confronted by the demands for justice of those dispossessed within global Weimer, the de-subjectified objects of law. In this confrontation, it can also play its part, taking care to understand better the opportunities and dangers posed by its faith in new universalisms.

17. Conclusions

Samo Bardutzky and Elaine Fahey

Exploring the idea that terms 'subject' and 'object' can become useful in researching and reflecting upon EU law, we had the privilege of gathering a diverse group of scholars who engaged with this idea and attempted to introduce it to their case studies on very different issues of EU law. After the first, to a large extent exploratory, workshop that we held in November 2015, some of the potential uses of the lexicon of subjects and objects gradually became identifiable. In the paper that we wrote while developing this project and that later evolved into what is now the introductory chapter of this volume, we proposed that the lexicon of subjects was particularly useful in observing three elements that define the character of EU law: transformations, crises and the external-internal nexus or dynamics of EU law.[1] The authors have all engaged with this background narrative provided in the introduction, for which we are grateful.

We thus drew upon these three elements to develop the structure of the project and organised the case studies presented in the book in three parts (Parts II–IV) that correspond to the three elements identified. We chose to open with an additional part (Part I) which joins the accounts with a more accentuated theoretical discussion rather than case study. As the edited volume grew, it also became more and more evident that the three elements appear side by side in a number of accounts presented here. For example, stories of EU law that are strong accounts of the EU's crises, or the external-internal dynamics of EU law are often also accounts of the transformations that EU law has undergone since its beginnings and how it has treated its subjects and objects along the way.

In Part I, in the theoretical section on reframing the subjects and objects of EU law: normative motivations and theoretical underpinnings, initial contributions were quite critical of the duality of subjects and objects. *Siniša Rodin*, writing from a judicial perspective on 'The subject

[1] See further in Chapter 1 of this volume.

and object in the interpretation of EU law', reminds us that it must not be forgotten that in all future situations the original statement of law, the utterance of the Court as the original subject will be objectified and reinterpreted by future contemporary subjects and that any future application will take place in different factual and legal interpretative contexts. He thus problematizes, from the perspective of EU law, roles of different actors, subjects of legal interpretation, and the relationship between them and legal rules as objects being interpreted by them and argues that the Court cannot envisage what is going to happen in the future even if it were its task to do so. *Damjan Kukovec*, in his chapter entitled 'Subject-object dialectics and social change', juxtaposes what he understands as the 'conventional story' of the subject of EU law, based on the conferral of different rights to an alternative vision where the subject is imagined within a web of relationships within law. *Emilios Christodoulidis*, in a piece entitled 'Subjects and technologies of European governance: reflections on suspect crossings', argues that the social dimension of EU integration is managed through devices that displace collective-democratic self-determination in favour of 'soft' forms of coordination that favour objective standards over subjective choices. The chapter considers the subtle forms of the displacements that such devices achieve in EU thinking, mainly in the use of indicators, and the reorganisation of the field of action and intervention they imply. *Joseph Corkin*, in a chapter entitled 'Who, then, in [European] law, is my neighbour? Limiting the argument from external effects', traces a growing illiberal nationalist challenge to the Liberal World Order to our diminishing subject-hood; resentment that we are increasingly the object of laws made elsewhere that spill over borders. Using a prominent critique of this argument, the chapter considered how we might limit it by grounding it in a universal (cosmopolitan) moral theory that also allows for a communitarian impulse to realise ourselves within bordered communities.

Part II focuses on the transformational character of subjects to objects and objects to subjects in EU law and contained a variety of case studies focusing upon their character and the omission there on account of this transformational character. *Sionaidh Douglas-Scott*, in her chapter 'Subjects and objects of EU human rights law', investigates the subjects and objects of EU Human Rights law, exploring the genesis in detail of the words 'subject' and 'object' and arguing that direct engagement with the subjects and objects of EU human rights laws is warranted precisely because they have provided the EU with more legitimacy and a human face. *Josephine van Zeben*, in 'Local governments as subjects and objects of EU law: legitimate limits?', focuses upon the important, albeit oft overlooked, case study of local government as an entity lacking status under EU law and explores local government as a possible subject and object of EU law and its relationship of exclusion to participation and principles of democracy. *Alina Tryfonidou*, in her topical account 'Citizenship-for-sale schemes and EU law: can third-country nationals buy their way into becoming subjects of EU law?', explores EU citizenship for sale as a route to becoming a subject of EU law, and examines the dominance of the Member States as the deciders of subject-hood through market-based principles. Finally, *Sara Poli*, in 'The turning of non-state entities from objects to subjects of EU restrictive measures', considers the dichotomy of the subjects and objects of EU law as to restrictive measures widely used to target third countries and many non-State actors. The Court and Council have played very different roles in the widening ambit of EU regulatory reach and she shows how shifts in distinct time periods are discernible.

In Part III, on the Internal/External Nexus of EU law and case studies exploring the outer limits of the nexus with respect to subjects and objects, *Andrés Delgado Casteleiro*, in a wonderfully reflective and argumentative piece, 'The EU as an international person between functionalism and constitutionalism', dissects the EU as an international subject from a range of intellectual and theoretical frames and explores what it means to be a subject and the consequences of being a subject. He considers how functionalism as a theory shows how the subject/object dichotomy cannot grasp the EU as an international actor. *Emilia Korkea-aho*, in her broad-ranging albeit conceptually neat case study, 'Evolution of the role of third countries in EU law – towards full legal subjectivity?', assesses how EU law conceives of third countries and how they are and could be the objects and subjects of EU law, especially as to law-making practices and principles in Article 11 TEU. She describes their evolution as one towards full legal subjectivity, albeit incomplete and uncertain. *Ilaria Vianello*, in 'From objects to subjects: paving the way for third countries and their natural and legal persons', explores carefully how a more encompassing definition of the subjects of EU law could help the application of the rule of law in the external domain and could challenge the classical approach of treating third states and their natural and legal persons as objects of EU law and policies. *Samantha Velluti*, in 'Beyond rhetoric? Social conditionality in the EU's external trade relations', considers the subjects and objects of EU law and practice in the promotion of social and labour rights in EU external trade relations. In a valuable account of the subject/object dichotomy, she argues that the non-state actors involved in the application and monitoring of social conditionality remain insufficiently meaningful.

Part IV deals with the shift in the subjects and objects of EU law, with respect to European crises. It is worth mentioning that, when first considering the directions we wanted this project to take, what we understood as 'crisis/crises' was predominantly the financial crisis; by the time we held our first workshop, it was joined by the refugee crisis of 2015. We then held our second workshop, only weeks before the fateful UK referendum in June 2016. And the final months of preparing the edited volume were a forceful illustration of how potent the crises of Europe can be in shaping the creative focus of students of the subjects and objects of EU law. *Matthias Ruffert*, in his piece 'European integration in a crisis scenario: easy steps to revitalise the EU as a subject and to avoid disintegration?' threads the *fil rouge*, or common thread, through the needles that he refers to as the multi-crisis of Europe and identifies the task of legal scholarship in the current situation. As *Dora Kostakopoulou* and *Anastasia Tataryn* write in their moving account, '*Homo objectus, homo subjectus* and Brexit', the Brexit vote amounts to as vivid a case study as can be provided with respect to the ingression of the object into an event, by focusing upon the status of EU citizens in the UK turning from subject to object. Finally, *Michelle Everson*, in a prescient piece entitled 'Who do we think we are? Citizenship post-Brexit', charts the mammoth event of Brexit and traces the question of legal subjects and objects in EU citizenship in this light. She traces the tension that is faced as to capital-driven economic liberalisation in the last few decades and how it has been expressed in Brexit, where social solidarity and individual voter participation sought to 'challenge' the EU status quo with venom and angst.

* * *

When surveying the case studies, the overall impression is that the authors have by and large embraced one of the first instincts when beginning to contemplate subjects and objects of EU law: that what can be captured by these terms in 2016 is a very wide spectrum of different entities compared to what we can imagine was or would be described by these words at the time when the Court of Justice issued its landmark judgment in *Van Gend en Loos*.

As a starting point for looking into the subjects and objects of EU law, the decision was that the project would be open to a variety of different understandings of 'subject' and 'object', as well as of the relationship between the two. There are numerous ways of understanding them and the richness of the project is also in remaining open to case studies drawing on these different aspects. In our introductory paper, we sought not to draw any sharp lines dividing the subjects and objects, aware of the implications of insisting on a stance of 'disengagement' of the subject in relation to the object.[2] Without overly generalising, we feel that a conclusion can be made that, in the majority of the accounts, a similarly flexible stance was taken: authors have explored the ways in which subjects can become objects and vice versa.

With that in mind, what one can further extract from the accounts is that the dominant view of the subject which the authors have woven into their case studies is what, in the introductory chapter, we decided to refer to as a 'liberal subject', an understanding of the subject roughly based on an idea of a rational, autonomous self.[3] This is a view of the subject as bearer of rights and duties or, somewhat differently, as the political subject, co-creator or co-author of the law. It is easy to establish the appeal of this particular understanding of a subject in the study of law as it offers what may seem a relatively straightforward relationship to the object. In so doing, it offers a readily available toolbox for discussing relationships in law.

It would seem that when one is invited to consider subjects as well as objects of EU law – in other words, encouraged to work with this dichotomy – this in turn seems to lead to an understanding of 'object' as 'object of regulation', 'what is regulated by law'. 'Object' meaning 'law' (whereas the subject has knowledge of, understands and interprets its object: the law) stays in the background.[4] This should probably not come as a surprise. So much of the discussion of European law is defined by questioning whether it does or does not regulate, or, differently, whether it should or should not regulate a certain area or issue. Considering the immense growth of the EU's scope of competences since its law was 'constitutionalised', it would seem that when discussing the subject-object relation in EU law, the meaning that will most readily come to mind will probably have to do with the dynamics of the subject creating law that applies to the object.

We can also conclude that the spectrum of case studies in this book corroborates an assertion that we have made in preparing this project. And that is that the lexicon of subjects and objects would be helpful in articulating the omissions of EU law, and potentially even help to address them. In a wealth of different meanings of 'subject' and 'object', many of the authors have indeed applied this lexicon to present accounts that

2 Chapter 1, Section 2.2.
3 Chapter 1, Section 1.2.
4 Chapter 1, Section 1.4. See Rodin, Chapter 2 of this volume.

articulate various shortcomings. This, we optimistically posit, may be the first step towards using the research platform proposed here in different projects of legal reform in EU law. EU law, increasingly in need of social legitimacy, might be able to rely more on its subjects to overcome the pull towards its self-referentiality.[5]

A careful reader would not miss the fact that a number of accounts that sought to identify omissions and shortcomings of EU law conclude with an appeal to go beyond law when embarking on a quest for solutions.[6] Drawing from this insight, it may well be that weaving the lexicon of subjects and objects into research on EU law possesses a hidden capacity to help us look beyond law.

---

[5] See Douglas-Scott, Chapter 6 of this volume.

[6] See for example Kostakopoulou and Tataryn, Chapter 15, and Everson, Chapter 16 of this volume.

Index